W. H. Hudson
A Bibliography

W. H. HUDSON
Photograph reproduced by kind permission of the Royal Society for the Protection of Birds

W. H. Hudson
A Bibliography

John R. Payne

Foreword by
Alfred A. Knopf

Dawson · Archon Books

First published in 1977

© John R. Payne 1977

All rights reserved. No part of this publication may be reproduced, stored in a retrieval system, or transmitted, in any form or by any means, electronic, mechanical, photocopying, recording or otherwise without the permission of the publishers:

Wm Dawson & Sons Ltd, Cannon House
Folkestone, Kent, England

Archon Books, The Shoe String Press, Inc
995 Sherman Avenue, Hamden, Connecticut 06514 USA

British Library Cataloguing in Publication Data

Payne, John R.
  W. H. Hudson: a bibliography.
  1. Hudson, William Henry, b. 1841-
  Bibliography
  016.828'808 Z8422 76-030003
  ISBN 0-7129-0750-5
  ISBN 0-208-01647-3 (Archon)

Printed in Great Britain
by W & J Mackay Limited, Chatham

For
Lois, John Tarver and Elisa

Hudson is at his best about the greatest living English stylist, that is the man whose heart and brain and ear work most perfectly together to let one into the core of his thoughts and visions. Besides this he is the finest living observer, and the greatest living lover of bird and animal life, and of Nature in her moods. Besides this he is the rarest spirit amongst us writers.

John Galsworthy to Alfred A. Knopf
4 January 1915

Contents

PREFACE ix
ACKNOWLEDGMENTS xi
FOREWORD by Alfred A. Knopf xiii
INTRODUCTION 1
MANUSCRIPTS AND LETTERS 4
CHRONOLOGY OF HUDSON'S MAJOR PUBLICATIONS 7
LIBRARY LOCATIONS 9
A Books and Pamphlets 11
B Contributions to Books 183
C Contributions to Periodicals 193
D Translations 213
E Books about W. H. Hudson 223
INDEX 227

Preface

This bibliography attempts to record all the important writings of W. H. Hudson: books and pamphlets, contributions to books, contributions to periodicals and translations.

Section A describes all first English and American editions and issues together with other editions that may be of interest to the scholar and collector, such as first illustrated editions, later collected editions of textual importance and finely printed editions. A typical entry contains the following information:

EDITION STATEMENT The introductory heading to each entry identifies the edition. The date is in parenthesis when the date does not appear on the title page.

TITLE PAGE Quasi-facsimile transcription.

COLLATION Full collational formula for all signatures; pagination showing the signing and inferred signing of all pages; size of pages to the nearest millimetre; type of paper, whether laid or wove. No distinction is made between actual handmade laid paper and simulated laid paper. All watermarks are transcribed.

PAGINATION Contents of each page; quasi-facsimile transcription of the verso of all title pages and of imprints at the close of each book.

CONTENTS When the text is a collection of short stories or separately identifiable articles or essays, the individual contents are described with cross references to Section C when appropriate.

ILLUSTRATIONS Identification of the artist and brief description of the number and kind of illustrations.

BINDING Colour of cloth; quasi-facsimile transcription of all stamping or printing on all covers; description of endpapers, edges of leaves and dust jackets.

NOTES The number of copies, publication date, price upon publication and summary of later printings are given in every case where this information was available through publishers' records or published reference works. Where the date of publication was not otherwise available the date of deposit is given for copies in the British Museum, the Bodleian Library or the Library of Congress.

Section B describes books with original contributions by Hudson.

Section C is a chronological list of Hudson's contributions to periodicals with cross references to Section A when appropriate.

Section D is a chronological list within language groups of translations of Hudson's books into foreign languages. Contributions to books and periodicals in translation have not been included.

Section E lists the most important books about Hudson.

Bibliographies have become increasingly complex and involved. To keep the descriptions here as simple as possible while including all essential information, bibliographical conventions such as the use of the Inter-Society Color Council – National Bureau of Standards centroid colour charts (ISCC–NBS) and the identification of type of binder's cloths and other forms of measurement sometimes used in bibliographies have been used only when necessary for identification or to avoid confusion.

While completeness and accuracy have been the goals, no one is more aware than I that there are omissions and errors in this bibliography. I will be grateful to have these called to my attention.

JRP

Acknowledgments

A bibliography necessarily requires the assistance of a great number of people. I would like to express first my appreciation to the late David A. Randall, Librarian, The Lilly Library, and William R. Cagle, Acting Librarian, The Lilly Library, who provided the initial direction and supervision for this work during my year as a Lilly Fellow, 1967–68. Thanks also to Joe Bennett, Bibliographer, The Lilly Library, for reading the typescript and making numerous suggestions for corrections and alterations.

I am also especially indebted to the late Harry H. Ransom, Chancellor Emeritus, The University of Texas at Austin, for providing a grant to allow me to pursue my research in the libraries of England during the spring of 1973; to F. W. Roberts, Director of the Humanities Research Center, who has consistently encouraged my work; and to Mrs Willie Belle Coker, formerly secretary to J. Frank Dobie and librarian of the Dobie Collection in the Humanities Research Center, 1961 to 1973.

My appreciation also goes to the following persons whose assistance was vital for the completion of this book:

LIBRARIANS Kathleen Blow, Reference Librarian, The University of Texas at Austin; D. W. Evans, Rare Book Librarian, The University of Birmingham; Harriet C. Jameson, Head, Department of Rare Books and Special Collections, The University of Michigan; Salvador Magno, Librarian, Asociacion Ornitologica del Plata, Buenos Aires; Ammiel Prochovnick, Assistant Librarian, The John Crerar Library; Lee Putnam, Reference Librarian, Field Museum of Natural History; Robert Rosenthal, Curator, Special Collections, University of Chicago; H. G. Tupper, Assistant Librarian, Brotherton Collection, University of Leeds; Walter W. Wright, Chief of Special Collections, Dartmouth College.

PUBLISHERS George W. Bauer, Cornell University Press; R. M. Cooper, Longman Group; John Cullen, Eyre Methuen; John Denton, Ernest Benn; Cornelia B. Foley, Cornell University Press; Walter E. Freese, Doubleday; Richard Garnett, Macmillan; David M. Glixon, Cardavon Press; Lord Horder, Gerald Duckworth; William A. Koshland, Alfred A. Knopf; Sir Robert Lusty, Hutchinson Publishing Group; John Macrae, Jr., E. P. Dutton; J. L. Marshall, J. M. Dent; Sir Francis Meynell, Nonesuch Press; Roger Palmer, Hodder and Stoughton; Robert K. Spencer, Appleton-Century-Crofts; William Targ, G. P. Putnam's Sons.

Special thanks to Dorothy Rook, Librarian of the Royal Society for the Protection of Birds, who provided complete access to the W. H. Hudson collection and personal archives in the Society's library and who assisted with various stages of my research.

Other persons who have assisted with this bibliography include H. Bradley Martin and George Spater who provided information about various Hudson books in their collections; the late Herbert Faulkner West, bookseller, Hanover, New Hampshire, who was long a lover of Hudson's works; Lesley Macdonald, The Society of Authors; Alicia Jurado, author, and biographer of Hudson, Buenos Aires; O. M. Brack, David R. Dewar and Eric S. Whittle. And I am indebted to the late G. F. Wilson for his earlier work on the bibliography of W. H. Hudson.

Foreword

While still an undergraduate at Columbia College (member of the class of 1912), I became interested in the work of John Galsworthy. I had picked up one or two of his novels in a second-hand bookstore in Harlem run by an old gentleman named Cox and his son Carol. In those days Joel B. Spingarn, still professor of comparative literature, offered three undergraduate literary prizes – one for a poem, one for a short story, and one for an essay. I decided to enter an essay about Galsworthy in the Spingarn competition. Being well endowed with what we Jews call *chutzpah* – one can almost tell the meaning of the word from its sound – I wrote Galsworthy of my plan and asked him for his *curriculum vitae*. He responded amiably and generously. I think the resulting essay must have been a very pedestrian affair (in any case it did not win the prize), but I felt it only proper to send Galsworthy a copy of it so that he would understand I had not asked him for information about himself out of idle curiosity. This started a correspondence between us which lasted until his death.

I was graduated at mid-year and rewarded by a generous father with a trip abroad. By early summer I was in London and in touch with the Galsworthys, who invited me to spend a night in their little cottage Wingstone in Devonshire. Someone met my train at Manaton and drove me by horse and trap to my hosts, who lived on the edge of the great moor over part of which J. G. and I walked that afternoon. Next morning I noticed pinned to the wall of the room on the ground floor where J. G. did his writing a photograph of a strange, elderly bird-like man with a small white beard. "Who is he?" I asked. "That," said Galsworthy, "is W. H. Hudson." "Who is he?" I asked again. "Do you mean to say that you Americans don't know Hudson and his *Green Mansions?*" I confessed that one American didn't and that I should at least have heard of him if he was read at all in the States. So when I returned to London I bought a copy of *Green Mansions*, read it, and fell in love with it. That autumn I started working for Doubleday, Page and Company at the Country Life Press at Garden City, where my job was using an adding machine and making postings to royalty ledgers. Several months later, despite the remoteness of this kind of work from anything editorial, I wrote Galsworthy about Hudson, assuming that the firm would seize an opportunity to publish a writer of whom Galsworthy held so high an opinion. Galsworthy's reply of 12 December 1913 to me tells much about Hudson:

> I have written to Hudson twice, and cannot write again. His first answer was that he was quite indifferent about America, the interest in him being less than it was in Canada.

This of course is enough to freeze any man of his great gifts, and I don't wonder at indifference, hostility almost.

In my second letter, I urged him strongly to give you and the American public another chance. Personally, I believe it is enormously a question of a publisher who is enthusiastic and will push him properly.

I would write to him as nicely as you can, if I were you, and see what happens.

I doubt that I followed up my friend's suggestion since my attempt to interest Eugene Saxton in the book was so ridiculously unsuccessful. Saxton, who later became a most brilliant editor at Harper's, in those days was taking care of advertising and book jackets at Garden City. He told me that he thought a fine opera could be based on the book if only someone at the Metropolitan could be persuaded to have a libretto made of it. So I made no further approach to Hudson.

But a year or so later I had left Doubleday and was working for Mitchell Kennerley, who, while he did indulge me to the extent of importing, in sheets, a small edition of Hudson's *Adventures Among Birds*, showed no interest whatever in *Green Mansions*. This was surprising in view of Kennerley's usual excellent taste and courage as a publisher.

Putnam had published *Green Mansions* in 1904. In those days one could secure United States copyright in a work of British origin only if it were printed from type set up in the United States. Since Putnam had imported the book in sheets from its London publisher, Duckworth, copyright over here for *Green Mansions* could never be secured, and so Hudson's masterpiece has always been in the public domain. Nevertheless, we decided, Blanche and I, to set up and print our edition over here. Knowing Galsworthy's fondness and admiration for Hudson and of the latter's – "poverty" – would I think be the correct word, I suggested that J. G. write an introduction for our edition. This would probably help with the booksellers and certainly with the reviewers. He agreed at once and wrote me 25 September 1915:

> I have finished the foreword to *Green Mansions* in rough and will let you have it in the course of a week or so. About twenty-three hundred words. I have pitched it strong, but no stronger than I feel – having been re-reading several of his books. He is the rarest spirit writing and the most valuable to our town-eaten-up age....
>
> If the war were not on, I would not have taken anything for the Hudson preface, but since all I can earn goes to Red Cross or other war funds, I will take what you'd like to give.

We were delighted. Such introductions were not then so common as they later became; Galsworthy's enthusiasm proved contagious, and the book caught on. Our most encouraging advance order – for one hundred copies – came from that old-fashioned gentleman and very fine bookseller C. C. Parker of Los Angeles. I should add that Major Putnam had written me a most gracious and generous letter (it has, alas, disappeared from our files), ceding the rights his firm had in the book and wishing us good luck with it.

When Blanche and I went to London in 1921 on the old *Carmania*, we had as a fellow passenger Sydney Pawling, the surviving partner of my great and favourite admiration among British publishers of the day, William Heinemann. Pawling, a generous man, gave me a desk and let me make the Heinemann office on Bedford Street off the Strand my office for the duration of our stay. One day I was told that a very strange little old man named Hudson was there to see me, and I saw the author of *Green Mansions* for the first time. Later Blanche and I had him and Edward Garnett, the critic, around to tea at the hotel at which we were staying – the Royal Palace, I think, in Kensington. The two old fellows were so glad to see each other and seemed to have so much to talk about that we soon felt ourselves as an all-but-unnecessary presence. We never met again but maintained a fairly steady correspondence until he died in 1922. Nor did we ever become in any proper sense of the word his publisher. Dent had taken over all his books in England and old J. M. worked very closely with his American opposite, John Macrae, the head of the firm of Dutton in New York, regarding me, I think, as an interloper, which I doubtless was. Nevertheless, it was our handling of *Green Mansions* that got Hudson his first largish audience over here and indeed launched our own firm on its way.

I need scarcely say that I feel privileged to add this purely personal note to Mr Payne's admirable bibliography.

ALFRED A. KNOPF

Introduction

W. H. Hudson's writing career began with contributions to the periodical press. His first published work appeared in a series of letters and articles in the *Proceedings of the Zoological Society of London*, 1869–1876. These were written while Hudson was still living in Quilmes, near Buenos Aires, Argentina. Except for his pseudonymous poem, "Wanted, A Lullaby", which appeared in *Cassell's Family Magazine* in February 1874, Hudson's next recorded publication was not until 1883, nine years after his move to England. "The London Sparrow" appeared in the July 1883 issue of *Merry England*. From this new beginning Hudson continued to submit manuscripts for publication in the monthly journals such as the *Gentleman's Magazine* and *Longman's Magazine* and later in the weeklies such as the *Saturday Review, Speaker, New Statesman* and others.

Much of Hudson's writing for the periodical press was later revised and expanded and makes up the contents of his books. One difficulty in tracing Hudson's periodical appearances to their later book publications is the large amount of rewriting he often did. Only bits and pieces would sometimes be used from an article, these rearranged, retitled and incorporated into a chapter in a book. Hudson also completely reworked some of his books, such as *Birds in a Village* and *Argentine Ornithology*. These contain substantial revisions with new text or prefatory matter. In contrast to these revisions, Hudson did little or no revision between successive printings of the same edition. Extensively revised editions are given separate entries and described in full in this bibliography. Later printings of an edition are not described unless they are known to have textual significance.

Hudson's livelihood in England depended upon his writing, and the importance of having an article accepted during the early years when he was establishing himself is indicated in his reminiscences in *Afoot in England*: "But I fancy the nearest crossing-sweeper did better and could afford to give himself a more generous dinner. It occasionally happened that an article sent to some magazine was not returned, and always after so many rejections to have one accepted and paid for with a cheque worth several pounds was a cause of astonishment and was as truly a miracle as if the angel of the sun had compassionately thrown us a handful of gold."

On Christmas Day, 1900, Hudson wrote to Morley Roberts, "I have a good many things out – articles, a book or two, etc. – but with the exception of some very small things the stuff does not go. . . ." By 1903 Hudson's popularity was on the rise and he wrote again to Roberts that he now had numerous requests for articles and was at work on some nature pieces for the *Speaker*. Within a year the demand for Hudson's work had increased dramatically as he reported to Roberts early in 1904: "As to literary work I can't touch it at present and can't think of anything to come. What revolts me is the thought that when I had not a penny and almost went down on my knees to Editors, publishers and literary agents I couldn't even get a civil word, and of ten – or perhaps twenty – MSS. sent nine (or nineteen) would be sent back. And now that I don't want the beastly money and care nothing for fame and am sick and tired of the whole thing they actually come to beg a book or article from me. I have had requests for a book from four publishers during the last few weeks and have not even replied to the letters sent me, and do not suppose I ever shall."

But even though Hudson was pursued by publishers and literary agents, he never became a popular author and never had a best seller until John Galsworthy introduced him to the American public in Alfred A. Knopf's edition of *Green Mansions* in 1916. The success of this edition is told in its proper place in this bibliography.

Perhaps the least known of Hudson's writings is the group of pamphlets written for and published by the Royal Society for the Protection of Birds. The Society's history dates back to 1889 when the fashion in women's clothes was for ornamentation with the plumes of brightly coloured birds. Milliners and dressmakers paid high prices to professional plume-hunters for choice feathers of the white heron, egret, ibis, pheasant and humming-bird. In February of that year a small group of ladies, distressed over the frightful loss of bird life, banded together in Manchester and pledged to refrain from wearing the feathers of any bird not killed for the purposes of food. They hoped that by enrolling a sufficiently large number of women the demand for ornamental plumes would cease and the supply would automatically come to an end. But their small number had little effect, and the trade in birds' feathers increased.

To strengthen their effectiveness the group was renamed the Society for the Protection of Birds in 1891 and elected the Duchess of Portland as its President, Mrs Edward Phillips, Vice-President, and Miss C. V. Hall, Honorary Treasurer. Within two years the Society's membership grew to over 5,000 and benefited from the strong patronage of influential members of English society. Hudson was involved with the Society's activities from the beginning. His *Osprey; Or, Egrets and Aigrettes* (1892) was one of the Society's earliest publications calling for the protection of British bird life.

Hudson's letter of 27 July 1893 to R. B. Cunninghame Graham indicates the early goals of the Society as well as his personal involvement. He enclosed a copy of the Constitution of the Society and wrote, "you may even care to pay your shilling and become an Associate. There are now about one hundred and twenty or thirty branches, and I am local Secretary to one, the North Kensington branch. One of our members has got a little Bird Protection Act through the Commons, but the Lords have made rather a muddle of it in Committee. Still, it shows that we are waking up to the fact that something must be done to preserve our bird life from destruction. When this Society numbers forty or fifty thousand members then I think we can safely go to Parliament and ask for a better Bill."

Much of Hudson's time and efforts over the following two years was devoted to the work of the Society and the writing of five additional pamphlets: *Feathered Women*, 1893; *Bird-Catching*, 1894; *Lost British Birds*, 1894, *The Barn Owl*, 1895 and *Letter to Clergymen, Ministers, and Others*, 1895. Because of the ephemeral nature of these pamphlets they are among the scarcest of all Hudson's work. The first printings of *Osprey* and *Kew Gardens and Old Deer Park*, for example, are known in only two and three copies respectively.

Hudson was instrumental in establishing the Bird and Tree Competition in 1901 which provided prizes to children for essays describing birds and trees they had studied in school. A few months before his death Hudson presented £1,000 to the Society to assist the continuation of the Bird and Tree Competition as well as other educational programmes. More importantly, Hudson provided in his will for all the income from his writing to go to the Society. To increase this fund he authorized the reprinting of *Argentine Ornithology* as *Birds of La Plata* in 1920, and, against the judgment of Morley Roberts, permitted *Fan* and *Ralph Herne* to be included in the Collected Edition of his works.

Hudson was greatly interested in the design and make-up of his published books, particularly the illustrations. His illustrators include some of the leading artists of the time, such as J. K. Keulemans, A. D. McCormick, Alfred Hartley, H. Grönvold and E. J. Detmold. Hudson was difficult to please and often returned unsatisfactory drawings to the artists. His letters and comments showing his concern for the illustrations of his books appear throughout this bibliography.

Manuscripts and Letters

The largest gathering of Hudson's surviving manuscripts and letters is in the library of the Royal Society for the Protection of Birds. These include chapters six, ten, twelve and a portion of chapter twenty-three of *Far Away and Long Ago*. There is also an exercise book containing a list of species of Argentine birds and notes on their appearance and songs, sixteen pages; notes on pre-natal suggestions in man and lower animals, thirteen pages; a list of Hudson's books, two pages; and miscellaneous notes, four pages.

Hudson's letters at the RSPB include seventy-five to Mrs George Hubbard, 1895–1903; thirty-four to Mrs Edward Phillips, 1892–1905; nine to Mr and Mrs Frank E. Lemon, 1900–1922; seven to Emily Hudson; one each to Miss Linda Gardiner, Miss C. V. Hall, and to an unidentified recipient.

Other Hudson manuscript material is held in the following libraries:

HUMANITIES RESEARCH CENTER, UNIVERSITY OF TEXAS AT AUSTIN
184 letters from Hudson to Margaret Alice Lilly Brooke, Lady Rani of Sarawak, 1912–1921; 11 other letters from Hudson to various recipients, 1900–1921. Related correspondence includes 1 letter from John Masefield to Hudson, 6 November 1919; 1 letter from Edith Palliser to Hudson, 15 December 1919; 12 letters from Morley Roberts and 1 letter from Joseph Dent to Lady Margaret Brooke, 1922 and 1923.

SPECIAL COLLECTIONS, DARTMOUTH COLLEGE LIBRARY, HANOVER, NEW HAMPSHIRE
51 letters from Hudson to R. B. Cunninghame Graham and Mrs Bontine, 1890–1922, typed copies of these letters as prepared for publication, printer's proof copy, layout design and other production material; one photostat copy of a nineteen-page letter to Albert Hudson, 14 April–6 May 1874, written during Hudson's voyage from South America to England. (See *William Henry Hudson's Diary* (A63);) 7 other letters to various correspondents including John Masefield, H. J. Massinghame and Mrs Hubbard; "The Pelican", four pages of notes with a letter from Edward Garnett to Agnes Redway, 9 July 1924, suggesting that this is a first draft of an article later rewritten for *Rare Vanishing & Lost British Birds*; "A Simple Story", twenty-one pages typescript with Hudson's autograph corrections; "Stonehenge", sixteen pages typescript with Hudson's autograph corrections; "Tom Rainger", nine pages typescript with Hudson's autograph corrections.

G. M. ADAMS COLLECTION, DEPARTMENT OF RARE BOOKS AND SPECIAL COLLECTIONS, UNIVERSITY OF MICHIGAN

13 letters from Hudson to Edward Garnett, 1902–1920; 9 letters to William Canton, 1887–1919: 4 letters to Miss E. A. Newton, 1920–1921; 1 letter to Emily Hudson, 1921; 1 letter to Morley Roberts, 1921, and 4 other letters to various correspondents. In addition to this correspondence the Adams Collection contains the copy of the first edition of *Fan* revised by Hudson for the Collected edition and the copy of "Ralph Herne" as it appeared in *Youth*, revised for the Collected edition.

LIBRARY, UNIVERSITY OF BIRMINGHAM

15 letters from Hudson to John Galsworthy, 1904–1922; the manuscript of Galsworthy's foreword to the American edition of *Green Mansions* published by Alfred A. Knopf in 1916; the manuscript of Galsworthy's article "A Note on W. H. Hudson" which appeared in the *New York Evening Post*, 16 September 1922; a letter from E. V. Lucas to John Galsworthy about Hudson, 27 July 1915, and a letter from Lady Margaret Brooke to John Galsworthy, 13 October 1922.

BROTHERTON LIBRARY, UNIVERSITY OF LEEDS

11 letters from Hudson to Morley Roberts, 1910–1921; 1 letter to Edward Clodd, July 1902; also the copy of the first edition of *Birds and Man* corrected by Hudson for the second edition, and part of Morley Roberts' transcript of Hudson's manuscript of *A Hind in Richmond Park*.

SMITHSONIAN INSTITUTION

6 letters from Hudson to Professor Spencer F. Baird, 1866–1868.

H. BRADLEY MARTIN. PRIVATE COLLECTION, NEW YORK CITY

299 letters from Hudson to Morley Roberts, 1903–1922; 69 letters to Edward Garnett, 1902–1921. With few exceptions these letters correspond to the published editions.

Hudson's intense desire to destroy the manuscripts of his books and the letters he had written and received is well known. His practice was to destroy the original manuscript of his books as soon as proofs were received and checked. Hudson's published letters to Morley Roberts and Edward Garnett tell of the destruction of whole volumes and masses of notes, including two complete books of poetry along with thousands of letters. On 1 April 1921 Hudson wrote to Roberts: "I have had to make a new will in a hurry to make sure that the small amount I'm leaving after a few legacies, will be used by the Bird Society in my way. Also to make sure that not a scrap of written paper or manuscript (barring the MS. of the book I'm doing) shall be kept. Of course I can't, dead or living, prevent people writing about me if they feel 'so disposed', but I would far rather be forgotten the instant I quit the scene." Following Hudson's death on 18 August 1921 Roberts wrote to Margaret Alice Lilly Brooke, Lady Rani of Sarawak: "As to unpublished sketches, I think he left none. I found him destroying tons of MSS., & all I saved was the long poem 'The Old Man in Kensington Gardens'." Wynnard Hooper and Ernest Bell, Hudson's literary executors, followed Hudson's instructions and burned additional bundles of letters and manuscripts.

Chronology of Hudson's Major Publications

A1	The Purple Land that England Lost	1885
A2	A Crystal Age	1887
A3	Argentine Ornithology	1888–1889
A4	Osprey; or, Egrets and Aigrettes	1891
A5	The Naturalist in La Plata	1892
A6	Fan	1892
A7	Idle Days in Patagonia	1893
A8	Birds in a Village	1893
A9	Feathered Women	1893
A10	Bird-Catching	1894
A11	Lost British Birds	1894
A12	British Birds	1895
A13	The Barn Owl	1895
A14	Letter to Clergymen, Ministers, and Others	1895
A15	Pipits	1897
A16	Birds in London	1898
A17	The Trade in Birds' Feathers	1898
A18	Kew Gardens and Old Deer Park	1900
A19	Nature in Downland	1900
A20	Birds and Man	1901
A21	El Ombú	1902
A22	Hampshire Days	1903
A23	Green Mansions	1904
A24	A Linnet for Sixpence	1904
A25	A Little Boy Lost	1905
A26	The Land's End	1908
A27	Afoot in England	1909
A28	South American Sketches	1909
A29	A Shepherd's Life	1910
A30	A Thrush that Never Lived	1911
A31	Adventures Among Birds	1913
A32	On Liberating Caged Birds	1914
A33	Tales of the Pampas	1916
A34	Far Away and Long Ago	1918
A35	Roff and a Linnet: Chain and Cage	1918

A36	Birds in Town and Village	1919
A37	The Book of a Naturalist	1919
A38	Birds of La Plata	1920
A39	Dead Man's Plack and an Old Thorn	1920
A40	A Traveller in Little Things	1921
A41	A Tired Traveller	1921
A42	Seagulls in London	1922
A43	A Hind in Richmond Park	1922
A44	Ralph Herne	1923
A45	Rare Vanishing & Lost British Birds	1923
A46	153 Letters from W. H. Hudson	1923
A47	Dead Man's Plack, an Old Thorn & Miscellany	1923
A48	A Hudson Anthology	1924
A49	Dead Man's Plack an Old Thorn & Poems	1924
A50	Men, Books and Birds	1925
A51	The Disappointed Squirrel	1925
A52	Three Water Birds	1926
A53	A Fairy Fauna	1927
A54	Mary's Little Lamb	1929
A55	Birds of Wing and Other Wild Things	1930
A56	South American Romances	1930
A57	W. H. Hudson's Letters to R. B. Cunninghame Graham	1941
A58	Tales of the Gauchos	1946
A59	Foreword	1947
A60	The Best of William H. Hudson	1949
A61	Letters on the Ornithology of Buenos Ayres	1951
A62	Two Letters on an Albatross	1955
A63	William Henry Hudson's Diary	1958
A64	Gauchos of the Pampas and their Horses	1963
A65	Birds and Green Places	1964

Library Locations

Listed below are the libraries where research was conducted for this bibliography. Each of these libraries has strong holdings of Hudson's works. Occasionally within the text of the bibliography the location of individual copies is given. This occurs only for particularly important titles, works known in extremely limited number, and variant copies.

Adams   G. M. Adams Collection, Department of Rare Books and Special Collections, University of Michigan, Ann Arbor.

Bodleian   Bodleian Library, Oxford.

BM   British Museum, London.

Brotherton   Edward Allen Brotherton Collection, The Brotherton Library, University of Leeds, Leeds.

Chicago   University of Chicago Library, Chicago.

Crerar   John Crerar Library, Chicago.

Dartmouth   Special Collections Department, Dartmouth College Library, Hanover, New Hampshire.

Dobie   J. Frank Dobie Collection, Humanities Research Center, University of Texas at Austin.

Field Museum   Library of the Field Museum of Natural History, Chicago.

Houghton   Houghton Library, Harvard University, Cambridge.

ISU   Illinois State University Library, Normal, Illinois.

Lilly   Lilly Library, Indiana University, Bloomington, Indiana.

Martin   Private Library of H. Bradley Martin.

RSPB   Royal Society for the Protection of Birds, Sandy, Bedfordshire.

Spater   Private Library of George Spater.

Texas   Humanities Research Center, University of Texas at Austin.

Zoological Society   Zoological Society of London.

A

Books and Pamphlets

A1a

THE PURPLE LAND THAT ENGLAND LOST

FIRST EDITION, FIRST ISSUE 1885

THE / PURPLE LAND THAT ENGLAND / LOST. / TRAVELS AND ADVENTURES IN THE BANDA / ORIENTAL, SOUTH AMERICA. / BY / W. H. HUDSON. / VOL. I. (VOL. II.) / LONDON: / SAMPSON LOW, MARSTON, SEARLE, AND RIVINGTON, / CROWN BUILDINGS, 188, FLEET STREET. / 1885. / [*All rights reserved.*]

Collation Volume I: [A]² B–T⁸ (–T8); pp. [i–iii] iv [1] 2–286; 189 × 127 mm.; printed on wove paper. *Volume II:* [A]² B–R⁸ S⁴ T1; pp. [i–iii] iv [1] 2–265 [266]; 189 × 127 mm.; printed on wove paper.

Pagination Volume I: p. [i], title; p. [ii], 'LONDON: / PRINTED BY WILLIAM CLOWES AND SONS, LIMITED, / STAMFORD STREET AND CHARING CROSS.'; pp. [iii]–iv, contents; pp. [1] 2–286, text; at bottom of p. 286, '[*rule*] / LONDON: PRINTED BY WILLIAM CLOWES AND SONS, LIMITED, / STAMFORD STREET AND CHARING CROSS.'. *Volume II:* p. [i], title; p. [ii], 'LONDON: / PRINTED BY WILLIAM CLOWES AND SONS, LIMITED, / STAMFORD STREET AND CHARING CROSS.'; pp. [iii]–iv, contents; pp. [1] 2–265, text; p. [266], 'LONDON: / PRINTED BY WILLIAM CLOWES AND SONS, LIMITED, / STAMFORD STREET AND CHARING CROSS.'.

Binding Moderate blue cloth (Centroid 182). Front cover printed in a decorative type face in brownish-red '[*rule*] / [*ornamental partial rule*] / THE PURPLE LAND / THAT ENGLAND LOST / [*leafy branch*] / W. H. HUDSON / [*ornamental partial rule*] / [*double thin thick rule*]'; spine stamped in gilt with decorations in brownish-red '[*rule*] / [*four type ornaments*] / [*rule*] / THE / PURPLE LAND / THAT / ENGLAND LOST / [*short rule*] / VOL. I. [VOL. II.] / W. H. HUDSON / [*rule*] / [*two fleurs-de-lis separated by a small star*] / [*rule*] / SAMPSON LOW & CO / [*double rule*]'. Top and fore edges untrimmed, bottom edges trimmed; green and white floral wove endpapers. *Binder's insert* following p. [266] of Volume II: a thirty-two page catalogue of books published by Sampson Low, Marston, Searle, & Rivington, dated October 1885.

Variants 1. Strong blue cloth (Centroid 178). Spine stamped in gilt 'THE / PURPLE LAND / THAT / ENGLAND / LOST / [*rule*] / VOL. I. [VOL. II.] / HUDSON / [*serifed initial letters*] SAMPSON LOW'. Yellow endpapers. No publisher's catalogue. 2. Same as variant 1 except that the author's name reads 'W. H. HUDSON' and 'SAMPSON' is misprinted 'SAPMSON' on spine of Volume I.

Notes Published at 21s. The BM copy is stamped 17 November 1885.

Chapter 3, "Story of a Piebald Horse", was reprinted with minor textual changes in *El Ombú* (A21). *The Purple Land* was collected in *South American Romances* (A56). Variants 1 and 2 are secondary bindings.

Reviews The Times 12 October 1885; *Saturday Review* 14 November 1885; *Whitehall Review* 26 November 1885; *Literary World* 4 December 1885; *Athenaeum* 26 December 1885; *Graphic* 2 January 1886; *Figaro* 9 January 1886; *Academy* 23 January 1886.

Like many first books, Hudson's *The Purple Land* had relatively few readers and much criticism. On 14 November 1885 a reviewer in *Saturday Review* wrote: "Never was so absolute a misnomer given to a book. *The Purple Land* is no record of genuine travel performed by a real traveller, but a very silly story of the imaginary adventures of an imaginary Mr. Lamb, who clandestinely married an imaginary Miss Romola Aveleyra in Buenos Ayres. . . . We feel bound to say that we have seldom been called upon to express an opinion on a more vulgar farrago of repulsive nonsense than is contained in the volumes to which the author has given so misleading a title."

This was followed by the *Athenaeum* on 26 December 1885. "Readers who are prejudiced by an obscure or unmeaning title may be reassured in the present instance. The 'land' is the Banda Oriental, or Republic of Uruguay, the epithet 'purple' being intended by the author to express the amount of purposeless bloodshed that has taken place there; but other South American republics might fairly dispute the pre-eminence of Uruguay in this respect. Beyond the title, however, and here and there a sentence of fine writing which might have been expunged, there is nothing to which we can take exception."

Professor A. H. Keane, writing in the *Academy*, 23 January 1886, found favour with the book, and Hudson referred to this review in a letter to Cunninghame Graham on 21 April 1890. "That heavy first chapter, also the heavy 'Mount of Expiation' chapter at the end would have disappeared in another edition. That there is 'too much love making' I was told by several critics, but I knew it first. For what you say about the gaucho dialogue thanks; and that also agrees with what was said by a very keen critic – whose name was also Keane by the way – in the *Academy*." Years later, in a letter to Morley Roberts on 28 February 1920, Hudson recalled again this favourable review by Keane: "I had a great regard for him. When my very first book came out and *The Saturday Review* and *Athenaeum* jumped on it as a farrago of indecent nonsense and lies, Keane wrote a glowingly favourable review in *The Academy*. The first taste of praise I ever had."

Because of its importance this review is quoted at length, though not in its entirety: "This enigmatical title, as is the fashion of the day, is explained by the more commonplace sub-title: 'Travels and Adventures in the Banda Oriental, South America'. But the enigmas of this altogether enigmatical book do not stop here; and it becomes necessary further to explain that the Banda Oriental, now more commonly known as the Republic of Uruguay, is called a 'purple land', not because 'she first catches the auroral hues on her shining hair and pale face turned towards the Atlantic', but because of 'the dark stains on her feet, ever washed with her children's blood'. Then the words, 'that England lost' are added regretfully at the somewhat ignominious surrender of Monte Video after its brief occupation by the British early in the present century. But now comes the real enigma respecting the authorship; for of the W. H. Hudson, whose name alone appears on the title-page, all we know is that he is not the author, or at least the author only of a short introductory chapter informing us that 'the real author is a young Englishman named Richard Lamb', whose personal adventures are supposed to be here related. These adventures take us back about a quarter of a century, to the time following the memorable ten years' siege of Monte Video, when 'strife and misgovernment, like bad weather in England, appeared to be the normal condition of the country'. But whether Richard Lamb himself is of more palpable substance than W. H. Hudson, or his adventures more real than those of Quentin Durward or Robinson Crusoe, is a problem which each reader will have to decide for himself.

Apart from this consideration the work is so clever, and, on the whole, so well written, that one wonders all the more why it should have been introduced to the British public surrounded by so much needless mystification. Whether real or fictitious, the scenes and characters are described with surprising vigour and vivacity. So uniformly truthful is the local colouring, so easy and natural the dialogue, so seldom are the limits of the strictly credible overstepped, that it really becomes a matter of secondary consideration whether we have here a story of actual experience, or merely a series of graphic pictures portraying an interesting historical period in the social and political life of the turbulent Spanish American States. In such characters as Eyebrows, Blas the Bearded, Demetria, Dolores, the hero's young wife Romola, and, of course, in the hero himself, with all his foibles and curious lack of 'high moral sentiment', we feel the same sympathetic interest that we do in Dick Swiveller, Becky Sharp, Olivia, and all the other heroes and heroines of English romance."

Copies Adams (Volume II only); Bodleian; Brotherton; Dartmouth; Dobie; LC; Lilly. *Variant copy 1* Adams; Texas. *Variant copy 2* ISU.

A1b

FIRST EDITION, SECOND ISSUE 1887

THE / PURPLE LAND THAT ENGLAND / LOST / TRAVELS AND ADVEN-TURES IN THE BANDA / ORIENTAL, SOUTH AMERICA. / BY / W. H. HUDSON. / *CHEAPER EDITION, IN ONE VOLUME.* / LONDON: / SAMPSON LOW, MARSTON, SEARLE, AND RIVINGTON, / CROWN BUILDINGS, 188, FLEET STREET. / 1887. / [*All rights reserved/*]

Collation [A]² B–T⁸ (–T8) B–R⁸S⁴T1; pp. [i–iii] iv [1] 2–286 [1] 2–265 [266]; 190 × 126 mm.; printed on wove paper.

Pagination p. [i], title; p. [ii], 'LONDON / PRINTED BY WILLIAM CLOWES AND SONS, LIMITED, / STAMFORD STREET AND CHARING CROSS.'; pp. [iii]–iv, contents; pp. [1] 2–286, text of chapters I–XVII; at end of p. 286 '[*rule*] / LONDON: PRINTED BY WILLIAM CLOWES AND SONS, LIMITED, / STAMFORD STREET AND CHARING CROSS.'; pp. [1] 2–265, text of chapters XVIII–XXX; p. [266], 'LONDON: / PRINTED BY WILLIAM CLOWES AND SONS, LIMITED, / STAMFORD STREET AND CHARING CROSS.'.

Binding Green cloth. Front cover stamped in a decorative type face in brownish-red 'THE PURPLE LAND / THAT ENGLAND LOST / [*short rule*] / W. H. HUDSON / [*tall grass design from lower left edge*]'; spine stamped in gilt '[*double rule*] / [*rule*] / [*first three words of title in a decorative type face*] THE / PURPLE / LAND / THAT / ENGLAND LOST / [*short rule*] / W. H. HUDSON / [*serifed*] SAMPSON·LOW & CO. / [*rule*] / [*double rule*]'. Top and fore edges untrimmed, bottom edges trimmed; black wove endpapers. *Binder's insert* following p. [266] of Volume II: a thirty-two page catalogue of books published by Sampson Low, Marston, Searle, & Rivington, dated October 1885.

Notes Published at 6s.

The sheets of the two volumes of A1a were bound into one volume and issued with a new title page as a "Cheaper Edition".

In a letter to Mrs Edward Phillips, Vice-president of the Society for the Protection of Birds, dated 7 July 1902, Hudson wrote: "[*The Purple Land*] was my first book, published before the 'Argentine Ornithology' was written, & it is full of faults, & the manner of it would seem rather quaint & out of date now. A small edition was published, which did not sell – except for waste paper, or as a remainder. Now it cannot be had. [Edward] Garnett advertised for a copy & failed to get one; he heard that if one were found it would cost 15/ or 18/. For a year or two there have been inquiries for it at the second-hand shops, & to all who have come to me about it I have said with truth 'I have no copy to lend.'"

Copies Adams; Dobie; ISU.

A1c

SECOND EDITION, REVISED; FIRST EDITION WITH THIS TITLE 1904

The Purple Land: Being the / Narrative of one Richard Lamb's / Adventures in the Banda Oriental, in / South America, as told by Himself / BY W. H. HUDSON / [ornament: *sea scape with coast and sun in the background*] / LONDON / DUCK-WORTH & CO. / 3, HENRIETTA STREET, COVENT GARDEN / 1904

Collation [A]⁴ B–Y⁸ Z¹⁰ (z5 signed "z2"); pp. [i–v] vi [vii] viii [1] 2–355 [356]; 188 × 124 mm.; printed on wove paper.

Pagination p. [i], half-title 'THE PURPLE LAND'; p. [ii], list of seven titles by the same author; p. [iii], title; p. [iv], 'ALL RIGHTS RESERVED / [*short rule*] / NEW EDITION'; pp. [v]–vi, preface to the new edition by Hudson, dated September 1904; pp. [vii]–viii, contents; pp. [1] 2–352, text; p. 353–355, appendix; p. [356], 'PLYMOUTH / WILLIAM BRENDON AND SON / PRINTERS'.

Binding Red cloth. The same ornamental design that appears on the title page is stamped in gilt in centre of front cover, enclosed within a single blind rule border; spine stamped in gilt '[*rule*] / THE / PURPLE / LAND / W. H. / HUDSON / DUCKWORTH & C⁰ / [*rule*]'; publisher's design blind stamped in centre of back cover. All edges trimmed; white wove endpapers.

Notes Published October 1904 at 6s. In response to my enquiry about publishing records, Lord Horder, Gerald Duckworth & Co., wrote on 9 March 1971, "Unfortunately our Hudson records and files here are far from complete, most of the former having been destroyed by a too zealous clerk in 1929."

This edition was revised by Hudson and contains a new preface. "Besides many small verbal corrections and changes, the deletion of some paragraphs and the insertion of a few new ones, I have omitted one entire chapter containing the Story of a Piebald Horse, recently reprinted in another book entitled *El Ombú* [A21]. I have also dropped the tedious introduction to the former edition, only preserving, as an appendix, the historical part, for the sake of such of my readers as may like to have a few facts about the land that England lost." [from Preface].

The second impression was issued in 1905 with E. P. Dutton's imprint (A1d) and the third impression was issued as The Readers' Library edition in 1911 (A1e).

Reviews *Spectator* 26 November 1904; *Saturday Review* 3 December 1904; *Daily News* 6 June 1905.

Hudson wrote to Edward Garnett 22 December 1904: "I'm glad to say *The Purple Land* has sold over 1000 copies – chiefly through *The Spectator* review, for no other journal has mentioned it decently."

A1d

FIRST AMERICAN ISSUE 1905

The Purple Land: Being the / Narrative of one Richard Lamb's / Adventures in the Banda Orientál, in / South America, as told by Himself / BY W. H. HUDSON / [*ornament: sea-scape with coast and sun in the background*] / NEW YORK / E. P. DUTTON AND CO. / 1905

Collation Same as A1c.

Pagination: same as A1c except title page and p. [iv] which reads 'ALL RIGHTS RESERVED / [*short rule*] / SECOND IMPRESSION / *Printed in Great Britain*'.

Binding Same as A1c except spine which reads 'DUTTON / & C<u>O</u>'.

Notes Published at $1.50. This is the second impression of the sheets of the 1904 revised edition (A1c) and the first appearance of this book in the United States.

Reviews *Saturday Review of Literature* 23 December 1905; *New York Times Book Review* 23 December 1905; *Outlook* 30 December 1905; *Dial* 1 January 1906; (*New York*) *Nation* 1 March 1906.

A1e

THE READERS' LIBRARY EDITION (1911)

The Purple Land: Being the / Narrative of one Richard Lamb's / Adventures in the Banda Orientál, in / South America, as told by Himself / BY W. H. HUDSON / AUTHOR OF "GREEN MANSIONS," ETC. / [*ornament: sea-scape with coast and sun in the background*] / LONDON / DUCKWORTH & CO. / 3, HENRIETTA STREET, COVENT GARDEN

Collation and *pagination* same as A1c except as follows: leaves measure 185 × 123

mm.; p. [ii], list of titles in The Readers' Library; p. [iv], '*Issued in "The Readers' Library*" 1911 / ALL RIGHTS RESERVED / [*short rule*] / THIRD IMPRESSION'; p. [356], 'PLYMOUTH / W. BRENDON AND SON, LIMITED / PRINTERS'.

Binding Blue cloth. Publisher's circular device blind stamped in centre of front cover; spine stamped in gilt '[*within a single rule panel*] THE / PURPLE / LAND / W. H. / HUDSON / [*in smaller single rule panel at bottom of spine*] DUCKWORTH'. All edges trimmed; white wove endpapers.

Notes Published March 1911 at 2s. 6d. See note to A1c for information on publishing records.

This is the third impression of the 1904 revised edition (A1c) and the first appearance in The Readers' Library series.

A1f

FIRST AMERICAN EDITION 1916

The Purple Land: Being the / Narrative of one Richard Lamb's / Adventures in the Banda Oriental, in / South America, as told by Himself / BY W. H. HUDSON / AUTHOR OF "GREEN MANSIONS," ETC. / WITH AN INTRODUCTORY NOTE / BY THEODORE ROOSEVELT / [*ornament: sea-scape with coast and sun in the background*] / NEW YORK / E. P. DUTTON AND COMPANY / 1916

Collation $[1]^8 ([1]4+\chi 1) [2-22]^8 [23]^6$; pp. [i–iv] v–vi [vii–viii] ix–x 1–355 [356]; 187×123 mm.; printed on laid paper. Leaves bulk 32 mm.

Pagination p. [i], half-title 'THE PURPLE LAND'; p. [ii], blank; p. [iii], title; p. [iv], 'PUBLISHED, 1916 / BY / E. P. DUTTON & COMPANY / Printed in the United States of America'; pp. v–vi, preface to the new edition by Hudson dated September 1904; p. [vii], contents; p. [viii], blank; pp. ix–x, introductory note by Theodore Roosevelt dated 14 August 1916; pp. 1–352, text; pp. 353–355, appendix; p. [356], blank.

Binding Purple cloth. Front cover stamped in gilt, enclosed within a single blind rule border '*The* / PURPLE LAND / ADVENTURES IN SOUTH AMERICA / [*thick rule*] / BY W. H. HUDSON / [*ornament: sea-scape with coast and sun in the background*]; spine stamped in gilt '*The* / PURPLE / LAND / [*rule*] W. H. HUDSON / E·P·DUTTON / [*two inverted heart designs*] & C⁰ [*two inverted heart designs*]'. All edges trimmed; white wove endpapers.

Variants 1. *Collation* $[1]^8 (\pm [1]2) ([1]4+\chi 1) [2-22]^8 [23]^6$; $\chi 1$ is introductory note by Theodore Roosevelt. 184×122 mm. Printed on wove paper. Leaves bulk 27 mm. Gilding is not so brilliant on front cover and spine, and cloth is a slightly different texture. 2. *Collation* [1]⁸ (±[1]₂) ([1]₃+χ1) [2–22]⁸ [23]⁶; χ1 is contents. 3. *Collation* [1]⁸ ([1]₃+χ1) [2–22]⁸ [23]⁶; χ1 is contents. Spine reads 'E. P. DUTTON'. 4. *Collation* [1–23]⁸; printed on wove paper. Page [356] contains ads for six of Hudson's books and last leaf ([23]₈) is blank. Spine reads 'E. P. Dutton'. 5. Same as variant 4 except spine reads 'E. P. DUTTON'.

Notes Published at $1.50. Ten editions to 1927.

Reviews New York Evening Sun 22 July 1916; *New York Independent* 28 August 1916; *New Republic* 23 September 1916; *Review of Reviews* September 1916; *Boston Transcript* 13 December 1916; *New York Times Book Review* 31 December 1916.

Copies Chicago; LC; Lilly; Texas (2). *Variant copy 1* Texas. *Variant copy 2* Dartmouth. *Variant copy 3* Texas (2). *Variant copy 4* Texas. *Variant copy 5* Adams; Dobie.

A1g

COLLECTED EDITION 1922

THE / [*in red*] PURPLE LAND / BEING THE NARRATIVE OF ONE RICHARD / LAMB'S ADVENTURES IN THE BANDA / ORIENTÁL IN SOUTH AMERICA, / AS TOLD BY HIMSELF / BY / W. H. HUDSON / [*publisher's device*] / MCMXXII / LONDON & TORONTO / [*in red*] J. M. DENT & SONS LTD. / NEW YORK: E. P. DUTTON & CO.

Collation π⁶ A–Z⁸; pp. [*six unnumbered pages*] [i–iv] v–vii [viii] 1–366 [367–368]; 220 × 148 mm.; printed on cream laid paper with oval watermark incorporating Hudson's name, a figure of a tree and two deer.

Pagination [*first unnumbered page*], blank; [*second unnumbered page*], 'THIS EDITION IS LIMITED TO 750 COPIES / FOR SALE IN ENGLAND, 100 FOR SALE / IN THE UNITED STATES OF AMERICA, / AND 35 PRESENTATION COPIES / THIS IS No [*autograph number written in blue ink*]'; [*third unnumbered page*], half-title 'THE / COLLECTED WORKS / *of* / W. H. HUDSON / [*short rule*] / IN TWENTY-FOUR / VOLUMES / THE PURPLE LAND'; [*fourth and fifth unnumbered pages*], blank; [*sixth unnumbered page*], frontispiece, drawing of Hudson by William Rothenstein; p. [i] title; p. [ii], '*All rights reserved* / PRINTED IN GREAT BRITAIN'; p. [iii], publisher's note about an appreciation of Hudson by Viscount Grey of Fallodon to be included in a later volume of the collected works (see *Dead Man's Plack*, A47a), and acknowledgments to other publishers for permission to include various works by Hudson in this Collected edition; p. [iv], blank; pp. v–vi, preface to the new edition of *The Purple Land*, reprinted from the 1904 edition; p. vii, contents; p. [viii], blank; pp. 1–363, text; pp. 364–366, Appendix, History of the Banda Oriental; p. [367], 'PRINTED BY / THE TEMPLE PRESS AT LETCHWORTH / IN GREAT BRITAIN'; p. [368], blank.

Binding Green cloth. Gold medallion profile portrait in centre of front cover enclosed within a single blind rule border; spine stamped in gilt 'W. H. HUDSON / [leafy branch] / The / Purple / Land / J·M·DENT / & SONS. LD.'. Blind rule border on back cover. Top edges trimmed and gilt, other edges untrimmed; cream laid endpapers. On front pastedown is a reproduction of pictorial bookplate with Hudson's name and dates. Maroon silk place marker.

Notes This is one of twenty-four volumes of Hudson's collected works. Eight hundred and eighty-five sets were published 1922–1923 for twenty-four guineas per set. The one hundred sets for sale in America were sold by E. P. Dutton for $192 per set. The collected works was reprinted in America by AMS Press in 1968 at $360.

The Uniform Edition of Hudson's works was published in 1951 by Dent and consists of seven titles: *The Purple Land, Nature in Downland, A Hind in Richmond Park; Green Mansions; Adventures Among Birds, Far Away and Long Ago. Idle Days in Patagonia* was added in 1954.

The Purple Land is gathered in 16's and the leaves measure 192 × 124 mm. Bound in red cloth. The author's name, title, a figure of a feather and the publisher's name are stamped in gilt on the spine. All edges trimmed; white wove endpapers. Green and white wove dust jacket printed in black. There is an introduction by David Garnett written especially for this edition, and the frontispiece is a previously unpublished photograph of Hudson about age twenty-five years.

The Collected edition of the works of W. H. Hudson was reviewed in the *New York Times Book Review*, 3 June 1923 and in the *Times Literary Supplement* 28 February 1924.

A1h

THE NEW READERS' LIBRARY EDITION (1927)

THE PURPLE LAND / *Being the Narrative of one Richard Lamb's* / *Adventures in the Banda Oriental, in* / *South America, as told by Himself* / by / W. H. HUDSON / AUTHOR OF / "GREEN MANSIONS," "A CRYSTAL AGE," ETC. / DUCKWORTH / 3 HENRIETTA STREET / LONDON, W. C. 2

Collation [A]¹⁶ B–L¹⁶ M⁸; pp. [i–v] vi [vii] viii [1] 2–355 [356–360]; 168 × 115 mm.; printed on wove paper.

Pagination p. [i], half-title 'THE NEW READERS LIBRARY / THE PURPLE LAND'; p. [ii], list of twenty-four titles published in the New Readers' Library series; p. [iii], title; p. [iv], '*All Rights Reserved / Reprinted (New Readers Library) 1927 / Made and Printed in Great Britain by / The Camelot Press Limited / London and Southampton*'; pp. [v]–vi, preface dated 1904; pp. [vii]–viii, contents; pp. [1] 2–355, text; p. [356], blank; pp. [357–360], ads for the New Readers' Library.

Binding Blue cloth. Spine stamped in gilt '[*rule*] / [*decorative rule*] / [*rule*] / THE / PURPLE / LAND / W. H. / HUDSON / DUCKWORTH / [*rule*] / [*decorative rule*] / [*rule*]'. All edges trimmed; white wove endpapers. Orange wove dust jacket printed in black.

Notes 3,000 copies published August 1927 at 3s 6d. No. 14 in The New Readers' Library.

A1i

FIRST ILLUSTRATED EDITION 1929

The Purple Land: / *Being the Narrative of one Richard Lamb's / Adventures in the Banda Oriental, in South / America, as told by Himself* / By W. H. HUDSON / ILLUSTRATED BY / KEITH HENDERSON / DUCKWORTH / 3 Henrietta Street, London / 1929

Collation [AL]⁸ BL–YL⁸; pp. [1–4] 5–368; 223 × 143 mm.; printed on laid paper.

Pagination p. [1], half-title 'THE PURPLE LAND'; p. [2], blank; *frontispiece*; p. [3], title; p. [4], '*First Published in 1885 / Reset and with illustrations by Keith Henderson, 1929 / Made and Printed in Great Britain by / The Camelot Press Limited / London and Southampton*'; pp. 5–6, preface to the second edition by Hudson dated September 1904; pp. 7–8, illustrations; pp. 9–366, text; pp. 367–368, appendix.

Illustrations Fifty-two woodblock illustrations by Keith Henderson; thirteen tipped in on calendered paper, thirty-nine within the text.

Binding Purple decorative paper boards with smooth purple cloth spine; spine stamped in gilt 'THE / PURPLE / LAND / W. H. / HUDSON / ILLUSTRATED BY / KEITH / HENDERSON / DUCKWORTH'. Top edges trimmed and stained purple, other edges untrimmed; white laid endpapers. Rose pictorial dust jacket printed in black.

Notes 3,000 copies published 4 November 1929 at 15s.

The sheets of this edition were issued by E. P. Dutton in 1930 with a cancel title page giving Dutton's imprint. The binding is orange cloth with purple cloth spine and corners with 'DUTTON' at foot of spine.

OTHER EDITIONS

A1j	1927	Everyman's Library. New York, Dutton.
A1k	1927	Modern Library edition. New York, The Modern Library. Introduction by William McFee.
A1l	1932	Braille edition. Mt. Healthy, Ohio, Clovernook Printing House for the Blind, 3 volumes.
A1m	1935	Penguin editions, no. 12. London, Penguin Books.
A1n	1937	Cameo Classics. New York, Grosset and Dunlap. Illustrated by Keith Henderson.
A1o	1942	Illustrated editions. Cleveland, World. Illustrated by Keith Henderson.
A1p	n.d.	New York, Three Sirens Press. Illustrated by Keith Henderson.
A1q	n.d.	Armed Services edition, no. 721. New York, Editions for the Armed Services.
A1r	n.d.	New York, Illustrated editions. Illustrated by Keith Henderson.
A1s	n.d.	Braille hand-copied edition for the National Library for the Blind (London), 4 volumes.

A2a

A CRYSTAL AGE

FIRST EDITION 1887

A CRYSTAL AGE / [*nine-line quotation from Darwin*] / LONDON / T. FISHER UNWIN / 26 PATERNOSTER SQUARE / 1887

Collation π^2 A–S^8; pp. [i–iv] [1] 2–287 [288]; 190 × 130 mm.; printed on wove paper.

Pagination p. [i], half-title 'A CRYSTAL AGE'; p. [ii], list of six titles included in The 4/6 Series of Novels published by T. Fisher Unwin; p. [iii], title; p. [iv], publisher's device; pp. [1] 2–287, text; p. [288], blank.

Binding Black cloth. Front cover printed in red 'A / CRYSTAL / AGE / [*four rules*] /

[*design of circle and crosses repeated three times*] / [*four rules*]'; spine stamped in gilt 'A / CRYSTAL / AGE / [*printed in red: four rules*] / [*printed in red: design of circle and crosses*] / [*printed in red: four rules*] / T. FISHER UNWIN'; back cover printed in red '[*publisher's device*] / [*four rules*] / [*four rules*]'. All edges untrimmed; green wove endpapers with floral design. *Binder's insert following p.* [288]: a thirty-two page catalogue of books published by T. Fisher Unwin dated 1886–7.

Variants 1. Copy with publisher's device omitted from back cover; publisher's catalogue omitted; light green endpapers with tree design rather than flowers. 2. Copy with publisher's name on spine in large and small caps. 3. Same as 2 but without publisher's catalogue. 4. Copy with twenty-four pages of undated ads. 5. Copy with publisher's device on back cover; publisher's catalogue omitted; light green endpapers with tree design rather than flowers. 6. Copy with publisher's device on back cover; publisher's catalogue omitted; green wove endpapers with floral design.

Notes Published at 4s. 6d. The BM copy is stamped 7 April 1887. In response to my enquiry about publishing information, John Denton, Managing Director, Ernest Benn Limited, wrote on 1 June 1972: "Your letter of May 25th has been passed on to us as we took over T. Fisher Unwin's business. Unfortunately the files were largely destroyed during the war and I am afraid that we can give you no information about Hudson's *A Crystal Age*."

The Humanities Research Center holds a copy of Variant 1 with the following inscription:

> This modest little book (by a modest little writer) is not a prophecy: we (optimists) believe that the future has higher things, although perhaps not imaginable, for the human race than such as are portrayed herein: nor is it a romance in spirit, but only in form, being nothing more than an expression of weariness at our too complex system of life, & the modernism which sums up variance with not a few of our finer feelings. –
>
> The traveller in a hot thirsty land delights his mind with images of cooling springs and shady groves: in like manner the author, at war with the time, & war-worn, has found a visionary relief in creating a more restful state than ours; – human beings, without ambition, pride or passion, following other, & in one sense lowlier, ideals. July 9, 1890.

Reviews Literary World 22 April 1887; *Jewish World* 29 April 1887; *Academy* 4 May 1887; *Bookman* December 1895.

Copies BM; Dobie; ISU; Texas. *Variant copy 1* Dartmouth; Texas. *Variant copy 2* Lilly. *Variant copy 3* Adams. *Variant copy 4, 5, 6* Spater.

A2b

SECOND, REVISED, EDITION 1906

[*in red*] A CRYSTAL AGE / BY / W. H. HUDSON / [*four lines of verse*] / [*circular design: snake with tail in mouth*] / LONDON / [*in red*] T. FISHER UNWIN / ADELPHI TERRACE / MCMVI

Collation π⁴ A–U⁸; pp. [i–iv] v–viii [1] 2–316 2[1–4]; 190 × 128 mm.; printed on wove paper.

Pagination p. [i], half-title 'A CRYSTAL AGE'; p. [ii], list of eight books by the same author; p. [iii], title; p. [iv], 'FIRST EDITION . . . . 1887 / SECOND EDITION . . . . 1906 / [*All rights reserved.*]'; pp. v–viii, preface to the second edition by Hudson, dated September 1906; pp. [1], 2–316, text; pp. 2[1–4], publisher's advertisements.

Binding Green cloth stamped in gold, white and blue. Woman playing a lyre astride a bull. Bull is standing on a pillar upon which is stamped in white 'A CRYSTAL / ▼▼▼▼▼ AGE ▼▼▼▼▼ / ▼▼▼▼ BY W. H. ▼ / HUDSON'. A floral vine stamped in gold flows from base of pillar up around the woman, all enclosed within a white decorative border. Floral vine stamped in gold on spine; spine stamped in white '[*within a white decorative border*] A / CRYSTAL / AGE / BY: W. H. / HUDSON / T. / FISHER / UNWIN'. Top edges gilt, others untrimmed; white laid endpapers.

Variants: 1. *Collation*: π⁴ (π1 and π2 are conjugate; π3 and π4 are nonconjugate and tipped in) A–T⁸ U⁸ (–U7, 8). No publisher's ads. Leaves measure 187 × 124 mm. 2. Light blue cloth stamped in black '[*fancy*] A CRYSTAL AGE / BY W. H. / HUDSON'; spine stamped in black '[*within a single rule panel*] [*fancy*] A / [*fancy*] CRYSTAL / [*fancy*] AGE / BY: W. H. / HUDSON / [*below panel*] T. Fisher Unwin'. All edges trimmed; white wove endpapers. Leaves measure 186 × 122 mm.

Notes Published October 1906 at 6s. See note to A2a for information on publishing records.

This edition, revised by the author, contains the author's name on the title page and a preface for the first time. The work is partly rewritten and several chapters are rearranged. The first edition contained eighteen chapters; this edition has twenty.

Reviews Tribune 13 October 1906; *New Age* 25 October 1906; *Aberdeen Free Press* 27 October 1906; *Times Literary Supplement* 2 November 1906; *Book Buyer* 15 November 1906; *Independent Review* November 1906; *Bookman*

December 1906; *Literary World* February 1907; *Nation* 11 April 1907; *Singapore Free Press* 11 April 1907.

Variant copy 1 Dobie; ISU. *Variant copy 2* Dartmouth; ISU.

A2c

FIRST AMERICAN ISSUE 1906

A CRYSTAL AGE/BY/W. H. HUDSON/[*four lines of verse*]/[*circular design: snake with tail in mouth*]/NEW YORK/E. P. DUTTON AND COMPANY/31 WEST TWENTY-THIRD STREET/1906

Collation π^4 ($\pm\pi 2$) A–U^8 (–U7,8); pp. [i–iv] v–viii [1] 2–316; 190 × 128 mm.; printed on wove paper.

Pagination Same as the second, revised, edition, except page [iv] which reads '[*Printed in Great Britain.*]/[*All rights reserved.*]', and the four pages of publisher's ads which have been cancelled.

Binding Same as the second, revised, edition, except that the spine reads 'DUTTON/ & Co'.

Notes Published at $1.50.

The sheets of the second, revised, edition with a cancel title page for the Dutton imprint, and cancelled publisher's advertisements at end.

Reviews New York Times Book Review 23 March 1907.

A2d

READERS' LIBRARY EDITION (1913)

A CRYSTAL AGE / BY / W. H. HUDSON / AUTHOR OF / "GREEN MANSIONS," "THE PURPLE LAND," "SOUTH AMERICAN SKETCHES," / ETC. / [*four lines of verse*] / [*publisher's device*] / LONDON: DUCKWORTH & CO. / 3 HENRIETTA STREET, COVENT GARDEN

Collation π^4 A–T^8 U^6; pp. [i–iv] v–viii [1] 2–316; 186 × 122 mm.; printed on wove paper.

Pagination p. [i], half-title 'A CRYSTAL AGE'; p. [ii], list of titles in The Readers' Library; p. [iii], title; p. [iv], '*Published in the Readers Library 1913 / All rights*

reserved'; pp. v–viii, preface to the second edition dated September 1906; pp. [1] 2–316, text.

Binding Blue cloth. Publisher's circular device blind stamped in centre of front cover; spine stamped in gilt '[*within a single rule panel*] A / CRYSTAL / AGE / W. H. / HUDSON / [*in smaller single rule panel at bottom of spine*] DUCKWORTH'; publisher's device blind stamped at lower left corner of back cover. All edges trimmed; white wove endpapers.

Notes Published March 1913 at 2s. 6d. See note to A1c for information on publishing records.

Copies RSPB.

A2e

SECOND AMERICAN ISSUE 1916

A CRYSTAL AGE / By / W. H. HUDSON / AUTHOR OF "THE PURPLE LAND," "A SHEPHERD'S LIFE," ETC, / WITH AN INTRODUCTION BY / DR. CLIFFORD SMYTH / [*four lines of verse*] / NEW YORK / E. P. DUTTON AND COMPANY / 681 FIFTH AVENUE / 1916

Collation π^4 ($-\pi 1 \pm \pi 2$) $[\chi]^6$ ($\pm \chi 1$) A–T^8 U^6; pp. [iii–iv] v–xix [xx] [1] 2–316; 190 × 128 mm.; printed on wove paper.

Pagination p. [iii], title; p. [iv], '[*Printed in Great Britain.*] / [*All rights reserved.*]'; pp. v–viii, preface to the second edition, dated September 1906; pp. ix–xix, 'A FOREWORD' by Clifford Smyth, dated 10 August 1916; [*at foot of p. ix:*] 'Copyright, 1916, by / E. P. DUTTON & Co.'; p. [xx], blank; pp. [1] 2–316, text.

Binding Light green cloth; decorations same as first American issue except stamping is inferior and top edge is not gilt.

Notes Published at $2.00 Three printings to 1937.
  $\pi 1$ is a cancelled half-title; $\pi 2$ is a cancellans title page; $\chi 1$ is a cancellans first page of Clifford Smyth's foreword.
  Clifford Smyth was an author and editor of the *New York Times Book Review* from 1913 to 1922. This is the first appearance of his foreword.

Reviews New York Times Book Review 31 December 1916; *Boston Transcript* 3 February 1917; *New York Independent* 19 March 1917; *ALA Booklist* March 1917; *Bookman* March 1917.

A2f

FIRST AMERICAN EDITION (1917)

A CRYSTAL AGE/BY/W. H. HUDSON/AUTHOR OF "THE PURPLE LAND," "A SHEPHERD'S LIFE," ETC./WITH AN INTRODUCTION BY/DR. CLIFFORD SMYTH/[*four lines of verse*]/NEW YORK/E. P. DUTTON & CO./618 FIFTH AVENUE

Collation [1–21]⁸; pp. [i–iv] v–viii [ix] x–xix [xx] χ1–316; 189 × 124 mm.; printed on wove paper.

Pagination p. [i], half-title 'A CRYSTAL AGE'; p. [ii], blank; p. [iii], title; p. [iv], 'PUBLISHED BY E. P. DUTTON & CO., 1917/[*short rule*]/ FOREWORD COPYRIGHT IN 1916, / BY E. P. DUTTON & CO. / 𝔓rinted in the 𝔘nited 𝔖tates of 𝔄merica'; pp. v–viii, preface dated September 1906; pp. [ix]x–xi x, foreword by Clifford Smyth dated 10 August 1916; p. [xx], blank; pp. 1–316, text.

Binding Light green cloth. White paper label printed in black in upper left corner of front cover '[*within a single rule frame*] A/CRYSTAL/AGE/∼/W. H. HUDSON'; identical label on spine. Foot of spine stamped in gilt 'E. P. DUTTON / & CO.'. All edges trimmed; white wove endpapers.

Variant Decorative binding as in first American issue (A2c). Brown wove dust jacket printed in black.

Notes Published November 1917 at $1.50. Three printings to 1937.

Reviews Nation 22 March 1917; *American Review of Reviews* May 1917; *Wilson Library Bulletin* May 1917; *Pittsburgh Monthly Bulletin* October 1917.

Variant copy ISU.

A2g

COLLECTED EDITION 1922

A / [*in red*] CRYSTAL AGE / BY / W. H. HUDSON / [*publisher's device*] / MCMXXII / LONDON & TORONTO/ [*in red*] J. M. DENT & SONS LTD. / NEW YORK: E. P. DUTTON & CO.

Collation π⁴ A–P⁸ Q⁴; pp. [*two unnumbered pages*] [i–iv] v–vi 1–246 [247–248]; 220 × 148 mm.; printed on cream laid paper with oval watermark incorporating Hudson's name, a figure of a tree and two deer.

Pagination [*first unnumbered page*], blank; [*second unnumbered page*], 'THIS EDITION IS LIMITED TO 750 COPIES / FOR SALE IN ENGLAND, 100 FOR SALE / IN THE UNITED STATES OF AMERICA, / AND 35 PRESENTATION COPIES'; p. [i], half-title 'THE / COLLECTED WORKS / of / W. H. HUDSON / [*short rule*] / IN TWENTY-FOUR / VOLUMES / A CRYSTAL AGE'; p. [ii], blank; p. [iii], title; p. [iv], '*All rights reserved* / PRINTED IN GREAT BRITAIN'; pp. v–vi, preface dated September 1906; pp. 1–246, text; p. [247], 'PRINTED BY / THE TEMPLE PRESS AT LETCHWORTH / IN GREAT BRITAIN'; p. [248], blank.

Binding Green cloth. Gold medallion profile portrait in centre of front cover enclosed within a single blind rule border; spine stamped in gilt 'W. H. / HUDSON / [*leafy branch*] / A / Crystal / Age / J·M·DENT / & SONS. LD.'. Blind rule border on back cover. Top edges trimmed and gilt, other edges untrimmed; cream laid endpapers. On front pastedown is a reproduction of pictorial bookplate with Hudson's name and dates. Maroon silk place marker.

Notes This is one of twenty-four volumes of Hudson's collected works. Eight hundred and eighty-five sets were published 1922–1923 for twenty-four guineas per set. The one hundred sets for sale in America were sold by E. P. Dutton for $192 per set. The collected works was reprinted in America by AMS Press in 1968 at $360.

A2h

THE NEW READERS' LIBRARY EDITION (1927)

A CRYSTAL AGE / by / W. H. HUDSON / AUTHOR OF / "GREEN MANSIONS," "THE PURPLE LAND," / "SOUTH AMERICAN SKETCHES," ETC. / [*four lines of verse*] / DUCKWORTH / 3 HENRIETTA STREET / LONDON, W.C.2

Collation $[1]^{16}$ 2–10^{16}; pp. [i–iv] v–viii [1] 2–316; 168 × 115 mm.; printed on wove paper.

Pagination p. [i], half-title 'THE NEW READERS' LIBRARY / A CRYSTAL AGE'; p. [ii], list of twenty-four titles published in the New Readers' Library series; p. [iii], title; p. [iv] '*Fourth Impression* . . . 1919 / *Reissued in "The New Readers' Library"* . . . 1927 / *All Rights Reserved* / *Printed in Great Britain by* / *Billing and Sons, Ltd., Guildford and Esher*'; pp. v–viii, preface dated 1906; pp. [1] 2–316, text.

Binding Blue cloth. Spine stamped in gilt '[*rule*] / [*decorative rule*] / [*rule*] / A / CRYSTAL / AGE / W. H. / HUDSON / DUCKWORTH / [*rule*] / [*decorative rule*] / [*rule*]'. All edges trimmed; white wove endpapers. Orange wove dust jacket printed in black.

Notes 2,000 copies published 22 September 1927 for 3s. 6d. No. 18 in the New Readers' Library.

OTHER EDITIONS

A2i   1950   New York, Doric Books.
A2j   n.d.   Armed Services edition no. G-196. New York, Editions for the Armed Services.

A3a

ARGENTINE ORNITHOLOGY

FIRST EDITION   1888-1889

Volume I
ARGENTINE ORNITHOLOGY. / A / DESCRIPTIVE CATALOGUE / OF THE / BIRDS OF THE ARGENTINE REPUBLIC. / BY / P. L. SCLATER, M.A., PH.D., F.R.S., ETC. / WITH NOTES ON THEIR HABITS / BY / W. H. HUDSON, C.M.Z.S., / LATE OF BUENOS AYRES. / [illustration] / THE CARIAMA. / [rule] / VOLUME I. / [rule] / LONDON: / R. H. PORTER, 6 TENTERDEN STREET, W. / 1888.

Collation [A]^8 (A1 + χ1) b^4 B-O^8; pp. [i-ii] [*two unnumbered pages*] [iii-v] vi-xiv [xv-xvii] xviii-xxiv [1] 2-208; 249 × 165 mm.; printed on wove paper.

Pagination p. [i], title; p. [ii], 'ALERE FLAMMAM / [*design of hand filling lamp with oil*] / PRINTED BY TAYLOR AND FRANCIS. / RED LION COURT, FLEET STREET.'; p. [*first unnumbered page*], notice of limitation 'ARGENTINE ORNITHOLOGY. / [*decorative short rule*] / THE Edition of this work being strictly limited to / 200 copies for Subscribers, each copy is numbered / and signed by the Authors. / [*capital script N n*] [*autograph number in blue ink*] / P. L. Sclater [*autograph signature in black ink*] / [*offset to left of a vertical rule*] Signed / W. H. Hudson [*autograph signature in black ink*]; p. [*second unnumbered page*], blank; p. [iii], preface to the first volume by Sclater dated 1 December 1887; p. [iv], blank; pp. [v] vi-xiv, contents of Volume I; p. [xv], list of plates in Volume I; p. [xvi], blank; pp. [xvii] xviii-xxiv, introduction; pp. [1] 2-208, text.

Illustrations Ten full-page coloured half-tone etchings from original drawings by J. G. Keulemans tipped in on a heavier stock of paper. Line etchings within the text.

Binding Greenish-grey paper boards printed in black 'ARGENTINE ORNITHOLOGY. / BY / P. L. SCLATER, M.A., PH.D., F.R.S., ETC., / AND / W. H. HUDSON, C.M.Z.S. / VOLUME I. / LONDON: / R. H. PORTER, 6 TENTERDEN STREET, W. / 1888. / [*rule*] / Subscription-price of the two Volumes, £2 15s., payable on the issue of Vol. 1.'; spine printed in black '[*thick-thin rule*] / ARGENTINE / ORNITHOLOGY. / [*double short rule*] / I. / [*double short rule*] / LONDON: / PORTER. / 1888. / [*thick-thin rule*]'. Back cover printed in black with publisher's ads. All edges untrimmed; white wove endpapers.

Volume II
ARGENTINE ORNITHOLOGY. / A / DESCRIPTIVE CATALOGUE / OF THE / BIRDS OF THE ARGENTINE REPUBLIC. / BY / P. L. SCLATER, M.A., PH.D., F.R.S., ETC. / WITH NOTES ON THEIR HABITS / BY / W. H. HUDSON, C.M.Z.S., / LATE OF BUENOS AYRES. / [*illustration*] / BURMEISTER'S CARIAMA / [*rule*] / VOLUME II. / [*rule*] / LONDON: / R. H. PORTER, 18 PRINCES STREET, CAVENDISH SQUARE, W. / 1889

Collation [A]^{10} B–P^8 Q^4 R^8 S^2; pp. [2] [i–iii] iv [v] vi–xv [xvi–xviii] [1] 2–220 [221] 222–232 [233] 234–251 [252]; 250 × 165 mm.; printed on wove paper.

Pagination [2], blank; p. [i], title; p. [ii], 'ALERE FLAMMAM / [*design of hand filling lamp with oil*] / PRINTED BY TAYLOR AND FRANCIS, / RED LION COURT, FLEET STREET.'; pp. [iii]–iv, preface to the second volume by Sclater dated 1 February 1889; pp. [v] vi–xv, contents of Volume II; p. [xvi], blank; p. [xvii], list of plates in Volume II; p. [xviii], blank; pp. [1] 2–220, text; pp. [221] 222–232, appendix; pp. [233] 234–251, index to Volumes I and II; p. [252], 'PRINTED BY TAYLOR AND FRANCIS, / RED LION COURT, FLEET STREET.'.

Illustrations Ten coloured illustrations by J. G. Keulemans tipped in on a heavier stock of paper. Black and white line drawings within the text.

Binding Greenish-grey paper boards printed in black 'ARGENTINE ORNITHOLOGY. / BY / P. L. SCLATER, M.A., PH.D., F.R.S., ETC., / AND / W. H. HUDSON, C.M.Z.S. / VOLUME II. / LONDON: / R. H. PORTER, 18 PRINCES STREET, CAVENDISH SQUARE, W. / 1889. / [*rule*] / Price of the two volumes, £3 3s.'; spine same as Volume I except reads 'II' and date '1889'. All edges untrimmed; white wove endpapers.

Variant The Library of Congress copy is in the original paper boards, and Volume I is inscribed 'Alfred Wingrove from W. H. Hudson. July, 1889'. In both the LC and BM copies the limitation notice is missing from Volume I and the introduction that normally appears in Volume I is bound in Volume II following [A10].

Collation Volume I: [A] B–O⁸; 259 × 167 mm.; *Volume II:* [A]¹⁰ b⁴ B–P⁸ Q⁴ R⁸ S²; 257 × 165 mm.

Notes 200 copies published 1888–1889 at £3 3s. The BM copy is stamped 1 February 1888.

"The present volume contains an account of the Passeres of the Argentine Republic, which, as at present known, number some 229 species. The second volume ... will be devoted to the history of the remaining Orders of Birds...."

All the personal observations recorded in these pages are due to Mr. Hudson, while I am responsible for the arrangement, nomenclature, and scientific portions of the work." (*Preface, Volume I, by P. L. Sclater*).

"This volume contains our account of all the Orders of Birds met with within the Argentine Republic except the Passeres, which were treated of in the First Volume. The Introduction is issued with this, but is intended to be bound up with the first volume, and is paged to follow the contents of that volume." (*Preface, Volume II, by P. L. Sclater*).

Argentine Ornithology incorporates, with slight textual changes, a large part of Hudson's contributions to the *Proceedings of the Zoological Society of London* 1869–1876 (C1–C22; C24–C28) and his article on the birds of the genus *Homorus* which appeared in *The Ibis* July 1885 (C39). In 1920 Hudson's portion of *Argentine Ornithology* was published as *Birds of La Plata* (A38), again with minor textual changes. Hudson's letters on the ornithology of Buenos Aires were collected in book form in *Letters on the Ornithology of Buenos Ayres*, 1951 (A61). See note preceding C1 for summary of the publication of this material.

Reviews Saturday Review 28 April 1888; *Nature* 18 October 1888.

The reviewer in the *Saturday Review* wrote: "[The reader will find that these] are not volumes to be dismissed too lightly; that, while they satisfy the strictest requirements of ornithological science, they are enlivened with ample notes, results of careful observation upon the habits and peculiarities of the particular birds described, which are not merely interesting in themselves, but are suggestive of curious questions of evolution and heredity and origin of species...."

In his review in *Nature* R. Bowdler Sharpe wrote: "Dr. Sclater and Mr. Hudson have combined their forces to produce one of the best books ever written on South American ornithology. Each is a master of his own portion of the subject, for no one is better acquainted with neotropical ornithology than Dr. Sclater, and Mr. Hudson has been known for many years as one of the best living observers of the habits of birds in the field."

Copies Adams; Dartmouth; Dobie; Martin; RSPB; Texas. *Variant copies* BM; LC.

A4a

OSPREY; OR, EGRETS AND AIGRETTES

FIRST EDITION (1891)

[*wrapper title*] SOCIETY FOR THE PROTECTION OF BIRDS. / (No. 3.) / OSPREY; / OR, / EGRETS AND AIGRETTES. / BY / W. H. HUDSON, C.M.Z.S., / *Author of* "*The Naturalist in La Plata,*" *and, jointly with Dr. P. L. Sclater,* / F.R.S., *of* "*Argentine Ornithology.*" / [*picture of an Egret*] / Any profits arising from the sale of this pamphlet will be devoted to / the SOCIETY FOR THE PROTECTION OF BIRDS. Copies at threepence / each, or two shillings per dozen, postage free, can be obtained from the / ladies whose addresses are given on the following page.

Collation [A]⁸; pp. [1–3] 4–14 [15–16]; 182 × 124 mm.; printed on laid paper.

Pagination p. [1], wrapper title; p. [2], list of officers and rules of the Society; p. [3] '[*decorative head piece*] / OSPREY; OR, EGRETS AND AIGRETTES. / [*text begins*]'; pp. 4–14, text; decorative tail piece at close of text; p. [15], blank; p. [16] '[*printer's device*] / CHISWICK PRESS:—C. WHITTINGHAM AND CO., TOOKS COURT, / CHANCERY LANE.'.

Binding Self-wrappers, stitched.

Notes Published at 3d. each or 2s. per dozen. The Bodleian Library copy is stamped 3 March 1892.

This first appeared in book form in *Dead Man's Plack An Old Thorn & Miscellanea* (A47).

This is without question the rarest of all Hudson's writings. G. F. Wilson had not seen a copy of the first printing when he published his bibliography of Hudson in 1922, although he later described a copy in the *Bookman's Journal*, February 1924. There is no copy in the library of the Royal Society for the Protection of Birds, and the only copies recorded are in the Bodleian Library and in the private library of H. Bradley Martin.

Copies Bodleian; Martin.

A4b

SECOND EDITION 1896

[*wrapper title*] Society for the Protection of Birds.–No. 3. / [*rule*] / OSPREY; / OR, EGRETS AND AIGRETTES. / BY / W. H. HUDSON. C.M.Z.S., / *Author of*

"*Birds in a Village,*" *etc.* / [*picture of an Egret*] / Copies of this leaflet, 1d. each, 9d. per doz., 5/- per 100, can be obtained from / the Society's Publishing Department, KNOWLEDGE Office, 326, High Holborn, / London, W.C.; or from the Hon. Sec. of the Society for the Protection of Birds, / Mrs. F. E. LEMON, Hillcrest, Redhill, Surrey. / [*short rule*] / 1896. / 6TH TO 10TH THOUSAND.

Collation [A]⁶; pp. [1–3] 4–10 [11–12]; 215 × 138 mm.; printed on wove paper.

Pagination p. [1], wrapper title; p. [2], blank; pp. [3] 4–10, text, p. [11], Postscript by Hudson dated 1 August 1896; p. [12], list of twenty-one publications by the Society; [*below a double rule*] '★*To be obtained post-free at* KNOWLEDGE *Office*, 326, *High Holborn, W. C.*, / *or from the Hon. Sec., Mrs.* F. E. LEMON, *Hillcrest, Redhill, Surrey; also assorted* / *packets at 6d., 1s., or upwards.*'.

Binding Self wrappers, stitched.

Notes 5,000 copies published at 1d. each or 9d. per dozen.
This is the first appearance of Hudson's postscript.

A5a

THE NATURALIST IN LA PLATA

FIRST EDITION 1892

THE / NATURALIST IN LA PLATA / BY / W. H. HUDSON, C.M.Z.S. / JOINT AUTHOR OF "ARGENTINE ORNITHOLOGY" / [*illustration*] / WHITE-BANDED MOCKING-BIRD / WITH ILLUSTRATIONS / LONDON-CHAPMAN AND HALL, LD. / 1892 / [*All rights reserved*]

Collation A⁴ B–Bb⁸ Cc²; pp. [i–iii] iv [v] vi–vii [viii] [1] 2–383 [384–385] 386–388; 225 × 145 mm.; printed on wove paper.

Pagination Frontispiece; p. [i], title; p. [ii], 'LONDON: / PRINTED BY GILBERT AND RIVINGTON, LD., / ST. JOHN'S HOUSE, CLERKENWELL, E.C.'; pp. [iii]–iv, preface dated 1891; pp. [v] vi–vii, contents; p. [viii], illustrations; pp. [1] 2–383, text; p. [384], blank; pp. [385] 386–388, index; at bottom of p. 388, '[*rule*] / PRINTED BY GILBERT AND RIVINGTON, LD., ST JOHN'S HOUSE, CLERKENWELL, E.C.'.

Contents The Desert Pampas – The Puma, or Lion of America –(first appeared in *Longman's Magazine* September 1886 (C44) and collected in *Harmsworth Natural History* (B3)) – A Wave of Life – Some Curious Animal Weapons – Fear in Birds – Parental and Early Instincts – The Mephitic Skunk – Mimicry and Warning Colours in Grasshoppers – Dragon-Fly Storms – Mosquitoes and Parasite Problems – Humble-Bees and other Matters – A Noble Wasp – Nature's Night-lights – Facts and Thoughts about Spiders – The Death-feigning Instinct – Humming Birds (first appeared in *Longman's Magazine* May 1886 (c43)) – The Crested Screamer (first appeared in *Gentleman's Magazine* September 1885 (c41)) – The Woodhewer Family – Music and Dancing in Nature (first appeared in *Longman's Magazine* April 1890 (c55)) – Biography of the Vizcacha (first appeared in the *Proceedings of the Zoological Society of London* 19 November 1872 (c20)) – The Dying Huanaco (first appeared in *Longman's Magazine* March 1891 (c58)) – The Strange Instincts of Cattle (first appeared in *Longman's Magazine* August 1891 (c59)) – Horse and Man – Seen and Lost (first appeared in *Longman's Magazine* August 1889 (c52)).

Illustrations Four full-page half-tone etchings by J. Smit, tipped in; twenty-three other half-tone etchings within the text.

Binding Dark green cloth. Illustration of a family of Coypú in water printed in black and white on front cover; spine stamped in gilt 'THE / NATURALIST / IN / LA PLATA / [rule] / W. H. HUDSON / CHAPMAN & HALL'; publisher's imprint stamped in black in centre of back cover. All edges untrimmed; white wove endpapers coated black. *Binder's insert following p. 388:* a forty-page catalogue listing books published by Chapman & Hall, dated February 1892.

Variant Publisher's catalogue dated April 1892.

Notes 1,000 copies published February 1892 at 16s. Six editions to 1922.

This was reprinted in June 1892 (750 copies). The "third edition", January 1895 (750 copies), was the first to contain an appendix.

The "fourth edition", June 1903, contained a new preface by Hudson which reads in part, "It has now been for some time out of print, and as a demand for it still exists, the author and his present publisher have been encouraged to issue this new and cheaper edition. The letter-press and the drawings in the text have been left as they were; the only change is in the form of the book and the substitution of new plates for the old ones."

An undetermined number of sheets of the "fourth edition" were imported by Dutton and issued with a printed slip tipped in over the Dent imprint on the title page which reads, 'IMPORTED BY / E. P. DUTTON & COMPANY / 31 WEST TWENTY-THIRD STREET / NEW YORK'.

Reviews Daily Chronicle 26 March 1892; *Spectator* 26 March 1892; *Nature* 14 April 1892; *Land and Water* 30 April 1892; *Natural Science* April 1892;

Observer 14 May 1892; *Athenaeum* 11 June 1892; *Science* 2 September 1892; *Quarterly Review* October 1892; *Scientific American* 19 November 1892; *Nation* 29 December 1892; *Nineteenth Century* May 1893.

The Naturalist in La Plata was Hudson's first book to realize a degree of success. The book was widely and favourably reviewed and Hudson, for the first time, came to the attention of the scientific world. Alfred R. Wallace's three-and-a-quarter page review in *Nature* was headed "A Remarkable Book on the Habits of Animals". He wrote: "It is, in fact, so far as the present writer knows, altogether unique among books on natural history. It is to be hoped that its success will be proportional to its merits, and that it will form the first of a series of volumes, by means of which residents in the various extra-European countries will make known to us the habits of the animals which surround them. What renders this work of such extreme value and interest is, that it is not written by a traveller or a mere temporary resident, but by one born in the country, to whom its various tribes of beasts, birds, and insects have been familiar from childhood; who is imbued with love and admiration for every form of life; and who for twenty years has observed carefully and recorded accurately everything of interest in the life-histories of the various species with which he has become acquainted. When we add to this the fact that the writer of this volume is well acquainted with the literature, both old and new, bearing upon his subject; that he groups his facts and observations so as to throw light on obscure problems, and often adduces evidence calculated to decide them; and, in addition to all this, that the book is written in an earnest spirit and in a clear and delightful style, it becomes evident that not all who attempt to follow in his steps can hope to equal their forerunner."

Wallace closed his review with the following: "Never has the present writer derived so much pleasure and instruction from a book on the habits and instincts of animals. He feels sure that it will long continue to be a storehouse of facts and observations of the greatest value to the philosophical naturalist, while to the general reader it will rank as the most interesting and delightful of modern books on natural history."

Variant copy Texas.

A5b

FIRST AMERICAN ISSUE 1892)

THE / NATURALIST IN LA PLATA / BY / W. H. HUDSON, C.M.Z.S. / JOINT AUTHOR OF "ARGENTINE ORNITHOLOGY." / [*illustration*] / WHITE-

BANDED MOCKING-BIRD / WITH ILLUSTRATIONS BY J. SMIT / NEW YORK / D. APPLETON AND COMPANY

Collation π^2 A^4 B–Bb^8 Cc^2; pp. [*two unnumbered pages*] [i–v] vi [vii] viii–ix [x] [1] 2–383 [384–385] 386–388; 225 × 145 mm.; printed on wove paper.

Pagination [*two unnumbered pages*], opinions of the press on *The Naturalist in La Plata*; p. [i], half-title 'THE NATURALIST IN LA PLATA.'; p. [ii], '*THE NATURALIST IN LA PLATA*. / Feb., 1892, 1000 *copies printed*.'; frontispiece; p. [iii], title; p. [iv], blank; pp. [v]–vi, preface; pp. [vii] viii–ix, contents; p. [x], illustrations; pp. [1] 2–383, text; p. [384], blank; pp. [385] 386–388, index; at bottom of p. 388, '[*rule*] / PRINTED BY GILBERT AND RIVINGTON, LD., ST JOHN'S HOUSE, CLERKENWELL, E. C.'.

Contents and *illustrations* same as first edition.

Binding Same as first edition except bottom of spine reads 'D. APPLETON & CO.'. No publisher's imprint on back cover and no publisher's catalogue.

Notes 1,000 copies issued at $2.00. In response to my enquiry about publishing information, Robert K. Spencer, Senior Editor, College Department of Appleton-Century-Crofts, wrote on 13 June 1972: "We have been researching our files to see if the information you need is still available. It is unfortunate but we no longer have publishing records for these books."

These are the English sheets with the addition of π^2 containing opinions of the press, and with A^4 reset.

Copies LC.

A5c

COLLECTED EDITION 1923

THE / [*in red*] NATURALIST / IN / LA PLATA / BY / W. H. HUDSON / [*publisher's device*] / MCMXXIII / LONDON & TORONTO / [*in red*] J. M. DENT & SONS LTD. / NEW YORK: E. P. DUTTON & CO.

Collation χ1 π^4 A–2A^8 2B^4; pp. [*two unnumbered pages*] [i–iv] v–vii [viii] [1] 2–392; 220 × 148 mm.; printed on cream laid paper with oval watermark incorporating Hudson's name, a figure of a tree and two deer.

Pagination p. [*first unnumbered page*], blank; p. [*second unnumbered page*], 'THIS EDITION IS LIMITED TO 750 COPIES / FOR SALE IN ENGLAND, 100 FOR SALE / IN THE UNITED STATES OF AMERICA, / AND 35 PRESENTATION COPIES'; p. [i], half-title

'THE / COLLECTED WORKS / of / W. H. HUDSON / [short rule] / IN TWENTY-FOUR / VOLUMES / THE NATURALIST IN LA PLATA'; p. [ii], blank; p. [iii], title; p. [iv], '*All rights reserved* / PRINTED IN GREAT BRITAIN'; pp. v–vi, preface to the first edition dated 1891; p. vii, contents; p. [viii], blank; pp. [1] 2–380, text; pp. 381–386, appendix; pp. 387–392, index; at bottom of p. 392 'PRINTED BY THE TEMPLE PRESS AT LETCHWORTH IN GREAT BRITAIN'.

Binding Green cloth. Gold medallion profile portrait in centre of front cover enclosed within a single blind rule border; spine stamped in gilt 'W. H. / HUDSON / [leafy branch] / The / Naturalist / in La Plata / J·M·DENT / & SONS. LD.'. Blind rule border on back cover. Top edges trimmed and gilt, other edges untrimmed; cream laid endpapers. On front pastedown is a reproduction of pictorial bookplate with Hudson's name and dates. Maroon silk place marker.

Notes This is one of twenty-four volumes of Hudson's collected works. Eight hundred and eighty-five sets were published 1922–1923 for twenty-four guineas per set. The one hundred sets for sale in America were sold by E. P. Dutton for $192 per set. The collected works was reprinted in America by AMS Press in 1968 at $360.

Following publication of the Collected Edition Dent issued a Popular Edition of thirteen of Hudson's books. *The Naturalist in La Plata* appeared in 1929 for 6s. It is gathered in 8's and the leaves measure 202 × 133 mm. Bound in blue cloth with a figure of a bird on a leafy branch blind stamped on the front cover. The author's name with a wavy thick-thin rule underneath, title with a printer's flower underneath, and the publisher's name are stamped in gilt on the spine. All edges trimmed and the top edges stained blue; white wove endpapers. Grey wove dust jacket printed in black. Illustrated by J. Smit.

OTHER EDITIONS

A5d   n.d.   Braille hand-copied edition for the National Library for the Blind (London), five volumes.

A6a

FAN

FIRST EDITION   1892

FAN / 𝕿𝖍𝖊 𝕾𝖙𝖔𝖗𝖞 𝖔𝖋 𝖆 𝖄𝖔𝖚𝖓𝖌 𝕲𝖎𝖗𝖑'𝖘 𝕷𝖎𝖋𝖊 / BY / HENRY HARFORD / *IN THREE VOLUMES* / VOL. I. (VOL. II.; VOL. III.) / LONDON: CHAPMAN AND HALL, LD. / 1892 / [*All rights reserved*]

Collation Volume I.: [A]² B–U⁸ X⁴; pp. [i–iv] [1] 2–310 [311–312]; 193 × 129 mm.; printed on wove paper.
Volume II.: [A]² B–T⁸ U²; pp. [i–iv] [1] 2–292; 193 × 129 mm.; printed on wove paper.
Volume III.: [A]² B–T⁸ U⁶; pp. [i–iv] [1] 2–298 [299–300]; 192 × 127 mm.; printed on wove paper.

Pagination Volume I.: p. [i], half-title 'FAN / VOL. I.'; p. [ii], blank; p. [iii], title; p. [iv], 'RICHARD CLAY & SONS, LIMITED, / LONDON & BUNGAY.'; pp. [1] 2–310, text; p. [311], 'RICHARD CLAY & SONS, LIMITED, / LONDON & BUNGAY,'; p. [312], blank.
Volume II.: p. [i], half-title 'FAN / VOL. II.'; p. [ii], blank; p. [iii], title; p. [iv], 'RICHARD CLAY & SONS, LIMITED, / LONDON & BUNGAY.'; pp. [1] 2–292, text.
Volume III.: p. [i], half-title 'FAN / VOL. III.'; p. [ii], blank; p. [iii], title; p. [iv], 'RICHARD CLAY & SONS, LIMITED, / LONDON & BUNGAY.'; pp. [1] 2–298, text; p. [299], 'RICHARD CLAY & SONS, LIMITED, / LONDON & BUNGAY.'; p. [300], blank.

Binding Green cloth. Front cover stamped in black '[*thick rule*] / [*double rule*] / [*thick rule*] / [*double rule*] / [*wide decorative band containing nineteen crosses*] / [*double rule*] / [*thick rule*] / [*double rule*] / [*thick rule*]'; spine stamped in gilt '[*thick rule*] / [*double rule*] / [*thick rule*] / [*fancy*] FAN [*short rule*] / HARFORD / VOL. I. (VOL. II.; VOL. III.) / CHAPMAN & HALL / [*thick rule*] / [*double rule*] / [*thick rule*]'. Publisher's initials stamped in blind in centre of back cover. All edges untrimmed; light yellow wove endpapers.

Variant Brown cloth as above except spine is stamped 'HARFORD'.

Notes Published 21 June 1892 at 31s. 6d.
In a letter to the editor of the *Bookman's Journal and Print Collector,* August 1923, G. F. Wilson gives the publication date and price of *Fan* as 21 June 1892 at 31s. 6d. He continues: "The edition, I understand, consisted of 350 copies, of which 250 were bound. . . . I would add that the unbound copies of the novel [in sheets], numbering about 100, were remaindered or otherwise disposed of to an exporter in 1895." Wilson's statement is undocumented and the publisher's records provided no information concerning the size of the press run or the remaindering of the sheets.
This edition was considerably revised by Hudson for the Collected edition. See notes under A6b.

Reviews Athenaeum 16 July 1892; *Spectator* 27 August 1892.
The reviewer in *Athenaeum* wrote: "*Fan* is as dull and badly put together as it is coarse and repulsive. It is unnecessary to say more about a book which

appears to be its author's first experiment in fiction. It is to be hoped it may also prove his last, if this is his idea of a readable novel."

Copies Adams; Bodleian; Dartmouth; ISU; Texas. *Variant* Brotherton (Morley Roberts' copy).

A6b

COLLECTED EDITION 1923

[*in red*] FAN / THE STORY OF / A YOUNG GIRL'S LIFE / BY / HENRY HARFORD / (W. H. HUDSON) / [*publisher's device*] / MCMXXIII / LONDON & TORONTO / [*in red*] J. M. DENT & SONS LTD. / NEW YORK: E. P. DUTTON & CO.

Collation π^4 ($\pi 1 + \chi 1$) A–NN^8; pp. [*2*] [i–viii] 1–576; 220 × 148 mm.; printed on cream laid paper with oval watermark incorporating Hudson's name, a figure of a tree and two deer.

Pagination [*2*], blank; p. [i], blank; p. [ii], 'THIS EDITION IS LIMITED TO 750 COPIES / FOR SALE IN ENGLAND, 100 FOR SALE / IN THE UNITED STATES OF AMERICA, / AND 35 PRESENTATION COPIES'; p. [iii], half-title 'THE / COLLECTED WORKS / of / W. H. HUDSON / [*short rule*] / IN TWENTY-FOUR / VOLUMES / FAN: A YOUNG GIRL'S LIFE'; p. [iv], blank; p. [v], title; p. [vi], 'All rights reserved / PRINTED IN GREAT BRITAIN'; p. [vii], publisher's note concerning the pseudonymous publication of *Fan* in 1892; p. [viii], blank; pp. 1–576, text; at bottom of p. 576, 'PRINTED BY THE TEMPLE PRESS AT LETCHWORTH IN GREAT BRITAIN'.

Binding Green cloth. Gold medallion profile portrait in centre of front cover enclosed within a single blind rule border; spine stamped in gilt 'W. H. / HUDSON / [*leafy branch*] / Fan / The Story of / a Young Girls / Life / J·M·DENT / & SONS. LD.'. Blind rule border on back cover. Top edges trimmed and gilt, other edges untrimmed; cream laid endpapers. On front pastedown is a reproduction of pictorial bookplate with Hudson's name and dates. Maroon silk place marker.

Note This is one of twenty-four volumes of Hudson's collected works. Eight hundred and eighty-five sets were published 1922–1923 for twenty-four guineas per set. The one hundred sets for sale in America were sold by E. P. Dutton for $192 per set. The collected works was reprinted in America by AMS Press in 1968 at $360.

Fan had been criticized from the first and Hudson never thought highly of it. On 1 July 1920 he wrote to Edward Garnett: "About the old novel: the title was *Fan*, but it is useless to bother about it as it is no good. Or at any rate, it is a book spoiled by one bad thing in it – the character of the heroine, a poor girl of the slums who develops into an impossibly refined creature. I remember the *Spectator's* good criticism, which was that the book made you angry because it was no better."

Morley Roberts tried to convince Hudson to suppress *Fan* and not permit it to be reprinted. But because Hudson had little concern for his own literary reputation and a strong desire to leave as large an estate as possible for the Royal Society for the Protection of Birds, he agreed the year before he died to have the book included in the Collected edition. A copy of the first edition containing extensive textual revisions by Hudson for the Collected edition is in the G. M. Adams Collection at the University of Michigan.

A6c

AMERICAN EDITION, REGULAR COPIES (1924)

[*within a single rule border*] FAN / THE STORY OF / A YOUNG GIRL'S LIFE / BY / HENRY HARFORD / (W. H. HUDSON) / [*publisher's device*] | NEW YORK | E. P. DUTTON & COMPANY | 681 Fifth Avenue

Collation π^2 A–S^{16}; pp. [i–iv] 1–576; 204 × 136 mm.; printed on wove paper.

Pagination p. [i], half-title 'FAN: A YOUNG GIRL'S LIFE'; p. [ii], list of thirteen books by the same author; p. [iii], title; p. [iv], 'NOTE / THE novel *Fan* was originally published / in 1892, under the pseudonym of / "Henry Harford." It now makes its / appearance under the name of W. H. / Hudson for the first time.'; pp. 1–576, text; at bottom of p. 576, 'PRINTED BY THE TEMPLE PRESS AT LETCHWORTH IN GREAT BRITAIN'.

Binding Grey cloth. Front cover stamped in gilt '[*within a single rule border*] FAN / [*rule*] / W. H. HUDSON'; spine stamped in gilt 'FAN / [*rule*] / W. H. HUDSON / E. P. DUTTON / & CO.'. Top edges trimmed, others untrimmed; white wove endpapers. Green wove dust jacket printed in black.

Notes Published 2 January 1924 at $3.00.

A6d

AMERICAN EDITION, LIMITED COPIES 1926

FAN / THE STORY OF / A YOUNG GIRL'S LIFE / BY / HENRY HARFORD / (W. H. HUDSON) / [*publisher's device*] / NEW YORK / E. P. DUTTON & COMPANY / 681 Fifth Avenue / 1926

Collation π⁴ (± π3) A–S¹⁶; pp. [2] [i–vi] 1–576; 203 × 135 mm.; printed on wove paper.

Pagination [2], blank; p. [i], half-title, 'FAN: A YOUNG GIRL'S LIFE'; p. [ii], blank; p. [iii], title; p. [iv], 'NOTE / THE novel *Fan* was originally published in 1892, under the / pseudonym of "Henry Harford." It now makes its appear- / ance under the name of W. H. Hudson for the first time. / *This edition is limited to 498 copies / of which 450 copies are for sale. / This is copy No.* — [*manuscript number in black ink*]'; p. [v], repeat of note about publication of *Fan*; p. [vi], blank; pp. 1–576, text; at bottom of p. 576, 'PRINTED BY THE TEMPLE PRESS AT LETCHWORTH IN GREAT BRITAIN'.

Binding Blue cloth. Purple paper label on upper right corner of front cover printed in black '[*row of seven type ornaments*] / [*fancy*] FAN / by / W. H. HUDSON / [*row of seven type ornaments*]; purple paper label on spine printed in black '[*row of four type ornaments*] / [*fancy*] FAN / [*short rule*] / HUDSON / [*row of four type ornaments*]'. All edges trimmed; white wove endpapers. Purple wove dust jacket printed in black.

Reviews New York Times Book Review 20 June 1926

A7a

IDLE DAYS IN PATAGONIA

FIRST EDITION, FIRST ISSUE   1893

IDLE DAYS IN PATAGONIA / BY / W. H. HUDSON, C.M.Z.S. / AUTHOR OF "THE NATURALIST IN LA PLATA;" AND JOINT AUTHOR OF / "ARGENTINE ORNITHOLOGY." / [*illustration*] / RHINOCRYPTA LANCEOLATA. / ILLUSTRATED BY ALFRED HARTLEY AND J. SMIT. / LONDON: CHAPMAN & HALL, LTD. / 1893 / [*All rights reserved*]

Collation [A]⁴ B–R⁸ S²; pp. [i–v] vi [vii–viii] [1] 2–251 [252–253] 254–256, 2[1] 2–3 [4]; 224 × 143 mm.; printed on wove paper.

Pagination p. [i], half-title 'IDLE DAYS IN PATAGONIA.'; p. [ii], '*This Edition consists of 1750 Copies. / January, 1893.*'; frontispiece; p. [iii], title; p. [iv], blank, pp. [v]–vi, contents; p. [vii], illustrations; p. [viii], notice of previous publications of parts of this book; pp. [1] 2–251, text; p. [252], blank; pp. [253] 254–256, index; at bottom of p. 256 '[*rule*] / GILBERT AND RIVINGTON, LD., ST. JOHN'S HOUSE, CLERKENWELL, E. C.'; pp. 2[1] 2–3, opinions of the press regarding Hudson's *The Naturalist in La Plata*; p. 2[4], publisher's ads.

Illustrations Frontispiece plus three other full-page half-tone etchings from original drawings tipped in. Twenty-two other half-tone etchings within the text. In a letter to R. B. Cunninghame Graham 13 February 1898 Hudson explained that he posed for the illustrations for Alfred Hartley, the English etcher.

Contents At Last, Patagonia! – How I Became an Idler – Valley of the Black River – Aspects of the Valley – A Dog in Exile – The War with Nature (first appeared as "The Settler's Recompense" in *Merry England* September 1883 (c30)) – Life in Patagonia (first appeared in *Gentleman's Magazine* July 1885 (c40)) – Snow, and the Quality of Whiteness – Idle Days (first appeared in *Gentleman's Magazine* November 1884 (c35)) – Bird Music in South America (first appeared in *Nature* 31 December 1885 (c42)) – Sight in Savages (first appeared in *Longman's Magazine* July 1888 (c49)) – Concerning Eyes (first appeared in *Gentleman's Magazine* April 1885 (c37)) – The Plains of Patagonia (first appeared in *Universal Review* August 1890 (c56)) – The Perfume of an Evening Primrose.

Binding Maroon buckram, bevelled edges. Design of a cross formed by four arrowheads stamped in gilt in centre of front cover; spine stamped in gilt 'IDLE DAYS / IN / PATAGONIA / [rule] / W. H. HUDSON / CHAPMAN & HALL'; publisher's device stamped in blind in centre of back cover. All edges untrimmed; white wove endpapers coated dark green. *Binder's insert following p. 256*: a forty page catalogue of books published by Chapman and Hall, dated January 1893.

Variants 1 Without publisher's device on back cover and without publisher's catalogue. 2 Closely woven maroon cloth. Front cover design made of broader arrow patterns and poorly stamped. Letters on spine are shorter and in a type face different from that used on regular bindings. Publisher's device is not present on back cover and edges are not bevelled. White wove endpapers coated black. Frontispiece misbound facing p. 1; lacking s^2 and first two pages of publisher's ads. 3 Cancel title page with collation $[A]^4 (\pm A2)$ $B-R^8$ S^2.

Notes 1,750 copies published January 1893 at 14s.

"The greatest part of the chapter on 'Sight in Savages' appeared originally in *Longman's Magazine*; the chapter entitled 'The Plains of Patagonia' is reprinted, with but little alteration, from *The Universal Review*. Of the other 12 chapters contained in this work, six are based on papers which have appeared in various periodicals." (page viii).

Reviews Land and Water 18 February 1893; Daily Chronicle 23 February 1893; Illustrated London News 25 February 1893; Academy 4 March 1893; Black and

White 4 March 1893; *Sketch* 15 March 1893; *Athenaeum* 18 March 1893; *Nature* 23 March 1893; *Westminster Review* April 1893; *Science* 5 May 1893; *Leisure Hour* June 1893; *Spectator* 5 August 1893; *Saturday Review* 23 September 1893; *Popular Science* September 1893.

Variant copy 1 Adams (2). *Variant copy 2* Texas. *Variant copy 3* BM; Lilly.

A7b

FIRST EDITION, SECOND ISSUE 1893

The Chapman & Hall sheets were later issued by Dent without alteration. The binding is maroon cloth with a wider weave than the earlier issue. The lettering and decoration are the same as the first issue binding except the foot of the spine which reads 'J·M·DENT· & CO.'. The Chapman & Hall design is not present on the back cover and their catalogue is omitted. White wove endpapers.

Variant Copy with spine reading 'J·M·DENT· & SONS LD'. s^2 omitted.

Notes 1,550 copies issued October 1893 for 14s.

Variant copy Texas.

A7c

FIRST AMERICAN EDITION (1917)

IDLE DAYS IN / PATAGONIA / BY / W. H. HUDSON / AUTHOR OF "THE PURPLE LAND," "A CRYSTAL AGE," / "A SHEPHERD'S LIFE," ETC. / [*ornament sea-scape with coast and sun in background*] / ILLUSTRATED BY / ALFRED HARTLEY AND J. SMIT / NEW YORK / E. P. DUTTON & CO. / 681 FIFTH AVENUE

Collation [1–15]⁸ [16]¹⁰; pp. [i–iv] v–vii [viii–x] 1–249 [250]; 187 × 125 mm.; printed on wove paper.

Pagination p. [i], half-title 'IDLE DAYS IN PATAGONIA'; p. [ii], list of four books by the same author; frontispiece; p. [iii], title; p. [iv], 'PUBLISHED 1917, / BY / E. P. DUTTON & COMPANY / 𝔓𝔯𝔦𝔫𝔱𝔢𝔡 𝔦𝔫 𝔱𝔥𝔢 𝔘𝔫𝔦𝔱𝔢𝔡 𝔖𝔱𝔞𝔱𝔢𝔰 𝔬𝔣 𝔄𝔪𝔢𝔯𝔦𝔠𝔞'; pp. v–vi, contents; p. vii, illustrations; p. [viii], blank; p. [ix], fly-title 'IDLE DAYS IN PATAGONIA'; p. [x], blank; pp. 1–244, text; pp. 245–249, index; p. [250], blank.

Contents Same as first edition.

Illustrations Frontispiece plus twenty-four other half-tone etchings by Alfred Hartley and J. Smit tipped in on calendered paper.

Binding Green cloth. Front cover stamped in gilt '[*within a single blind rule border*] IDLE DAYS / IN PATAGONIA / [*rule*] / W. H. HUDSON / [*four arrowheads forming a cross*]'; spine stamped in gilt 'IDLE DAYS / IN / PATAGONIA / [*rule*] / HUDSON / E. P. DUTTON / & CO.'. All edges trimmed; white wove endpapers.

Variants 1 Foot of spine omits ' & CO.'. 2 p. [ii] blank.

Notes Published March 1917 at $1.50. Four printings to November 1926.

Reviews Boston Transcript 14 March 1917; *New York Times Book Review* 18 March 1917; *Nation* 3 May 1917; *Springfield Republican* 14 May 1917; *New York Call* 20 May 1917; *ALA Booklist* May 1917; *American Review of Reviews* May 1917; *Catholic World* June 1917; *New York Independent* 7 July 1917; *Yale Review* July 1917.

Variant copy 1 LC. *Variant copy* 2 Texas.

A7d

COLLECTED EDITION 1923

[*in red*] IDLE DAYS / IN / [*in red*] PATAGONIA / BY / W. H. HUDSON / [*publisher's device*] / MCMXXIII / LONDON & TORONTO / [*in red*] J. M. DENT & SONS LTD. / NEW YORK: E. P. DUTTON & CO.

Collation π^6 A–P^8; pp. [2]; [i–viii] ix [x] [1] 2–237 [238] [2]; 220 × 148 mm.; printed on cream laid paper with oval watermark incorporating Hudson's name, a figure of a tree and two deer.

Pagination [2], blank; p. [i], blank; p. [ii], 'THIS EDITION IS LIMITED TO 750 COPIES / FOR SALE IN ENGLAND, 100 FOR SALE / IN THE UNITED STATES OF AMERICA, / AND 35 PRESENTATION COPIES'; p. [iii], half-title 'THE / COLLECTED WORKS / of / W. H. HUDSON / [*short rule*] / IN TWENTY-FOUR / VOLUMES / IDLE DAYS IN PATAGONIA'; pp. [iv–v], blank; p. [vi], facsimile of a postcard from Hudson to Morley Roberts, 24 May 1918; p. [vii], title; p. [viii], '*All rights reserved* | PRINTED IN GREAT BRITAIN'; p. ix, contents; p. [x], blank; pp. [1] 2–232, text; pp. 233–237, index; at bottom of p. 237 'PRINTED BY THE TEMPLE PRESS AT LETCHWORTH IN GREAT BRITAIN'; p. [238], blank; [2], blank.

Contents Same as first edition.

Illustrations Facsimile of a postcard from Hudson to Morley Roberts, 24 May 1918.

Binding Green cloth. Gold medallion profile portrait in centre of front cover enclosed within a single blind rule border; spine stamped in gilt 'W. H. / HUDSON / [*leafy branch*] / Idle Days / in / Patagonia / J·M·DENT / & SONS. LD.'. Blind rule border on back cover. Top edges trimmed and gilt, other edges untrimmed; cream laid endpapers. On front pastedown is a reproduction of a pictorial bookplate with Hudson's name and dates. Maroon silk place marker.

Notes This is one of twenty-four volumes of Hudson's collected works. Eight hundred and eighty-five sets were published for twenty-four guineas per set. The one hundred sets for sale in America were sold by E. P. Dutton for $192 per set. The collected works was reprinted in America by AMS Press in 1968 at $360.

Following publication of the Collected Edition Dent issued a Popular Edition of thirteen of Hudson's books. *Idle Days in Patagonia* appeared in 1923 for 6s. It is gathered in 8's and the leaves measure 203 × 133 mm. Illustrated by Alfred Hartley and J. Smit. Bound in blue cloth with a figure of a bird on a leafy branch blind stamped on the front cover. The author's name with a wavy thick-thin rule underneath, title with a printer's flower underneath, and the publisher's name are stamped in gilt on the spine. All edges trimmed and the top edges stained blue; white wove endpapers. Grey wove dust jacket printed in black.

The Uniform Edition of Hudson's works was published in 1951 by Dent and consists of seven titles: *The Purple Land, Nature in Downland; A Hind in Richmond Park; Green Mansions; Adventures Among Birds; Far Away and Long Ago. Idle Days in Patagonia* was published in the Uniform Edition in 1954. It contains an introduction by David Dewar written especially for this edition. "Birds of the Rio Negro of Patagonia" is here reprinted from the *Proceedings of the Zoological Society of London*, 26 April 1872 (C17), and there is a two-page "Select Bibliography" of Hudson's works. It is gathered in 16's and the leaves measure 192 × 124 mm. Bound in red cloth. The author's name, title, a figure of a feather and the publisher's name are stamped in gilt on the spine. All edges trimmed; white wove endpapers. Green and white wove dust jacket printed in black.

A8a

BIRDS IN A VILLAGE

FIRST EDITION 1893

[*in red*] BIRDS IN A VILLAGE / BY / W. H. HUDSON, C.M.Z.S., / AUTHOR OF / "IDLE DAYS IN PATAGONIA," "THE NATURALIST IN LA PLATA," ETC. / [*in red*] LONDON: CHAPMAN & HALL, Ld. / 1893. / (ALL RIGHTS RESERVED.)

Collation π1 [A]⁴ B–Q⁸; pp. [i–x] [1–3] 4–82 [83–85] 86–112 [113–115] 116–125 [126–129] 130–142 [143–145] 146–162 [163–165] 166–183 [184–187] 188–232; 2[1] 2 [3] 4 [5] 6 [7–8]; 203 × 150 mm.; printed on laid paper.

Pagination p. [i], half-title '[*in red*] BIRDS IN A VILLAGE'; p. [ii], blank; p. [iii], title; p. [iv], blank; p. [v], dedication to Mrs Edward Phillips; p. [vi], blank; p. [vii], note regarding previous publications of parts of this book; p. [viii], blank; p. [ix], contents; p. [x], blank; p. [1], section-title 'BIRDS IN A VILLAGE.'; p. [2], blank; pp. [3] 4–82, text; p. [83], section-title 'EXOTIC BIRDS FOR BRITAIN.'; p. [84], blank; pp. [85] 86–112, text; p. [113], section-title 'MOOR-HENS IN HYDE PARK.'; p. [114], blank; pp. [115] 116–125, text; p. [126], blank; p. [127], section-title 'THE EAGLE AND THE CANARY.'; p. [128], blank; pp. [129] 130–142, text; p. [143] section-title 'CHANTICLEER.'; p. [144], blank; pp. [145] 146–162, text; p. [163], section-title 'IN A GARDEN.'; p. [164], blank; pp. [165] 166–183, text; p. [184], blank; p. [185], section-title 'BY WAY OF APPENDIX.'; p. [186], blank; pp. [187] 188–232, text; at bottom of p. 232, 'PRINTED BY WILLIAM CLOWES AND SONS, LIMITED, LONDON AND BECCLES.'; pp. 2[1–8], opinions of the press and publisher's advertisements.

Contents Birds in a Village – Exotic Birds for Britain (first appeared in *Murray's Magazine* March 1889 (c50)) – Moor-hens in Hyde Park – The Eagle and the Canary (first appeared in *Gentleman's Magazine* February 1888 (c48)) – Chanticleer (first appeared in *Longman's Magazine* December 1887 (c46)) – In a Garden – By Way of Appendix.

Binding Chocolate buckram, bevelled edges. Leaf device embodying the author's initials stamped in gilt on front cover; spine stamped in gilt 'BIRDS / IN A / VILLAGE / [*rule*] / *W. H. HUDSON* / CHAPMAN & HALL'. All edges untrimmed; white wove endpapers coated dark green.

Variants 1 Chocolate binding as above but with publisher's initials stamped in blind in centre of back cover. 2 Light green cloth. Front cover stamped in brown. 'BIRDS IN A VILLAGE / *W. H. HUDSON* / [*A floral design with three birds forms a partial top and left side border*]'; spine stamped in gilt 'BIRDS / IN A / VILLAGE / [*short rule*] / *W. H. HUDSON* / CHAPMAN & HALL'. Publisher's initials stamped in brown in centre of back cover. All edges untrimmed; dark green wove endpapers. 3. Same as variant 2 but with cream crackled glass design endpapers. Leaves measure 200 × 146 mm. 4. Terra cotta cloth. Otherwise same as variant 2.

Notes Published August 1893 at 7s. 6d.

Republished with revisions as *Birds in Town & Village* (A36).

Reviews Graphic 5 August 1893; *Daily Chronicle* 16 August 1893; *Academy* 26 August 1893; *Nature* 31 August 1893; *Manchester Guardian* 5 September 1893; *New York Times Book Review* 17 September 1893; *Athenaeum* 30 September 1893.

Variant copy 1 Adams; Chicago; Texas (2); Zoological Society. *Variant copy 2* ISU. *Variant copy 3* Dartmouth; Dobie; Texas. *Variant copy 4* ISU; Lilly; RSPB.

A8b

AMERICAN ISSUE 1893

[*in red*] BIRDS IN A VILLAGE / BY / W. H. HUDSON, C.M.Z.S., / AUTHOR OF / "IDLE DAYS IN PATAGONIA," "THE NATURALIST IN LA PLATA," ETC. / PHILADELPHIA: / [*in red*] J. B. LIPPINCOTT COMP.^{Y} / LONDON: CHAPMAN & HALL LD. / 1893. / (ALL RIGHTS RESERVED.)

Collation, pagination and *contents* same as first edition.

Binding Same as variant 3 above.

Notes The English sheets with a cancel title page for the Lippincott imprint.

Copies Texas.

OTHER EDITIONS

A8c   1920   King's Treasuries of Literature edition. London, Dent.
A8d   n.d.   Braille hand-copied edition for the National Library for the Blind (London), three volumes.

A9a

FEATHERED WOMEN

FIRST SEPARATE EDITION 1893

[*printed at top*] 𝔖ociety for the 𝔓rotection of 𝔅irds. – 𝔑o. 10. / [*rule*] / FEATHERED WOMEN. / [*double rule*] / TO THE EDITOR OF THE TIMES. / [*text follows in double column*]

Collation Broadside, 264 × 210 mm.; printed on laid paper.

Pagination [*On recto*] title as above followed by the text, signed at end 'H. [*sic*] H. HUDSON. / *October 17th, 1893*.'; [*across bottom of page*] [*rule*] / Copies of Leaflet 1d. each, 6d. per doz., and 2/6 per 100, post free, with other publications and cards of membership (registration fee / 2d.), may be obtained from Mrs. PHILLIPS, or from the Treasurer, Miss C. V. HALL, 11, Morland Road, Croydon, or from the / Secretary, Mrs. LEMON, Hillcrest, Redhill.' [*On verso*] a reprint of the leading article from *The Times*, 17 October 1893.

Notes 5,000 copies published at 1d. The BM copy is stamped 27 June 1894.

This first appeared in *The Times*, 17 October 1893 (C62), and was reprinted in *Nature Notes* in November 1893 (C63). It was reprinted by the Society for the Protection of Birds in a smaller format in 1902, and first appeared in book form in *Dead Man's Plack An Old Thorn & Miscellanea* (A47).

Copies BM; Martin.

A10a

BIRD-CATCHING

FIRST EDITION (1894)

Society for the Protection of Birds. – No. 12. / [*rule*] / BIRD-CATCHING. / [*short ornamental rule*] / [*text begins*]

Collation [A]²; pp. [1] 2–4; 214 × 137 mm.; printed on wove paper.

Pagination p. [1], title and beginning of text; p. 2, end of text, signed 'W. H. HUDSON.'; beginning of 'LINNETS, LARKS AND GOLDFINCHES.'; pp. 3–4, text of "Linnets, Larks and Goldfinches," signed 'W. L. WOODROFFE.'; [*across bottom of p. 4*] '[*rule*] / Copies of Leaflet, 3d. per doz., or 1/9 per 100, post free, also Cards of Membership can / be obtained from Mrs. Phillips, Vaughan House, Croydon; Miss C. V. Hall, 11, Morland / Road, Croydon; or the Hon. Sec., Mrs. Lemon, Redhill, Surrey.'.

Contents Bird-Catching by W. H. Hudson – Linnets, Larks and Goldfinches by W. L. Woodroffe.

Binding Self-wrappers, folded.

Notes Published at 3d per dozen. The BM copy is stamped 27 June 1894.

Copies BM; Bodleian; Martin.

This first appeared in book form in *Dead Man's Plack An Old Thorn & Miscellanea* (A47).

A11a

LOST BRITISH BIRDS

FIRST EDITION, FIRST PRINTING (1894)

Society for the Protection of Birds. – 14. / [*rule*] / LOST BRITISH BIRDS / BY / W. H. HUDSON / *Member of the British Ornithologists' Union; Author of* "*Birds in a Village,*" *&c., &c.* / [*illustration of a St. Kilda Wren perched on the skull of an extinct bird*] / WITH 15 DRAWINGS BY A. D. MCCORMICK / Sevenpence, Post Free

Collation B–C^8; pp. [1] 2–30 [31] 32; 217 × 139 mm.; printed on wove paper.

Pagination p. [1], 'LOST BRITISH BIRDS. / [*short rule with diamond shape in centre*] / [*text begins*]'; pp. 2–30, text; pp. [31]–32, conclusion.

Illustrations Cover illustration plus fourteen line etchings within the text by A. D. McCormick, the Irish painter.

Binding Light green wove paper wrappers printed in black with title as above. On back cover within a single rule frame is a list of fourteen publications of the Society for the Protection of Birds; at bottom of back cover '[*short rule*] / To be obtained from Mrs. E. Phillips or Miss C. V. Hall (Hon. Treasurer), / 11, Mortand [*sic*] Road, Croydon, and from Mrs. Lemon (Hon. Secre- / tary), Redhill, Surrey; also assorted packets at 6d., 1s., or / upwards, post free.'.

Notes Published June 1894 at 7d.

This first appeared in book form in *Dead Man's Plack An Old Thorn & Miscellanea* (A47).

This was revised and expanded and published in 1923 as *Rare Vanishing & Lost British Birds* (see A45).

On 5 December 1921 Hudson wrote to Morley Roberts: "I have had 25 coloured plates made [for *Lost British Birds*] – they are just being finished now and I think them very good, better even than the coloured figures in *Birds of La Plata*."

Reviews Nature 17 May 1894.

A11b

FIRST EDITION, SECOND PRINTING 1894

Same as the first printing except for the removal of the price and the following addition to the front wrapper: 'LONDON: CHAPMAN & HALL, LTD. / 1894'.

Copies Bodleian.
 The Bodleian Library copy is stamped 8 October 1894.

A11c

FIRST EDITION, THIRD PRINTING 1894

Same as the second printing except for the following changes: removal of 'LONDON: CHAPMAN & HALL, LTD.' from the front cover; on the back cover the eighteenth publication of the Society is the last one listed; the note at the bottom of the back cover, changed slightly, reads 'To be obtained from Mrs. E. Phillips or Miss C. V. Hall, 11, Morland / Road, Croydon, and from Mrs. Lemon, Hillcrest, Redhill, Surrey; / also assorted packets at 6d., 1s., or upwards, post free.'.

A12a

BRITISH BIRDS

FIRST EDITION 1895

BRITISH BIRDS / BY / W. H. HUDSON, C.M.Z.S. / WITH A CHAPTER ON STRUCTURE AND CLASSIFICATION / BY FRANK E. BEDDARD, F.R.S. / *With 8 Coloured Plates from Original Drawings by A. Thorburn* / *and 8 Plates and 100 Figures in black and white from Original Drawings by G. E. Lodge* / *and 3 Illustrations from Photographs from Nature by R. B. Lodge* / LONDON / LONGMANS, GREEN, AND CO. / AND NEW YORK / 1895 / *All rights reserved*

Collation [A]^8 a^4 B–Z^8 AA^4 BB^2; pp. [2] [i–v] vi–xiv [xv] xvi–xviii [xix] xx–xxii [1] 2–352 [353] 354–363 [364]; 200 × 138 mm.; printed on wove paper.

Pagination [2], blank; p. [i], half-title 'BRITISH BIRDS'; p. [ii], advertisement of five books included in the Out-Door World Library by Longmans, Green & Co.; frontispiece; p. [iii], title; p. [iv], blank; pp. [v] vi–xiv, contents; pp. [xv] xvi–

xviii, illustrations; pp. [xix] xx–xxii, introduction by Hudson; pp. [1] 2–352, text; pp. [353] 354–363, index; at bottom of p. 363, 'PRINTED BY / SPOTTISWOODE AND CO., NEW-STREET SQUARE / LONDON'; p. [364], blank.

Illustrations Eight coloured half-tone etchings from original drawings by A. Thorburn on heavier stock paper tipped in with protective tissue; seven half-tone etchings from original drawings by G. E. Lodge tipped in, with one included in the text; one hundred line etchings and three illustrations from photographs by G. E. Lodge included within the text.

Binding Green cloth. Front cover stamped in gilt with a rule at top and bottom edges and a song-thrush on a woody branch in the centre; spine stamped in gilt '[*rule*] / BRITISH / BIRDS / *HUDSON* / LONGMANS & CO. / [*rule*]'. Top edges gilt, fore edges rough trimmed, lower edges trimmed; white wove endpapers coated black.

Variant Short gilt rule on spine between title and author's name.

Notes Published 14 August 1895 at 12s. 6d. In response to my enquiry about publishing information R. M. Cooper, Longman Group Limited, wrote on 6 October 1972: "I am able to answer only some of your questions. Because a very great quantity of our archives were destroyed in the blitz on London in 1940 I am not able to give you the total number of copies of the first printings."

Erratum slip tipped in at p. 108.

This was reprinted in 1897. The title page was reset with the additional note 'NEW EDITION'. It was reprinted again in 1902. The erratum from p. 108 of the first printing was corrected in the 1902 reprint by moving an illustration from p. 108 to its proper position on p. 84. This was accomplished by omitting ten lines of text that originally appeared on p. 85 of the first printing to accommodate the illustration on p. 84, and by adding a new paragraph on pp. 109–110.

Reviews Nation 21 November 1895; *Critic* 30 November 1895; *Dial* 1 December 1895; *Spectator* 25 January 1896; *Athenaeum* 7 March 1896; *Nature* 21 May 1896; *Popular Science* May 1896.

Variant copy RSPB.

A12b

COLLECTED EDITION 1923

[*in red*] BRITISH BIRDS / BY / W. H. HUDSON / [*publisher's device*] / WITH A CHAPTER ON / ANATOMY AND CLASSIFICATION / BY FRANK E. BEDDARD,

F. R. S. / MCMXXIII / LONDON & TORONTO / [in red] J. M. DENT & SONS LTD. / NEW YORK: E. P. DUTTON & CO.

Collation π^{12} A–2F^8 2G^{12}; pp. [2] [i–vi] vii–xxi [xxii] [1] 2–475 [476] 477–488; 220 × 148 mm.; printed on cream laid paper with oval watermark incorporating Hudson's name, a figure of a tree and two deer.

Pagination pp. [2], blank; p. [i], blank; p. [ii], 'THIS EDITION IS LIMITED TO 750 COPIES / FOR SALE IN ENGLAND, 100 FOR SALE / IN THE UNITED STATES OF AMERICA / AND 35 PRESENTATION COPIES'; p. [iii], half-title 'THE / COLLECTED WORKS / of / W. H. HUDSON / [short rule] / IN TWENTY-FOUR / VOLUMES / BRITISH BIRDS'; p. [iv], blank; p. [v], title; p. [vi], '*All rights reserved* / PRINTED IN GREAT BRITAIN'; pp. vii–x, introduction; pp. xi–xx, contents; p. xxi, illustrations; p. [xxii], blank; pp. [1] 2–51, chapter on the anatomy of a bird by Frank E. Beddard; pp. 52–58, chapter on the classification of birds; pp. 59–475, text; p. [476], blank; pp. 477–488, index; at bottom of p. 488, 'PRINTED BY / THE TEMPLE PRESS AT LETCHWORTH IN GREAT BRITAIN'.

Illustrations Seventeen line drawings illustrating the chapter on the anatomy of a bird.

Binding Green cloth. Gold medallion profile portrait in centre of front cover enclosed within a single blind rule border; spine stamped in gilt 'W. H. / HUDSON / [leafy branch] / British / Birds / J·M·DENT / & SONS. LD.'. Blind rule border on back cover. Top edges trimmed and gilt, other edges untrimmed; cream laid endpapers. On front pastedown is a reproduction of pictorial bookplate with Hudson's name and dates. Maroon silk place marker.

Notes This is one of twenty-four volumes of Hudson's collected works. Eight hundred and eighty-five sets were published 1922–1923 for twenty-four guineas per set. The one hundred sets for sale in America were sold by E. P. Dutton for $192 per set. The collected works was reprinted in America by AMS Press in 1968 at $360.

A13a

THE BARN OWL

FIRST EDITION 1895

Society for the Protection of Birds. – No. 19. / [rule] / THE BARN OWL / *A reprint of Waterton's Essay, with Introductory Remarks,* / BY / W. H. HUDSON,

C.M.Z.S. / [*illustration of the Barn Owl*] / (Messrs. GURNEY & JACKSON, of No. 1, Paternoster Row, have kindly lent / this illustration of the Barn Owl from Yarrell's "British Birds.") / [*short rule*] / 1895.

Collation [1]⁶; pp. [1-3] 4-11 [12]; 217 × 140 mm.; printed on wove paper.

Pagination p. [1], title; p. [2], blank; p. 3, 'SOMETHING ABOUT THE OWL / [*text begins*]'; pp. 4-5, text; pp. 6-11, text of Charles Waterton's essay "The Habits of the Barn Owl, and the Benefits it Confers on Man."; p. [12], list of seventeen publications by the Society for the Protection of Birds; at bottom of p. [12], '[*rule*] / To be obtained from Mrs. E. Phillips, or Miss C. V. Hall, / 11, Morland Road, Croydon, and from Mrs. Lemon, / Hillcrest, Redhill, Surrey; also assorted packets at 6d., / 1s., or upwards, post free.'.

Contents Hudson's essay Something about the Owl – Charles Waterton's essay The Habits of the Barn Owl and the Benefits it Confers on Man.

Illustrations Illustration of the barn owl by T. Thompson, from Yarrell's *British Birds*.

Binding Self-wrappers, stapled.

Notes Published at 1d. The Bodleian Library copy is stamped 30 July 1895.
  Reprinted with an additional note by Hudson in May 1902.
  This first appeared in book form in *Dead Man's Plack An Old Thorn & Miscellanea* (A47).

Copies BM; Bodleian; Field Museum; RSPB.

A14a

LETTER TO CLERGYMEN, MINISTERS, AND OTHERS

FIRST EDITION (1895)

Society for the Protection of Birds. – No. 25. / [*rule*] / *LETTER to CLERGY-MEN, MINISTERS, and others.* / [*short rule with diamond shape in centre*] / The following is a copy of a letter which was sent to / upwards of 10,000 clergymen and ministers throughout the / United Kingdom in November, 1895: – / [*text begins*]

Collation [1]²; pp. [1] 2-4; 222 × 140 mm., printed on wove paper.

Pagination p. [1], title and beginning of text; pp. 2-4, text, signed at end

'W. H. Hudson'; at bottom of p. 4, '[rule] / Copies of this Leaflet, 3d. per doz., or 1/9 per 100, and other publications of the / Society, can be obtained from the Society's Publishing Department, Knowledge / Office, 326, High Holborn, W. C. Cards of Membership and information respecting / the Society from the Hon. Sec., Mrs. F. E. Lemon, Hillcrest, Redhill, Surrey.'.

Binding Self-wrappers, folded.

Notes 10,000 copies published November 1895 at 3d. per dozen.
    Reprinted in *Nature Notes* January 1896 (C70).
    This first appeared in book form in *Dead Man's Plack An Old Thorn & Miscellanea* (A47).

Copies BM; Field Museum; RSPB.

A15a

PIPITS

FIRST EDITION (1897)

𝔖𝔬𝔠𝔦𝔢𝔱𝔶 𝔣𝔬𝔯 𝔱𝔥𝔢 𝔓𝔯𝔬𝔱𝔢𝔠𝔱𝔦𝔬𝔫 𝔬𝔣 𝔅𝔦𝔯𝔡𝔰. / EDUCATIONAL SERIES. Edited by H. E. DRESSER, F.L.S., F.Z.S. / [*decorative short rule*] / No. 21. – PIPITS. / By W. H. HUDSON, C.M.Z.S. / [*illustration*] / TREE PIPIT. / [*text begins*]

Collation [A]²; pp. [1] 2–4; 253 × 189 mm.; printed on wove paper.

Pagination p. [1], title and beginning of text; pp. 2–4, text; at bottom of p. 4, below a double rule, advertisement for the Educational Series listing twenty-four titles; '[*short rule*] / Copies of the above may be obtained from the Society's Publishing Department, *Knowledge* Office, / 326, High Holborn, W. C., or from the Hon. Sec., Mrs. F. E. LEMON, Hillcrest, Redhill, on the following / terms:– Post free; three copies of any one number of the Series, 1d.; one dozen, 3d.; 100, 1s. 6d. / Assorted packets, one copy of any six numbers, 2d.; one copy of any twelve, or two copies of any six / numbers, 4d.; or 50 assorted numbers, 1s. Special terms for larger quantities, and to County Councils, the Constabulary, and Schools. / [*rule*] / The Society's Publishing Office, *Knowledge*, 326, High Holborn, London, W. C. 1897.'.

Illustrations Two illustrations from Hudson's *British Birds*.

Binding Self-wrappers, folded.

Notes See note above for cost.
Reprinted from Hudson's *British Birds* (A12). No. 21 in the Educational Series published by the Society.

Copies Adams; BM (2); Field Museum; LC; RSPB.

A16a

BIRDS IN LONDON

FIRST EDITION 1898

BIRDS IN LONDON / BY / W. H. HUDSON, F.Z.S. / ILLUSTRATED BY BRYAN HOOK, A. D. MCCORMICK / AND FROM PHOTOGRAPHS FROM NATURE BY R. B. LODGE / LONGMANS, GREEN, AND CO. / 39 PATERNOSTER ROW, LONDON / NEW YORK AND BOMBAY / 1898 / All rights reserved

Collation [A]^8 B–Y^8 Z^2; pp. [i–v] vi–viii [ix] x–xiv [xv] xvi [1] 2–329 [330–331] 332–339 [340]; 220 × 144 mm.; printed on wove paper.

Pagination p. [i], half-title 'BIRDS IN LONDON'; p. [ii], blank; *frontispiece*; p. [iii], title; p. [iv], blank; pp. [v] vi–viii, preface by Hudson, dated April 1898; pp. [ix] x–xiv, contents; pp. [xv] –xvi, illustrations; pp. [1] 2–329, text; p. [330], bibliography; pp. [331] 332–339, index; at bottom of p. 339, 'PRINTED BY / SPOTTISWOODE AND CO., NEW-STREET SQUARE / LONDON'; p. [340], blank.

Contents The Birds and the Book – Crows in London – The Carrion Crow in the Balance – The London Daw – Expulsion of the Rooks – Recent Colonists – London's Little Birds – Movements of London Birds (first appeared in *Saturday Review* 13 March 1897 (C80)) – A Survey of the Parks: West London – North-West and North London – East London – South-East London – South-West London – Protection of Birds in The Parks – The Cat Question – Birds for London.

Illustrations Frontispiece plus sixteen other full-page illustrations on calendered paper, tipped in; fifteen smaller illustrations within the text by Bryan Hook, A. D. McCormick and R. B. Lodge.

Binding Green cloth. Front cover stamped in gilt with a single rule border enclosing a design "Fieldfares at the Tower"; spine stamped in gilt '[*double rule*] / BIRDS / IN / LONDON / [*short rule*] / *HUDSON* / LONGMANS & CO. / [*double rule*]'. Top edges gilt, other edges rough-trimmed; white wove endpapers coated black. Tan wove dust jacket printed in black.

Variants 1. Copy with forty-page publisher's catalogue dated November 1902; spine reads 'Cº 2. Copy with forty-page publisher's catalogue dated January 1903; spine reads 'Cº'. 3. Copy without publisher's catalogue; spine reads 'Cº'.

Notes Published 3 May 1898 at 12s. See note to A12a for information on publishing records.

All of the material in this book appears for the first time with the exception of part of chapter VIII on London birds.

Reviews The Times 4 April 1898; *Globe* 5 May 1898; *Daily Telegraph* 18 May 1898; *Standard* 19 May 1898; *Athenaeum* 28 May 1898; *Literature* 28 May 1898; *Daily Chronicle* 31 May 1898; *Nature* 28 June 1898; *Academy* 5 July 1898; *Speaker* 16 July 1898; *Nature Notes* July 1898; *Knowledge* 1 September 1898; *Literary Gazette* 15 September 1898; *Spectator* 8 October 1898; *Country Life* 26 November 1898; *Forest and Stream* 18 February 1899; *Critic* February 1899.

Variant copy 1 Spater. *Variant copy 2* Texas. *Variant copy 3* Adams; ISU; RSPB.

A16b

COLLECTED EDITION 1923

BIRDS / [*in red*] IN LONDON / BY / W. H. HUDSON / [*publisher's device*] / MCMXXIII / LONDON & TORONTO / [*in red*] J. M. DENT & SONS LTD. / NEW YORK: E. P. DUTTON & CO.

Collation π^8 A–P^8 Q^6; pp. [2] [i–vi] vii–xiv [1] 2–243 [244] 245–251 [252]; 220 × 148 mm.; printed on cream laid paper with oval watermark incorporating Hudson's name, a figure of a tree and two deer.

Pagination pp. [2], blank; p. [i], blank; p. [ii], 'THIS EDITION IS LIMITED TO 750 COPIES / FOR SALE IN ENGLAND, 100 FOR SALE / IN THE UNITED STATES OF AMERICA, / AND 35 PRESENTATION COPIES'; p. [iii], half-title 'THE / COLLECTED WORKS / of / W. H. HUDSON / [*short rule*] / IN TWENTY-FOUR / VOLUMES / BIRDS IN LONDON'; p. [iv], blank; frontispiece: sketch of Hudson by A. D. McCormick; p. [v], title; p. [vi], '*All rights reserved* / PRINTED IN GREAT BRITAIN'; pp. vii–viii, preface dated April 1898; pp. ix–xiv, contents; pp. [1] 2–242, text; p. 243, bibliography; p. [244], blank; pp. 245–251, index; p. [252], 'PRINTED BY / THE TEMPLE PRESS AT LETCHWORTH / IN GREAT BRITAIN'.

Illustrations Sketch of Hudson by A. D. McCormick and a map of the County of London.

Contents Same as first edition.

Binding Green cloth. Gold medallion profile portrait in centre of front cover enclosed within a single blind rule border; spine stamped in gilt 'W. H. / HUDSON / [leafy branch] / Birds / in / London / J·M·DENT / & SONS. LD.'. Blind rule border on back cover. Top edges trimmed and gilt, other edges untrimmed; cream laid endpapers. On front pastedown is a reproduction of pictorial bookplate with Hudson's name and dates. Maroon silk place marker.

Notes This is one of twenty-four volumes of Hudson's collected works. Eight hundred and eighty-five sets were published 1922–1923 for twenty-four guineas per set. The one hundred sets for sale in America were sold by E. P. Dutton for $192 per set. The collected works was reprinted in America by AMS Press in 1968 at $360.

Following publication of the Collected Edition Dent issued a Popular Edition of thirteen of Hudson's books. *Birds in London* appeared in 1924 for 6s. It is gathered in 8's and the leaves measure 202 × 133 mm. Bound in blue cloth with a figure of a bird on a leafy branch blind stamped on the front cover. The author's name with a wavy thick-thin rule underneath, title with a printer's flower underneath, and the publisher's name are stamped in gilt on the spine. All edges trimmed and the top edges stained blue; white wove endpapers. Grey wove dust jacket printed in black. Illustrated with photographs and drawings by A. D. McCormick and Bryan Hook.

A16c

THE NEW READERS' LIBRARY EDITION (1928)

BIRDS IN LONDON / by / W. H. HUDSON / DUCKWORTH / 3 HENRIETTA STREET / LONDON, W.C.2

Collation [1]⁸ 2–16⁸; pp. [i–vi] vii–viii 9–255 [256]; 170 × 113 mm.; printed on wove paper.

Pagination p. [i], half-title 'THE NEW READERS LIBRARY / BIRDS IN LONDON'; p. [ii], list of thirty-four titles published in the New Readers' Library; p. [iii], title; p. [iv], '*First Published in The New Readers Library 1928 / by arrangement with Messrs. J. M. Dent & Sons, Ltd. / All rights reserved*'; p. [v], contents; p. [vi], blank; pp. vii–viii, preface dated April 1898; pp. 9–255, text; p. [256], bibliography; at bottom of p. [256], '[rule] / Printed in Great Britain by Ebenezer Baylis & Son, Ltd., The Trinity Press, / Worcester.'.

Contents Same as first edition.

Binding Blue cloth. Spine stamped in gilt '[*rule*] / [*decorative rule*] / [*rule*] / BIRDS IN / LONDON / W. H. / HUDSON / DUCKWORTH / [*rule*] / [*decorative rule*] / [*rule*]'. All edges trimmed; white wove endpapers. Orange wove dust jacket printed in black.

Notes 3,000 copies published 31 May 1928 at 3s. 6d. No. 33 in the New Readers' Library.

OTHER EDITIONS

A16d 1969 Facsimile reprint edition of the 1898 edition. Devon, David & Charles (Publishers). Introduction by Richard Fitter.

A17a

THE TRADE IN BIRDS' FEATHERS

FIRST SEPARATE EDITION   1898

Society for the Protection of Birds. No. 28. / [*rule*] / THE TRADE IN BIRDS' FEATHERS. / (REPRINTED FROM THE TIMES.) / [*illustration*] / "THE SHUDDERING ANGEL." / (*From a photograph of a picture being painted by G. F. Watts, R. A., representing* / *an angel standing over an altar covered with birds' wings.*) / LONDON: / PRINTED AND PUBLISHED BY GEORGE EDWARD WRIGHT, / AT THE TIMES OFFICE, PRINTING HOUSE SQUARE. / 1898.

Collation [A]⁴; pp. [1] 2–8; 215 × 135 mm.; printed on wove paper.

Pagination p. [1], 'THE TRADE IN BIRDS' FEATHERS. / [*short rule with diamond shape in centre*] / TO THE EDITOR OF THE TIMES. / [*text begins*]'; pp. 2–4 text, signed at end 'W. H. HUDSON.'; beginning of text of the leading article in *The Times*, 25 December 1897; pp. 5–6, text of leading article; letter to the Editor of *The Times* by "A PERPLEXED LADY"; beginning of a letter to the Editor of *The Times* by Sydney Buxton; pp. 7–8, text of letter by Buxton, signed 'SYDNEY BUXTON.'; at bottom of p. 8, '[*rule*] / Copies of this Pamphlet, 1d. each, or 5s. per 100, and other publications of / the Society, can be obtained from the Hon. Secretary, at the Society's London / Office, 326, High Holborn, W. C.'.

Contents Letter by Hudson to the Editor of *The Times*, 25 December 1897 – leading article from *The Times*, 25 December 1897 – letter by "A Perplexed Lady" to the Editor of *The Times*, Christmas Day, 1897 – letter by Sydney Buxton to the Editor of *The Times*, 30 December 1897.

Illustrations Photograph of the painting 'The Shuddering Angel' by G. F. Watts, R. A.

Binding White wove paper wrappers. Front wrapper printed in black with title as above. All edges trimmed.

Notes Published at 1d. The BM copy is stamped 2 June 1898.

This is a reprint of Hudson's letter to The Editor of *The Times* 25 December 1897 (C85).

The second edition (6th to 10th thousand), June 1899, was reset and expanded to twelve pages. The following note was added to the wrapper title below the description of the photograph: "This picture, when finished in 1899, was exhibited at the New Gallery, under the / title, 'A Dedication to all who love the beautiful and mourne over the senseless and / cruel destruction of bird life and beauty.' / June, 1899."

This first appeared in book form in *Dead Man's Plack An Old Thorn & Miscellanea* (A47).

Hudson wrote George Gissing 19 January 1898: "It is enough to fight the barbarian of this beautiful land, and this I have just been doing in a long letter to *The Times* apropos of the wholesale destruction of bird life all the world over for the ornamentation of our tender-hearted women. It was a hasty, badly written letter, as I was ill and in a depressed state, but the good old thunderer backed it up with a powerful leading article; and so a long correspondence followed, and numberless articles in other papers, and a considerable noise was made."

Copies BM.

A18a

KEW GARDENS AND OLD DEER PARK

FIRST SEPARATE EDITION 1900

The careful perusal of the following letter from / *the pen of W. H. Hudson, F. L.* [sic] *S., author of* "*Birds* / *in London,*" *&c., &c., is most earnestly requested.* / [Reprinted from "The Times" of April 14th, 1900.] / 𝕶𝖊𝖜 𝕲𝖆𝖗𝖉𝖊𝖓𝖘 𝖆𝖓𝖉 𝕺𝖑𝖉 𝕯𝖊𝖊𝖗 𝕻𝖆𝖗𝖐. / [wavy rule] / TO THE EDITOR OF THE "TIMES." / [text begins]

Collation [A]²; pp. [1] 2–3 [4]; 184 × 114 mm.; printed on wove paper; watermark: 'CHARTA / REGIA / BRITANNICA / [floral design]'.

Pagination p. [1], title and beginning of text; pp. 2–3, text, signed 'W. H. HUDSON.'; p. [4], blank.

Binding Self-wrappers, folded.

Notes Published 1900.

This is a reprint of Hudson's letter to The Editor of *The Times*, 14 April 1900 (C98). This was not sold, but distributed free to protest against the decision of the Government to erect the National Physical Laboratory in Old Deer Park.

On 10 May 1900 Hudson wrote Mrs F. E. Lemon, Honorary Secretary of the Society for the Protection of Birds: "The Government sent down last Sat. & had the ground examined & discussed the whole thing with Dr. Gunther, one of the leading residents at Kew. The result is that they have altered the original plan to build alongside the Queen's C[ottage] grounds; but the building will be placed some distance off. Mr. Akers-Douglas in reply on Monday to the question asked by a member, assumed an aggrieved air, & said exaggerated statements had been made in the papers. There was only one statement – mine in *The Times*, & no other paper said anything about it. If I had not written the letter the original plans would have been carried out.'.

Copies RSPB (3).

A19a

NATURE IN DOWNLAND

FIRST EDITION 1900

[*in red*] NATURE IN DOWNLAND / BY / W. H. HUDSON / AUTHOR OF "BIRDS IN LONDON," ETC. / [*illustration*] / WITH ILLUSTRATIONS / [*in red*] LONGMANS, GREEN, AND CO. / 39 PATERNOSTER ROW, LONDON / NEW YORK AND BOMBAY / 1900 / *All rights reserved*

Collation π^6 A–T^8 U^2; pp. [i–iv] v–ix [x] xi–xii [1] 2–307 [308]; 225 × 143 mm.; printed on wove paper.

Pagination p. [i], half-title 'NATURE IN DOWNLAND'; p. [ii], blank; frontispiece; p. [iii], title; p. [iv], blank; pp. v–ix, contents; p. [x], blank; pp. xi–xii, illustrations; pp. [1] 2–298, text; pp. 299–307, index; at bottom of p. 307, 'Printed by BALLANTYNE, HANSON & Co. / Edinburgh & London'; p. [308], blank.

Contents Thistle-Down – Charm of the Downs – The Living Garment (first appeared in *Longman's Magazine* May 1898 (C89)) – A Fairy Fauna (see A53 for separate publication) – Wild Life – The Shepherd of the Downs – Shepherds and Wheatears – Silence and Music – Summer Heat – Swallows and Churches – Autumn – West of the Adur – The Maritime District – Chichester – Winter in West Downland.

Illustrations Frontispiece plus eleven other full-page half-tone etchings tipped in on calendered paper. Fourteen line etchings within the text.

Binding Light green cloth. Front cover stamped in gilt with figure of a leaf. Inside leaf is a landscape of a setting sun, and below the sun in decorative letters 'Nature / in / Downland'; spine stamped in gilt '[*design of a leaf and two snails*] / NATURE / IN / DOWNLAND / [*design of a leaf enclosing a setting sun*] / W. H. HUDSON / LONGMANS & C9'. Top edges untrimmed, other edges rough trimmed. Four binder's leaves of off-white wove paper sewn in front and four sewn in back serving as endpapers; the first and last are pasted down.

Notes Published 25 May 1900 at 10s. 6d. Four printings by 1906. See note to A12a for information on publishing records.

The author's corrected proof copy is in the Humanities Research Center. Hudson's annotations and corrections include the titling of illustrations, marking the title page for correct inking and dozens of slight changes in wording and punctuation throughout the text.

Reviews Standard 13 February 1900; *Amateur Photographer* 15 March 1900; *Outlook* 9 June 1900; *Academy* 16 June 1900; *Eastbourne Gazette* 16 June 1900; *Literature* 16 June 1900; *Navy & Army Illustrated* 16 June 1900; *St. James's Gazette* 20 June 1900; *Daily Telegraph* 22 June 1900; *Pall Mall Gazette* 25 June 1900; *Westminster Budget* 29 June 1900; *Speaker* 30 June 1900; *Spectator* 30 June 1900; *Daily News* 13 July 1900; *Pilot* 14 July 1900; *New York Commercial Advertiser* 28 July 1900; *Graphic* 4 August 1900; *Athenaeum* 18 August 1900; *Nature* 30 August 1900; *Good Words* August 1900; *Dial* 1 September 1900; *New York Tribune* 9 September 1900; *Field* 15 September 1900; *Guardian* 19 September 1900; *Public Opinion* 5 October 1900; *Boston Transcript* 17 October 1900; *Literary World* 7 September 1900.

A19b

COLLECTED EDITION   1923

[*in red*] NATURE / IN / [*in red*] DOWNLAND / BY / W. H. HUDSON / [*publisher's device*] / WITH A NOTE BY / EDWARD GARNETT / MCMXXIII / LONDON &

TORONTO / [*in red*] J. M. DENT & SONS LTD. / NEW YORK: E. P. DUTTON & CO.

Collation π^{10} A–S^8; pp. [i–vi] vii–xiii [xiv] xv–xx [1] 2–287 [288]; 220 × 148 mm.; printed on cream laid paper with oval watermark incorporating Hudson's name, a figure of a tree and two deer.

Pagination p. [i], blank; p. [ii], 'THIS EDITION IS LIMITED TO 750 COPIES / FOR SALE IN ENGLAND, 100 FOR SALE / IN THE UNITED STATES OF AMERICA, / AND 35 PRESENTATION COPIES'; p. [iii], half-title 'THE / COLLECTED WORKS / *of* / W. H. HUDSON / [*short rule*] / IN TWENTY-FOUR / VOLUMES / NATURE IN DOWNLAND'; p. [iv], blank; p. [v], title; p. [vi], '*All rights reserved* / PRINTED IN GREAT BRITAIN'; pp. vii–xiii, 'A NOTE ON HUDSON'S LITERARY ART' by Edward Garnett dated February 1923; p. [xiv], blank; pp. xv–xx, contents; pp. [1] 2–278, text; pp. 279–287, index; p. [288], 'PRINTED BY / THE TEMPLE PRESS AT LETCHWORTH / IN GREAT BRITAIN'.

Contents Same as first edition.

Binding Green cloth. Gold medallion profile portrait in centre of front cover enclosed within a single blind rule border; spine stamped in gilt 'W. H. / HUDSON / [*leafy branch*] / Nature / in / Downland / J·M·DENT / & SONS. LD.'. Blind rule border on back cover. Top edges trimmed and gilt, other edges untrimmed; cream laid endpapers. On front pastedown is a reproduction of pictorial bookplate with Hudson's name and dates. Maroon silk place marker.

Notes This is one of twenty-four volumes of Hudson's collected works. Eight hundred and eighty-five sets were published 1922–1923 for twenty-four guineas per set. The one hundred sets for sale in America were sold by E. P. Dutton for $192 per set. The collected works was reprinted in America by AMS Press in 1968 at $360.

This is the first appearance of Edward Garnett's note on Hudson's literary art.

Following publication of the Collected Edition Dent issued a Popular Edition of thirteen of Hudson's books. *Nature in Downland* appeared in 1923 for 6s. It is gathered in 8's and the leaves measure 202 × 133 mm. Bound in blue cloth with a figure of a bird on a leafy branch blind stamped on the front cover. The author's name with a wavy thick-thin rule underneath, title with a printer's flower underneath, and the publisher's name are stamped in gilt on the spine. All edges trimmed and the top edges stained blue; white wove endpapers. Grey wove dust jacket printed in black. See A19c for the first American issue of this edition.

The Uniform Edition of Hudson's works was published in 1951 by Dent and consists of seven titles: *The Purple Land, Nature in Downland, A Hind in Richmond Park; Green Mansions; Adventures Among Birds; Far Away and Long Ago. Idle Days in Patagonia* was added in 1954.

Nature in Downland is gathered in 16's and the leaves measure 192 × 124 mm. Bound in red cloth. The author's name, title, a figure of a feather and the publisher's name are stamped in gilt on the spine. All edges trimmed; white wove endpapers. Green and white wove dust jacket printed in black. This edition reprints the note on Hudson's literary art by Edward Garnett that first appeared in the Collected edition.

A19c

FIRST AMERICAN ISSUE 1923

[*within a single rule border*] NATURE / IN / DOWNLAND / [*publisher's device*] / BY / W. H. HUDSON / 1923 / J. M. DENT & SONS LTD. / LONDON & TORONTO / PARIS: J. M. DENT ET FILS

Collation π^6 A–S^8; pp. [2] [i–iv] v–x [1] 2–287 [288]; 207 × 137 mm.; printed on wove paper.

Pagination [2], blank; p. [i], half-title 'NATURE IN DOWNLAND'; p. [ii], blank; p. [iii], title; p. [iv], 'All rights reserved / PRINTED IN GREAT BRITAIN'; pp. v–x, contents; pp. [1] 2–278, text; pp. 279–287, index; p. [288], 'PRINTED BY / THE TEMPLE PRESS AT LETCHWORTH / IN GREAT BRITAIN'.

Contents Same as first edition.

Binding Grey cloth. Front cover stamped in gilt '[*within a single rule border*] NATURE / IN DOWNLAND / [*rule*] / W. H. HUDSON'; spine stamped in gilt 'NATURE / IN / DOWNLAND / [*short rule*] / W. H. HUDSON / E. P. DUTTON / & CO.'. Top edges trimmed; others untrimmed; white wove endpapers.

Notes Published at $2.00.

The sheets of the 1923 Popular edition published by J. M. Dent. The only indication that this is the American issue is Dutton's name on the spine and dust jacket.

Copies ISU.

OTHER EDITIONS

A19d 1932 [with *An Old Thorn*] The Open-Air Library edition. London, Dent. Edited, with a foreword and wood-engravings by Eric Fitch Daglish

A19e 1932 [with *An Old Thorn*] The Open-Air Library edition. New York,

Dutton. Edited, with a foreword and wood-engravings by Eric Fitch Daglish.

A19f 1940 Literature of Yesterday and To-day edition. London, Dent.

A19g n.d. [with *An Old Thorn*] Braille hand-copied edition for the National Library for the Blind (London), four volumes.

A20a

BIRDS AND MAN

FIRST EDITION 1901

[*in red*] BIRDS AND MAN / BY / W. H. HUDSON, F.Z.S. / AUTHOR OF "BIRDS IN LONDON," "NATURE IN DOWNLAND" / "THE NATURALIST IN LA PLATA," ETC. / [*publisher's device*] / [*in red*] LONGMANS, GREEN, AND CO. / 39 PATERNOSTER ROW, LONDON / NEW YORK AND BOMBAY / 1901 / *All rights reserved*

Collation [A]^4 B–X^8; pp. [*2*] [i–vi] [*1*] 2–311 [*312*] 313–317 [*318*] [*2*]; 202 × 138 mm.; printed on wove paper.

Pagination [*2*], blank; p. [i], half-title 'BIRDS AND MAN'; p. [ii], list of three books by the same author; p. [iii], title; p. [iv], blank; p. [v], contents; p. [vi], note regarding previous publications of parts of this book; pp. [1] 2–311, text; p. [*312*], blank; pp. 313–317, index; at bottom of p. 317 '*Printed by* R. & R. CLARK, LIMITED, *Edinburgh*.'; p. [318], blank; [*2*], blank.

Contents Birds at their Best – Birds and Man (first appeared in *Longman's Magazine* December 1896 (C79)) – Daws in the West Country – A Wood Wren at Wells (first appeared in *Longman's Magazine* October 1896 (C77)) – Ravens in Somerset (first appeared in *Longman's Magazine* October 1896 (C78)) – The Secret of the Willow Wren (first appeared in *Longman's Magazine* March 1898 (C87)) – A Secret of the Charm of Flowers (first appeared in *Saturday Review* 11 March 1899 (C94)) – Owls in a Village (first appeared in the *Idler* June 1898 (C90)) – The Strange and Beautiful Sheldrake – Geese: An Appreciation and a Memory (first appeared in *Badminton Magazine of Sports and Pastimes* October 1899 (C95)) – Early Spring in Savernake Forest (first appeared in *Longman's Magazine* April 1897 (C81)) – The Dartford Warbler (first appeared in *Humane Review* April 1900 (C97)) – Birds in London (first appeared in *Longman's Magazine* March 1899 (C93)) – Selborne (first appeared in *Contemporary Review* February 1896 (C71)).

Binding Light green cloth. Publisher's design stamped in gilt in centre of front cover, enclosed within a single blind rule border; spine stamped in gilt '[*double rule*] BIRDS / AND / MAN / *HUDSON* / LONGMANS & Cº / [*double rule*]'. All edges rough trimmed; white wove endpapers coated black. Cream wove dust jacket printed in reddish-brown.

Notes Published 28 November 1901 at 6s. See note to A12a for information on publishing records.

Hudson's "working copy" of *Birds and Man* containing corrections and additions for the second edition was left to Morley Roberts in Hudson's will and is now in the Brotherton Library, University of Leeds. There are brief marginal notes on eight pages; a long note on the charm of flowers and on names of flowers that was incorporated at the end of chapter VII in the second edition; and a long note on the difficulty of passing bird protection legislation that was incorporated at the end of chapter XII. Morley Roberts identified the landowner / collector mentioned by Hudson as Lord Grey of Fallodon.

Reviews Scotsman 9 December 1901; *Land and Water* 14 December 1901; *Nottinghamshire Daily Guardian* 14 December 1901; *Glasgow Herald* 20 December 1901; *Manchester Guardian* 20 December 1901; *Gloucester Journal* 28 December 1901; *Pall Mall Gazette* 2 January 1902; *Daily News* 19 January 1902; *Guardian* 22 January 1902; *Nature* 30 January 1902; *Literary World* 28 February 1902; *Animals Friend* February 1902; *Speaker* 1 March 1902; *Outlook* 8 March 1902; *Spectator* 8 March 1902; *Morning Post* 13 March 1902; *Ibis* 15 March 1902; *Standard* 27 March 1902; *Athenaeum* 5 April 1902; *Humane Review* April 1902; *Indian Field* 8 May 1902; *Times Literary Supplement* 16 May 1902; *New York Times Book Review* 17 May 1902; *Bookman* May 1902; *Saturday Review* 21 June 1902; *Times of India* 22 November 1902; *Field* 28 December 1902.

A20b

SECOND EDITION (FIRST DUCKWORTH EDITION)   1915

[*in red*] BIRDS AND MAN / BY / W. H. HUDSON / LONDON / [*in red*] DUCKWORTH & CO. / 3 HENRIETTA STREET, COVENT GARDEN, W.C. / 1915

Collation π^4 A–T^8 U^2; pp. [i–viii] 1–301 [302] 303–306 [307–308]; 216 × 137 mm.; printed on wove paper.

Pagination p. [i], half-title 'BIRDS AND MAN'; p. [ii], list of thirteen books by the same author; coloured frontispiece; p. [iii], title; p. [iv], blank; p. [v], note regarding this new edition; p. [vi], blank; p. [vii], contents; p. [viii], blank;

pp. 1–301, text; p. [302], blank; pp. 303–306, index; p. [307], 'PRINTED BY / TURNBULL AND SPEARS, / EDINBURGH'; p. [308], blank.

Contents Same as first edition except "Birds in London" is omitted and the following two chapters are added: "Vert – Vert; or Parrot Gossip" (first appeared in *Saturday Review* 15 June 1901 (C104)) and "Something Pretty in a Glass Case" (first appeared in *Saturday Review* 10 February 1906 (C135)).

Binding Green cloth. Front cover stamped in gilt '[*within a single blind rule border*] BIRDS AND MAN / W. H. HUDSON'; spine stamped in gilt 'BIRDS / & MAN / [*ornament*] / W. H. HUDSON / DUCKWORTH'. Publisher's device stamped in blind at lower left corner of back cover. All edges trimmed; white wove endpapers.

Notes Published September 1915 at 6s. See note to A1C for information on publishing records.

This edition was extensively revised by Hudson. New material was added throughout the book; two new chapters were added and the order in which the chapters originally appeared was rearranged. "Birds in London" was omitted because it was treated more fully in the book by the same title (A16).

Reviews Athenaeum 16 October 1915; *Nature* 25 November 1915; *Bookman* December 1915; *Spectator* 29 January 1916.

A20c

FIRST AMERICAN ISSUE 1916

[*in red*] BIRDS AND MAN / BY / W. H. HUDSON / [*publisher's device*] / [*rule*] / [*in red*] ALFRED A. KNOPF / NEW YORK MCMXVI

Collation π^4 ($-\pi$ 1,2) ($+\pi$ 1.2) A–T^8 U^2; pp. [i–viii] 1–301 [302] 303–306 [307–308]; 220 × 142 mm.; printed on wove paper.

Pagination pp. [i], half-title 'BIRDS AND MAN'; p. [ii], blank; p. [iii], title; p. [iv], 'PRINTED IN GREAT BRITAIN / BY TURNBULL AND SPEARS, EDINBURGH'; p. [v], note regarding this new edition; p. [vi], blank; p. [vii], contents; p. [viii], blank; pp. 1–301, text; p. [302], blank; pp. 303–306, index; p. [307], 'PRINTED BY / TURNBULL AND SPEARS, / EDINBURGH'; p. [308], blank.

Contents Same as second edition.

Binding Green cloth. Front cover stamped with double blind rule border; white paper label on spine printed in green '[*rule*] / BIRDS / & MAN / [*rule*] / W ▼ H ▼ / HUDSON / [*rule*] / [*publisher's device: a borzoi*] / ALFRED ▼ A ▼ KNOPF / [*rule*]'. Top edges trimmed and stained green, other edges untrimmed; white wove endpapers.

Notes Published at $2.25. Reprinted in 1920. In response to my enquiry about publishing information William A. Koshland, President, Alfred A. Knopf Incorporated, wrote on 4 August 1972: "When the information is missing it means that it is unobtainable from our records; and where I have merely listed month and year, it means I have no record as to the exact date of first publication."

The second edition sheets with the first two leaves cancelled.

Reviews New York Times Book Review 11 June 1916; *Nation* 15 June 1916; *Bookman* July 1916.

A20d

FIRST AMERICAN EDITION 1923

[*in green*] BIRDS AND MAN / *by* / W. H. HUDSON / WITH AN INTRODUCTION BY / EDWARD GARNETT / [*publisher's device in green*] / NEW YORK / ALFRED ▼ A ▼ KNOPF / 1923

Collation [1–17]⁸; pp. [i–vi] vii–xiii [xiv] [1–2] 3–257 [258]; 203 × 141 mm.; printed on wove paper.

Pagination p. [i], half-title 'BIRDS / AND MAN'; p. [ii], list of six books by the same author; p. [iii], title; p. [iv], 'COPYRIGHT, 1923, BY / ALFRED A. KNOPF, INC. / Published, February, 1923 / Set up, electrotyped, and printed by the Vail-Ballou Co., Binghamton, N.Y. / Paper furnished by W. F. Etherington & Co., New York. / Bound by H. Wolff Estate, New York. / MANUFACTURED IN THE UNITED STATES OF AMERICA'; p. [v], contents; p. [vi], blank; pp. vii–xiii, preface; p. [xiv], blank; p. [1], fly-title 'BIRDS / AND MAN'; p. [2], blank; pp. 3–257, text; p. [258], blank.

Contents Same as second edition.

Binding Reddish-brown cloth. Front cover stamped in green '[*rule*] / BIRDS AND MAN / [*rule*]'; spine stamped in green '[*rule*] / BIRDS / AND / MAN / [*rule*] / BY W.H. / HUDSON / ALFRED·A·KNOPF'. Publisher's device stamped in blind in lower right corner of back cover. Top edges trimmed and stained green, other edges untrimmed; white wove endpapers.

Variants 1 Brown cloth stamped as above. Leaves measure 208 × 139 mm. All edges trimmed. 2 As variant 1 except top edges stained green.

Notes 2,000 copies published February 1923 at $2.50.
  This is the first appearance of Edward Garnett's introduction.

Variant copy 1 Texas. *Variant copy 2* Texas.

A20e

COLLECTED EDITION   1923

BIRDS / [*in red*] AND MAN / BY / W. H. HUDSON / [*publisher's device*] / MCMXXIII / LONDON & TORONTO / [*in red*] J. M. DENT & SONS LTD. / NEW YORK: E. P. DUTTON & CO.

Collation π^6 A–Q^8; pp. [i–vi] vii–xi [xii] [1] 2–249 [250] 251–255 [256]; 220 × 148 mm.; printed on cream laid paper with oval watermark incorporating Hudson's name, a figure of a tree and two deer.

Pagination p. [i], blank; p. [ii], 'THIS EDITION IS LIMITED TO 750 COPIES / FOR SALE IN ENGLAND, 100 FOR SALE / IN THE UNITED STATES OF AMERICA, / AND 35 PRESENTATION COPIES'; p. [iii], half-title 'THE / COLLECTED WORKS / of / W. H. HUDSON / [*short rule*] / IN TWENTY-FOUR / VOLUMES / BIRDS AND MAN'; p. [iv], blank; p. [v], title; p. [vi], '*All rights reserved* / PRINTED IN GREAT BRITAIN'; pp. vii–xi, contents; p. [xii], blank; pp. [1] 2–249, text; p. [250], blank; pp. 251–255, index; p. [256], 'PRINTED BY / THE TEMPLE PRESS AT LETCHWORTH / IN GREAT BRITAIN'.

Contents Same as second edition.

Binding Green cloth. Gold medallion profile portrait in centre of front cover enclosed within a single blind rule border; spine stamped in gilt 'W. H. / HUDSON / [*leafy branch*] / Birds / and / Man / J·M·DENT / & SONS. LD.'. Blind rule border on back cover. Top edges trimmed and gilt, other edges untrimmed; cream laid endpapers. On front pastedown is a reproduction of pictorial bookplate with Hudson's name and dates. Maroon silk place marker.

Notes This is one of twenty-four volumes of Hudson's collected works. Eight hundred and eighty-five sets were published 1922–1923 for twenty-four guineas per set. The one hundred sets for sale in America were sold by E. P. Dutton for $192 per set. The collected works was reprinted in America by AMS Press in 1968 at $360.

  Following publication of the Collected Edition Dent issued a Popular Edition of thirteen of Hudson's books. Dent did not acquire publication rights to *Birds and Man* for this edition.

  In 1924 Duckworth published *Birds and Man* in a size and binding similar to volumes in the Popular edition. The binding is blue cloth with a single rule border blind stamped on front cover. The author's name without the rule underneath, title, with printer's device underneath, and publisher's name are stamped in gilt on spine. The publisher's device is stamped in blind in lower left corner of back cover. White wove endpapers, all edges trimmed, top edges stained blue. Even though this volume was not published by Dent and cannot be considered a part of the Popular edition, it was published by Duckworth in an obvious attempt to make it uniform with other volumes in that set and will therefore be desired by collectors of Hudson's books.

A20f

THE NEW READERS' LIBRARY EDITION (1927)

BIRDS AND MAN / by / W. H. HUDSON / DUCKWORTH / 3 HENRIETTA STREET / LONDON, W. C. 2

Collation [A]⁸ B–Q⁸; pp. [1–6] 7 [8] 9–252 [253–256]; 168 × 114 mm.; printed on wove paper.

Pagination p. [1], half-title 'THE NEW READERS LIBRARY / BIRDS AND MAN'; p. [2], list of twenty titles published in the New Readers' Library series; p. [3], title; p. [4], '*First Published* 1915 / *First issue in New Readers Library* 1927 / ALL RIGHTS RESERVED / *Printed in Great Britain*'; p. [5], note regarding this new edition; p. [6], blank; p. 7, contents; p. [8], blank; pp. 9–252, text; at bottom of p. 252 '*Printed by Burleigh Ltd., at* THE BURLEIGH PRESS, *Bristol*'; pp. 253–256, ads for the New Readers' Library.

Contents Same as second edition.

Binding Blue cloth. Spine stamped in gilt '[*rule*] / [*decorative rule*] / [*rule*] / BIRDS / AND / MAN / W. H. / HUDSON / DUCKWORTH / [*rule*] / [*decorative rule*] / [*rule*]'. All edges trimmed; white wove endpapers. Orange wove dust jacket printed in black.

Notes 2,000 copies published July 1927 at 6s. No. 9 in the New Readers' Library.

OTHER EDITIONS

A20g 1929 Bayswater edition. New York, Knopf. Introduction by Edward Garnett.
A20h n.d. Crown Library edition. London, Duckworth.

A21a

EL OMBÚ

FIRST EDITION, PAPER WRAPPERED ISSUE 1902

W. H. HUDSON / [*rule*] / [*to left of centre*] EL OMBÚ / BY / W. H. HUDSON / AUTHOR OF "NATURE IN DOWNLAND," "THE NATURALIST IN / LA PLATA," ETC. / *Cada comarca en la tierra* / *Tiene su rasgo prominente,* / *Brazil tiene su sol ardiente,* / *Minas de plata el Perú:* / *Buenos Ayres – patria hermosa –* / *Tiene su Pampa grandiosa;* / *La Pampa tiene el Ombú.* / LONDON / DUCKWORTH & CO., / 3 HENRIETTA STREET, W.C. / MDCCCCII

Collation [A]⁴ B–M⁸ N⁴; pp. [i–viii] [1] 2–68 [69] 70–88 [89] 90–124 [125] 126–173 [174] 175–182 [*2*]; 184 × 123 mm.; printed on wove paper.

Pagination p. [i], half-title 'EL OMBÚ'; p. [ii], list of two titles published in The Greenback Library; p. [iii], title; p. [iv], 'PRINTED BY R. FOLKARD AND SON, / 22, DEVONSHIRE STREET, QUEEN SQUARE, BLOOMSBURY, / LONDON, W.C.'; p. [v], dedication to R. B. Cunninghame Graham; p. [vi], note regarding previous publication of parts of this book; p. [vii], contents; p. [viii], blank; pp. [1] 2–68, El Ombú; pp. [69] 70–88, Story of a Piebald Horse; pp. [89] 90–124, Niño Diablo; pp. [125] 126–173, Marta Riquelme; pp. [174] 175–182, Appendix to El Ombú; [*2*], blank.

Contents El Ombú – Story of a Piebald Horse – Niño Diablo – Marta Riquelme – Appendix to El Ombú.

Binding Green paper wrappers. Front cover printed in black with a single rule border enclosing three single rule compartments of varying size. 'EL OMBÚ / W. H. HUDSON / [*circular design of a tree*] / Duckworth's Greenback Library'; spine printed in black 'HUDSON / [*short rule*] / EL / OMBÚ / 1/6 / Net / Duckworth's / Greenback / Library'. All edges trimmed; white wove endpapers.

Notes 1,250 copies issued April 1902 at 1s. 6d.

"Story of a Piebald Horse" first appeared in *The Purple Land That England Lost* (A1). "Niño Diablo" first appeared in *Macmillan's Magazine* February 1890 (C53). "Marta Riquelme" and "El Ombú" appear now for the first time except for the incidents of the English invasion related in "El Ombú," and the "Appendix to El Ombú", which previously appeared in an article describing the game of El Pato in the *Badminton Magazine* October 1898 (C91).

El Ombú was published without textual change in 1909 with the title *South*

American Sketches (A28). It first appeared in the United States in 1916 with the title *Tales of the Pampas* (A33). This edition contained two additional stories, "Pelino Viera's Confession" which had previously appeared in *Cornhill Magazine* October 1883 (C31) and "Tecla and the Little Men". It was collected with *The Purple Land* and *Green Mansions* in 1930 under the title *South American Romances* (A56).

In the introduction to his edition of Hudson's letters, Edward Garnett relates how he met Hudson in September 1901 on his last day as reader for Heinemann. A few weeks earlier Garnett had tried to convince William Heinemann that El Ombú was "a work of genius and that he must publish it". Heinemann delayed and Garnett took it to Duckworth's and arranged for its publication.

Hudson wrote to R. B. Cunninghame Graham in 1902: "I should like to have your permission to inscribe these little gaucho tales to you.

"They are of small merit, whatever Garnett may say – he is not infallible, as MY still small voice assures me – but the two or three dedicatory words will at least serve to show that I can appreciate something better, and will [show] others [who do not know] where it may be found." Graham in turn dedicated to Hudson his *Hernando de Soto*, London: Heinemann, 1903.

Reviews The Times 26 April 1902; *Sheffield Telegraph* 30 April 1902; *Humane Review* April 1902; *Spectator* 10 May 1902; *Athenaeum* 17 May 1902; *Anglo-Argentine* 30 August 1902; *Academy & Literature* 6 December 1902; *Lady* 15 January 1903; *Morning Leader* 11 April 1903; *Daily Chronicle* 19 April 1903.

A21b

FIRST EDITION, CLOTH BOUND ISSUE 1902

Same as A21a except that the sheets measure 180 × 120 mm. and are bound in green cloth. The spine reads '2/- Net', and the publisher's design is stamped in black on the back cover.

Notes 1,960 copies issued April 1902 at 2s.

A21c

THE READERS' LIBRARY EDITION (1920)

El Ombú by W. H. Hudson / Author of "Green Mansions," "The Purple Land," "A / Crystal Age," "A Little Boy Lost" / [*7 lines of verse*] / LONDON / DUCKWORTH & CO. / 3 HENRIETTA STREET, COVENT GARDEN

Collation [A]⁴ (— A 1,2) (+ A1.2) B–M⁸ N⁴; pp. [i–viii] [1] 2–182 [2]; 186 × 122 mm.; printed on wove paper.

Pagination p. [i], half-title 'EL OMBÚ'; p. [ii], advertisement for The Readers' Library; p. [iii], title; p. [iv], 'First Published 1902. | Reissued under the title of "South American Sketches" 1909 | Published in the Readers Library 1920 | All rights reserved | Printed in Great Britain by R. Folkard & Son, London'; p. [v], dedication to R. B. Cunninghame Graham; p. [vi], note regarding previous publication of parts of this book; p. [vii], contents; p. [viii], blank; pp. [1] 2–68, El Ombú; pp. [69] 70–88, Story of a Piebald Horse; pp. [89] 90–124, Niño Diablo; pp. [125] 126–173, Marta Riquelme; pp. [174] 175–182, Appendix to El Ombú; [2], blank.

Contents Same as first edition.

Binding Blue cloth. Publisher's circular device blind stamped in centre of front cover; spine stamped in gilt '[*within a single-rule panel*] EL / OMBÚ / W. H. / HUDSON / [*in smaller single-rule panel at bottom of spine*] DUCKWORTH'; publisher's device blind stamped at lower left corner of back cover. All edges trimmed; white wove endpapers.

Notes Published August 1920 at 5s. See note to A1c for information on publishing records.

The first edition sheets with the first two leaves cancelled.

A21d

COLLECTED EDITION 1923

[*in red*] EL OMBÚ / TOGETHER WITH THE / STORY OF A PIEBALD HORSE / PELINO VIERA'S CONFESSION / NIÑO DIABLO / MARTA RIQUELME / AND / RALPH HERNE / BY / W. H. HUDSON / [*publisher's device*] / MCMXXIII / LONDON & TORONTO / [*in red*] J. M. DENT & SONS LTD. / NEW YORK: E. P. DUTTON & CO.

Collation π⁶ A–T⁸ U⁴; pp. [i–viii] ix [x–xii] 1–310 [311–312]; 220 × 148 mm.; printed on cream laid paper with oval watermark incorporating Hudson's name, a figure of a tree and two deer.

Pagination p. [i], blank; p. [ii], 'THIS EDITION IS LIMITED TO 750 COPIES / FOR SALE IN ENGLAND, 100 FOR SALE / IN THE UNITED STATES OF AMERICA, / AND 35 PRESENTATION COPIES'; p. [iii], 'THE / COLLECTED WORKS / *of* / W. H. HUDSON / [*short rule*] / IN TWENTY-FOUR / VOLUMES / EL OMBÚ'; p. [iv], blank; p. [v], title; p.

[vi], 'All rights reserved / THIS VOLUME IS INCLUDED IN THE / AMERICAN COL-
LECTED EDITION BY / THE KINDLY COURTESY OF MR. / ALFRED A. KNOPF, WHO HAS
COPY- / RIGHTED IT IN THE UNITED STATES / OF AMERICA / PRINTED IN GREAT
BRITAIN'; p. [vii], note regarding the inclusion of *Ralph Herne* in the Collected
edition; p. [viii], blank; p. ix, contents; p. [x], blank; p. [xi], section-title 'EL
OMBÚ'; p. [xii], blank; pp. 1–310, text; p. [311], 'PRINTED BY / THE TEMPLE
PRESS AT LETCHWORTH / IN GREAT BRITAIN'; p. [312], blank.

Contents El Ombú (A21a) – Story of a Piebald Horse (see A1) – Pelino Viera's
Confession (see A33) – Niño Diablo (C53) – Marta Riquelme (A21a) – *Ralph
Herne* (C41).

Binding Green cloth. Gold medallion profile portrait in centre of front cover
enclosed within a single rule border; spine stamped in gilt. 'W. H. / HUDSON /
[*leafy branch*] / El Ombú / and other / South American / Stories / J·M·DENT /
& SONS. LD.'. Blind rule border on back cover. Top edges trimmed and gilt, other
edges untrimmed; cream laid endpapers. On front pastedown is a reproduction
of pictorial bookplate with Hudson's name and dates. Maroon silk place marker.

Notes This is one of twenty-four volumes of Hudson's collected works. Eight
hundred and eighty-five sets were published 1922–1923 for twenty-four guineas
per set. The one hundred sets for sale in America were sold by E. P. Dutton for
$192 per set. The collected works was reprinted in America by AMS Press in
1968 at $360.

This is the first book appearance of *Ralph Herne*. It first appeared in *Youth*,
1889, (C47) and was first published in the United States in May 1923 (A44).

A21e

THE NEW READERS' LIBRARY EDITION (1927)

EL OMBÚ / by / W. H. HUDSON / DUCKWORTH / 3 HENRIETTA STREET /
LONDON, W.C.2

Collation [1]⁸ 2–12⁸; pp. [1–12] 13–78 [79–80] 81–98 [99–100] 101–132 [133–134]
135–179 [180–182] 183–190 [191–192]; 168 × 115 mm.; printed on wove paper.

Pagination p. [1], half-title 'THE NEW READERS LIBRARY / EL OMBÚ'; p. [2], list of
twenty-six titles published in the New Readers' Library; p. [3], title; p. [4],
'First Published ... 1902 / Issued in the New Readers Library ... 1927 / *Printed
in Great Britain by* / *Percy Lund, Humphries & Co. Ltd.* / *London and Bradford*'; p.
[5], note regarding previous publications of parts of this book; p. [6], blank;

p. [7] dedication to R. B. Cunninghame Graham; p. [8], blank; p. [9], section-title 'EL OMBÚ'; p. [10], blank; p. [11], contents; p. [12], blank; pp. 13–78, text; p. [79], section-title 'STORY OF A PIEBALD HORSE'; p. [80], blank; pp. 81–98, text; p. [99], section-title 'NIÑO DIABLO'; p. [100], blank; pp. 101–132, text; p. [133], section-title 'MARTA RIQUELME'; p. [134], blank; pp. 135–179, text; p. [180], blank; p. [181], section-title 'APPENDIX TO EL OMBÚ'; p. [182], blank; pp. 183–190, text; pp. [191–192], blank.

Contents Same as first edition.

Binding Blue cloth. Spine stamped in gilt '[rule] / [decorative rule] / [rule] / EL / OMBÚ / W. H. / HUDSON / DUCKWORTH / [rule] / [decorative rule] / [rule]'. All edges trimmed; white wove endpapers. Orange wove dust jacket printed in black. *Binder's insert following p. [192]*: eight pages of publisher's advertisements.

Notes 2,000 copies published 29 November 1927 at 3s. 6d. No. 23 in the New Readers' Library.

OTHER EDITIONS

A21f   n.d.   Braille hand-copied edition for the National Library for the Blind (London), two volumes.

A22a

HAMPSHIRE DAYS

FIRST EDITION, FIRST ISSUE   1903

[*in red*] HAMPSHIRE DAYS / BY / W. H. HUDSON / AUTHOR OF / "BIRDS AND MAN," "NATURE IN DOWNLAND," ETC. / [*illustration*] / *WITH ILLUSTRA-TIONS* / [*in red*] LONGMANS, GREEN, AND CO / 39 PATERNOSTER ROW, LONDON / NEW YORK AND BOMBAY / 1903 / *All rights reserved*

Collation π^8 A–X^8 Y^4; pp. [i–viii] ix–xiii [xiv] xv–xvi [1] 2–344; 220 × 143 mm.; printed on wove paper.

Pagination p. [i], '*'; p. [ii], blank; p. [iii], half-title 'HAMPSHIRE DAYS'; p. [iv], list of four books by the same author; frontispiece; p. [v], title; p. [vi], blank; p. [vii], notice of previous publication of parts of this book; p. [viii], blank; pp. ix–xiii, contents; p. [xiv], blank; pp. xv–xvi, illustrations; pp. [1] 2–336, text; p. 337–344, index; at bottom of p. 344 'Printed by BALLANTYNE, HANSON & Co. / Edinburgh & London'.

Illustrations Eleven full-page half-tone etchings from the artist's drawings tipped in on calendered paper; thirty-six other line etchings within the text by J. Smit, D. Sulman and others.

Binding Green cloth. Front cover stamped in gilt '[*within a gilt design of branches embodying two butterflies*] HAMPSHIRE / DAYS'; spine stamped in gilt '[*floral design with two butterflies*] / HAMPSHIRE / DAYS / [*floral design*] / HUDSON / LONGMANS & Cº'. Top edges trimmed, other edges untrimmed; white wove endpapers coated black; two fly leaves of white laid paper inserted front and back. Binder's insert following p. 344: forty-page publisher's catalogue dated January 1903.

Notes Published May 1903 at 10s. 6d. See note to A12a for information on publishing records.

The BM copy is stamped 15 May 1903. In his article "The Real First Edition of Hudson's *Hampshire Days*, and Other Notes" in the *Bookman's Journal and Print Collector* (March 1923) pp. 170–171, G. F. Wilson gives the number of copies of the first issue as about six. This information is presumably based on the publisher's records, but because these records were not available this figure has not been verified. It should be noted however that the only copy located of the first issue was in the BM, whereas ten copies of the second issue were examined.

The greater part of the matter contained in this volume appears for the first time. Other material has been taken from "A More or Less Happy Family" (*Badminton Magazine* May 1901 (C101)) as well as from four articles that previously appeared in *Longman's Magazine*: "Summer in the Forest" (January 1900 (C96)), "Wolmer Forest," (August 1897 (C84)), "A Summer's End on the Itchen," (May 1901 (C102)) and "Selborne Revisited" (March 1902 (C106)).

A portion of Chapter XII, "Three Common River Birds" was published separately as *Three Water Birds* (A52).

The author's corrected proof copy is in the Humanities Research Centre. Hudson's annotations and corrections include marking the title page for correct inking, a comment on the accuracy of one illustration, numerous slight changes in wording and punctuation, and the expansion of the last paragraph of Chapter VI with the addition of 105 words.

Hudson's continuing concern for the appropriate illustrations for his books is evident in his letter to Edward Garnett 31 August 1902: "I wish I could find some clever young artists to do a few drawings for me. I am having a few done by J. Smit, who did some things for *Idle Days* but he can't manage some of my subjects at all."

On 4 October 1902 Hudson wrote again to Garnett: "Alas! good old animal-drawer Smit sends me drawings which will not do, and so I return them to him, and I must go on hunting all about for someone able to draw a mouse or sparrow or bug."

Copies BM.

A22b

FIRST EDITION, SECOND ISSUE 1903

Same as first issue except as follows:
1 The endpapers are white wove paper.
2 A dedication to Sir Edward and Lady Grey, printed on a stock of paper differing from the text stock, is tipped in between pp. [vi] and [vii].
3 No publisher's catalogue.

Notes Published 12 May 1903. See note to A12a for information on publishing records.

Reviews Daily Chronicle 6 May 1903; *Hants Chronicle* 16 May 1903; *World* 26 May 1903; *Nottinghamshire Daily Guardian* 27 May 1903; *Daily Telegraph* 29 May 1903; *Academy & Literature* 30 May 1903; *Liverpool Daily Post* 2 June 1903; *Daily Chronicle* 5 June 1903; *Manchester Guardian* 9 June 1903; *Work of the Book World* 10 June 1903; *Nature* 11 June 1903; *The Times* 12 June 1903; *Birmingham Daily Post* 19 June 1903; *Standard* 19 June 1903; *St. James's Gazette* 25 June 1903; *Graphic* 27 June 1903; *Literary World* 3 July 1903; *Field* 4 July 1903; *Lancet* 4 July 1903; *Week's Survey* 4 July 1903; *Fishing Gazette* 18 July 1903; *Nature Notes* July 1903; *Athenaeum* 8 August 1903; *Public Opinion* 14 August 1903; *Studio* 15 August 1903; *Leisure Hour* 19 August 1903; *Bournemouth Graphic* 27 August 1903; *Speaker* 29 August 1903; *Athenaeum* 12 September 1903; *Pall Mall Gazette* 3 October 1903; *Pilot* 17 October 1903; *Saturday Review* 17 October 1903; *Daily Mail* 26 October 1903; *London Quarterly Review* October 1903; *Animal's Friend* 1 November 1903; *New York Times Book Review* 14 November 1903; *New York Tribune* 29 January 1904; *World's Work* July 1904.

Copies Adams; Crerar; Dartmouth; Dobie; LC; Lilly; RSPB; Texas (2); Zoological Society.

A22c

FIRST AMERICAN ISSUE 1923

[*within a single rule border*] HAMPSHIRE / DAYS / [*publisher's device*] / BY / W. H.

HUDSON / 1923 / J. M. DENT & SONS LTD. / LONDON & TORONTO / PARIS: J. M. DENT ET FILS

Collation π⁶ A–T⁸ U⁶; pp. [iii–viii] ix–xiii [xiv] 1–315 [316]; 201 × 133 mm.; printed on wove paper.

Pagination p. [iii], half-title 'HAMPSHIRE DAYS'; p. [iv], blank; p. [v], title; p. [vi], 'All rights reserved / PRINTED IN GREAT BRITAIN'; p. [vii] dedication to Sir Edward and Lady Grey; p. [viii], blank; pp. ix–xiii, contents; p. [xiv], blank; pp. 1–306, text; pp. 307–315, index; p. [316], 'PRINTED BY / THE TEMPLE PRESS AT LETCHWORTH / IN GREAT BRITAIN'.

Binding Grey cloth. Front cover stamped in gilt '[within a single rule border] HAMPSHIRE DAYS / [rule] / W. H. HUDSON'; spine stamped in gilt 'HAMPSHIRE / DAYS / [rule] / W. H. HUDSON / E. P. DUTTON / & CO.'. Top edges trimmed, others untrimmed; white wove endpapers. Green wove dust jacket printed in black.

Notes Published at $3.00. The publishing records of E. P. Dutton are in the library at Syracuse University, New York. At the time of the preparation of this bibliography they were uncatalogued and unavailable for research. Thus full information regarding the number of copies printed, exact date of publication and price have not been recorded.

The sheets of the Popular Edition were bound in Dutton's binding for sale in the United States. The only difference is Dutton's name on spine and on spine of dust jacket.

Copies ISU; Texas (2).

A22d

COLLECTED EDITION 1923

[in red] HAMPSHIRE / [in red] DAYS / BY / W. H. HUDSON / [publisher's device] / MCMXXIII / LONDON & TORONTO / [in red] J. M. DENT & SONS LTD. / NEW YORK: E. P. DUTTON & CO.

Collation π⁸ A–T⁸ U⁶; pp. [2] [i–viii] ix–xiii [xiv] 1–315 [316]; 220 × 148 mm.; printed on cream laid paper with oval watermark incorporating Hudson's name, a figure of a tree and two deer.

Pagination [2], blank; p. [i], blank; p. [ii], 'THIS EDITION IS LIMITED TO 750 COPIES / FOR SALE IN ENGLAND, 100 FOR SALE / IN THE UNITED STATES OF AMERICA, / AND 35 PRESENTATION COPIES'; p. [iii], half-title 'THE / COLLECTED WORKS / of / W. H. HUDSON / [short rule] / IN TWENTY-FOUR / VOLUMES / HAMPSHIRE DAYS';

p. [iv], blank; p. [v], title; p. [vi], '*All rights reserved* / PRINTED IN GREAT BRITAIN'; p. [vii], dedication to Sir Edward and Lady Grey; p. [viii], blank; pp. ix–xiii, contents; p. [xiv], blank; pp. 1–306, text; pp. 307–315, index; p. [316], 'PRINTED BY / THE TEMPLE PRESS AT LETCHWORTH / IN GREAT BRITAIN'.

Illustrations Three line drawings.

Binding Green cloth. Gold medallion profile portrait in centre of front cover enclosed within a single blind rule border; spine stamped in gilt 'W. H. / HUDSON / [*leafy branch*] / Hampshire / Days / J·M·DENT / & SONS. LD.'. Blind rule border on back cover. Top edges trimmed and gilt, other edges untrimmed; cream laid endpapers. On front pastedown is a reproduction of pictorial bookplate with Hudson's name and dates. Maroon silk place marker.

Notes This is one of twenty-four volumes of Hudson's collected works. Eight hundred and eighty-five sets were published 1922–1923 for twenty-four guineas per set. The one hundred sets for sale in America were sold by E. P. Dutton for $192 per set. The collected works was reprinted in America by AMS Press in 1968 at $360.

Following publication of the Collected Edition Dent issued a Popular Edition of thirteen of Hudson's books. *Hampshire Days* appeared in 1923 for 6s. It is gathered in 8's and the leaves measure 202 × 133 mm. Bound in blue cloth with a figure of a bird on a leafy branch blind stamped on the front cover. The author's name with a wavy thick-thin rule underneath, title with a printer's flower underneath, and the publisher's name are stamped in gilt on the spine. All edges trimmed and the top edges stained blue; white wove endpapers. Grey wove dust jacket printed in black.

A22e

THE NEW READERS' LIBRARY EDITION (1928)

HAMPSHIRE DAYS / by / W. H. HUDSON / DUCKWORTH / 3 HENRIETTA STREET / LONDON, W.C.2

Collation [1]^{16} 2–9^{16}; pp. [1–7] 8–288; 168 × 114 mm.; printed on wove paper.

Pagination p. [1], half-title 'THE NEW READERS LIBRARY / HAMPSHIRE DAYS'; p. [2], list of thirty-four titles published in the New Readers' Library; p. [3], title; p. [4], '*First issued in The New Readers Library . . . 1928 / by arrangement with Messrs. J. M. Dent & Sons Ltd. / All rights reserved*'; p. [5], dedication to Sir Edward and Lady Grey; p. [6], blank; pp. [7] 8–288, text; at bottom of p. 288 '[*rule*] /

Printed in Great Britain by Ebenezer Baylis & Son, Ltd., The Trinity Press, / Worcester.'.

Binding Blue cloth. Spine stamped in gilt '[rule] / [decorative rule] / [rule] / HAMPSHIRE / DAYS / W. H. / HUDSON / DUCKWORTH / [rule] / [decorative rule] / [rule]'. All edges trimmed; white wove endpapers. Orange wove dust jacket printed in black. *Binder's insert following p. 288*; sixteen pages of publisher's advertisements.

Notes 3,000 copies published May 1928 at 3s. 6d. No. 30 in the New Readers' Library.

OTHER EDITIONS

A22f 1973 New edition. Reading, Barry Shurlock.
A22g n.d. Braille hand-copied edition for the National Library for the Blind (London), four volumes.

A23a

GREEN MANSIONS

FIRST EDITION, REGULAR ISSUE 1904

Green Mansions: A Romance of / the Tropical Forest by W. H. Hudson / [*illustration: snake in underbrush*] / LONDON / DUCKWORTH & CO. / 1904

Collation [A]² B–U⁸ X⁶; pp. [i–iv] [1] 2–315 [316]; 186 × 125 mm.; printed on wove paper.

Pagination p. [i], half-title 'GREEN MANSIONS'; p. [ii], list of six books by the same author; p. [iii], title; p. [iv], blank; pp. [1] 2–6, prologue; pp. 7–315, text; p. [316], 'PLYMOUTH / WILLIAM BRENDON AND SON / PRINTERS'.

Early Binding Green cloth. Front cover stamped in gilt 'GREEN MANSIONS'; spine stamped in gilt 'GREEN / MANSIONS / [*47 mm. below title*] W. H. / HUDSON / DUCKWORTH & CO'. All edges trimmed; white wove endpapers.

Later Binding As above but with publisher's device stamped in blind on back cover. Author's name 29 mm. below title on spine.

Notes Published February 1904 at 6s. See note to A1c for information on publishing records.

It was Duckworth's practice to blind stamp their device on the back cover of their publications. This stamping was inadvertently omitted from the earliest bound copies of *Green Mansions*, quantity unknown. When this oversight was discovered all succeeding copies were stamped. Among the earlier bindings are copies inscribed to Mrs George Hubbard dated 2 February 1904; to Morley Roberts dated 6 February 1904; to J. Wingrave, undated. The BM and Bodleian copies, both in the earlier binding, are stamped 3 February 1904 and 20 February 1904 respectively.

A proof copy of *Green Mansions* is in Bradley Martin's library. The volume contains Hudson's corrections, three trial title pages, and an original drawing by A. D. McCormick.

Hudson criticized *Green Mansions* in a letter to Edward Garnett, 12 December 1903: "I left the MS. for my wife to forward, so I daresay you have got it. I had a look at the first few chapters before tying it up and was again struck painfully by the cumbersomeness of the form. Perhaps some little alteration might be made here: the whole of the story should perhaps come more direct from Abel's lips through memory.

All through the story is told in a leisurely way and very minutely, but the introductory chapters seem too slow: the story doesn't move at all, it simply sits still and stews contentedly in its own juice; and it doesn't even stew, or boil, *à barbolloner*, but simmers placidly away, like a saucepot of cocoa-nibs that has all the day before it. This too might be remedied to some extent.

There are, I daresay, some good points in the book, especially the hero's feeling for nature; and he being a Venezuelan some might say that it is all wrong. But of course it is a delusion that this feeling is confined to our race and that it is a thing of to-day. It is as strong in some of the old Spanish poets as in some of the modern English poets which show it most, and I have known S. Americans with that passion as strong in them as any Englishman. The fault here is that the hero expresses the feeling too well – in English – to be convincing."

Reviews Pall Mall Gazette 13 February 1904; *Week's Survey* 20 February 1904; *Spectator* 27 February 1904; *Daily Chronicle* 1 March 1904; *To-day* 2 March 1904; *Nature* 3 March 1904; *Literary World* 4 March 1904; *The Times* 4 March 1904; *Speaker* 5 March 1904; *Daily News* 8 March 1904; *Vanity Fair* 10 March 1904; *Daily Telegraph* 11 March 1904; *Globe* 14 March 1904; *Saturday Review* 4 April 1904; *Illustrated London News* 30 April 1904; *British Weekly* 26 May 1904; *Standard* 17 June 1904.

Copies Early Binding: BM; Bodleian; Brotherton; Dartmouth; Texas (2). Later Binding: Adams; Chicago; Dobie; Lilly; Martin; Texas (2).

A23b

FIRST EDITION, COLONIAL ISSUE 1904

DUCKWORTH'S COLONIAL LIBRARY / [rule] / GREEN MANSIONS / *A Romance of the Tropical Forest* / BY / W. H. HUDSON / [publisher's device] / LONDON / DUCKWORTH & CO. / 3 HENRIETTA STREET, COVENT GARDEN, W.C. / 1904

[A]² is reset as follows: p. [i], half-title 'GREEN MANSIONS / *This Edition is intended for circulation only in the British / Colonies and India.*'; p. [ii], list of Duckworth & Co.'s new novels; p. [iii], title; p. [iv], '*All Rights Reserved.*' Printed on laid paper.

The remainder of the collation and pagination are the same as the first edition, regular issue, except the leaves measure 180 × 122 mm.

Binding Green cloth. Front cover stamped in black 'GREEN★★ / Mansions★ / By W. H. Hudson / [leaf figure repeated six times on three lines] / Colonial / Edition'; spine stamped in black 'GREEN / MANSIONS / W. H. / HUDSON / COLONIAL / EDITION / DUCKWORTH / ·· & ··'. Publisher's device stamped in black in centre of back cover. All edges trimmed; white wove endpapers.

Notes Number of sets of sheets thus issued unknown. See note to A1c for information on publishing records.

Copies Texas.

A23c

FIRST EDITION, AMERICAN ISSUE 1904

Green Mansions: A Romance of / the Tropical Forest by W. H. Hudson / [*illustration: snake in underbrush*] / NEW YORK: G. P. PUTNAM'S SONS / LONDON: DUCKWORTH & CO. / 1904

[A]² is reset as follows: p. [i], half-title 'GREEN MANSIONS'; p. [ii], blank; p. [iii], title; p. [iv], blank.

Binding Green cloth, lighter in colour and more widely woven than first edition, regular issue. Bottom of spine reads 'PUTNAM'.

Notes Number of sets of sheets thus issued unknown. Copies sold at $1.20. In response to my enquiry about publishing information, William Targ, Vice-President and Editor in Chief, G. P. Putnam's Sons, wrote on 27 May 1972:

"Putnam's 1904 files are non existant!" See note to A1C for information on Duckworth's publishing records.

Reviews New York Times Book Review 3 September 1904.

Copies Adams; Dartmouth; Dobie.

A23d

READERS' LIBRARY EDITION (1910)

Green Mansions: A Romance of / the Tropical Forest by W. H. Hudson / [*illustration*] / LONDON / DUCKWORTH & CO. / 3 HENRIETTA STREET, COVENT GARDEN

Collation [A]² B–W⁸ X⁶; pp. [i–iv] [1] 2–315 [316]; 184 × 132 mm.; printed on wove paper.

Pagination p. [i], half-title 'GREEN MANSIONS'; p. [ii], list of titles in The Readers' Library; p. [iii] title; p. [iv] '*Published in The Readers' Library 1910 / All rights reserved*'; pp. [1] 2–6, prologue; pp. 7–315, text; p. [316] 'PRINTED BY / WILLIAM BRENDON AND SON, LTD. / PLYMOUTH'.

Binding Blue cloth. Publisher's circular device blind stamped in centre of front cover; spine stamped in gilt '[*within a single rule panel*] GREEN / MANSIONS / W. H. / HUDSON / [*in smaller single rule panel at bottom of spine*] DUCKWORTH'; publisher's device blind stamped at lower left corner of back cover. All edges trimmed; white wove endpapers.

Notes Published March 1910 at 2s. 6d. Ten printings to 1926. See note to A1C for information on publishing records.

A23e

FIRST AMERICAN EDITION, REVISED 1916

Green Mansions: A Romance of / the Tropical Forest by W. H. Hudson / With an Introduction by / John Galsworthy / New York [*publisher's device*] MCMXVI / Alfred A Knopf

Collation [1–23]⁸; pp. [i–vi] vii–xvi [xvii–xviii] 1–7 [8] 9–350; 195 × 130 mm.; printed on wove paper.

Pagination p. [i], half-title 'Green Mansions: A Romance of / the Tropical Forest by W. H. Hudson'; p. [ii], list of eleven titles of 'MR. KNOPF'S NEW

BOOKS'; p. [iii], title; p. [iv], 'COPYRIGHT, 1916, BY / ALFRED A. KNOPF / PRINTED IN AMERICA'; p. [v], 'FOREWORD'; p. [vi], blank; pp. vii–xvi, text of foreword by John Galsworthy dated September 1915; p. [xvii], fly-title 'GREEN MANSIONS'; p. [xviii], blank; pp. 1–7, prologue; p. [8], blank; pp. 9–350, text.

Binding Purple cloth. Front cover stamped in green '[*rule*] / GREEN MANSIONS / [*rule*]'; spine stamped in green '[*rule*] / GREEN MANSIONS / [*rule*] / BY – W. H. / HUDSON / ALFRED A ▼ / KNOPF'. Top edges trimmed and stained brownish-red, bottom and fore edges untrimmed; white wove endpapers.

Variant Rose cloth. Stamped as above with the addition of the publisher's device blind stamped in lower right corner of back cover.

Notes Published 10 March 1916 at $1.50. Twenty-two printings to 1925. See note to A20c for information on publishing records.

This is the first appearance of Galsworthy's introduction. See Alfred Knopf's introduction to this bibliography for additional information about this edition.

The financial success of this edition is indicated in Hudson's letter to Knopf, 7 July 1917: "Your two letters one enclosing cheque for $661 have been received & I am glad of the money & grateful to you for having made the book such a success. It has been like bringing a dead thing to life again. I used to think that after my death some of my books, *Green Mansions* included, would get a new lease but I (not being a spiritualist) would know nothing about it." By this date Knopf had paid Hudson $1,876.75.

Reviews Boston Transcript 11 March 1916; *New York Sun* 19 March 1916; *New York Times Book Review* 19 March 1916; *Springfield Republican* 26 March 1916; *New York Evening Sun* 1 April 1916; *Los Angeles Times* 2 April 1916; *Knickerbocker Press* 8 April 1916; *Chicago Tribune* 15 April 1916; *San Francisco Chronicle* 16 April 1916; *Washington D. C. Evening Star* 16 April 1916; *Harper's Weekly* 22 April 1916; *New York Independent* 1 May 1916; *Nation* 18 May 1916; *New Republic* 17 June 1916; *Dial* 22 June 1916; *Bookman* June 1916; *Review of Reviews* June 1916; *ALA Booklist* July 1916; *Wilson Library Bulletin* November 1916.

Variant copy Dartmouth.

A23f

COLLECTED EDITION 1923

[*in red*] GREEN / [*in red*] MANSIONS / A ROMANCE OF THE / TROPICAL FOREST / BY / W. H. HUDSON / [*publisher's device*] / MCMXXIII / LONDON & TORONTO / [*in red*] J. M. DENT & SONS LTD. / NEW YORK: E. P. DUTTON & CO.

Collation π⁶ A–T⁸ U¹⁰; pp. [*two unnumbered pages*] [i–iv] v–ix [x] 1–323 [324]; 220 × 148 mm.; printed on cream laid paper with oval watermark incorporating Hudson's name, a figure of a tree and two deer.

Pagination p. [*first unnumbered page*], blank; p. [*second unnumbered page*], 'THIS EDITION IS LIMITED TO 750 COPIES / FOR SALE IN ENGLAND, 100 FOR SALE / IN THE UNITED STATES OF AMERICA, / AND 35 PRESENTATION COPIES'; p. [i], half-title 'THE / COLLECTED WORKS / of / W. H. HUDSON / [*short rule*] / IN TWENTY-FOUR / VOLUMES / GREEN MANSIONS'; p. [ii], blank; frontispiece: facsimile of four-page letter from Hudson to Edward Garnett referring to *Green Mansions*, 12 December 1903; p. [iii], title; p. [iv], '*All rights reserved* / PRINTED IN GREAT BRITAIN'; pp. v–ix, 'A NOTE ON HUDSON'S ROMANCES' by Edward Garnett, dated April 1923; p. [x], blank; pp. 1–6, prologue; pp. 7–323, text; p. [324], 'PRINTED BY / THE TEMPLE PRESS AT LETCHWORTH / IN GREAT BRITAIN'.

Illustrations Facsimile of four-page letter from Hudson to Edward Garnett, 12 December 1903.

Binding Green cloth. Gold medallion profile portrait in centre of front cover enclosed within a single blind rule border; spine stamped in gilt 'W. H. / HUDSON / [*leafy branch*] / Green / Mansions / J·M·DENT / & SONS. LD.'. Blind rule border on back cover. Top edges trimmed and gilt, other edges untrimmed; cream laid endpapers. On front pastedown is a reproduction of pictorial bookplate with Hudson's name and dates. Maroon silk place marker.

Notes This is one of twenty-four volumes of Hudson's collected works. Eight hundred and eighty-five sets were published 1922–1923 for twenty-four guineas per set. The one hundred sets for sale in America were sold by E. P. Dutton for $192 per set. The collected works was reprinted in America by AMS Press in 1968 at $360.

This is the first book appearance of Garnett's note on Hudson's romances.

The Uniform Edition of Hudson's works was published in 1951 by Dent and consists of seven titles: *The Purple Land*; *Nature in Downland*; *A Hind in Richmond Park*; *Green Mansions*; *Adventures Among Birds*; *Far Away and Long Ago*. *Idle Days in Patagonia* was added in 1954.

Green Mansions is gathered in 16's and the leaves measure 192 × 124 mm. Bound in red cloth. The author's name, title, a figure of a feather and the publisher's name are stamped in gilt on the spine. All edges trimmed; white wove endpapers. Green and white wove dust jacket printed in black. Edward Garnett's note on Hudson's romances is reprinted from the Collected edition.

A23g

FIRST ILLUSTRATED EDITION, REGULAR COPIES 1926

GREEN MANSIONS / *A Romance of the Tropical Forest* / BY / W. H. HUDSON / ILLUSTRATED BY / KEITH HENDERSON / [*publisher's device*] / DUCKWORTH / 3 HENRIETTA STREET, LONDON, W. C. / 1926

Collation [AG]⁸ BG–TG⁸ UG⁴ WG⁸; pp. [1–4] 5–325 [326] [2]; 220 × 144 mm.; printed on laid paper.

Pagination p. [1], half-title 'GREEN MANSIONS'; p. [2], blank; frontispiece; p. [3], title; p. [4], '*First published in 1904 / Reset and with illustrations by Keith Henderson, 1926 / Made and Printed in Great Britain by / The Camelot Press Limited, / London and Southampton*; pp. 5–6, illustrations; pp. 7–13, prologue; pp. 14–325, text; p. [326], blank; [2], blank.

Illustrations Fifty-eight woodblock illustrations; twelve on coated paper, tipped in; forty-six within the text by Keith Henderson.

Binding Green decorative paper boards with smooth green cloth spine; spine stamped in gilt 'GREEN / MANSIONS / W. H. / HUDSON / DUCKWORTH'. All edges trimmed, top edges stained green; white wove endpapers.

Notes 2,000 copies published 4 November 1926 at 15s.

The illustration to face p. 90 is misbound as the frontispiece in the RSPB copy.

Copies RSPB.

A23h

FIRST ILLUSTRATED EDITION, LIMITED COPIES 1926

Same as regular copies except as follows: 1. leaves measure 232 × 148 mm. 2. printed on laid paper. Watermarks: 'F. J. Head & Co.' and 'Hand Made'. 3. Page [4], '*Of this illustrated edition of* GREEN / MANSIONS, *on hand-made paper, / numbered and signed by the artist, / 165 copies only have been printed, of / which 150 are for sale throughout / the world. / Copy No.* [numbered and signed by the artist in blue ink] / *Made and Printed in Great Britain by / The Camelot Press Limited, / London and Southampton*'. 4. all edges untrimmed. Green wove dust jacket decorated in gilt.

Notes 165 copies published 15 November 1926 at £2 2s.

Copies Adams; BM; Dobie.

A23i

THE NEW READERS' LIBRARY EDITION (1927)

GREEN MANSIONS / *A Romance of The Tropical Forest* / by / W. H. HUDSON / DUCKWORTH / 3 HENRIETTA STREET / LONDON, W.C.2

Collation [A]¹⁶ B–K¹⁶; pp. [i–iv] [1] 2–315 [316]; 168 × 115 mm.; printed on wove paper.

Pagination p. [i], half-title 'THE NEW READERS LIBRARY / GREEN MANSIONS'; p. [ii] list of twenty titles published in the New Readers' Library; p. [iii], title; p. [iv], 'All Rights Reserved / First Issue in New Readers Library 1927 / Made and Printed in Great Britain by / The Camelot Press Limited / London and Southampton'; pp. [1] 2–6, prologue; pp. 7–315, text; p. [316], blank.

Binding Blue cloth. Spine stamped in gilt '[*rule*] / [*decorative rule*] / [*rule*] / GREEN / MANSIONS / W. H. / HUDSON / DUCKWORTH / [*rule*] / [*decorative rule*] / [*rule*]'. All edges trimmed; white wove endpapers. Orange wove dust jacket printed in black. *Binder's insert following p. [316]*: eight pages of publisher's advertisements.

Notes 2,000 copies published May 1927 at 3s. 6d. No. 1 in the New Readers' Library.

A23j

THE LIMITED EDITIONS CLUB EDITION 1935

[*coloured illustration*] / [*open letters*] GREEN MANSIONS / A ROMANCE OF THE TROPICAL FOREST / BY / W. H. HUDSON / [*coloured illustration*] / *With an Introduction by* WM. BEEBE / *and Illustrations by* EDWARD A. WILSON / [*rule*] / THE LIMITED EDITIONS CLUB / NEW YORK / 1935

Collation [1–14]⁸; pp. [i–vi] vii–x [xi–xii] xiii–xvi 1–206 [207–208]; 260 × 173 mm.; printed on laid paper.

Pagination p. [i], half-title 'GREEN MANSIONS'; p. [ii], blank; p. [iii], title; p. [iv], 'The Special Contents of this Edition / are Copyright 1935 by / The Limited Editions Club, Inc.'; p. [v], 'INTRODUCTION'; p. [vi], blank; pp. vii–x, text of introduction by William Beebe; p. [xi], fly-title 'GREEN MANSIONS / A ROMANCE OF THE TROPICAL FOREST'; p. [xii], blank; pp. xiii–xvi, prologue; pp. 1–206, text; p. [207], blank; p. [208], '*This edition of* / GREEN MANSIONS / *consists of fifteen hundred copies* / *printed at the* / *Franklin Printing Company* / *Philadelphia* / *for the* members of / The Limited Editions Club / The edition was designed by / Carl J. H. Anderson / and the illustrations were drawn by / Edward A. Wilson / [design] / THIS COPY IS NUMBER / [autograph number in aqua blue ink] / SIGNED BY / [autograph signature of Edward A. Wilson in aqua blue ink]'.

Illustrations Twenty-five coloured offset lithographic illustrations by Edward A. Wilson throughout text. Wilson is known for his work in advertising art and, as a student of Howard Pyle, is recognized for his flamboyant book illustrations in the romantic-adventure tradition.

Binding Green cloth boards with foliage design; tan cloth spine stamped in red '[*reading from bottom to top*] GREEN MANSIONS'. Top edges trimmed, others untrimmed; white laid endpapers. Enclosed within a green paper board box with white spine label printed in red '[*reading from bottom to top*] GREEN MANSIONS'.

Notes 1,500 copies published 25 February 1935 at $10.00.

A23k

THE HERITAGE PRESS EDITION (1936)

GREEN MANSIONS / *A Romance of The Tropical Forest* / BY W. H. HUDSON / ILLUSTRATED BY MIGUEL COVARRUBIAS / [*coloured illustration*] / NEW YORK / FOR THE MEMBERS OF THE HERITAGE CLUB

Collation [1]^8 (1₁ + χ1) [2–20]^8 [21]^6 [22]^8; pp. [1–8] 9–15 [16] 17–346 [347–350]; 240 × 161 mm.; printed on laid paper.

Pagination p. [1], half-title, 'Green Mansions'; p. [2], blank; p. [3], title; p. [4], 'COPYRIGHT, 1916, BY ALFRED A. KNOPF, INC. / THE SPECIAL CONTENTS OF THIS EDITION ARE COPYRIGHT, 1936, / BY THE HERITAGE CLUB / PRINTED IN THE UNITED STATES OF AMERICA'; p. [5], illustrations; p. [6], blank; p. [7], fly-title, '*Green Mansions*'; p. [8], blank; pp. 9–15, prologue; p. [16], blank; pp. 17–346, text; pp. [347–348], blank; p. [349], 'THIS EDITION OF "GREEN MANSIONS" / WAS ILLUSTRATED BY / MIGUEL COVARRUBIAS, / DESIGNED BY / FREDERIC WARDE / AND PRINTED BY THE STRATFORD PRESS, NEW YORK CITY / FOR THE MEMBERS OF / THE HERITAGE CLUB'; p. [350], blank.

Illustrations Eight coloured illustrations, tipped in, and twenty-one line drawings within the text. The illustrations were drawn by Miguel Covarrubias in full colour and in pen and ink. The coloured illustrations are reproduced in four-colour offset lithography; the pen and ink drawings are reproduced by lineplates through the photo-engraving process. Covarrubias, the Mexican painter, caricaturist and illustrator, is also known for his books on Bali and the Isthmus of Tehuantepec.

Binding Coloured pictorial cloth. '[*The binding is*] lithographed in full colour from a painting by Miguel Covarrubias, and then varnished.' All edges trimmed, top edges stained green; coloured wove pictorial endpapers. In a green paper board box.

Notes 1,500 copies published 26 October 1936 at $3.75.

Reprinted in The Heritage Reprint series, 1944, with an introduction by Carl Van Doren.

A separate issue of this book was distributed with a variant title page giving the joint imprint of The Heritage Press and The Nonesuch Press. This is printed on finer paper than that used in the volume for members of The Heritage Club. The illustrations are more brilliant in colour and there is a full-page note on page [349] concerning the production of this book.

In response to my enquiry about the two issues of this edition, a member of the editorial board of The Cardavon Press, (publishers of books for The Limited Editions Club, The Heritage Club, and The Readers Club), replied that the Heritage Press promotional methods varies; sometimes the Club imprint appears on editions distributed both to the members and in the trade, and sometimes the Press imprint differentiates a trade edition. It was not known exactly how *Green Mansions* was distributed.

Correspondence in the publishing files of Alfred A. Knopf, Inc., and the George Macy Archives, both in the Humanities Research Center, The University of Texas at Austin, illustrate Alfred Knopf's position towards the American copyright, or lack of copyright, of *Green Mansions*. The exchange of correspondence between Knopf and Macy also illustrates the terms generally followed by reprint publishers in America.

On 28 March 1930 George Macy asked permission of Alfred Knopf to include *Green Mansions* in the Limited Editions Club edition and offered a courtesy fee of $250.00. This offer was refused by Blanche Knopf on 29 March. Macy wrote again two days later explaining that he wanted Edward A. Wilson to do the illustrations. "No artist in the world is so well equipped (in my opinion) to make the ideal illustrations for this book. It seems to me a shame that we should have to wait until the copyright expires and then pounce upon it, before we can give any present-day classic its ideal setting."

On 1 April 1930 Mrs Knopf refused permission again with a reminder that they had three editions of *Green Mansions* in print at the time: the regular edition, the Borzoi Pocket Book edition, and the Borzoi Classics edition.

Macy proceeded with his plans to publish *Green Mansions* for members of the

Limited Editions Club with publication occurring on 25 February 1935 (A23j).

In April 1936 Knopf learned that Macy planned The Heritage Press edition of *Green Mansions* with illustrations by Miguel Covarrubias. Knopf wrote to Cedric R. Crowell, Doubleday, Doran & Co., "This is the first I have heard of this, although *Green Mansions* is, of course, our book. While I recognize that it is not copyrighted in this country, still we are its only authorized publishers and other reprint houses of standing and repute, as for example The Modern Library and Grosset & Dunlap, have always recognized this fact and made their arrangements with us. I cannot believe that The Heritage Press will wish to take advantage of a technical lack of copyright and ignore our rights simply because they have only moral and no legal support."

Macy wrote Knopf on 1 June asking what steps Knopf would like him to take in arranging to produce the Heritage Press edition. Knopf replied on 4 November, "You will recall discussing with Mr. Lesser back in June the question of your edition of *Green Mansions*. I understand that you offered Mr. Lesser at that time a courtesy fee of $150.00 for this edition, but that he, quite rightly I think, rejected this offer as inadequate and suggested a royalty of five percent on your sales. This you considered too high.

In view of all the facts of the case, facts of which you are fully aware, I confess myself very astonished that you have proceeded with the publication of this book without making any arrangement with me. You are legally quite within your rights, of course, but I cannot believe that you intend to take advantage of that fact. I trust, therefore, that you will now make a proposal without further delay which I can accept.

On the basis of what other reputable publishers are paying us for their use of *Green Mansions*, I would say that if you paid us fifteen cents a copy that would be about right – a little bit in your favor."

On 9 November Macy replied, "Although I do not feel that the tone of your note is pleasant, or that your position is justified, I will take the action you suggest.

But I must call to your attention the fact that you seem irritated because I did not ask your permission to issue an illustrated edition of *Green Mansions*; yet you forget that, when I once did ask for this permission, it was refused to me. There are many other recently published books which are unfortunately not protected by copyright; in many cases, notably the case of *South Wind*, the American publisher (Dodd, Mead) does not seem to feel that he is entitled to a royalty from reprint publishers when he does not hold a copyright. I can clearly see the position you take, and do not disagree with that position. But I think you should see with equal clearness, that you do not have the right to refuse reprint permission to any reputable publisher."

Knopf replied on 16 November, "I confess I was disturbed at your having proceeded with the publication of your edition of *Green Mansions* without making any further effort to come to an agreement with us regarding it.

Perhaps I ought to explain my attitude regarding books that are technically not copyrighted. If they are in the public domain because the copyright has expired then I certainly don't feel the original publisher is entitled to any consideration whatever. If again the original publisher has taken advantage of the technical lapse of copyright to make no payment or only nominal payment to the author or the foreign holder of copyright, then I don't think *that* publisher is entitled to any consideration either. But when the original publisher, regardless of the technical lack of copyright, treats with the author without taking unreasonable advantage of that fact, then I think ethically on every score that original publisher is entitled to fair treatment from reprinters. Now I always paid W. H. Hudson royalties, usually our maximum of fifteen percent on the retail price on my sales of his books, regardless of their copyright position. I paid these royalties until the day came that Hudson himself requested me to make him a lump payment in lieu of future royalties. Then I fell in with his wishes, although I do not ordinarily like to buy books outright. So you see we have some justification for hoping that others will treat us as we in turn have treated others.

I am particularly glad, therefore, that you have agreed to pay us a royalty of fifteen cents per copy on the Covarrubias edition of *Green Mansions*...."

A23l

DEFINITIVE EDITION 1943

[*figure of a tree trunk encircled with branches and birds, printed in black, tan and blue*] / [*printed in tan*] GREEN MANSIONS / A Romance of the Tropical Forest by W. H. Hudson / With a Foreword by John Galsworthy · Paintings & / Drawings by Horacio Butler / *Alfred A. Knopf* [*figure of a Borzoi*] New York 1943

Collation [1]¹⁰ (— [1]₈) [2–17]⁸; pp. [2] [i–vi] vii–x [xi–xiv] 1–4 [5–6] 7–230 [231–234]; 266 × 187 mm.; printed on wove paper.

Pagination [2], blank; p. [i], half-title 'GREEN MANSIONS / A ROMANCE OF THE TROPICAL FOREST'; p. [ii], blank; p. [iii], title; p. [iv], 'COPYRIGHT 1916, 1943 BY ALFRED A. KNOPF, INC. / [*seven-line rights reserved notice*]'; p. [v] 'FOREWORD'; p. [vi], blank; pp. vii–x [xi], foreword by John Galsworthy dated September 1915; p. [xii], blank; p. [xiii], fly-title 'GREEN MANSIONS'; p. [xiv], blank; pp. 1–4 [5], Prologue; p. [6], blank; pp. 7–230

[231], text; p. [232], blank; p. [233], 'NOTES ON / THE PRODUCTION OF THIS VOLUME'. [*This note reads in part*: 'The entire volume was designed by and produced under the supervision of Rudolph Ruzicka. It was composed, printed, and bound by THE PLIMPTON PRESS, Norwood, Massachusetts.']; p. [234], blank.

Illustrations Thirteen full-page coloured lithographic etchings tipped in and twenty-three line engravings within the text by Horacio Butler. "The paintings were reproduced by Colorgraphic Offset Company, Inc., in offset lithography from color separations prepared by Louis Schwarz; the plates for the chapterhead decorations were engraved by The Beck Engraving Company, Inc., New York." [*from the "Notes on the Production of this Volume"*].

Binding Orange cloth. Front cover stamped in blue '[*to the right of a gilt stamped design of a snake, a bird and foliage*] GREEN MANSIONS / A Romance of the Tropical / Forest by W. H. HUDSON / PAINTINGS AND DRAWINGS BY / HORACIO BUTLER'; spine stamped in gilt [*design of footprints and foliage repeated four times, separated by triple blue rules*] [*between first and second design*] 'GREEN / MANSIONS / W. H. HUDSON / [*at foot of spine*] Alfred A. Knopf'. Lower right corner of back cover stamped in blue with a figure of a Borzoi, a leaf design, and '*BORZOI*'. All edges trimmed; coloured decorative endpapers. White wove dust jacket printed in brown and blue and with a reproduction of a coloured painting by Horacio Butler.

Notes Published 18 October 1943 at $5.00 pre-publication price, $6.00 postpublication price.

This edition was reprinted in 1959 with a new preface by Alfred A. Knopf telling how he first came to publish *Green Mansions* in 1916, and an essay by Louis J. Halle, Jr.

Reviews Chicago News 17 November 1943; *New York Times Book Review* 21 November 1943; *Boston Herald* 1 December 1943; *Pasadena, Texas Star-News* 4 December 1943; *Publisher's Weekly* 4 December 1943; *Atlanta, Georgia Journal* 26 December 1943; *Philadelphia Inquirer* 2 January 1944; *Springfield Sunday Union-Republican* 2 January 1944.

OTHER EDITIONS

A23m	1925	Borzoi Classics edition. New York, Knopf. Introduction by John Galsworthy.
A23n	1925	School edition. New York, Knopf.
A23o	1929	Students' Library of Contemporary Fiction edition. New York, Knopf. Introduction by Thomas E. Rankin.

A23p	1931	London, Duckworth. Illustrated by Keith Henderson.
A23q	(1932)	New York, Three Sirens Press. Illustrated by Keith Henderson.
A23r	1932	New York, The Book League of America.
A23s	1932	The Jacket Library edition no. 3. New York, National Home Library.
A23t	1935	Mrs Emma (Gelders) Stern. *Far Town Road*. Acted and Read. Illustrated by Reginald Birch. New York, Dodd, Mead. Contains *Green Mansions* dramatized from the book.
A23u	1936	Cameo Classics edition. New York, Grosset and Dunlap. Illustrated by Keith Henderson.
A23v	1938	Hampton Court edition. New York, Sun Dial Press.
A23w	1939	London, Classics Book Club.
A23x	1939	University Classics edition. Greenwich, Connecticut, Appleby.
A23y	1941	New York, Court Book Company.
A23z	1942	New York, World. Illustrated by Keith Henderson.
A23aa	1943	Toronto, Ryerson Press. Foreword by John Galsworthy and illustrated by Horacio Butler.
A23bb	1943	Deluxe artists' edition. New York, Peter Pauper Press. Illustrated by John de Martelly.
A23cc	1944	The Heritage Reprints edition. New York, Heritage Press. Introduction by Carl Van Doren and illustrated by Miguel Covarrubias.
A23dd	1944	New York, Random House. Illustrated by E. McKnight Kauffer. An undetermined number of copies were bound by Bennett Book Studio (New York) in calf, with leather labels on spine, stamped in gold, silver, red, blue and green.
A23ee	1944	Illustrated Modern Library edition. New York, Modern Library. Introduction by John Galsworthy and illustrated by E. McKnight Kauffer.
A23ff	1944	New York, Carlton House. Introduction by John Galsworthy.
A23gg	1946	New York, Bantam.
A23hh	1949	Great Illustrated Classics edition. New York, Dodd, Mead. Introductory biographical sketch and anecdotal captions by Edwin Way Teale. Illustrated with drawings and photographs.
A23ii	1950	Guild Books paperback edition no. 420. London, Duckworth.

A23jj	1951	Classics illustrated edition. New York, Gilberton. An adaptation by Albert L. Kanter.
A23kk	1951	Harper's Modern Classics. New York, Harper & Brothers. Introduction by Louise Bogan.
A23ll	1954	Hollywood, California, Metro-Goldwyn-Mayer. Film-script by Alan Jay Lerner. A mimeo script in blue wrappers, 100 pages. This script was not used; another version was written by Dorothy Kingsley in 1957. See A23nn.
A23mm	1954	Mount Vernon, Peter Pauper Press. Illustrated by John de Martelly.
A23nn	1957	Hollywood, California, Metro-Goldwyn-Mayer. Film-script by Dorothy Kingsley. A mimeo script in blue wrappers, 124 pages. This script was preceded by an earlier version written by Alan Jay Lerner in 1954. See A23ll. *Green Mansions* was released by M-G-M in 1959, produced by Edmund Grainger and directed by Mel Ferrer. Anthony Perkins played Abel; Audrey Hepburn played Rima; Lee J. Cobb played Nuflo.
A23oo	1957	New York, Fine Editions Press. Introduction by Charles Dwoskin.
A23pp	1957	Collins Classics edition. London, Collins. Introduction by H. E. Bates.
A23qq	1957	New York, Norton.
A23rr	1958	Readers' Digest Condensed Books edition. Pleasantville, New York. Essay by Edwin Way Teale.
A23ss	1959	Bantam Fifty. New York, Bantam.
A23tt	1960	*Four Novels for Adventure*, edited by Edmund Fuller and Olga Achtenhagen. New York, Harcourt Brace. Includes *Green Mansions*.
A23uu	1962	Bantam Classics edition. New York, Bantam.
A23vv	1963	Harper's Modern Classics edition. Evanston, Illinois, Harper & Row. Introduction by Jean A. Wilson.
A23ww	1965	New York, Bantam Pathfinder edition. Introduction by Carlos Barker.
A23xx	1965	An Airmont Classic. New York, Airmont. Introduction by N. R. Teitel.
A23yy	1967	New York, Dell.
A23zz	1967	Large-type edition. New York, Franklin Watts. Ontario, Ambassador Books. Foreword by John Galsworthy and illustrated by E. McKnight Kauffer.

A23aaa	1968	Everyman's Library. London, Dent. Introduction by Edward Garnett.
A23bbb	1968	Magnum Easy Eye Books edition. New York, Lancer Books.
A23ccc	1971	New York, Amsco School Publications.
A23ddd	n.d.	Universal Library. New York, Grosset & Dunlap.
A23eee	n.d.	Modern Library edition. New York, Boni and Liveright. Introduction by John Galsworthy.
A23fff	n.d.	New York, Hartsdale House. Illustrated by Keith Henderson.
A23ggg	n.d.	World's Popular Classics. Art-Type edition. New York, Books.
A23hhh	n.d.	New Readers' Library, pocket edition. London, Duckworth.
A23iii	n.d.	Duo-tone classics, library edition. New York, Books.
A23jjj	n.d.	Registered Guild library edition. New York, Books.
A23kkk	n.d.	Best Books edition. London, Humphries.
A23lll	n.d.	Armed Services edition no. c-71. New York, Editions for the Armed Services. Introduction by John Galsworthy.
A23mmm	n.d.	New York Illustrated Editions. Illustrated by Keith Henderson.
A23nnn	n.d.	New York, Parnassus. Illustrated by Keith Henderson.
A23ooo	n.d.	Illustrated Classics. London, Strato Publications.
A23ppp	n.d.	International Collectors Library edition. New York. Illustrated by Keith Henderson.
A23qqq	n.d.	Popular Classics of the World. New York, Caxton House.
A23rrr	n.d.	Literary Guild of America. N.p. Introduction by Carl Van Doren.
A23sss	n.d.	New York, Windsor Press. Illustrated by Keith Henderson.
A23ttt	n.d.	Braille edition. London, Royal National Institute for the Blind, three volumes.
A23uuu	n.d.	Braille hand-copied edition for the National Library for the Blind (London), four volumes.
A23vvv	n.d.	Braille edition. Talladega, Alabama, Alabama Institute for Deaf and Blind, four volumes, grade 1 1/2; five volumes, grade 1 1/2.

A24a

A LINNET FOR SIXPENCE

FIRST EDITION   1904

[*on left, coloured illustration of The Linnet*] [*on right*] 'A . . . / Linnet . . . / for . . . / Sixpence.' / [*rule*] / [*shorter rule*] / [*decorative double rule*] / THE LINNET (in Summer Plumage). / *Reproduced from an Original Drawing by* J. SMIT. / [*text begins*]

Collation [A]⁴; pp. [1] 2–8; 204 × 125 mm.; printed on wove paper.

Pagination p. [1], title and beginning of text; pp. 2–8, text; at bottom of p. 8 'Leaflet No. 50. Published by the Society for the Protection of Birds, / 3, Hanover Square, London, W., of whom copies may be obtained at 1d. / each; 9d. per doz.; 5s. per 100. / [*rule*] / 2704] WITHERBY & Co., Printers, 326, High Holborn, London, W. C. 1904. / Telephone No. 92 Holborn.'.

Illustrations Coloured half-tone etching of The Linnet from a drawing by J. Smit.

Binding Self-wrappers, stapled.

Notes Published at 1d. The BM copy is stamped 1 July 1904.

This was reprinted in 1907 with the addition of Hudson's name at the end of the text and with the address of the Society changed to Queen Anne's Gate, London.

This first appeared in book form in *Dead Man's Plack An Old Thorn & Miscellanea* (A47).

Copies BM; Bodleian.

A25a

A LITTLE BOY LOST

FIRST EDITION   1905

[*printed in red*] A LITTLE BOY LOST / BY / W. H. HUDSON / ILLUSTRATED BY A. D. M'CORMICK / [*publisher's device*] / LONDON / [*printed in red*] DUCKWORTH & CO. / 3 HENRIETTA STREET, COVENT GARDEN, W. C / 1905

Collation π⁴ A–M⁸ N⁶; pp. [i–vi] vii–viii 1–201 [202–204]; 195 × 145 mm.; printed on wove paper.

Pagination p. [i], half-title 'A LITTLE BOY LOST'; p. [ii], list of eight books by the same author; p. [iii], blank, p. [iv], frontispiece; p. [v], title; p. [vi], '*All rights reserved*'; pp. vii–viii, contents; pp. 1–201, text; p. [202], 'PRINTED BY / TURNBULL AND SPEARS / EDINBURGH'; p. [203], advertisements of three works by Richard Jefferies; p. [204], advertisements of three works by W. H. Hudson.

Illustrations Thirteen full-page line etchings and seventeen line etchings within the text by A. D. McCormick. Twenty-five to thirty illustrations had originally been planned by Hudson as indicated in a letter to George Gissing 6 June 1905.

Binding Beige crash canvas. Front cover stamped with a design of a ship at sea [*in black*] sailing toward a setting sun [*in gilt*]; stamped in green below the design 'A / LITTLE BOY / [*design of a seagull*] LOST [*design of a seagull*] / W. H. HUDSON'; spine stamped in gilt 'A LITTLE / BOY LOST / [*design of two seagulls*] / W. H. / HUDSON / DUCKWORTH / & CO.'; publisher's device blind stamped in centre of back cover. All edges trimmed, top edges gilt; white wove endpapers.

Notes Published October 1905 at 3s. 6d. See note to A1c for information on publishing records.

Chapter 2 appeared earlier as "The Vision of the Great Spoonbill" in *Sunday Magazine*, March 1896 (C72).

Hudson had little regard for *A Little Boy Lost*. He wrote to R. B. Cunninghame Graham on 28 July 1905 that the book was a very slight thing and lacked guts. After its publication, in January 1926, he wrote again to Graham: "I didn't send you or Mrs. Bontine *A Little Boy Lost* because it was only a very little boy's book and I suspected that it was not a particularly good one."

Over the years Hudson changed his opinion and in 1917 agreed with Alfred A. Knopf for the publication of an American edition. See Hudson's letter to Knopf at A25b.

Reviews Speaker 9 December 1905; *Spectator* 9 December 1905; *Outlook* 16 December 1905; *Daily Chronicle* 21 December 1905.

A25b

FIRST AMERICAN EDITION 1918

A LITTLE BOY / LOST, By W. H. Hudson / Illustrated by A. D. M'CORMICK / [*publisher's device*] / NEW YORK: ALFRED A. KNOPF / MCMXVIII

Collation [1-14]⁸; pp. [1-10] 11-215 [216-218] 219-222 [2]; 200 × 154 mm.; printed on wove paper.

Pagination p. [1], half-title 'A LITTLE BOY LOST / [*publisher's design*]'; p. [2], list of four books by the same author; p. [3], blank; p. [4], frontispiece; p. [5], title; p. [6], 'COPYRIGHT, 1918, BY / ALFRED A. KNOPF, INC. / *Published, September, 1918* / PRINTED IN THE UNITED STATES OF AMERICA'; p. [7], contents; p. [8], blank; p. [9], fly-title 'A LITTLE BOY LOST'; p. [10], blank; pp. 11-215, text; p. [216], blank; p. [217], note by Alfred A. Knopf regarding a special foreword by Hudson for the American edition of *A Little Boy Lost*; p. [218], blank; pp. 219-222, postscript: letter from Hudson to Alfred A. Knopf dated 14 November 1917 explaining Hudson's reasons for writing the book; [2], blank.

Illustrations Same as first edition.

Binding Grey cloth. Front cover stamped in gilt on a blue panel 'A LITTLE BOY LOST', enclosed within a gilt, single rule border, enclosed within a printed decorative frame formed by two interwoven thick blue rules. Stamped in gilt below frame 'W. H. HUDSON'; spine stamped in gilt on a blue panel '[*reading from top to bottom*] A LITTLE BOY LOST – W. H. HUDSON', enclosed within a gilt, single rule border, enclosed within a printed decorative frame formed by one interwoven thick blue rule. Top edges trimmed and stained blue, others rough trimmed; white wove endpapers. Cream wove dust jacket printed in blue and orange.

Notes Published 28 September 1918 at $1.50. Thirteen printings to November 1941. See note to A20c for information on publishing records.

This is the first publication of Hudson's letter to Knopf.

In July 1917 Hudson wrote to Knopf about the proposed American edition of *A Little Boy Lost*: "No, I certainly don't dislike *Little Boy Lost*, & hope you will republish it, as I should like to hear what the little readers on the other side would say of it. I do not possess a copy I find but will look at one by & by just to see if a foreword would be of any use.... One thing I remember is that the artist made one ridiculous mistake in an illustration in which the little boy is depicted lying on a raft with his clothes on. He should have been naked as in the two best pictures in the book – one where he is by the water in a gloomy wood & the other where he is surrounded by vultures in the shape of small men. McCormick, who did the illustrations is one of our really good imaginative artists exhibits works every year in our Royal Academy."

Reviews Boston Transcript 9 November 1918; *New York Times Book Review* 17 November 1918; *Nation* 30 November 1918; *New York Evening Post* 14

December 1918; *American Review of Reviews* December 1918; *ALA Booklist* January 1919.

A25c

ILLUSTRATED EDITION 1920

A LITTLE BOY / LOST / BY / W ▼ H ▼ HUDSON / *Author of* "GREEN MANSIONS," *Etc.* / ILLUSTRATED BY / DOROTHY ▼ P ▼ LATHROP / [*illustration*] / NEW YORK / ALFRED ▼ A ▼ KNOPF / MCMXX

Collation [1–10]⁸ [11]⁶; pp. [1–12] 13–187 [188]; 270 × 205 mm.; printed on wove paper. Watermark: 'WARREN'S / OLDE STYLE'.

Pagination p. [1], half-title 'A LITTLE BOY LOST'; p. [2], list of four books by the same author; p. [3], blank recto of frontispiece; p. [4], frontispiece; p. [5], title; p. [6], 'COPYRIGHT, 1920, BY / ALFRED A. KNOPF, INC. / PRINTED IN THE UNITED STATES OF AMERICA'; p. [7], contents; p. [8], blank; p. [9], illustrations; p. [10], blank; p. [11], fly-title 'A LITTLE BOY LOST'; p. [12], blank; pp. 13–183, text; pp. 184–187, postscript; letter from Hudson to Alfred A. Knopf dated 14 November 1917; p. [188] blank.

Illustrations Eight full-page coloured half-tone etchings tipped in on calendered paper, included in the pagination; four full-page black and white line etchings; thirty-four small black and white line etchings at beginnings and endings of chapters by Dorothy P. Lathrop, the American painter, illustrator and engraver.

Binding Green cloth. Front cover stamped in gilt 'A LITTLE BOY / LOST / W ▼ H ▼ HUDSON / [*illustration*] / ILLUSTRATED BY / DOROTHY ▼ P ▼ LATHROP'; spine stamped in gilt 'A / LITTLE / BOY / LOST / By / W ▼ H / HUDSON / With / Pictures / by / DOROTHY ▼ P ▼ / LATHROP / ALFRED ▼ A ▼ / KNOPF'. Top edges gilt, others untrimmed; white wove endpapers.

Notes 2,000 copies published 18 September 1920 at $4.00. Five printings to January 1939.

A25d

ILLUSTRATED EDITION, ENGLISH ISSUE (1921)

A LITTLE BOY / LOST / BY / W ▼ H ▼ HUDSON / *Author of* "Green Mansions," *Etc.* / ILLUSTRATED BY / DOROTHY ▼ P ▼ LATHROP / [*illustra-*

tion] / LONDON / DUCKWORTH AND CO. / 3, HENRIETTA STREET, COVENT GARDEN

Collation [1]⁸(±1₁,₂) [2–10]⁸ [11]⁶(±11₄; −11₅,₆); pp. [1–12] 13–182 [183–184]; 270 × 205 mm.; printed on wove paper. Watermark: 'WARREN'S / OLDE STYLE'.

Pagination p. [1], half-title 'A LITTLE BOY LOST'; p. [2], blank; p. [3], blank recto of frontispiece; p. [4], frontispiece; p. [5], title; p. [6], '*First published 1921* / *All rights reserved* / PRINTED IN THE UNITED STATES OF AMERICA'; p. [7], contents; p. [8], blank; p. [9], illustrations; p. [10], blank; p. [11], fly-title 'A LITTLE BOY LOST'; p. [12], blank; pp. 13–182 [183], text; p. [184], blank.

Illustrations Same as American issue.

Binding Blue cloth. Front cover stamped in gilt 'A LITTLE BOY / LOST / W. H. HUDSON / [*illustration of boy in lower right corner*]'; spine stamped in gilt 'A / LITTLE / BOY / LOST / W. H. HUDSON / DUCKWORTH'; publisher's device blind stamped in lower left corner of back cover. All edges trimmed; white wove endpapers. Grey wove dust jacket printed in blue. Coloured illustration pasted in on upper right corner of front of jacket.

Notes Issued 21 October 1921 at 21s. See note to A1c for information on publishing records.

The sheets of the American issue with the first two leaves reset and tipped in. The last page of text (p. [183]) is reset and tipped in. Hudson's letter to Alfred A. Knopf, which served as a postscript in the American issue, is cancelled in this issue.

A25e

COLLECTED EDITION   1923

A / [*in red*] LITTLE BOY LOST / TOGETHER WITH THE POEMS OF / W. H. HUDSON / [*publisher's device*] / MCMXXIII / LONDON & TORONTO / [*in red*] J. M. DENT & SONS LTD. / NEW YORK: E. P. DUTTON & CO.

Collation π⁸ A–M⁸ N⁶; pp. [4]; [i–viii] ix [x–xii] 1–200 [201–202] [2]; 220 × 148 mm.; printed on cream laid paper with oval watermark incorporating Hudson's name, a figure of a tree and two deer.

Pagination [4], blank; p. [i], blank; p. [ii], 'THIS EDITION IS LIMITED TO 750 COPIES / FOR SALE IN ENGLAND, 100 FOR SALE / IN THE UNITED STATES OF AMERICA, /

AND 35 PRESENTATION COPIES'; p. [iii], half-title 'THE / COLLECTED WORKS / of / W. H. HUDSON / [short rule] / IN TWENTY-FOUR / VOLUMES / A LITTLE BOY LOST / AND VARIOUS POEMS'; p. [iv], blank; p. [v], title; p. [vi], 'All rights reserved / PRINTED IN GREAT BRITAIN'; p. [vii], publisher's note about collecting Hudson's verse writings in this volume and about this being the first publication of the ballad, "The Old Man of Kensington Gardens"; p. [viii], blank; p. ix, contents; p. [x], blank; p. [xi], section-title 'A LITTLE BOY LOST'; p. [xii], blank; pp. 1–146, text; p. [147], section-title 'POEMS'; p. [148], blank; pp. 149–154, "The London Sparrow"; pp. 155–157, "In the Wilderness"; p. 158, "Gwendoline"; pp. 159–170, "Tecla and the Little Men"; pp. 171–200, "The Old Man of Kensington Gardens"; p. [201], 'PRINTED BY / THE TEMPLE PRESS AT LETCHWORTH / IN GREAT BRITAIN'; p. [202], blank; [2], blank.

Contents A Little Boy Lost – The London Sparrow (first appeared in *Merry England* July 1883 (C29)) – In the Wilderness (first appeared in *Merry England* June 1884 (C32)) – Gwendoline (first appeared in *Merry England* June 1885 (C38)) – Tecla and the Little Men (first appeared in *Tales of the Pampas* (A33)) – The Old Man of Kensington Gardens.

Binding Green cloth. Gold medallion profile portrait in centre of front cover enclosed within a single blind rule border; spine stamped in gilt 'W. H. / HUDSON / [leafy branch] / A / Little Boy / Lost & / Various / Poems / J·M·DENT / & SONS. LD.' Blind rule border on back cover. Top edges trimmed and gilt, other edges untrimmed; cream laid endpapers. On front pastedown is a reproduction of pictorial bookplate with Hudson's name and dates. Maroon silk place marker.

Notes This is one of twenty-four volumes of Hudson's collected works. Eight hundred and eighty-five sets were published for twenty-four guineas per set. The one hundred sets for sale in America were sold by E. P. Dutton for $192 per set. The collected works was reprinted in America by AMS Press in 1968 at $360.
 This is the first publication of "The Old Man of Kensington Gardens".

OTHER EDITIONS

A25f 1938 Borzoi books edition. New York, Knopf. Illustrated by A. D. McCormick.
A25g 1938 Ryerson Press edition. New York, Ryerson Press.
A25h n.d. Braille edition. London, Royal National Institute for the Blind, one volume.
A25i n.d. Braille hand-copied edition for the National Library for the Blind (London), one volume.

A26a

THE LAND'S END

FIRST EDITION 1908

THE LAND'S END / A NATURALIST'S IMPRESSIONS / IN WEST CORN-WALL / BY / W. H. HUDSON / WITH FORTY-NINE ILLUSTRATIONS BY / A. L. COLLINS / London: HUTCHINSON & CO. / Paternoster Row [*printer's flower*] 1908

Collation [A]⁴ B–X⁸ Y⁴; pp. [i–vi] vii–viii [1] 2–317 [318] 319–323 [324–328]; 218 × 140 mm.; printed on wove paper.

Pagination p. [i], half-title 'THE LAND'S END'; p. [ii], list of nine books by the same author; frontispiece; p. [iii], title,; p. [iv], blank; p. [v], contents; p. [vi], note regarding previous publication of parts of this book; pp. vii–viii, illustrations; pp. [1] 2–317, text; p. [318], blank; pp. 319–323, index; at bottom of p. 323, 'WILLIAM BRENDON AND SON, LTD. / PRINTERS, PLYMOUTH'; p. [324], blank; pp. [325–328], publisher's advertisements of six books.

Contents Wintering in West Cornwall – Gulls at St. Ives (first appeared in the *Speaker* 24 February 1906 (C136)) – Cornwall's Connemara (first appeared in the *Speaker* 24 March 1906 (C138)) – Old Cornish Hedges – Bolerium: The End of all the Land (first appeared in the *Speaker* 28 April 1906 (C139)) – Castles by the Sea – The British Pelican (first appeared in *Saturday Review* 16 February 1907 (C144)) – Bird Life in Winter – The People and the Farms – An Impression of Penzance – Manners and Morals – Cornish Humour – The Poetic Spirit – Winter Aspects and a Bird Visitation – A Great Frost – A Native Naturalist – The Coming of Spring – Some Early Flowers – The Furze in its Glory – Pilgrims at The Land's End.

Illustrations Eight full-page illustrations on calendered paper, tipped in, and forty-one pen and ink sketches within the text by A. L. Collins.

Binding Blue cloth. Front cover stamped in gilt with a figure of a mermaid enclosed within a single rule border; spine stamped in gilt '[*double rule*] / THE / LAND'S / END / W. H. HUDSON / HUTCHINSON & CO. / [*double rule*]'. All edges trimmed, top edges gilt; white wove endpapers.

Variant Sheets measure 192 × 135 mm. Front cover stamped in blind with a single rule border; spine stamped in gilt '[*rule*] / The / Land's / End / Hudson / Hutchinson & Co / [*rule*]. All edges trimmed.

Notes Published May 1908 at 10s. 6d. In response to my enquiry about publishing information Sir Robert Lusty, Managing Director, Hutchinson Publishing Group wrote on 1 June 1972: "I am afraid I cannot reply very helpfully as all the records of this organisation were destroyed during the War."

The RSPB copy is inscribed by Hudson and dated 16 May 1908. The BM copy is stamped 11 June 1908.

The proof sheets with numerous changes in wording and punctuation by the author are in the Lilly Library.

Hudson wrote to Morley Roberts 28 May 1908: "The St. Ives people are very angry with me for exposing their bird-torturing practices, I see in to-day's *Telegraph*. I'm very glad they are angry: perhaps they will now mend their ways a little." And on 16 July 1908 Hudson wrote again to Roberts: "I've just received a delightful letter from a gentleman at Camborne, inviting me on behalf of the Literary Society to go and discuss Cornish character with the Cambornites, who will be delighted to meet me face to face and hear what I have to say to justify my charges against the people of Cornwall. They want me to know what Cornishmen really are, etc., etc. The Cambornites have a name for roughness: they very nearly killed Will Thorne (general secretary of the National Union of General Workers) when *he* went to meet them face to face, and I shall have to ask you to come with your gun to back me up. On the other hand the Editor of the Penzance paper *The Cornishman* has just concluded a series of 5 long articles on my book and tho' he begins by being a little angry he concludes that he is now convinced of my perfect sincerity and much more in my praise."

Reviews Daily Telegraph 18 May 1908; *Scotsman* 25 May 1908; *Daily Chronicle* 1 June 1908; *Globe* 4 June 1908; *The Times* 4 June 1908; *Outlook* 13 June 1908; *Sunday Sun* 21 June 1908; *Standard* 29 June 1908; *Truth* 1 July 1908; *Cornishman* 9 July 1908; *Spectator* 11 July 1908; *Nation* 18 July 1908; *Guardian* 29 July 1908; *Humanitarian* July 1908; *Bookman* August 1908; *Athenaeum* 12 September 1908; *Saturday Review* 19 September 1908.

Variant copy Spater.

A26b

FIRST AMERICAN ISSUE 1908

THE LAND'S END / A NATURALIST'S IMPRESSIONS / IN WEST CORN-WALL / BY / W. H. HUDSON / WITH FORTY-NINE ILLUSTRATIONS BY / A. L. COLLINS / NEW YORK / D. APPLETON AND COMPANY / 1908.

Collation Same as first edition except [A]⁴ is reset and the last two leaves are cancelled.

Pagination p. [i], half-title, 'THE LAND'S END'; p. [ii], blank; frontispiece; p. [iii], title; p. [iv], blank; p. [v], contents; p. [vi], note regarding previous publication of parts of this book; pp. vii–viii, illustrations; pp. [1] 2–317, text; p. [318], blank; pp. 319–323, index; at bottom of p. 323, 'WILLIAM BRENDON AND SON, LTD. / PRINTERS, PLYMOUTH'; p. [324], blank.

Contents and *illustrations* Same as first edition.

Binding Same as first edition except spine reads 'APPLETONS' instead of 'HUTCHINSON & Cº'.

Notes Published at $3.00. See note to A5b for information on publishing records. The English sheets with [A]⁴ reset and the last four pages cancelled.

Reviews Nation 31 December 1908; *New York Times Book Review* 31 October 1908.

A26c

COLLECTED EDITION   1923

THE / [*in red*] LAND'S END / A / NATURALIST'S IMPRESSIONS / IN WEST CORNWALL / BY / W. H. HUDSON / [*publisher's device*] / MCMXXIII / LONDON & TORONTO / [*in red*] J. M. DENT & SONS LTD. / NEW YORK: E. P. DUTTON & CO.

Collation π⁸ A–S⁸ T¹⁰; pp. [*2*] [i–viii] ix–xiv 1–307 [308]; 220 × 148 mm.; printed on cream laid paper with oval watermark incorporating Hudson's name, a figure of a tree and two deer.

Pagination [*2*], blank; p. [i], blank; p. [ii], 'THIS EDITION IS LIMITED TO 750 COPIES / FOR SALE IN ENGLAND, 100 FOR SALE / IN THE UNITED STATES OF AMERICA, / AND 35 PRESENTATION COPIES'; p. [iii], half-title 'THE / COLLECTED WORKS / of / W. H. HUDSON / [*short rule*] / IN TWENTY-FOUR / VOLUMES / THE LAND'S END'; p. [iv], blank; p. [v], title; p. [vi], '*All rights reserved* / PRINTED IN GREAT BRITAIN'; p. [vii], note regarding previous publication of parts of this book; p. [viii], blank; pp. ix–xiv, contents; pp. 1–302, text; pp. 303–307, index; p. [308], 'PRINTED BY / THE TEMPLE PRESS AT LETCHWORTH / IN GREAT BRITAIN'.

Contents Same as first edition.

Binding Green cloth. Gold medallion profile portrait in centre of front cover enclosed within a single blind rule border; spine stamped in gilt 'W. H. / HUDSON / [*leafy branch*] / The / Land's / End / J·M·DENT / & SONS. LD.'. Blind rule border on back cover. Top edges trimmed and gilt, other edges untrimmed; cream laid endpapers. On front pastedown is a reproduction of a pictorial bookplate with Hudson's name and dates. Maroon silk place marker.

Notes This is one of twenty-four volumes of Hudson's collected works. Eight hundred and eighty-five sets were published 1922–1923 for twenty-four guineas per set. The one hundred sets for sale in America were sold by E. P. Dutton for $192 per set. The collected works was reprinted in America by AMS Press in 1968 at $360.

Following publication of the Collected Edition Dent issued a Popular Edition of thirteen of Hudson's books. *The Land's End* appeared in 1923 for 6s. It is gathered in 8's and the leaves measure 202 × 133 mm. Bound in blue cloth with a figure of a bird on a leafy branch blind stamped on the front cover. The author's name with a wavy thick-thin rule underneath, title with a printer's flower underneath, and the publisher's name are stamped in gilt on the spine. All edges trimmed and the top edges stained blue; white wove endpapers. Grey wove dust jacket printed in black.

A26d

FIRST AMERICAN EDITION 1927

[*within a single rule frame, within a red spiral frame*] [*printed in red*] The Land's End / A Naturalist's Impressions / in West Cornwall / W. H. Hudson / [*printed in red*] [*publisher's device*] / Alfred·A·Knopf / NEW YORK MCMXXVII

Collation [1–19]^8 [20]^6; pp. [i–iv] v–ix [x–xii] 1–293 [294] 295–299 [300–302] [2]; 221 × 148 mm.; printed on laid paper.

Pagination p. [i], half-title, 'THE LAND'S END'; p. [ii], list of seven books by the same author; p. [iii], title; p. [iv], 'MANUFACTURED IN THE / UNITED STATES OF AMERICA'; pp. v–ix, contents; p. [x], blank; p. [xi], fly-title, 'THE LAND'S END'; p. [xii], blank; pp. 1–293, text; p. [294], blank; pp. 295–299, index; p. [300], blank; p. [301], 'A NOTE ON THE TYPE IN WHICH THIS BOOK IS SET / [*12 lines of description*] / [*publisher's device*] / TITLE PAGE DESIGNED BY ELMER ADLER / SET UP, ELECTRO-TYPED, PRINTED AND / BOUND BY THE QUINN & BODEN / COMPANY, RAHWAY, N. J.·PAPER / MANUFACTURED BY W. C. HAM- / ILTON & SONS, MIQUON, PA., / AND FURNISHED BY W. F. / ETHERINGTON & CO., NEW / YORK'; p. [302], blank; [2], blank.

Contents Same as first edition.

Binding Purplish blue cloth. Front cover printed in yellow, '[*rule*] / THE LAND'S

END / [rule]'; spine printed in yellow, '[rule] / THE / LAND'S / END / [rule] / BY
– W. H. / HUDSON / ALFRED·A·KNOPF'. Top edges trimmed, others rough-trimmed;
white wove endpapers.

Notes 1,800 copies published 6 May 1927 at $2.50.

Reviews New York Times Book Review 29 May 1927.

A27a

AFOOT IN ENGLAND

FIRST EDITION 1909

AFOOT IN ENGLAND / BY / W. H. HUDSON / London: HUTCHINSON &
CO. / Paternoster Row [*leaf ornament*] 1909

Collation [A]⁴ B–U⁸; pp. [i–viii] [1] 2–303 [304]; 218 × 140 mm.; printed on
wove paper.

Pagination p. [i], half-title, 'AFOOT IN ENGLAND'; p. [ii], list of ten books by the
same author; p. [iii], title; p. [iv], blank; p. [v], notice of previous publications
of parts of this book; p. [vi], blank; p. [vii], contents; p. [viii], blank; pp. [1]
2–303 text; at bottom of p. 303, 'PRINTED BY / WILLIAM BRENDON AND SON, LTD. /
PLYMOUTH'; p. [304], blank.

Contents Guide Books: An Introduction (first appeared in the *Speaker* 2 April
1904 (C117)) – On Going Back – Walking and Cycling (first appeared in the
Speaker 14 July 1906 (C147)) – Seeking a Shelter – Wind, Wave, and Spirit – By
Swallowfield – Roman Calleva – A Cold Day at Silchester (first appeared in
the *Speaker* 31 October 1903 (C111)) – Rural Rides (first appeared in *Saturday
Review* 28 December 1901 (C105)) – The Last of his Name – Salisbury and its
Doves (first appeared in the *Speaker* 9 January 1904 (C114)) – Whitesheet Hill
(first appeared in the *Speaker* 27 May 1905 (C125)) – Bath and Wells Revisited
(first appeared in the *Speaker* 18 March 1905 (C123)) – The Return of the Native
(first appeared in the *Speaker* 30 September 1905 (C129)) – Summer Days on the
Otter – In Praise of the Cow (first appeared in the *Speaker* 6 February 1904
(C115)) – An Old Road Leading Nowhere – Branscombe (first appeared in
Longman's Magazine October 1898 (C92)) – Abbotsbury (first appeared in
Saturday Review 5 September 1896 (C75)) – Salisbury Revisited – Stonehenge
(first appeared in the *English Review* December 1908 (C148)) – The Village and
'The Stones' – Following a River – Troston – My Friend Jack.

Binding Green cloth. Front cover stamped in gilt with single rule border; spine stamped in gilt '[*rule*] / AFOOT / IN / ENGLAND / W.H. / HUDSON / HUTCHINSON & Cº. / [*rule*]'. All edges trimmed, top edges gilt; white wove endpapers.

Notes Published June 1909 at 10s. 6d. See note to A26a for information on publishing records.

The BM copy is stamped 9 August 1909.

About half the matter in this book appeared earlier in various periodicals such as the *Saturday Review, Speaker, Morning Post, English Review, Longman's Magazine.*

At the end of 1921 Hudson was finalizing plans with Alfred A. Knopf for the publication of an American edition of *Afoot in England.* On 10 December Hudson wrote Morley Roberts: "Will you give me back your copy of *Afoot in England*? I promise you to return you another by and by, but I want one immediately, and as my books are locked up at Tower House I can't get at my own. If I fail to get one soon I will give you mine when I return. The thing is this. Knopf has arranged to publish the book in Spring and has failed to get a copy in America after advertising for one during the last six months. I, on my part, have advertised for one through *three* different booksellers and not one of them can get a copy. So it is wanted at once, and if you can't give me yours I must appeal to some other friend – perhaps the Ranee would give me her copy. But if you can give me yours please post it to me at once as there is little time to get it to America in time for the Spring season." And on 16 December Hudson writes again to Roberts: "The Ranee gave me her copy of *Afoot* and it is on its way to New York, with some corrections I put in it."

Reviews Morning Post 24 June 1909; *The Times* 1 July 1909; *Nation* 3 July 1909; *Planet* 3 July 1909; *Daily Chronicle* 6 July 1909; *Pall Mall Gazette* 6 July 1909; *Globe* 7 July 1909; *Evening Standard* 8 July 1909; *Truth* 21 July 1909; *Glasgow Evening News* 22 July 1909; *Graphic* 24 July 1909; *Daily News* 25 July 1909; *Tatler* 28 July 1909; *Manchester Guardian* 29 July 1909; *Liverpool Courier* 30 July 1909; *Observer* 1 August 1909; *Irish Times* 6 August 1909; *Standard* 6 August 1909; *T. P.'s Weekly* 6 August 1909; *Spectator* 7 August 1909; *Athenaeum* 4 September 1909; *Family Herald* 4 September 1909; *Field* 11 September 1909; *Guardian* 23 September 1909; *Bookman* October 1909.

A27b

FIRST AMERICAN EDITION 1922

AFOOT IN ENGLAND / W. H. HUDSON / [*publisher's device*] / NEW YORK / ALFRED ▼ A ▼ KNOPF / 1922

Collation [1–19]⁸ [20]⁴; pp. [1–8] 9–309 [310] [2]; 205 × 139 mm.; printed on wove paper.

Pagination p. [1], half-title, 'AFOOT IN / ENGLAND'; p. [2], list of six titles by the same author; p. [3], title; p. [4], 'COPYRIGHT, 1922, BY / ALFRED A. KNOPF, INC. / Published, May, 1922 / Set up, electrotyped, and printed by the Vail-Ballou Co., Binghamton, N.Y. / Paper (Warren's) furnished by Henry Lindenmeyr & Sons, New York, N.Y. / Bound by the Plimpton Press, Norwood, Mass. / MANUFACTURED IN THE UNITED STATES OF AMERICA'; pp. [5–6], contents; p. [7], fly-title, 'AFOOT IN / ENGLAND'; p. [8], blank; pp. 9–309, text; p. [310], blank; [2], blank.

Contents Same as first edition, with slight textual changes and the addition of a paragraph at the close of chapter XVIII.

Binding Rose cloth. Front cover stamped in green, '[*rule*] / AFOOT IN ENGLAND / [*rule*]'; spine stamped in green, '[*rule*] / AFOOT IN / ENGLAND / [*rule*] / BY – W. H. / HUDSON / ALFRED ▼ A ▼ KNOPF'; publisher's design stamped in blind in lower right corner of back cover. Top edges trimmed, others untrimmed; white wove endpapers. Yellow wove dust jacket printed in black; Hudson's photograph on front cover.

Notes 2,000 copies published May 1922 at $3.50. Seven printings to 1941.

Reviews Boston Transcript 27 May 1922; *New York Times Book Review* 18 June 1922; *Booklist* July 1922; *Wilson Library Bulletin* July 1922; *New York Freeman* 2 August 1922; *ALA Bookman* August 1922; *New York Evening Post Literary Review* 23 September 1922; *Nation* 10 January 1923.

A27c

COLLECTED EDITION   1923

AFOOT / [*in red*] IN ENGLAND / BY / W. H. HUDSON / [*publisher's device*] / MCMXXIII / LONDON & TORONTO / [*in red*] J. M. DENT & SONS LTD. / NEW YORK: E. P. DUTTON & CO.

Collation π⁸ A–T⁸ U⁴; pp. [i–viii] ix–xvi [1] 2–312; 220 × 148 mm.; printed on cream laid paper with oval watermark incorporating Hudson's name, a figure of a tree and two deer.

Pagination p. [i], blank; p. [ii], 'THIS EDITION IS LIMITED TO 750 COPIES / FOR SALE IN ENGLAND, 100 FOR SALE / IN THE UNITED STATES OF AMERICA, / AND 35 PRESENTATION COPIES'; p. [iii], half-title 'THE / COLLECTED WORKS / of / W. H.

HUDSON / [*short rule*] / IN TWENTY-FOUR / VOLUMES / AFOOT IN ENGLAND'; p. [iv], blank; frontispiece: sketch of Hudson by A. D. McCormick; p. [v], title; p. [vi], '*All rights reserved* / PRINTED IN GREAT BRITAIN'; p. [vii], notice of previous publication of parts of this book; p. [viii], blank; pp. ix–xvi, contents; pp. [1] 2–306, text; pp. 307–312, index; at bottom of p. 312, 'PRINTED BY / THE TEMPLE PRESS AT LETCHWORTH IN GREAT BRITAIN'.

Illustrations Frontispiece sketch of Hudson by A. D. McCormick.

Contents Same as first edition.

Binding Green cloth. Gold medallion profile portrait in centre of front cover enclosed within a single blind rule border; spine stamped in gilt 'W. H. / HUDSON / [*leafy branch*] / Afoot / in / England / J·M·DENT / & SONS.LD.'. Blind rule border on back cover. Top edges trimmed and gilt, other edges untrimmed; cream laid endpapers. On front pastedown is a reproduction of pictorial bookplate with Hudson's name and dates. Maroon silk place marker.

Notes This is one of twenty-four volumes of Hudson's collected works. Eight hundred and eighty-five sets were published 1922–1923 for twenty-four guineas per set. The one hundred sets for sale in America were sold by E. P. Dutton for $192 per set. The collected works was reprinted in America by AMS Press in 1968 at $360.

Following publication of the Collected Edition Dent issued a Popular Edition of thirteen of Hudson's books. *Afoot in England* appeared in 1924 for 6s. It is gathered in 8's and the leaves measure 202 × 133 mm. Bound in blue cloth with a figure of a bird on a leafy branch blind stamped on the front cover. The author's name with a wavy thick-thin rule underneath, title with a printer's flower underneath, and the publisher's name are stamped in gilt on the spine. All edges trimmed and the top edges stained blue; white wove endpapers. Grey wove dust jacket printed in black.

OTHER EDITIONS

A27d	1926	Cheaper edition. New York, Knopf.
A27e	1927	Wayfarer's Library edition, no. 127. London, Dent.
A27f	1929	Bayswater edition. New York, Knopf.
A27g	1929	Braille edition. Los Angeles, Universal Braille Press, two volumes.
A27h	1933	Open Air Library edition. London, Dent. Illustrated by Eric Fitch Daglish.
A27i	1945	Guild Books edition. Stockholm, A B Ljus Förlag for the British Publishers Guild. (Guild Books No. C4).

A27j 1952 Penguin Books edition. London, Penguin Books. Introduction by Richard Curle.

A27k n.d. Braille hand-copied edition for the National Library for the Blind (London), three volumes.

A28a

SOUTH AMERICAN SKETCHES

FIRST EDITION 1909

SOUTH / AMERICAN / SKETCHES / BY / W. H. HUDSON / Author of / "THE PURPLE LAND" / "GREEN MANSIONS" / "NATURE IN DOWNLAND," etc. / LONDON: / DUCKWORTH & CO / 3 HENRIETTA ST., COVENT GARDEN, W.C. / 1909

Collation [A]⁴ (— A1,2) (+ A1,2) B–M⁸ N⁴; pp. [i–viii] [1] 2–68 [69] 70–88 [89] 90–124 [125] 126–173 [174] 175–182 [2]; 184 × 125 mm.; printed on wove paper.

Pagination p. [i], half-title, 'SOUTH AMERICAN SKETCHES'; p. [ii], blank; p. [iii], title; p. [iv], 'This volume is a re-issue of the stories which / appeared in the "Greenback Library" / in 1902 under the title of *El Ombú*.'; p. [v], dedication to R. B. Cunninghame Graham; p. [vi], note regarding previous publication of "Story of a Piebald Horse" and "Niño Diablo" and notice that "El Ombú" and "Marta Riquelme" are here printed for the first time; p. [vii], contents; p. [viii], blank; pp. [1] 2–68, El Ombú; pp. [69] 70–88, Story of a Piebald Horse; pp. [89] 90–124, Niño Diablo; pp. [125] 126–173, Marta Riquelme; pp. [174] 175–182, Appendix to El Ombú; [2], blank.

Contents El Ombú.– Story of a Piebald Horse. – Niño Diablo. – Marta Riquelme. – Appendix to El Ombú.

Binding Blue cloth. Front cover stamped in blind '[*rule*] / [*rule*] / SOUTH / AMERICAN / SKETCHES / W. H. HUDSON / [*rule*] / [*rule*]'; spine stamped in gilt [*thick-thin rule*] / SOUTH / AMERICAN / SKETCHES / W. H. / HUDSON / [*blind rule with 8 blind rules extending 108 mm. down spine to another blind rule*] / DUCKWORTH / [*double, thin thick rule*]'. Publisher's device stamped in blind in lower left corner of back cover. All edges trimmed, top edges stained blue; white wove endpapers.

Notes Published March 1909 at 1s. See note to A1c for information on publishing records.

This is a reissue of *El Ombú* (A21). This first appeared in the United States with an expanded text in 1916 under the title *Tales of the Pampas* (A33). It was collected with *The Purple Land* and *Green Mansions* in 1930 under the title *South American Romances* (A56).

OTHER EDITIONS

A28b   n.d.   Two shilling net series. London, Duckworth.

A29a

A SHEPHERD'S LIFE

FIRST EDITION (1910)

A SHEPHERD'S LIFE / IMPRESSIONS OF THE SOUTH WILTSHIRE DOWNS / BY / W. H. HUDSON / ILLUSTRATED BY / BERNARD C. GOTCH / [*illustration of Stonehenge*] / METHUEN & CO. LTD. / 36 ESSEX STREET W.C. / LONDON

Collation [a]⁴ b² 1–22⁸ 23⁴ 23*²; pp. [i–iv] v [vi] vii [viii] ix–xi [xii] [1] 2–361 [362] [2]; 220 × 140 mm.; printed on wove paper.

Pagination p. [i], half-title 'A SHEPHERD'S LIFE'; p. [ii], list of eleven books by the same author; frontispiece; p. [iii], title; p. [iv], '*First Published in 1910*'; p. v, note regarding previous publication of parts of this book; p. [vi], blank; p. vii, contents; p. [viii], blank; pp. ix–xi, illustrations; p. [xii], blank; pp. [1] 2–354, text; pp. 355–361, index; p. [362], 'ABERDEEN: THE UNIVERSITY PRESS'; [2], blank.

Illustrations Coloured frontispiece plus sixty-four line etchings within the text by Bernard C. Gotch.

Binding Green cloth. Front cover stamped in gilt '[*within a single rule border*] A SHEPHERD'S LIFE / W. H. HUDSON / [*illustration of Stonehenge*]'; spine stamped in gilt '[*double rule*] / A / SHEPHERD'S / LIFE / W. H. / HUDSON / METHUEN / [*double rule*]'. Top edges trimmed, others rough-trimmed; white wove endpapers. *Binder's insert following p. [362]*: thirty-two page catalogue of books published by Methuen, dated April 1910.

Variants 1 Publisher's catalogue dated August 1910. 2 Purple cloth. Spine stamped in gilt 'A / SHEPHERD'S / LIFE / HUDSON'. All edges trimmed, white wove endpapers. Publisher's catalogue dated August 1910.

Notes 1,500 copies published 22 September 1910 at 7s. 6d. Twenty-three printings to 1957.

Parts of 'A Shepherd of the Downs' which first appeared in *Longman's Magazine* September 1902 (C108), are incorporated into different chapters of this book. With this exception, the whole of the contents now appears for the first time.

Hudson wrote to Edward Garnett 11 October 1910: "Thanks for your letter – you said so much in praise of *A Shepherd's Life* I had to wait to get cool before replying. But you are always too generous to your friends and (I can't help thinking) especially to me. The reason of it is that you are to some extent under an illusion. A man is so much better than his books! – take the best thing you have done – don't you feel how little of all the best in you it contains – and that little how poorly expressed? I don't like even to look at a book of mine after it is finished. I suppose when you know a man intimately and have an affection for him, you get into the way of expecting to find him – something worthy of him – in his book. Hence the illusion."

Reviews Morning Post 26 September 1910; *The Times* 29 September 1910; *Evening Standard* 5 October 1910; *Punch* 5 October 1910; *Daily Chronicle* 7 October 1910; *Truth* 7 October 1910; *Observer* 9 October 1910; *Field* 15 October 1910; *Daily Telegraph* 19 October 1910; *Nation* 22 October 1910; *Saturday Review* 22 October 1910; *Spectator* 22 October 1910; *New Age* 24 October 1910; *Daily News* 16 November 1910; *Tatler* 23 November 1910; *Guardian* 25 November 1910; *Country Life* 13 December 1910; *Bookman* December 1910.

Variant copy 1 Adams; Dartmouth; Lilly. *Variant copy 2* Dobie.

A29b

FIRST AMERICAN ISSUE 1910

A SHEPHERD'S LIFE / IMPRESSIONS OF THE SOUTH WILTSHIRE DOWNS / BY / W. H. HUDSON / ILLUSTRATED BY / BERNARD C. GOTCH / [*illustration of Stonehenge*] / NEW YORK / E. P. DUTTON AND COMPANY / 31 WEST TWENTY-THIRD STREET / 1910

Collation Same as first edition except title page is a cancellans.

Pagination p. [i], half-title, 'A SHEPHERD'S LIFE'; p. [ii], blank; frontispiece; p. [iii], title; p. [iv], blank; p. v, note regarding previous publication of parts of this book; p. [vi], blank; p. vii, contents; p. [viii], blank; pp. ix–xi, illustrations; p. [xii], blank; pp. [1] 2–354, text; pp. 355–361, index; p. [362], 'ABERDEEN: THE UNIVERSITY PRESS'; [2], blank.

Illustrations Same as first edition.

Binding Same as first edition except foot of spine reads 'DUTTON' and there is no publisher's catalogue.

Notes 1,500 copies issued at $2.50. See note to A22c for information on publishing records.

The English sheets with a cancel title page for the Dutton imprint.

Reviews Dial 16 December 1910; *Outlook* 31 December 1910; *ALA Booklist* April 1911; *Nation* 13 July 1911.

A29c

FIRST AMERICAN EDITION   1921

A SHEPHERD'S LIFE / IMPRESSIONS OF THE / SOUTH WILTSHIRE DOWNS / BY / W. H. HUDSON / ILLUSTRATED BY / BERNARD C. GOTCH / [*illustration of Stonehenge*] / NEW YORK / E. P. DUTTON & COMPANY / 681 FIFTH AVENUE / 1921

Collation [1–22]⁸; pp. [i–vi] vii [viii] ix–xi [xii–xiv] 1–338; 204 × 139 mm.; printed on wove paper.

Pagination p. [i], half-title 'A SHEPHERD'S LIFE'; p. [ii], list of nine books by the same author; frontispiece; p. [iii], title; p. [iv], 'New American Edition / Entirely re-set / Published 1921 / By E. P. DUTTON & COMPANY / [*short rule*] / All Rights Reserved / PRINTED IN THE UNITED STATES OF AMERICA'; p. [v], note regarding previous publication of parts of this book; p. [vi], blank; p. vii, contents; p. [viii], blank; pp. ix–xi, illustrations; p. [xii], blank; p. [xiii], fly-title, 'A SHEPHERD'S LIFE'; p. [xiv], blank; pp. 1–332, text; pp. 333–338, index.

Illustrations Frontispiece plus sixty-four line etchings within the text by Bernard C. Gotch.

Binding Brown cloth. Front cover stamped in gilt 'A SHEPHERD'S LIFE / [*rule*] / W. H. HUDSON'; spine stamped in gilt 'A / SHEPHERD'S / LIFE / [*diamond design*] / HUDSON / E. P. DUTTON / & CO.'. Top and bottom edges trimmed, fore edges rough trimmed; white wove endpapers.

Variant Purple cloth.

Notes Published at $3.00. See note to A22c for information on publishing records.

Reviews New York Times Book Review 1 January 1922.

Variant copy Dobie.

A29d

COLLECTED EDITION 1923

A / [*in red*] SHEPHERD'S LIFE / IMPRESSIONS OF THE SOUTH / WILTSHIRE DOWNS / BY / W. H. HUDSON / [*publisher's device*] / MCMXXIII / LONDON & TORONTO / [*in red*] J. M. DENT & SONS LTD. / NEW YORK: E. P. DUTTON & CO.

Collation π⁸ A–U⁸ X¹⁰; pp. [i–viii] ix–xv [xvi] 1–337 [338] [2]; 220 × 148 mm.; printed on cream laid paper with oval watermark incorporating Hudson's name, a figure of a tree and two deer.

Pagination p. [i], blank; p. [ii], 'THIS EDITION IS LIMITED TO 750 COPIES / FOR SALE IN ENGLAND, 100 FOR SALE / IN THE UNITED STATES OF AMERICA, / AND 35 PRESENTATION COPIES'; p. [iii], half-title 'THE / COLLECTED WORKS / *of* / W. H. HUDSON / [*short rule*] / IN TWENTY-FOUR / VOLUMES / A SHEPHERD'S LIFE'; p. [iv], blank; p. [v], title; p. [vi], '*All rights reserved* / PRINTED IN GREAT BRITAIN'; p. [vii], author's note regarding a previously published article; p. [viii], blank; pp. ix–xv, contents; p. [xvi], blank; pp. 1–332, text; pp. 333–337, index; p. [338], 'PRINTED BY / THE TEMPLE PRESS AT LETCHWORTH / IN GREAT BRITAIN'; [2], blank.

Contents Same as first edition.

Binding Green cloth. Gold medallion profile portrait in centre of front cover enclosed within a single blind rule border; spine stamped in gilt 'W. H. / HUDSON /[*leafy branch*] / A / Shepherd's / Life / J·M·DENT / & SONS. LD.'. Blind rule border on back cover. Top edges trimmed and gilt, other edges untrimmed; cream laid endpapers. On front pastedown is a reproduction of pictorial bookplate with Hudson's name and dates. Maroon silk place marker.

Notes This is one of twenty-four volumes of Hudson's collected works. Eight hundred and eighty-five sets were published 1922–1923 for twenty-four guineas per set. The one hundred sets for sale in America were sold by E. P. Dutton for $192 per set. The collected works was reprinted in America by AMS Press in 1968 at $360.

OTHER EDITIONS

A29e 1932 Modern Classics edition. London, Methuen.
A29f 1936 Everyman's Library edition no. 926. London, Dent. Introduction by Ernest Rhys.

A29g 1961 [with *An Old Thorn*] Everyman's Library edition. London, Dent. Introduction by Ernest Rhys.
A29h n.d. [Selections from *A Shepherd's Life*]. Edited by Yoshio Nannichi. N.p., The Seibundo Press.
A29i n.d. Braille edition. London, Royal National Institute for the Blind, three volumes.
A29j n.d. Braille hand-copied edition for the National Library for the Blind (London), five volumes.

A30a

A THRUSH THAT NEVER LIVED

FIRST EDITION (1911)

[*coloured illustration of a thrush reproduced from a painting by H. Grönvold*] / A Thrush that Never Lived / [*text follows*]

Collation [A]²; pp. [1-4]; 222 × 143 mm.; printed on wove calendered paper.

Pagination p. [1], title and beginning of text; pp. [2-4], text; at bottom of p. [4], '[*rule*] / Copies of this Leaflet, 6d. per dozen, 3s. 6d. per 100, may be obtained from the / Royal Society for the Protection of Birds, 23 Queen Anne's Gate, London, S. W. / [*short rule*] / THE CAMPFIELD PRESS, ST. ALBANS'.

Illustrations Coloured half-tone etching of a thrush from the original drawing by H. Grönvold.

Binding Self-wrappers, folded.

Notes Published at 3d.

The 2nd printing, undated, gives the address of the Society as 82 Victoria Street, London.

This first appeared in book form in *Dead Man's Plack An Old Thorn & Miscellanea* (A47). See also C 109.

A31a

ADVENTURES AMONG BIRDS

FIRST EDITION 1913

ADVENTURES / AMONG BIRDS / *By* / W. H. HUDSON / WITH A PORTRAIT / LONDON / HUTCHINSON & CO. / PATERNOSTER ROW / 1913

Collation π⁴ 1–19⁸ 20⁶; pp. [i–vi] vii–viii [1] 2–311 [312] 313–316; 219 × 142 mm.; printed on wove paper.

Pagination p. [i], half-title '*ADVENTURES | AMONG BIRDS*'; p. [ii], list of twelve books by the same author (*South American Sketches* mistitled *South American Stretches*); frontispiece tipped in with protective tissue; p. [iii], title; p. [iv], blank; p. [v], notice of previous publications of parts of this book; p. [vi], eight-line quotation by Meredith; pp. vii–viii, contents; pp. [1] 2–311, text; p. [312], blank; pp. 313–316, index; at bottom of p. 316, '[*rule*] | *Printed by Hazell, Watson & Viney, Ld., London and Aylesbury.*'.

Contents The Book: An Apology – Cardinal: The Story of My First Caged Bird (first appeared in *Sunday Magazine* October 1895 (c69); reprinted in *Cornhill Magazine* July 1910 (c161)) – Wells-Next-The-Sea, Where Wild Geese Congregate (first appeared in *Saturday Review* 30 April 1910 (c155)) – Great Bird Gatherings – Birds in Authority – A Wood by the Sea (first appeared in *Saturday Review* 21 May 1910 (c157)) – Friendship in Animals – The Sacred Bird (first appeared in *Saturday Review* 3 October 1908 (c147)) – A Tired Traveller (*Turdus iliacus*) (first appeared in *Saturday Review* 2 January 1909 (c149); published separately in 1921 (A41)) – White Duck (first appeared in *English Review* May 1910 (c156)) – An Impression of Axe Edge (first appeared in *Saturday Review* 21 January 1911 (c162)) – Birds of the Peak (first appeared in *Saturday Review* 28 January 1911 (c163)) – The Ring-Ouzel as a Songster (first appeared in *Saturday Review* 4 February 1911 (c164)) – Bird Music – In a Green Country in Quest of Rare Songsters (first appeared in four parts in *Saturday Review* 29 June, 6 July, 20 July and 27 July 1912 (c170, c171, c172, c173)) – In a Hampshire Village – The Furze-Wren or Furze-Fairy – Back to the West Country – Avalon and a Blackbird – The Lake Village – The Marsh Warbler's Music – Goldfinches at Ryme Intrinsica (first appeared in *English Review* May 1909 (c150); reprinted in *English Review* July 1925) – The Immortal Nightingale (first appeared in *Cornhill Magazine* April 1910 (c154)) – The Clerk and the Last Ravens – The Temples of the Hills (first appeared in *Cornhill Magazine* March 1912 (c168)) – Autumn, 1912 – Wild Wings: A Farewell (first appeared in *English Review* January 1913 (c175); reprinted in *English Review* August 1925).

Binding Green cloth. Front cover stamped in gilt with single rule border; spine stamped in gilt '[*rule*] | ADVENTURES | AMONG | BIRDS | W. H. HUDSON | HUTCHINSON & C⁰ | [*rule*]'. All edges trimmed, top edges gilt; white wove endpapers.

Notes Published May 1913 at 10s. 6d. See note to A26a for information on publishing records.

The BM copy is stamped 24 May 1913.

The proof sheets with numerous changes in wording and punctuation by the author are in the Lilly Library. Included in the proofs are six different settings for the title page.

Reviews Times Literary Supplement 22 May 1913; *Globe* 24 May 1913; *Evening Standard* 29 May 1913; *Newcastle Weekly Chronicle* 31 May 1913; *Outlook* 31 May 1913; *Observer* 1 June 1913; *Truth* 1 June 1913; *Daily Express* 6 June 1913; *Queen* 7 June 1913; *Aberdeen Free Press* 10 June 1913; *Manchester Guardian* 10 June 1913; *Westminster Gazette* 14 June 1913; *Birmingham Daily Post* 20 June 1913; *Church Family Newspaper* 20 June 1913; *New Statesman* 21 June 1913; *Pall Mall Gazette* 26 June 1913; *Daily News and Leader* 27 June 1913; *Liverpool Daily Post* 2 July 1913; *Daily Telegraph* 4 July 1913; *Irish Times* 11 July 1913; *Field* 12 July 1913; *Nottingham Guardian* 26 August 1913; *Bookman* August 1913; *Humanitarian* August 1913; *Spectator* 27 September 1913.

A31b

FIRST AMERICAN ISSUE 1915

ADVENTURES / AMONG BIRDS / By / W. H. HUDSON / WITH A PORTRAIT / [*publisher's device*] / NEW YORK / MITCHELL KENNERLEY / 1915

Collation and pagination same as first edition except leaves measure 217 × 140 mm.

Contents Same as first edition.

Binding Greenish blue cloth. Front cover stamped in gilt 'ADVENTURES / AMONG BIRDS / BY / W ▼ H ▼ HUDSON'; spine stamped in gilt 'ADVENTURES / AMONG / BIRDS / W ▼ H ▼ / HUDSON / Mitchell / Kennerley'. All edges trimmed; white wove endpapers.

Notes Published at $2.50.

On 29 November 1916 Hudson wrote to Alfred A. Knopf: "About *Adventures Among Birds*, Hutchinson sold his remainder to America & not a copy is to be had here as I lately discovered when I wanted 10 copies for prize books."

These are the remaindered sheets, quantity unknown, with the title page reset for Mitchell Kennerley's imprint and '*Printed in Great Britain*' added to the verso of title page.

Reviews Dial 9 December 1915; *New York Times Book Review* 19 March 1916.

117 / BOOKS AND PAMPHLETS

A31c

FIRST AMERICAN EDITION 1920

[*within a double rule frame*] ADVENTURES / AMONG BIRDS / BY / W. H. HUDSON / AUTHOR OF "FAR AWAY AND LONG AGO," "THE PURPLE LAND," / "A SHEPHERD'S LIFE," "IDLE DAYS IN PATAGONIA," ETC. / [*illustration*] / NEW YORK / E. P. DUTTON & COMPANY / 681 FIFTH AVENUE / 1920

Collation [1–21]⁸; pp. [i–iv] v–x [xi–xii] [1] 2–319 [320] [4]. 210 × 140 mm., printed on wove paper.

Pagination p. [i], half-title 'ADVENTURES / AMONG BIRDS'; p. [ii], list of seven titles by the same author; p. [iii], title; p. [iv], 'PUBLISHED, 1920, BY / E. P. DUTTON & COMPANY / [*short rule*] / All Rights Reserved / [*illustration*] / The Illustrations in this Volume are / Reproductions of the Original Woodcuts / from "A History of British Birds" by / Bewick (1826). / Printed in the United States of America'; p. v, notice of previous publications of parts of this book; p. vi, eight-line quotation from Meredith; pp. vii–viii, contents; pp. ix–x, illustrations; p. [xi], fly-title 'ADVENTURES / AMONG BIRDS'; p. [xii], blank; pp. [1] 2–314, text; pp. 315–319, index; p. [320], blank; [4], blank.

Contents Same as first edition.

Illustrations Twenty-seven illustrations of birds by Bewick at chapter openings; small vignettes by the same artist throughout the book, generally at chapter closings.

Binding Blue cloth. Front cover stamped in gilt '[*within a single blind rule border*] ADVENTURES / AMONG BIRDS / [*rule*] / ▼▼ W. H. HUDSON ▼▼ / [*illustration of bird on a tree limb within a double rule circle*]'; spine stamped in gilt 'ADVENTURES / AMONG / BIRDS / [*rule*] / HUDSON / E. P. DUTTON / AND COMPANY'. Top edges trimmed, others untrimmed; white wove endpapers.

Notes Published April 1920 at $4.00. The LC copy is stamped 29 April 1920. See note to A22c for information on publishing records.

Reviews New York Times Book Review 6 June 1920; Auk October 1920.

A31d

COLLECTED EDITION 1923

[*in red*] ADVENTURES / [*in red*] AMONG BIRDS / BY / W. H. HUDSON /

[*publisher's device*] / MCMXXIII / LONDON & TORONTO / [*in red*] J. M. DENT & SONS LTD. / NEW YORK: E. P. DUTTON & CO.

Collation π⁸ A–T⁸ U⁶; pp. [*2*]; [*two unnumbered pages*]; [i–vi] vii–xii 1–313 [314] [*2*]; 220 × 148 mm.; printed on cream laid paper with oval watermark incorporating Hudson's name, a figure of a tree and two deer.

Pagination pp. [*2*], blank; [*first unnumbered page*], blank; [*second unnumbered page*], 'THIS EDITION IS LIMITED TO 750 COPIES / FOR SALE IN ENGLAND, 100 FOR SALE / IN THE UNITED STATES OF AMERICA, / AND 35 PRESENTATION COPIES'; p. [i], half-title 'THE / COLLECTED WORKS / *of* / W. H. HUDSON / [*short rule*] / IN TWENTY-FOUR / VOLUMES / ADVENTURES AMONG BIRDS'; p. [ii], blank; p. [iii], title; p. [iv], '*All rights reserved* / PRINTED IN GREAT BRITAIN'; p. [v], notice of previous publication of parts of this book; p. [vi], eight-line quotation by Meredith; pp. vii–xii, contents; pp. 1–308, text; pp. 309–313, index; p. [314], 'PRINTED BY / THE TEMPLE PRESS AT LETCHWORTH / IN GREAT BRITAIN'; [*2*], blank.

Contents Same as first edition.

Binding Green cloth. Gold medallion profile portrait in centre of front cover enclosed within a single blind rule border; spine stamped in gilt 'W. H. / HUDSON / [*leafy branch*] / Adventures / Among / Birds / J·M·DENT / & SONS. LD.'. Blind rule border on back cover. Top edges trimmed and gilt, other edges untrimmed; cream laid endpapers. On front pastedown is a reproduction of pictorial bookplate with Hudson's name and dates. Maroon silk place marker.

Notes This is one of twenty-four volumes of Hudson's collected works. Eight hundred and eighty-five sets were published 1922–1923 for twenty-four guineas per set. The one hundred sets for sale in America were sold by E. P. Dutton for $192 per set. The collected works was reprinted in America by AMS Press in 1968 at $360.

Following publication of the Collected Edition Dent issued a Popular Edition of thirteen of Hudson's books. *Adventures Among Birds* appeared in 1924 for 6s. It is gathered in 8's and the leaves measure 202 × 133 mm. Bound in blue cloth with a figure of a bird on a leafy branch blind stamped on the front cover. The author's name with a wavy thick-thin rule underneath, title with a printer's flower underneath, and the publisher's name are stamped in gilt on the spine. All edges trimmed and the top edges stained blue, white wove endpapers. Grey wove dust jacket printed in black.

The Uniform Edition of Hudson's works was published in 1951 by Dent and consists of seven titles: *The Purple Land; Nature in Downland; A Hind in Richmond Park; Green Mansions; Adventures Among Birds; Far Away and Long Ago. Idle Days in Patagonia* was added in 1954.

Adventures Among Birds is gathered in 16's and the leaves measure 192 × 124 mm. Bound in red cloth. The author's name, title, a figure of a feather and the publisher's name are stamped in gilt on the spine. All edges trimmed; white wove endpapers. Green and white wove dust jacket printed in black. There is an introduction by Richard Curle, reprinted from his *Caravansary and Conversation* (London: Cape, 1937).

OTHER EDITIONS

A31e 1927 King's Treasuries of Literature edition. London, Dent.
A31f n.d. Braille hand-copied edition for the National Library for the Blind (London), four volumes.

A32a

ON LIBERATING CAGED BIRDS

FIRST EDITION (1914)

ON LIBERATING CAGED BIRDS / By W. H. HUDSON / [*coloured illustration of a Crossbill enclosed within a single rule frame*] / THE CROSSBILL. / Reproduced from the original Painting by H. Grönvold. / Royal Society for the Protection of Birds / 23, Queen Anne's Gate, S.W.

Collation [A]²; pp. [1–4]; 217 × 139 mm.; printed on wove paper.

Pagination pp. [1–4], text; at bottom of p. [4], '[*rule*] / Leaflet No. 73. Published by the Royal Society for the Protection of Birds, / 23, Queen Anne's Gate, London, S.W., of whom copies may be obtained at / 1d. each; 9d. per doz.; 5s. per 100. / [*rule*] / J. Miles & Co. Ltd., Wardour St., W.'.

Illustrations Coloured half-tone etching of a crossbill from the original drawing by H. Grönvold.

Binding White calendered paper wrappers, stapled, printed in black.

Notes Published at 3d.

A later printing, undated, gives the address of the Society as 82 Victoria Street (London).

This previously appeared in *Bird Notes and News*, spring 1915 (C181), and first appeared in book form in *Dead Man's Plack An Old Thorn & Miscellanea* (A47).

A33a

TALES OF THE PAMPAS

FIRST EDITION 1916

[*within a double and a triple rule border*] TALES / OF THE PAMPAS / BY / W. H. HUDSON / [*publisher's device*] / NEW YORK / ALFRED ▼ A ▼ KNOPF / MCMXVI

Collation [1-16]⁸ 17⁴; pp. [i-viii] [1] 2-69 [70-72] 73-92 [93-94] 95-133 [134-136] 137-172 [173-174] 175-225 [226-228] 229-242 [243-244] 245-253 [254-256]; 193 × 131 mm., printed on wove paper.

Pagination p. [i], half-title 'TALES / OF THE PAMPAS'; p. [ii], list of three titles by the same author; p. [iii], title; p. [iv], 'COPYRIGHT, 1916, BY / ALFRED A. KNOPF / All Rights Reserved / PRINTED IN THE UNITED STATES OF AMERICA'; p. [v], contents; p. [vi], blank; p. [vii], section-title 'EL OMBÚ'; p. [viii], blank; pp. [1] 2-69, text; p. [70], blank; p. [71], section-title 'STORY OF A PIEBALD HORSE'; p. [72], blank; pp. 73-92, text; p. [93], section-title 'PELINO VIERA'S CONFESSION'; p. [94], blank; pp. 95-133, text; p. [134], blank; p. [135], section-title 'NIÑO DIABLO'; p. [136], blank; pp. 137-172, text; p. [173], section-title 'MARTA RIQUELME'; p. [174], blank; pp. 175-225, text; p. [226], blank; p. [227], section-title, 'TECLA AND THE LITTLE MEN'; p. [228], blank; pp. 229-242, text; p. [243], section-title 'APPENDIX TO EL OMBÚ'; p. [244], blank; pp. 245-253, text; p. [254], blank; pp. [255-256], ads for Borzoi books.

Contents El Ombú. – Story of a Piebald Horse. – Pelino Viera's Confession. – Niño Diablo. – Marta Riquelme. – Tecla and the Little Men. – Appendix to El Ombú.

Binding Green cloth. Front cover stamped in pink '[*rule*] / TALES OF THE PAMPAS / [*rule*]'; spine stamped in pink '[*rule*] / TALES / OF THE / PAMPAS / [*rule*] / BY – W. H. / HUDSON / ALFRED ▼A▼ / KNOPF'; publisher's device blind stamped in lower right corner of back cover. Top edges trimmed and stained green, fore edges rough trimmed, lower edges untrimmed; white wove endpapers. Yellow wove dust jacket printed in green.

Notes Published 13 October 1916 at $1.50. See note to A20c for information on publishing records.

This first appeared in 1902 under the title *El Ombú* (A21). It was reissued in 1909 as *South American Sketches* (A28). This edition, the first to appear in the United States, contains two new pieces not previously included, "Pelino Viera's

Confession" which first appeared in *Cornhill Magazine* October 1883 (C31), and the long poem "Tecla and the Little Men". This was collected with *The Purple Land* and *Green Mansions* in 1930 under the title *South American Romances* (A56), with the text as it originally appeared in *El Ombú*.

Hudson wrote to John Galsworthy 19 May 1916: "If you have not written already to [Alfred] Knopf I wish you would tell him that if he makes up his mind to my edition of *El Ombú* I can send him a copy of the book with corrections & some additional matter to be included. There is a story called 'Pelino Viera's Confessions' which appeared many years ago in the *Cornhill* (Edited then by James Payn who liked the story very well), & is an account of feathered witch women who have their meeting place at Trapalanda, the lost city of Patagonia; it is founded on a gaucho story or legend I heard on the pampas & is, I fancy as good a story as I have written: but Garrett refused to include it in *El Ombú* because, he said, there was a story about feathered women in *The Golden Ass*. I daresay there are other stories in the universe about feathered women, but I would like this one included in the book all the same. Also I think, another piece – a legend I heard from old gauchos. And the original title of *El Ombú* should be retained. I suppose the only reason Duckworth would be able to give for the title he used of 'South American Sketches' is that (some name of a place is somewhere in S. America) – also that the tales are not sketches. Anyhow he made a mess of it, & I don't quite see what he will have to do with an American edition if Knopf chooses to bring one out."

Reviews New Republic 9 December 1916; *Boston Transcript* 13 December 1916; *Springfield Republican* 24 December 1916; *New York Times Book Review* 31 December 1916; *American Review of Reviews* December 1916; *Nation* 18 January 1917.

A33b

FIRST ILLUSTRATED EDITION 1939

[*within a frame formed by a thick rule top and bottom, and thin rules and decorative border on either side*] W. H. HUDSON'S / Tales of / the Pampas / [*outside of frame*] NEW YORK *Alfred A. Knopf* MCMXXXIX / [*publisher's device*]

Collation [1–16]⁸ (Signatures [2], [7] and [12] are sewn within an extra 2-leaf fold which contains illustrations on the rectos; these are not included in the pagination); pp. [i–viii] [1–2] 3–68 [69–70] 71–90 [91–92] 93–130 [131–132] 133–167 [168–170] 171–217 [218–220] 221–234 [235–236] 237–245 [246] [2]; 223 × 140 mm., printed on laid paper.

Pagination p. [i], blank; p. [ii], list of three other Borzoi books by the same author; p. [iii], half-title, '*Tales of the Pampas*'; p. [iv], '[*within a decorative rule frame*] ILLUSTRATED BY / ROGER DUVOISIN'; p. [v], title; p. [vi], '[*type ornament*] PUBLISHED OCTOBER 1916; / REPRINTED FOUR TIMES; ILLUSTRATED EDITION / SEPTEMBER, 1939. COPYRIGHT 1916 BY ALFRED A. / KNOPF, INC. ALL RIGHTS RESERVED. NO PART OF / THIS BOOK MAY BE REPRODUCED IN ANY FORM / WITHOUT PERMISSION IN WRITING FROM THE PUB- / LISHER, EXCEPT BY A REVIEWER WHO MAY QUOTE / BRIEF PASSAGES OR REPRODUCE NOT MORE THAN / THREE ILLUSTRATIONS IN A REVIEW TO BE PRINTED / IN A MAGAZINE OR NEWSPAPER. MANUFACTURED IN / THE UNITED STATES OF AMERICA'; p. [vii], contents; p. [viii], blank; p. [1], section-title for "*El Ombú*"; p. [2], blank; pp. 3–68, text; p. [69], section-title for "*Story of a Piebald Horse*"; p. [70], blank; pp. 71–90, text; p. [91], section-title for "*Pelino Viera's Confession*"; p. [92], blank; p. 93–130, text; p. [131], section-title for "*Niño Diablo*"; p. [132], blank; pp. 133–167, text; p. [168], blank; p. [169], section-title for "*Marta Riquelme*"; p. [170], blank; pp. 171–217, text; p. [218], blank; p. [219], section-title for "*Tecla and the Little Men*"; p. [220], blank; pp. 221–234, text; p. [235], section-title for *Appendix to El Ombú*; p. [236], blank; pp. 237–245, text; p. [246], note on the type face in which this book is set; [2], blank.

Contents Same as first edition.

Illustrations Six full-page gravure illustrations on regular text stock, sewn around gatherings [2], [7] and [12] by Roger A. Duvoisin, the Swiss–American illustrator and cartoonist.

Binding Greenish-grey cloth. Publisher's device enclosed within a circular frame formed by interlacing leafy branches stamped in blue in centre of front cover; spine stamped in blue '[*decorative piece*] / [*thick-thin double rule*] / W. H. Hudson / [*rule*] / [*fancy*] Tales / [*fancy*] of the / [*fancy*] Pampas / [*thick-thin double rule*] / [*decorative piece*] / ALFRED·A·KNOPF'; publisher's device stamped in blue in lower right corner of back cover. All edges trimmed, top edges stained yellow; white laid endpapers. Coloured illustrated dust jacket printed in red, black, brown and white and lettered in black, tan and white.

Notes 5,200 copies published 5 September 1939 at $2.00.

For publication history see Notes for A33a.

OTHER EDITIONS

A33c 1926 Borzoi pocket book edition. New York, Knopf.
A33d n.d. Armed services edition no. 0-5. New York, Editions for the Armed Services.

A34a

FAR AWAY AND LONG AGO

FIRST EDITION 1918

[*within a double rule border*] [*printed in green*] FAR AWAY / [*printed in green*] AND LONG AGO / A HISTORY / OF MY EARLY LIFE / BY / W. H. HUDSON / [*printed in green: publisher's device*] / 1918 / LONDON & TORONTO / [*printed in green*] J. M. DENT AND SONS, LTD / NEW YORK E. P. DUTTON & CO

Collation [A]⁶ B–X⁸ Y⁶; pp. [i–iv] v–xii [1] 2–332; 210 × 141 mm.; printed on wove paper. Sheets bulk 33 mm.

Pagination p. [i], half-title 'FAR AWAY / AND LONG AGO'; p. [ii], blank; frontispiece; p. [iii], title; p. [iv], blank; pp. v–xii, contents; pp. [1] 2–332, text; at bottom of p. 332, '[*rule*] / PRINTED IN GREAT BRITAIN BY RICHARD CLAY & SONS, LIMITED, / BRUNSWICK ST., STAMFORD ST., S.E. I, AND BUNGAY, SUFFOLK.'

Illustrations Frontispiece photograph of Hudson.

Binding Dark green cloth. Front cover printed in black with a border of one thick and two thin rules enclosing the publisher's device; spine stamped in gilt '[*thick-thin rule printed in black*] / [*within a frame formed by two horizontal rules at top and single vertical rules on either side, joining to form a circle at the bottom*] FAR AWAY / AND / LONG AGO / [*orn: knot*] / W. H. HUDSON / [*orn: knot*] / [*below the frame*] J·M·DENT / &·SONS· LD / [*thick-thin rule printed in black*]'. All edges trimmed, top edges stained dark green; white wove endpapers. Grey wove dust jacket printed in black.

Variant Coarse green cloth; sheets bulk 26 mm.

Notes 3,160 copies published 21 September 1918 at 15s.

Chapter 1 "Earliest Memories" appeared in *English Review* January 1916 (C190). Chapter 13 "A Patriarch of the Pampas" appeared in *Eye Witness* 7 September 1911 (C166.).

A portion of chapter 22 "Boyhood's End" was recorded in 1952 by Peter Pears and Noel Mewton-Wood and released in 1953 by Argo. It was reissued in 1965 by Michael Tippett (No DA34). The text was printed on a leaflet and inserted with the 1965 recording.

Hudson sent a copy of the manuscript of *Far Away and Long Ago* for Edward Garnett's reading. On 14 December 1917 Hudson responded to Garnett's criticism and expressed his own opinion of the book: "Of course those middle chapters would interest you more in the book, but the real interest of the book is the feeling for nature and wild life – and *that* appeals only to those who have it in them, in whom it is a passion and more to them than interest in human character and affairs. If the book is worth anything, it is that in it and nothing else – at all events, it is certainly not in the human portrait."

Hudson's letter to Edward Garnett, 22 October 1918, shows his lack of interest in critics' opinions of his work. "It is always grateful to me to hear of a friend or individual who has found some pleasure in a book of mine, but nothing do I care for the stuff in the papers and I daresay when you suppose I'm 'overwhelmed' it was 'writ sarkastic.' Good God, no! all those twenty or thirty columns of it I've seen so far had not one thought in it all to give me any pleasure."

Reviews Times Literary Supplement 26 September 1918; *Daily News & Leader* 19 October 1918; *Spectator* 9 November 1918; *Athenaeum* December 1918; *Bookman* December 1918; *Geographical Journal* February 1919; *Villager* 13 March 1920.

Variant copy Dobie.

A34b

FIRST AMERICAN EDITION 1918

[*within a double rule frame*] FAR AWAY / AND LONG AGO / A HISTORY / OF MY EARLY LIFE / BY / W. H. HUDSON / AUTHOR OF "IDLE DAYS IN PATAGONIA," "THE PURPLE LAND," / "A CRYSTAL AGE," "ADVENTURES AMONG BIRDS," ETC. / [*publisher's device of J. M. Dent*] / NEW YORK / E. P. DUTTON & COMPANY / 681 FIFTH AVENUE / 1918

Collation [1]^{10} (16 + χ1) [2–20]^8 [21]^{10}; pp. [i–iv] v–xii [xiii–xiv] [1] 2–332; 202 × 135 mm. printed on wove paper.

Pagination p. [i], half-title, 'FAR AWAY AND LONG AGO'; p. [ii], blank; frontispiece; p. [iii], title; p. [iv], 'COPYRIGHT, 1918, / BY E. P. DUTTON & COMPANY / [*short rule*] / All Rights Reserved / Printed in the United States of America'; pp. v–xii, contents; p. [xiii], fly-title, 'FAR AWAY AND LONG AGO'; p. [xiv], blank; pp. [1] 2–332, text.

Illustrations Frontispiece photograph of Hudson.

Binding Blue cloth. Front cover stamped in gilt '[*within a single blind rule border*] FAR AWAY / AND LONG AGO / *A HISTORY OF MY EARLY LIFE* / [*rule*] / W. H.

HUDSON'; spine stamped in gilt 'FAR AWAY / AND / LONG AGO / [short rule] / HUDSON / E. P. DUTTON / & CO.' All edges trimmed; white wove endpapers.

Notes Published 23 October 1918 at $2.50. Twenty-four printings to February 1936. See note to A22c for information on publishing records.

Reviews New York Times Book Review 3 November 1918; *Boston Transcript* 23 November 1918; *Outlook* 4 December 1918; *Dial* 14 December 1918; *Publisher's Weekly* 28 December 1918; *Bookman* December 1918; *ALA Booklist* January 1919; *Current Opinion* January 1919; *Nation* 25 January 1919; *New York Times Book Review* 2 March 1919; *Nature* 13 March 1919.

A34c

COLLECTED EDITION 1923

[in red] FAR AWAY / [in red] AND LONG AGO / A HISTORY OF MY EARLY LIFE / BY / W. H. HUDSON / [publisher's device] / WITH A FOREWORD BY / JOHN GALSWORTHY / MCMXXIII / LONDON & TORONTO / [in red] J. M. DENT & SONS LTD. / NEW YORK: E. P. DUTTON & CO.

Collation π^{10} A–X^8 Y^{10}; pp. [i–vi] vii–xi [xii] xiii–xx 1–353 [354] [2]; 220 × 148 mm.; printed on cream laid paper with oval watermark incorporating Hudson's name, a figure of a tree and two deer.

Pagination p. [i], blank; p. [ii], 'THIS EDITION IS LIMITED TO 750 COPIES / FOR SALE IN ENGLAND, 100 FOR SALE / IN THE UNITED STATES OF AMERICA, / AND 35 PRESENTATION COPIES'; p. [iii], half-title 'THE / COLLECTED WORKS / of / W. H. HUDSON / [short rule] / IN TWENTY-FOUR / VOLUMES / FAR AWAY AND LONG AGO'; p. [iv], blank; frontispiece photograph of Hudson; p. [v], title; p. [vi], '*All rights reserved* / PRINTED IN GREAT BRITAIN'; pp. vii–xi, foreword by John Galsworthy; p. [xii], blank; pp. xiii–xx, contents; pp. 1–348, text; pp. 349–353, index; p. [354], 'PRINTED BY / THE TEMPLE PRESS AT LETCHWORTH / IN GREAT BRITAIN'; [2], blank.

Illustrations Frontispiece photograph of Hudson.

Binding Green cloth. Gold medallion profile portrait in centre of front cover enclosed within a single blind rule border; spine stamped in gilt 'W. H. HUDSON / [leafy branch] / Far Away / and / Long Ago / J·M·DENT / & SONS. LD.'. Blind rule border on back cover. Top edges trimmed and gilt, other edges untrimmed; cream laid endpapers. On front pastedown is a reproduction of pictorial bookplate with Hudson's name and dates. Maroon silk place marker.

Notes This is one of twenty-four volumes of Hudson's collected works. Eight hundred and eighty-five sets were published 1922–1923 for twenty-four guineas per set. The one hundred sets for sale in America were sold by E. P. Dutton for $192 per set. The collected works was reprinted in America by AMS Press in 1968 at $360.

John Galsworthy's foreword is reprinted, with slight revision, from the first American edition of *Green Mansions* (A23d).

Following publication of the Collected Edition Dent issued a Popular Edition of thirteen of Hudson's books. *Far Away and Long Ago* appeared in 1923 for 6s. It is gathered in 8's and the leaves measure 202 × 133 mm. Bound in blue cloth with a figure of a bird on a leafy branch blind stamped on the front cover. The author's name with a wavy thick-thin rule underneath, title with a printer's flower underneath, and the publisher's name are stamped in gilt on the spine. All edges trimmed and the top edges stained blue; white wove endpapers. Grey wove dust jacket printed in black. Contains a frontispiece photograph of Hudson and a foreword by John Galsworthy reprinted with slight changes from the first American edition of *Green Mansions* (A23e).

The Uniform Edition of Hudson's works was published in 1951 by Dent and consists of seven titles: *The Purple Land; Nature in Downland; A Hind in Richmond Park; Green Mansions; Adventures Among Birds; Far Away and Long Ago. Idle Days in Patagonia* was added in 1954.

Far Away and Long Ago is gathered in 16's and the leaves measure 192 × 124 mm. Bound in red cloth. The author's name, title, a figure of a feather and the publisher's name are stamped in gilt on the spine. All edges trimmed; white wove endpapers. Green and white wove dust jacket printed in black. Contains an introduction by R. B. Cunninghame Graham dated 1931 and a frontispiece photograph of Hudson.

A34d

FIRST ILLUSTRATED, REVISED EDITION, REGULAR COPIES (1931)

FAR AWAY / AND LONG AGO / A HISTORY OF MY EARLY LIFE / BY / W. H. HUDSON / WITH WOOD-ENGRAVINGS / BY ERIC FITCH DAGLISH / [*illustration of an owl*] / AND AN INTRODUCTION BY / R. B. CUNNINGHAME GRAHAM / LONDON & TORONTO / J. M. DENT & SONS LTD. / NEW YORK: E. P. DUTTON & CO. INC.

Collation [A]^8 B–2A^8; pp. [i–vi] vii–xiii [xiv] xv–xxiii [xxiv] [1] 2–337 [338]; 218 × 145 mm.; printed on wove paper.

Pagination p. [i], half-title 'FAR AWAY / AND LONG AGO'; pp. [ii–iii], blank; p. [iv], frontispiece; p. [v], title; p. [vi], 'ALL RIGHTS RESERVED / PRINTED IN GREAT BRITAIN AT / THE TEMPLE PRESS, LETCHWORTH, HERTS / FIRST PUBLISHED IN 1918 / REVISED EDITION, ILLUSTRATED WITH WOOD-ENGRAVINGS, 1931'; pp. vii–xiii, introduction dated 1931; p. [xiv], illustration; pp. xv–xxii, contents; p. xxiii, list of full-page illustrations; p. [xxiv], illustration; pp. [1] 2–332, text; pp. 333–337, index; p. [338] '[*printed across a drawing of a small flower*] MADE AT THE / TEMPLE PRESS / LETCHWORTH / IN / GREAT BRITAIN'.

Illustrations Twelve full-page wood engravings by Eric Fitch Daglish. Smaller engravings throughout the text.

Binding Blue cloth. Figure of an owl stamped in gilt in centre of front cover, enclosed within a single rule blind stamped border; spine stamped in gilt 'FAR AWAY / AND / LONG AGO / [*figure of a leaf*] / W. H. HUDSON / J. M. DENT / & SONS L$^\text{D}$'. All edges trimmed, top edges stained blue; white wove endpapers. Blue wove pictorial dust jacket printed in black and white.

Notes 3,150 copies published 15 October 1931 at 10s. 6d. An undetermined number of copies were sold in the United States at $3.75.

A34e

FIRST ILLUSTRATED, REVISED EDITION, LIMITED COPIES (1931)

Title same as regular copies.

Collation A^8 ($\pm$ A2) B^8 C^8 ($\pm$ C2) D–E^8 F^8 ($\pm$ F2, F8) G^8 ($\pm$ G7) H–I^8 ($\pm$ I4) K^8 L^8 ($\pm$ L2) M^8 N^8 ($\pm$ N3) O^8 ($\pm$ O4) P^8 Q^8 ($\pm$ Q6) R–T^8 U^8 ($\pm$ U2) X^8 ($\pm$ X7) Y–2A^8; pagination same as regular copies; 253 $\times$ 193 mm.; printed on wove paper. Watermarks: 'UNBLEACHED ARNOLD' and 'MADE IN ENGLAND'.

Pagination Same as regular copies except p. [ii] reads '*This large-paper edition is limited to* / *one hundred and ten sets, of which fifty* / *are for sale in Great Britain and fifty* / *in the United States of America.* / *This is No.* [*autograph number in black ink*]'.

Illustrations Same as regular copies except the full page illustrations are tipped in as cancellans and there is an extra wood engraving, 150 $\times$ 105 mm. signed by the artist and tipped in.

Binding Vellum. Small rectangular inset in centre of front cover; gilt owl on a green background with a gilt border; spine stamped in gilt 'FAR AWAY / AND /

LONG AGO / [branch with three leaves] / W. H. HUDSON / J. M. DENT / & SONS L__D__. Top edges gilt, other edges untrimmed; white wove endpapers. Red cloth marker.

Notes 110 copies published 15 October 1931 at 42s. in England and $25.00 in the United States.

This is the first appearance of R. B. Cunninghame Graham's introduction.

A34f

LIMITED EDITIONS CLUB EDITION 1943

FAR AWAY / AND LONG AGO / A HISTORY OF MY EARLY LIFE / *by W. H. Hudson* / WITH AN INTRODUCTION / *by R. B. Cunninghame Graham* / AND ILLUSTRATIONS / *by Raúl Rosarivo* / [*illustration of thistles*] / PRINTED FOR THE MEMBERS OF THE LIMITED EDITIONS CLUB / BY GUILLERMO KRAFT LTDA. / BUENOS AIRES / 1943

Collation [1–2]⁴ [3–20]⁸ [21–23]⁴; pp. [i–ix] x–xiv [xv–xvi] [1] 2–306 [307–310] [2]; 268 × 202 mm.; printed on laid paper.

Pagination pp. [i–ii], blank; p. [iii], half-title 'FAR AWAY AND LONG AGO'; p. [iv], blank; frontispiece; p. [v], title; p. [vi], 'PRINTED IN ARGENTINA'; p. [vii], contents; at bottom of p. [vii] 'WITH 32 FULL PAGE ILLUSTRATIONS BY / RAUL ROSARIVO'; p. [viii], blank; pp. [ix] x–xiv, introduction by R. B. Cunninghame Graham; p. [xv], fly-title 'FAR AWAY AND LONG AGO'; p. [xvi], blank; pp. [1] 2–306 [307], text; p. [308], blank; p. [309], '*This edition of* / FAR AWAY AND LONG AGO / *consists of fifteen hundred copies* / *printed by* / *Guillermo Kraft Limitada S. A.* / *Buenos Aires* / *for the members of* / *The Limited Editions Club* / [*publisher's device*] / *The edition was designed by* / *Alberto Kraft* / *and the illustrations were drawn by* / *Raúl Rosarivo* / THIS COPY IS NUMBER / [*autograph number in aqua-blue ink*] / SIGNED BY / *Alberto Kraft. RW Rosarivo* [*autograph signatures in aqua-blue ink*]'; p. [310], blank; [2], blank.

Illustrations Thirty-two full-page half-tone lithographic etchings from the original drawings by Raúl Rosarivo, tipped in with protective tissues.

Binding The top third of the binding is smooth white leather, printed diagonally in brown ink 'Far / away and / long ago / [*diagonal line*]'; a fancy letter 'H' printed in brown on spine; the lower two-thirds of the cover are black and white or brown and white cowhide, hair side out. All edges and line between top and bottom parts of the covers are laced with a strip of cowhide. Brown suede endpapers, with an extra white laid free endpaper front and back. Top edges trimmed and stained brown; others untrimmed. Tan laid dust jacket printed in brown; in a brown box with tan paper label, printed in brown.

Notes The correspondence between George Macy and Alberto Kraft in the George Macy Archives, Humanities Research Center, shows that 1,520 copies were printed. Fifteen hundred were numbered consecutively; twenty copies were not numbered. All copies were signed on the colophon page by Alberto Kraft and Raúl Rosarivo. The exact date of publication is not recorded, but the books were received in George Macy's office on 12 December 1943. Because the books had been delayed three months in shipment from Argentina it is assumed they were distributed immediately to members of the Limited Editions Club.

There is a question about additional copies, quantity unknown, that may have been issued in Argentina. Alberto Kraft wrote to George Macy on 8 March 1944: "Now there is a matter on which I have to consult you. It will be remembered that when the price of this edition was arranged, I told you it would not be possible to make any profit, but that I expected to break even more or less. This, unfortunately, has not been the case, as the job shows a dead loss of slightly over $10,000 Argentine currency, which is attributable to a great extent to the increased cost of materials and so forth. However, there might be a suitable solution whereby part of this loss could be recovered. We have a limited number of copies that might be sold immediately to bibliophiles and members of the American and British colonies who are anxious to acquire the edition, and have been informed that we are not at liberty to sell without a written authorization from you.

It would be a great help if you could allow us to dispose of these volumes, and if you agree, I will be glad to have your suggestions as to the declaration that should appear on the colophon page."

Macy's reply to this enquiry is not in the files, and no copy of a special Argentine issue of the book has been seen.

Reviews New York Times Book Review 5 March 1944.

OTHER EDITIONS

A34g 1925 School edition. New York, Dutton.
A34h (1933– Popular edition. Toronto, McClelland and Stewart.
      1937)
A34i 1936 Braille edition. Mt. Healthy, Ohio. Clovernook Printing House for the Blind. Three volumes.
A34j 1939 Everyman's Library edition no. 956. London, Dent.

A34k 1940 Literature of Yesterday and Today edition. London, Dent.
A34l n.d. Tokyo, Nan-un-do. Edited by I. Nobusada.
A34m n.d. Braille edition. London, Royal National Institute for the Blind. Three volumes.
A34n n.d. Braille hand-copied edition for the National Library for the Blind (London). Five volumes.

A35a

ROFF AND A LINNET: CHAIN AND CAGE

FIRST EDITION 1918

ROFF AND A LINNET: / Chain and Cage. / By / W. H. HUDSON. / HUMANITARIAN LEAGUE, / 53 CHANCERY LANE, / LONDON. / 1918.

Collation [A]⁴; pp. 1–7 [8]; 186 × 124 mm.; printed on wove paper; watermark: 'CHARIOT / [*figure of a horse and chariot*] / FINE WOVE'.

Pagination p. 1, 'ROFF AND A LINNET. / CHAIN AND CAGE. / [*short rule*] / BY W. H. HUDSON. / [*text begins*]'; pp. 2–7 [8], text; at bottom of p. [8] 'HUMANITARIAN LEAGUE, / 53, CHANCERY LANE, LONDON, W. C. / [*rule*] / Printed by BONNER & Co., 38, Cursitor Street, London, E. C. 4.'.

Binding Grey stiff wrappers, stapled. Title printed in black on front wrapper as above. The aims and objects of the Humanitarian League are printed on the inside of the back wrapper. All edges trimmed.

Notes The BM copy is stamped 26 September 1918.

This is reprinted from *New Statesman*, 29 May 1915 (C184).

This first appeared in book form in *Dead Man's Plack An Old Thorn & Miscellanea* (A47).

Copies BM; Bodleian; RSPB.

A36a

BIRDS IN TOWN & VILLAGE

FIRST EDITION 1919

[*in green*] BIRDS IN TOWN / [*in green*] & VILLAGE / BY / W. H. HUDSON / [*illustration of a pheasant*] / WITH PICTURES IN COLOUR / BY / E. J.

DETMOLD / 1919 / LONDON & TORONTO / [*in green*] J. M. DENT & SONS LTD. / NEW YORK: E. P. DUTTON & CO.

Collation π⁴ *² A–R⁸; pp. [i–iv] v–vii [viii] ix–[x] [1–2] 3–274; 196 × 140 mm.; printed on wove paper.

Pagination p. [i], half-title 'BIRDS IN TOWN AND VILLAGE'; p. [ii], '*All rights reserved*'; frontispiece; p. [iii], title; p. [iv], blank; pp. v–vi, author's preface dated September 1919; p. vii, contents; p. [viii], blank; p. ix, coloured illustrations; p. [x], blank; p. [1], fly-title 'BIRDS IN A VILLAGE'; p. [2], blank; pp. 3–274, text; at bottom of p. 274 'THE / TEMPLE PRESS [*picture of a little flower*] LETCHWORTH / ENGLAND'.

Contents Birds in a Village (a revision and expansion of *Birds in a Village* (see A8)) – Exotic Birds for Britain (first appeared in *Murray's Magazine* March 1889 (C50)) – Moor-hens in Hyde Park – The Eagle and the Canary (first appeared in *Gentleman's Magazine* February 1888 (C48)) – Chanticleer (first appeared in *Longman's Magazine* December 1887 (C46)) – In an Old Garden – Birds in a Cornish Village.

Illustrations Eight coloured half-tone etchings on calendered paper by E. J. Detmold. Detmold is best known for his etchings of birds and animals of remarkable technical ability. He is the twin brother of the animal painter and etcher, Charles Maurice.

Binding Light green cloth. Front cover stamped in gilt '[*within a single blind rule border*] [*scene of country village within single and double rule frame*] / BIRDS·IN·TOWN / AND / VILLAGE / [*publisher's device*]'; spine stamped in gilt '[*interlacing strapwork*] / BIRDS / IN TOWN / & / VILLAGE / [*three small squares*] / W. H. HUDSON / WITH / PICTURES / BY / E. J. DETMOLD / [*interlacing strapwork*] / J·M·DENT / &·SONS·Lᴅ'. All edges trimmed, top edges stained green; white wove endpapers. Tan wove dust jacket printed in black and red.

Variant Light green cloth. Blind rule border around top, bottom and outside edges only; spine stamped in gilt as above except the following is stamped in blind 'J. M. DENT / & SONS LT (overstamped to read LD)'. Top edges stained brown.

Notes 2,550 copies published 21 October 1919 at 10s.6d.

This work is more than a reprint of *Birds in a Village*, 1893 (A8). "The first portion, 'Birds in a Village,' has been mostly rewritten with some fresh matter added, mainly later observations and incidents introduced in illustration of the various subjects discussed. For the concluding portion of the old book ["By

Way of Appendix"], which has been discarded, I have substituted entirely new matter – the part entitled 'Birds in a Cornish Village'." [preface].

Hudson wrote to Morley Roberts 4 October 1919 that he was sending him a copy of his most recent book, *Birds in Town & Village*, "an old one in a new dress". There are some fresh things in it. "The flower chapter has a little added to it too as a concession to several persons who attacked my views about expression in flowers and its cause – you among others."

Roberts wrote complimenting Hudson on the illustrations in *Birds in Town & Village*, and Hudson responded on 28 September 1919: "I sent your letter about 'Birds in Town etc.' to Dent on account of what you said about the pictures. He was delighted and says he sent the letter on to Detmold to encourage him. He thinks he has found a genius in young Detmold."

Reviews Times Literary Supplement 23 October 1919; *Athenaeum* 31 October 1919; *Observer* 2 November 1919; *Spectator* 6 December 1919; *Bookman* December 1919; *Saturday Review* 31 January 1920; *Nature* 22 July 1920.

Variant copy Texas.

A36b

FIRST AMERICAN EDITION 1920)

BIRDS IN TOWN / & VILLAGE / BY / W. H. HUDSON, / F.Z.S. / AUTHOR OF "THE PURPLE LAND," "IDLE DAYS IN / PATAGONIA," "FAR AWAY AND LONG AGO," ETC. / [*illustration of a pheasant*] / WITH PICTURES IN COLOUR / BY / E. J. DETMOLD / NEW YORK / E. P. DUTTON & COMPANY / 681 FIFTH AVENUE

Collation [1–21]⁸; pp. [i–v] vi–vii [viii] ix [x–xii] [1] 2–323 [324]; 208 × 140 mm.; printed on wove paper.

Pagination p. [i], half-title, 'BIRDS IN TOWN / & VILLAGE'; p. [ii], list of seven titles by the same author; frontispiece; p. [iii], title; p. [iv], 'COPYRIGHT, 1920 / By E. P. DUTTON & COMPANY / [*short rule*] / All Rights Reserved / Printed in the United States of America'; pp. [v]–vi, author's preface dated September, 1919; p. vii, contents; p. [viii], blank; p. ix, list of coloured illustrations; p. [x], blank; p. [xi], fly-title 'BIRDS IN TOWN / & VILLAGE'; p. [xii], blank; pp. [1] 2–323, text; p. [324], blank.

Contents Same as first edition.

Illustrations Eight coloured half-tone etchings by E. J. Detmold. Line etchings at chapter headings and closings.

Binding Blue cloth. Front cover stamped in gilt '[*within a single blind rule border*] BIRDS IN / TOWN & VILLAGE / [*rule*] / W. H. HUDSON / [*illustration of a pheasant*]'; spine stamped in gilt 'BIRDS / IN / TOWN & / VILLAGE / [*rule*] / ▼ HUDSON ▼ / E. P. DUTTON / AND COMPANY'. Top edges trimmed, others untrimmed; white wove endpapers.

Variants 1. Collation [1]⁸ (1₃ + χ²) [2–21]⁸. Paginated as above. 2. Pages vii and [x] were interchanged during printing, resulting in the following arrangement: [x], blank; [viii], blank; ix, list of coloured illustrations; vii, contents. 3. Green cloth. Front cover stamped in gilt as copy above except border is also in gilt. Foot of spine reads ' & CO.'.

Notes Published 26 January 1920 at $4.00. See note to A22c for information on publishing records.

Reviews Saturday Review 31 January 1920; *New York Times Book Review* 7 March 1920; *Outlook* 10 March 1920; *Springfield Republican* 19 March 1920; *ALA Booklist* April 1920; *New York Weekly Review* 14 July 1920; *Boston Transcript* 28 July 1920; *Auk* October 1920.

Variant copy 1 Texas. *Variant copy 2* LC. *Variant copy 3* ISU.

A36c

COLLECTED EDITION   1923

[*in red*] BIRDS IN TOWN / [*in red*] & VILLAGE / BY / W. H. HUDSON / [*publisher's device*] / MCMXXIII / LONDON & TORONTO / [*in red*] J. M. DENT & SONS LTD. / NEW YORK: E. P. DUTTON & CO.

Collation π⁶ A–P⁸ Q⁶; pp. [2] [i–vi] vii [viii] ix [x] [1–2] 3–243 [244] 245–249 [250] [2]; 220 × 148 mm.; printed on cream laid paper with oval watermark incorporating Hudson's name, a figure of a tree and two deer.

Pagination [2], blank; p. [i], blank; p. [ii], 'THIS EDITION IS LIMITED TO 750 COPIES / FOR SALE IN ENGLAND, 100 FOR SALE / IN THE UNITED STATES OF AMERICA, / AND 35 PRESENTATION COPIES'; p. [iii], half-title 'THE / COLLECTED WORKS / OF / W. H. HUDSON / [*short rule*] / IN TWENTY-FOUR / VOLUMES / BIRDS IN TOWN AND VILLAGE'; p. [iv], blank; p. [v], title; p. [vi], '*All rights reserved* / PRINTED IN GREAT BRITAIN'; p. vii, preface dated September 1919; p. [viii], blank; p. ix, contents; p. [x], blank; p. [1], section-title 'BIRDS IN A VILLAGE'; p. [2], blank; pp. 3–243, text; p. [244], blank; pp. 245–249, index; p. [250], 'PRINTED BY / THE TEMPLE PRESS AT LETCHWORTH / IN GREAT BRITAIN'; [2], blank.

Contents Same as first edition.

Binding Green cloth. Gold medallion profile portrait in centre of front cover enclosed within a single blind rule border; spine stamped in gilt 'W. H. / HUDSON / [*leafy branch*] / Birds / In Town / and / Village / J·M·DENT / & SONS. LD.'. Blind rule border on back cover. Top edges trimmed and gilt, other edges untrimmed; cream laid endpapers. On front pastedown is a reproduction of pictorial bookplate with Hudson's name and dates. Maroon silk place marker.

Notes This is one of twenty-four volumes of Hudson's collected works. Eight hundred and eighty-five sets were published 1922–1923 for twenty-four guineas per set. The one hundred sets for sale in America were sold by E. P. Dutton for $192 per set. The collected works was reprinted in America by AMS Press in 1968 at $360.

Following publication of the Collected Edition Dent issued a Popular Edition of thirteen of Hudson's books. *Birds in Town & Village* appeared in 1924 for 6s. It is gathered in 8's and the leaves measure 202 × 133 mm. Bound in blue cloth with a figure of a bird on a leafy branch blind stamped on the front cover. The author's name with a wavy thick-thin rule underneath, title, with a printer's flower underneath, and the publisher's name are stamped in gilt on the spine. All edges trimmed and the top edges stained blue; white wove endpapers. Grey wove dust jacket printed in black.

A37a

THE BOOK OF A NATURALIST

FIRST EDITION (1919)

THE BOOK OF / A NATURALIST / BY / W. H. HUDSON / Author of / 'The Naturalist in La Plata' / [*picture of a moth*] / HODDER AND STOUGHTON / LONDON NEW YORK TORONTO

Collation [A]⁴ B–Z⁸ 2A⁴; pp. [i–iv] v–viii 1–360; 223 × 146 mm.; printed on wove paper.

Pagination p. [i], half-title 'THE BOOK OF A NATURALIST'; p. [ii], blank; p. [iii], title; p. [iv], blank; pp. v–vi, preface by Hudson; pp. vii–viii, contents; pp. 1–356, text; pp. 357–360, index; at bottom of p. 360 '*Printed in Great Britain by* R. & R. CLARK, LIMITED, *Edinburgh.*'.

Contents Life in a Pine Wood (first appeared in *The National and English Review*

June 1916 (C196)) – Hints to Adder-Seekers (a four-line quote from this text first appeared in *The Book of the Open Air*, edited by Edward Thomas, 1907 (B2) – Bats (first appeared in *Speaker* 24 December 1904 (C121)) – Beauty of the Fox – A Sentimentalist on Foxes (first appeared in *Country Life* 17 April 1915 (C182)) – The Discontented Squirrel (first appeared in *Chambers's Journal of Popular Literature, Science and Art* 11 March 1916 (C193)) – My Neighbour's Bird Stories (first appeared in *New Statesman* 4 October 1913 (C176)) – The Toad as Traveller (first appeared in *Country Life* 13 November 1915 (C189)) – The Heron: A Feathered Notable – The Heron as a Table-Bird – The Mole Question (first appeared in *Country Life* 6 November 1915 (C188)) – Cristiano: A Horse – Mary's Little Lamb (see A54 for separate publication) – The Serpent's Tongue (first appeared in *Fortnightly Review* August 1893 (C61)) – The Serpent's Strangeness (first appeared in *Fortnightly Review* April 1894 (C64)) – The Bruised Serpent (first appeared in *Macmillan's Magazine* April 1893 (C60)) – The Serpent in Literature (first appeared in the *Monthly Review* August 1905 (C128)) – Wasps (first appeared in *Speaker* 24 June 1905 (C126)) – Beautiful Hawk-Moths – The Strenuous Mole (first appeared in *New Statesman* 18 July 1914 (C180)) – A Friendly Rat – The Little Red Dog (first appeared in *Speaker* 24 December for 26 December 1903 (C113); collected in *The Book of the Open Air* edited by Edward Thomas, 1907 (B2) – Dogs in London (first appeared in *National and English Review* May 1915 (C183)) – The Great Dog Superstition (first appeared in *Macmillan's Magazine* April 1889 (C51)) – My Friend the Pig (first appeared in the *National and English Review* March 1917 (C198)) – The Potato at Home and in England (first appeared in *National and English Review* April 1917 (C199)) – John-Go-To-Bed-At-Noon – The Chequered Daffodil (first appeared in *Speaker* 21 November 1903 (C112)); collected in *The Book of the Open Air* edited by Edward Thomas, 1907 (B2) – Concerning Lawns and Earthworms.

Binding Green cloth. Front cover stamped in gilt '[*within a double blind rule panel, within a single blind rule border*] THE BOOK OF / A NATURALIST / [*figure of a bat repeated 3 times*] / W. H. HUDSON'; spine stamped in gilt '[*blind rule*] / THE BOOK / OF A / NATURALIST / W. H. / HUDSON / HODDER & STOUGHTON / [*blind rule*]'. Bottom and fore edges untrimmed, top edges trimmed; white wove endpapers.

Notes Published 17 October 1919 at 12s. In response to my enquiry about publishing information Roger Palmer, Contracts Department, Hodder & Stoughton, wrote on 30 May 1972: "We published W. H. Hudson's *The Book of a Naturalist* on the 17th October 1919 and the price was in fact 12/- rather than 10/6d. Unfortunately at this stage it is impossible to ascertain the number of copies first printed...."

"Some of the chapters in this volume now appear for the first time; more of them, however, are taken from or based on articles which have appeared in various periodicals: the *Fortnightly Review*, *National Review*, *Country Life*, *Nation*, the *New Statesman*, and others. I am obliged to the Editors of The *Times* and *Chambers's Journal* for permission to use two short copyright articles on the Rat and Squirrel which appeared in those journals." (from Preface.)

Hudson explained his trouble with a title for this book in the preface. In a letter to Morley Roberts 11 October 1917 Hudson elaborated on his feelings: "Each morning and evening when I rise and lie down I devoutly curse Ray Lankester for anticipating me in his *Diversions of a Naturalist*. 'Idle Hours of a Naturalist' doesn't like me and nothing is left but 'Half-hour breathing intervals of a laborious Naturalist' which is long, so to speak, and lacks charm." Nearly two years later Hudson was still fooling with the title, however humorously. He wrote to Roberts in June 1919: "I don't think very highly of your suggestions for a title. Still I might improve on them and call the book – *The inconsequent demi-semi divagations of Indolence* (?) with an explanatory sub-title so that any fool would be able to understand what it was all about."

Reviews Times Literary Supplement 6 November 1919; *Nature* 22 July 1920.

A37b

FIRST AMERICAN EDITION (1919)

THE BOOK OF / A NATURALIST / BY / W. H. HUDSON / Author of / "The Naturalist in La Plata" / "Green Mansions," etc. / [*picture of a moth*] / NEW [*publisher's device*] YORK / GEORGE H. DORAN COMPANY

Collation [1–23]⁸ [24]⁴; pp. [2] [i–iv] v–viii [ix–x] 1–360 [4]; 223 × 148 mm.; printed on wove paper.

Pagination [2], blank; p. [i], half-title 'THE BOOK OF A NATURALIST / [*rule*] / W. H. HUDSON'; p. [ii], blank; p. [iii], title; p. [iv], 'COPYRIGHT, 1919 / BY GEORGE H. DORAN COMPANY / PRINTED IN THE UNITED STATES OF AMERICA'; pp. v–vi, preface by Hudson; pp. vii–viii, contents; p. [ix], fly-title 'THE BOOK OF A NATURALIST'; p. [x], blank; pp. 1–356, text; pp. 357–360, index; [4], blank.

Contents Same as first edition.

Binding Green cloth. Front cover stamped in gilt 'THE BOOK OF / A NATURALIST / [*figure of a bat repeated three times*] / W. H. HUDSON'; spine stamped in gilt 'THE

BOOK / OF A / NATURALIST / [*diamond design*] / W. H. HUDSON / DORAN'. Top edges trimmed, bottom and fore edges untrimmed; white wove endpapers. White wove dust jacket printed in green and with a coloured illustration on front.

Notes Published October 1919 at $3.50. In response to my enquiry about publishing information, Walter E. Freese, Vice-President, Doubleday & Company, wrote on 6 June 1972: "We have checked our records and, as you expected, they are not complete that far back. These books were published by George H. Doran before they merged with Doubleday in 1927. We have been able to locate all except the first print quantities."

A portion of this text was published as *The Disappointed Squirrel and Other Stories from "The Book of a Naturalist"* by Doran in 1925. See A51.

Reviews Boston Transcript 11 October 1919; *New York Times Book Review* 19 October 1919; *Dial* 1 November 1919; *Outlook* 17 December 1919; *ALA Booklist* December 1919; *Wilson Library Bulletin* December 1919; *New York Weekly Review* 31 January 1920.

A37c

E. P. DUTTON ISSUE (1919)

THE BOOK OF / A NATURALIST / BY / W. H. HUDSON / Author of / "The Naturalist in La Plata" / "Green Mansions", etc. / [*picture of a moth*] / NEW YORK / E. P. DUTTON & COMPANY / 681 FIFTH AVENUE.

Collation, pagination, contents, and *binding* same as A37b except the title page is a cancellans.

Notes First American edition sheets with a cancel title page for the Dutton imprint. See note to A22c for information on publishing records.

Copies ISU.

A37d

COLLECTED EDITION 1923

[*in red*] THE BOOK / OF / [*in red*] A NATURALIST / BY / W. H. HUDSON / [*publisher's device*] / MCMXXIII / LONDON & TORONTO / [*in red*] J. M. DENT & SONS LTD. / NEW YORK: E. P. DUTTON & CO.

Collation π⁶ A–U⁸ X¹⁰; pp. [2] [i–vi] vii–x [1] 2–339 [340]; 220 × 148 mm.; printed on cream laid paper with oval watermark incorporating Hudson's name, a figure of a tree and two deer.

Pagination [2], blank; p. [i], blank; p. [ii], 'THIS EDITION IS LIMITED TO 750 COPIES / FOR SALE IN ENGLAND, 100 FOR SALE / IN THE UNITED STATES OF AMERICA, / AND 35 PRESENTATION COPIES'; p. [iii], half-title 'THE / COLLECTED WORKS / of / W. H. HUDSON / [short rule] / IN TWENTY-FOUR / VOLUMES / THE BOOK OF A NATURALIST'; p. [iv], blank; p. [v], title; p. [vi], '*All rights reserved* / PRINTED IN GREAT BRITAIN'; pp. vii–viii, preface; pp. ix–x, contents; pp. [1] 2–334, text; pp. 335–339, index; p. [340], 'PRINTED BY / THE TEMPLE PRESS AT LETCHWORTH / IN GREAT BRITAIN'.

Contents Same as first edition.

Binding Green cloth. Gold medallion profile portrait in centre of front cover enclosed within a single blind rule border; spine stamped in gilt 'W. H. / HUDSON / [leafy branch] / The / Book of a / Naturalist / J·M·DENT / & SONS. LD.'. Blind rule border on back cover. Top edges trimmed and gilt, other edges untrimmed; cream laid endpapers. On front pastedown is a reproduction of pictorial bookplate with Hudson's name and dates. Maroon silk place marker.

Notes This is one of twenty-four volumes of Hudson's collected works. Eight hundred and eighty-five sets were published 1922–1923 for twenty-four guineas per set. The one hundred sets for sale in America were sold by E. P. Dutton for $192 per set. The collected works was reprinted in America by AMS Press in 1968 at $360.

Following publication of the Collected Edition Dent issued a Popular Edition of thirteen of Hudson's books. *The Book of a Naturalist* appeared in 1924 for 6s. It is gathered in 8's and the leaves measure 202 × 133 mm. Bound in blue cloth with a figure of a bird on a leafy branch blind stamped on the front cover. The author's name with a wavy thick-thin rule underneath, title with a printer's flower underneath, and the publisher's name are stamped in gilt on the spine. All edges trimmed and the top edges stained blue; white wove endpapers. Grey wove dust jacket printed in black.

OTHER EDITIONS

A37d 1927   Edinburgh Library edition. Toronto, Nelson.
A37e 1939   Black Jacket series. London, Hodder & Stoughton. Illustrated by Winifred Thridgould.

A38a

BIRDS OF LA PLATA

FIRST EDITION, ENGLISH ISSUE, REGULAR COPIES 1920

[*printed in red*] BIRDS / [*printed in red*] OF LA PLATA / BY / W. H. HUDSON / [*picture of a pheasant*] / *WITH TWENTY-TWO COLOURED* / *ILLUSTRATIONS BY* / *H. GRONVOLD* / VOLUME ONE (VOLUME TWO) / 1920 / LONDON & TORONTO / [*printed in red*] J. M. DENT & SONS LTD. / NEW YORK: E. P. DUTTON & CO.

Collation Volume I: π^{10} A–O^8 P^{10}; pp. [2] [i–iv] v–xvii [xviii] [1] 2–244; 245 × 175 mm.; printed on thick wove paper.

Volume II: π^6 A–P^8; pp. [2] [i–iv] v–ix [x] [1] 2–240; 245 × 177 mm.; printed on thick wove paper.

Pagination Volume I: [2], blank; p. [i], half-title 'BIRDS OF LA PLATA'; p. [ii], '*All rights reserved*'; frontispiece; p. [iii], title; p. [iv], '*There have been printed of this Edition 1500 Copies for England and* / *1500 Copies for United States of America, also a Large Paper Edition* / *of 200 Copies, and the type then distributed.*'; pp. v–xii, introduction by Hudson dated October, 1920; pp. xiii–xvi, contents; p. xvii, illustrations; p. [xviii], blank; pp. [1] 2–240, text; pp. 241–244, index to Volume I; at bottom of p. 244 'THE / TEMPLE PRESS [*picture of a flower*] LETCHWORTH / ENGLAND'.

Volume II: [2], blank; p. [i], half-title 'BIRDS OF LA PLATA'; p. [ii], '*All rights reserved*'; frontispiece; p. [iii], title; p. [iv], '*There have been printed of this Edition 1500 Copies for England and* / *1500 Copies for United States of America, also a Large Paper Edition* / *of 200 Copies, and the type then distributed.*'; pp. v–viii, contents; p. ix, illustrations; p. [x], blank; pp. [1] 2–236, text; pp. 237–240, index to Volume II; at bottom of p. 240, 'THE TEMPLE PRESS, PRINTERS, LETCHWORTH, ENGLAND'.

Illustrations Volumes I and II: Eleven coloured half-tone etchings from original drawings by H. Grönvold tipped in on calendered paper in each volume.

Binding Volumes I and II: Green cloth with tan cloth spine. Centre of front cover stamped in gilt with figure of a pheasant inside a single rule circle; spine stamped in gilt 'BIRDS / OF / L^A PLATA / [*figure of a bird in flight*] / W·H· / HUDSON / VOL·I [VOL·II] / J·M·DENT / & SONS. LD.' Fore edges untrimmed, others trimmed, top edges stained dark green; white wove endpapers. Brown wove dust jacket printed in brown.

Notes 1,500 copies issued 28 October 1920 at 37s. 6d.

Birds of La Plata is a new publication of Hudson's portion of *Argentine Ornithology* (A3). It is here slightly revised and contains a new introduction by the author and new illustrations by H. Grönvold. See also *Letters on the Ornithology of Buenos Ayres* (A61) for a separate edition of Hudson's letters.

The corrected proofs of *Birds of La Plata* are in the British Museum. Grönvold's original drawings were given to the Sociedad Ornitológica del Plata, Buenos Aires, by Jorge Casares in 1934.

On 26 October 1920 Hudson wrote to Morley Roberts: "I am sending you the book – the very sight of which is a weariness to me. It was my poverty that made me allow it to be re-published. It wasn't worth it."

Hudson's demands for accuracy on the part of the artists who illustrated his books is evident in his letter of 16 March 1917 to H. Grönvold. "I am now returning the book of plates with thanks for letting me see them. But they do not help me in any way. I cannot say I admire them as the attitudes seem too stiff & the colours too hard & in some cases too dark. It may be partly the fault of the process in colour-printing, but to some extent it is owing to your having to paint from long dead specimens in which the plumage has lost as is always the case the brilliant flower-like freshness seen in the plumage of the living bird – or in freshly-killed specimens.

There are 14 species known to me in the lot – 1. Rhea 2. Rufous tinamu 3. Martineta tinamu 4. C. maculosa 5. C. picazuro 6. Rallus rhytirhynchus 7. A-ypecaha 8. Podiceps major 9 Larus-wing-spotted 10. Thin. rumicivorus 11. Arg. lapwing 12 Char. falklandicus 13 Tree duck viduata 14. Wigeon. In the Martineta tinamu you have got the rich black & straw-colour of the back very well, & the plumage of the Wigeon is also very natural. In most of the others the colour is too hard & dark & the whole appearance of the bird too solid & wooden. In the living bird the feathers do not lie so prone as it were on the body, & this gives some of the pictures a look of having too big a head, too much legs, as in the Aramides ypecaha – a splendid bird when seen alive in its own marshes. Their grey & solemn colours, also the olive trunk have a lovely softness too in the living bird. That was one of the species I had thought of as a subject. I had also thought of the tree duck – D. viduata, but I don't like it as it appears in this plate.

These pictures are not nearly so good – so real to the natural loveliness of a bird – as your warblers. But you can I suppose *imagine* what the plumage is like in the living bird & freshen the colour more than it appears in the Museum specimens; & you can certainly get better attitudes than these, as you have done with the Arg. lapwing in the sketch you sent; also in the second sketch of the Black-faced Ibis. In the Thin. rumicivorus or Seed-snipe the principal beauty of the bird is in the soft fresh appearance of the feathers, which is lost in your picture...."

Hudson's descriptions of ten birds from *Birds of La Plata* were used in *Birds from my Homeland* by Antonio Frasconi. This volume contains ten hand-coloured woodcuts by Frasconi, printed on hand-made Hosho paper from Japan in an edition of 200 numbered copies. The printing was by Igal Roodenko in New York in 1958.

Reviews Times Literary Supplement 28 October 1920; *Times Literary Supplement* 4 November 1920; *Manchester Guardian* 11 November 1920; *Observer* 19 December 1920; *Nation* 24 December 1920; *Field* 29 January 1921; *Auk* January 1921.

A38b

FIRST EDITION, AMERICAN ISSUE, REGULAR COPIES   1920

Title page, collation, pagination, and illustrations same as first edition, English issue.

Binding Volumes I and II: Dark yellowish green cloth (centroid 137); tan cloth spine. Centre of front cover stamped in gilt with figure of a pheasant inside a single rule circle; spine stamped in gilt 'BIRDS / OF / L^A PLATA / [*figure of a bird in flight*] / W·H· / HUDSON / VOL·I [VOL·II] / E·P·DUTTON / [*figure of a leaf*] & CO [*figure of a leaf*]'. Top edges trimmed and stained green, other edges rough trimmed; white wove endpapers. Brown wove dust jacket printed in brown with Dutton's imprint on front and spine.

Variant Moderate green cloth (centroid 145). Centre of front cover stamped in gilt with figure of a pheasant inside a single rule circle; spine stamped in gilt 'Birds / of / La Plata / [*figure of a bird in flight*] / W·H· / HUDSON / VOI . I [VOL. II] / DUTTON'. All edges trimmed, top edges stained green; white wove endpapers. Brown wove dust jacket printed in brown with Dutton's imprint on front cover and spine.

Notes 1,500 copies issued 28 October 1920 at $15.00.

Reviews Nation 12 January 1921; *New York Evening Post* 29 January 1921; *New York Times Book Review* 11 September 1921.

Variant copy Texas.

A38c

FIRST EDITION, LIMITED COPIES
1920

Same as regular copies except as follows:
1 The limitation notice on p. [iv] Volume I reads '200 Copies of this Edition, signed by the Author, have / been printed; 75 of which are for Great Britain, 50 for / United States of America, and 75 for South America / [*Hudson's signature*]'.
2 No limitation notice in Volume II, page [iv] being blank.
3 No captions below coloured illustrations; illustrations are protected with tissue.
4 Spine is of rose buckram. Top edges trimmed and stained green; other edges untrimmed.
5 Leaves measure 286 × 215 mm.
6 The two volumes are accompanied by an extra set of plates mounted on Japan paper contained in a separate green thick-paper envelope. Envelope printed in red 'TWENTY-TWO ILLUSTRATIONS / TO THE / BIRDS OF LA PLATA / [*publisher's device*]'.

Notes 200 copies issued 1 December 1920 at 84s. in England and $35.00 in America.

Copies Adams; BM; Dartmouth; Dobie.

A38d

COLLECTED EDITION
1923

[*in red*] BIRDS / [*in red*] OF LA PLATA / BY / W. H. HUDSON / [*publisher's device*] / WITH A NOTE BY / R. B. CUNNINGHAME GRAHAM / MCMXXIII / LONDON & TORONTO / [*in red*] J. M. DENT & SONS LTD. / NEW YORK: E. P. DUTTON & CO.

Collation π^{12} A–2A^8 2B^{12}; pp. [2] [i–vi] vii–xxii 1–397 [398] 399–405 [406] [2]; 220 × 148 mm.; printed on cream laid paper with oval watermark incorporating Hudson's name, a figure of a tree and two deer.

Pagination [2], blank; p. [i], blank; p. [ii], 'THIS EDITION IS LIMITED TO 750 COPIES / FOR SALE IN ENGLAND, 100 FOR SALE / IN THE UNITED STATES OF AMERICA, / AND 35 PRESENTATION COPIES'; p. [iii], half-title 'THE / COLLECTED WORKS / of / W. H. HUDSON / [*short rule*] / IN TWENTY-FOUR / VOLUMES / BIRDS OF LA PLATA';

p. [iv], blank; p. [v], title; p. [vi], '*All rights reserved* / PRINTED IN GREAT BRITAIN'; pp. vii–viii, introductory note by R. B. Cunninghame Graham; p. ix–xiv, introduction by W. H. Hudson dated October 1920; pp. xv–xxii, contents; pp. 1–397, text; p. [398], blank; pp. 399–405, index; p. [406], 'PRINTED BY / THE TEMPLE PRESS AT LETCHWORTH / IN GREAT BRITAIN'; [2], blank.

Binding Green cloth. Gold medallion profile portrait in centre of front cover enclosed within a single blind rule border; spine stamped in gilt 'W. H. / HUDSON / [*leafy branch*] / Birds / of / La Plata / J·M·DENT / & SONS. LD.'. Blind rule border on back cover. Top edges trimmed and gilt, other edges untrimmed; cream laid endpapers. On front pastedown is a reproduction of pictorial bookplate with Hudson's name and dates. Maroon silk place marker.

Notes This is one of twenty-four volumes of Hudson's collected works. Eight hundred and eighty-five sets were published 1922–1923 for twenty-four guineas per set. The one hundred sets for sale in America were sold by E. P. Dutton for $192 per set. The collected works was reprinted in America by AMS Press in 1968 at $360.

This is the first appearance of the note on Hudson by R. B. Cunninghame Graham.

OTHER EDITIONS

A38e 1938 New popular edition. New York, Dutton.
A38f 1952 The King Penguin Books edition, No. 66. London, Penguin Books. Introduction by Richard Curle. Colour plates by S. Magno. The drawings were first used in *Pájaros Nuestros*, Buenos Aires, Kraft.

A39a

DEAD MAN'S PLACK AND AN OLD THORN

FIRST EDITION 1920

[*in green*] DEAD MAN'S PLACK / AND / AN OLD THORN / BY / W. H. HUDSON / [*in green: publisher's device*] / 1920 / LONDON & TORONTO / [*in green*] J. M. DENT & SONS LTD. / NEW YORK: E. P. DUTTON & CO.

Collation [A]⁸ (A2 + χ2) B–O⁸; pp. [2] [i–viii] [1–3] 4–145 [146–148] 149–189 [190–192] 193–205 [206–216]; 186 × 126 mm.; printed on laid paper.

Pagination [2], blank; p. [i], half-title 'DEAD MAN'S PLACK'; p. [ii], '*First Published* in 1920. / *All rights reserved*'; frontispiece; p. [iii], title; p. [iv], blank; p. [v], contents; p. [vi], blank; p. [vii], illustrations; p. [viii], blank; p. [1], section-title 'DEAD MAN'S PLACK'; p. [2], blank; pp. [3] 4-13, preamble to Dead Man's Plack; pp. 14-145, text; p. [146], blank; p. [147], section-title 'AN OLD THORN'; p. [148], blank; pp. 149-189, text; p. [190], blank; p. [191], section-title 'POSTSCRIPT'; p. [192], blank; pp. 193-205, text; p. [206], 'PRINTED IN GREAT BRITAIN BY / RICHARD CLAY & SONS, LIMITED, / BRUNSWICK ST., STAMFORD ST., S.E.1, / AND BUNGAY, SUFFOLK.'; pp. [207-215], publisher's advertisements; p. [216], blank.

Contents Dead Man's Plack – An Old Thorn (first appeared in *English Review* May 1911 (C165)) – Postscript to Dead Man's Plack and Postscript to An Old Thorn.

Illustrations Two line etchings.

Binding Ribbed green cloth. Front cover stamped in blind with a single rule border enclosing publisher's device of three trees; spine stamped in gilt '[*within a frame formed by branches*] DEAD / MAN'S / PLACK / & / AN OLD / THORN / W. H. HUDSON / [*below frame*] J. M. DENT / & SONS. L^D'. All edges trimmed, top edges stained green; white wove endpapers. Tan wove dust jacket printed in green.

Variants 1 Smooth green cloth. 2 Red cloth. Border formed by three blind stamped rules on front cover. Spine stamped in gilt '[*four blind rules*] / DEAD / MAN'S / PLACK / ETC. / [*rule*] / HUDSON / [*five blind stamped compartments, every other one enclosing a blind stamped device*] / [*double blind rule*]'. All edges trimmed; white wove endpapers.

Notes 2,500 copies published 30 November 1920 at 7s. 6d.

An uncorrected proof copy is in the Dartmouth College Library. The writing of 'Dead Man's Plack' bothered Hudson, for he felt he was stealing time from *A Hind in Richmond Park*. He sent copies of the story to Morley Roberts and Edward Garnett asking whether or not it was worth printing. On 29 May 1920 Hudson wrote Garnett: "I am now sending you the story which you see is the old historical one of Edgar and Elfrida, a subject most unsuitable for me, which was forced on me so to speak; and so I should not be surprised to hear that I am out of it here and that it is no good. Well, you will tell me; and all I can say is I will not rewrite it, as I've now finished with it and very glad too; as I should have preferred one of my own natural history subjects – the book I had half written before I came down in fact. But when I came down I put [out] some old envelopes, each containing some notes I had made on some subjects which had interested me at one time. I thought it best to bring them down and look over them to destroy most of them as now useless, when I turned out and looked at the Edgar and E. note I had made years ago. I thought I might just try to make a little thing of three or four thousand words and get rid of it in that way instead of destroying it. But the confounded subject would not let me go until I had made this long short story which runs to over 21,000 words. And now I'm fairly sick of it and can do nothing beyond mending any glaringly wrong passage. But you will tell me about that. . . .

What I feel about this thing is that I haven't succeeded in producing the effect aimed at in the character of the woman as the whole and sole interest is in that – the woman who was capable of a horrible crime and who was yet essentially noble in spirit. But as to its being a story of a thousand years ago, that doesn't matter at all seeing that human passions then were what they are to-day and always, and all the archaeology stuff is left out. You must say Use it or Burn it and I'll obey."

On 2 June 1920 Hudson wrote to Garnett: "Very many thanks for your helpful letter. I had seen when correcting the MS that a lot of sentences and phrases ought to come out – and that Fisher allusion and things like that. But about style – the moment it looks artificial it revolts me. . . . I'm glad you like the passages I like and think [best.] I sent a copy to Morley Roberts at the same time and *he* says those are the wrong passages – that Elfreda's monologues must all be cut short to make the story better."

A new and expanded edition of *Dead Man's Plack and an Old Thorn* appeared in 1924. See A49. Five poems were added: "The London Sparrow", "In the Wilderness"; "Gwendoline"; "Tecla and the Little Men"; and "The Old Man of Kensington Gardens". See also the Collected Edition of Hudson's works, 1922–1923 with the title *A Little Boy Lost Together with the Poems of W. H. Hudson* (A25e).

Reviews Times Literary Supplement 9 December 1920; *Manchester Guardian* 17 December 1920; *Bookman* 1 January 1921; *Athenaeum* 14 January 1921; *Nation* 22 January 1921; *Tatler* 26 January 1921; *Plain English* 12 February 1921; *Gloucester Journal* 12 March 1921; *John O'London's Weekly* 19 March 1921; *Dublin Evening Herald* 26 March 1921.

Variant copy 1 Texas. *Variant copy 2* Texas.

A39b

FIRST AMERICAN EDITION (1920)

[*within a double rule frame*] DEAD MAN'S PLACK / *and* / AN OLD THORN / BY / W. H. HUDSON / *AUTHOR OF* / "THE PURPLE LAND," "BIRDS IN TOWN

AND VILLAGE," / "FAR AWAY AND LONG AGO," ETC., ETC. / [*publisher's device of J. M. Dent*] / NEW YORK / E. P. DUTTON & COMPANY / 681 FIFTH AVENUE

Collation [1–12]⁸; pp. [i–iv] v [vi] [1–2] 3–132 [133–134] 135–170 [171–172] 173–185 [186]; 210 × 140 mm.; printed on wove paper.

Pagination p. [i], half-title 'DEAD MAN'S PLACK / *and* / AN OLD THORN'; p. [ii], list of eight books by the same author; p. [iii], title; p. [iv], 'Copyright 1920, by / E. P. DUTTON & COMPANY / [*short rule*] / *All rights reserved* / *Printed in the United States of America*'; p. v, contents; p. [vi], blank; p. [1], section-title 'DEAD MAN'S PLACK'; p. [2], blank; pp. 3–12, Preamble; pp. 13–132, text; p. [133], section-title 'AN OLD THORN'; p. [134], blank; pp. 135–170, text; p. [171], section-title 'POSTSCRIPT'; p. [172], blank; pp. 173–185, text; p. [186], blank.

Binding Brown cloth. Front cover stamped in gilt '[*within a single gilt border*] DEAD MAN'S PLACK / *and* / AN OLD THORN / [*rule*] / ▼▼▼ W. H. HUDSON ▼▼▼'; spine stamped in gilt 'DEAD / MAN'S / PLACK / *and* / AN OLD / THORN / [*short rule*] / HUDSON / E. P. DUTTON / AND COMPANY'. Top edges trimmed, others untrimmed; white wove endpapers.

Notes Published 30 November 1920 at $2.50. See note to A22c for information on publishing records.

Hudons wrote to Morley Roberts 11 January 1921: "A pile of books from America with letters, etc. *Dead Man's Plack* a much nicer book than Dent's edition."

Reviews New York Times Book Review 19 December 1920; *Outlook* 19 January 1921; *Bookman* February 1921.

OTHER EDITIONS

A39c n.d. [*An Old Thorn*, with *Nature in Downland*] Braille hand-copied edition for the National Library for the Blind (London), four volumes.

A40a

A TRAVELLER IN LITTLE THINGS

FIRST EDITION 1921

A / TRAVELLER / IN LITTLE THINGS / BY / W. H. HUDSON / [*publisher's device*] / 1921 / LONDON AND TORONTO / J. M. DENT & SONS LTD.

Collation π⁴ A–Q⁸ R⁴; pp. [i–iv] v–vi [vii–viii] [1] 2–257 [258] 11–5 [6]; 209 × 141 mm.; printed on wove paper.

Pagination p. [i], half-title 'A TRAVELLER / IN LITTLE THINGS'; p. [ii], '*All rights reserved*'; p. [iii], title; p. [iv], blank; pp. v–vi, contents; p. [vii], notice of previous publication of parts of this book; p. [viii], blank; pp. [1] 2–257, text; p. [258], '[*printed across a picture of a flower*] THE / TEMPLE PRESS / LETCHWORTH / ENGLAND'; pp. 11–5 [6], publisher's advertisements of six books by Hudson.

Contents How I Found My Title – The Old Man's Delusion (first appeared in *New Statesman* 4 September 1915 (C186)) – As a Tree Falls – "Blood": A Story of Two Brothers – A Story of Long Descent – A Second Story of Two Brothers – A Third Story of Two Brothers – The Two White Houses: A Memory – Dandy: A Story of a Dog (first appeared in *Animals' Friend* August 1919 (C201)) – The Samphire Gatherer – A Surrey Village – A Wiltshire Village – Her Own Village – Apple Blossoms and a Lost Village (first appeared in *Reveille* November 1918 (C200)) – The Vanishing Curtsey (first appeared in *Speaker* 7 January 1905 (C122)) – Little Girls I Have Met (first appeared in *Cornhill Magazine* February 1916 (C192)) – Millicent and Another – Freckles – On Cromer Beach – Dimples – Wild Flowers and Little Girls – A Little Girl Lost – A Spray of Southernwood (first appeared in *Saturday Review* 14 August 1909 (C152)) – In Porchester Churchyard (first appeared in *Saturday Review* 21 August 1909 (C153)) – Homeless – The Story of a Skull (first appeared in *Country Life* 1 January 1916 (C191)) – A Story of a Walnut (first appeared in *Speaker* 25 August 1906 (C142)) – A Story of a Jackdaw – A Wonderful Story of a Mackerel (first appeared in *Saturday Review* 9 September 1911 (C167)) – Strangers Yet – The Return of the Chiff-Chaff – A Wasp at Table – Wasps and Men – In Chitterne Churchyard – A Haunter of Churchyards – The Dead and the Living – A Story of Three Poems (reprints Hudson's poem "The Visionary" which first appeared in *Nature Notes: The Selborne Society's Magazine* March 1898 (C86)).

Binding Green cloth. Front cover stamped in blind with a single rule border enclosing the publisher's device; spine stamped in gilt 'A / TRAVELLER / IN / LITTLE / THINGS / [*orn: floral branch*] / W. H. / HUDSON / J·M·DENT· &·S⁰NS·L^D'. All edges trimmed, top edges stained dark green; white wove endpapers. Tan wove dust jacket printed in green.

Variant Blue cloth. Front cover stamped in black around top, bottom and fore edges with a single rule border; spine stamped in black as copy described above. All edges trimmed; white wove endpapers.

Notes 2,400 copies published 26 September 1921 at 10s. 6d.

On 1 May 1921 Hudson wrote to his wife's nephew, Horace Wingrave: "I am never interested in 1st Editions:– they are never so good as the later ones, & I like the American Editions of my books much better than the English. Besides, they *are* better in every way. They have *Adventures Among Birds* illustrated; *A Little Boy Lost* in two editions – one with large coloured plates. *The Purple Land* with introduction by Roosevelt (late president). *Green Mansions* with introduction by Galsworthy, & *A Crystal Age* with Introduction by Clifford Smyth, the Literary Editor of the *New York Times*. *Dead Man's Plack* is much better too in the American Edition. So is *El Ombú* with a lot of additional matter. But all my books have a much greater sale over there, & I hear 1st Editions sell from 5 to 20 pounds – much higher than in England."

Reviews Times Literary Supplement 29 September 1921; *Morning Post* 30 September 1921; *Daily News* 1 October 1921; *Observer* 2 October 1921; *Outlook* 8 October 1921; *Sunday Times* 9 October 1921; *Nation & Athenaeum* 22 October 1921; *Westminster Gazette* 10 December 1921; *New Statesman* 15 October 1921; *Manchester Guardian* 20 October 1921; *Bazaar Exchange & Mart* 21 October 1921; *Tatler* 8 March 1922.

Variant copy Dobie.

A40b

FIRST AMERICAN EDITION (1921)

[*within a double rule frame*] A TRAVELLER IN / LITTLE THINGS / BY / W. H. HUDSON / AUTHOR OF "THE PURPLE LAND," / "FAR AWAY AND LONG AGO," ETC. / [*publisher's device of J. M. Dent*] / NEW YORK / E. P. DUTTON & COMPANY / 681 FIFTH AVENUE

Collation [1–22]⁸; pp. [i–vi] vii–viii [ix–x] [1] 2–339 [340] [2]; 204 × 140 mm.; printed on wove paper.

Pagination p. [i], half-title, 'A TRAVELLER IN / LITTLE THINGS'; p. [ii], list of nine books by the same author; p. [iii], title; p. [iv], 'Copyright, 1921, / By E. P. DUTTON & COMPANY / [*short rule*] / All rights reserved / *Printed in the United States of America*'; p. [v], note regarding previous publication of parts of this book; p. [vi], blank; pp. vii–viii, contents; p. [ix], fly-title, 'A TRAVELLER IN / LITTLE THINGS'; p. [x], blank; pp. [1] 2–339, text; p. [340], blank; [2], blank.

Contents Same as first edition.

Binding Blue cloth. Front cover stamped in gilt '[*within a single blind rule border*] A TRAVELLER IN / LITTLE THINGS / [*rule*] / W. H. HUDSON / [*circular device*]'; spine stamped in gilt, 'A / TRAVELLER / IN / LITTLE / THINGS / [*diamond design*] / HUDSON / E. P. DUTTON / & CO.'. Top edges trimmed, others untrimmed; white wove endpapers. Grey wove dust jacket printed in black.

Notes Published 27 October 1921 at $2.00. See note to A22c for information on publishing records.

Reviews New York Times Book Review 1 January 1922; *ALA Booklist* January 1922; *Springfield Republican* 15 October 1921; *Saturday Review* 5 November 1921; *Outlook* 23 November 1921; *Nation* 28 December 1921.

A40c

COLLECTED EDITION 1923

[*in red*] A TRAVELLER / IN / [*in red*] LITTLE THINGS / BY / W. H. HUDSON / [*publisher's device*] / WITH A NOTE BY / EDWARD GARNETT / MCMXXIII / LONDON & TORONTO / [*in red*] J. M. DENT & SONS LTD. / NEW YORK: E. P. DUTTON & CO.

Collation π⁸ A–Q⁸ R⁴; pp. [i–vi] vii–xiii [xiv] xv–xvi [1] 2–257 [258] 259–261 [262] [*2*]; 220 × 148 mm.; printed on cream laid paper with oval watermark incorporating Hudson's name, a figure of a tree and two deer.

Pagination p. [i], blank; p. [ii], 'THIS EDITION IS LIMITED TO 750 COPIES / FOR SALE IN ENGLAND, 100 FOR SALE / IN THE UNITED STATES OF AMERICA, / AND 35 PRESENTATION COPIES'; p. [iii], half-title 'THE / COLLECTED WORKS / *of* / W. H. HUDSON / [*short rule*] / IN TWENTY-FOUR / VOLUMES / A TRAVELLER / IN LITTLE THINGS'; p. [iv], blank; p. [v], title; p. [vi], 'All rights reserved / PRINTED IN GREAT BRITAIN'; pp. vii–xiii, 'A NOTE ON HUDSON'S SPIRIT' by Edward Garnett; p. [xiv], notice of previous publication of parts of this book; pp. xv–xvi, contents; pp. [1] 2–257, text; p. [258], blank; pp. 259–261, index; p. [262], 'PRINTED BY / THE TEMPLE PRESS AT LETCHWORTH / IN GREAT BRITAIN'; [*2*], blank.

Contents Same as first edition.

Binding Green cloth. Gold medallion profile portrait in centre of front cover enclosed within a single blind rule border; spine stamped in gilt 'W. H. / HUDSON / [*leafy branch*] / A / Traveller / in Little / Things / J·M·DENT / & SONS. LD.'. Blind rule border on back cover. Top edges trimmed and gilt, other edges untrimmed; cream laid endpapers. On front pastedown is a reproduction of pictorial bookplate with Hudson's name and dates. Maroon silk place marker.

Notes This is one of twenty-four volumes of Hudson's collected works. Eight hundred and eighty-five sets were published 1922–1923 for twenty-four guineas per set. The one hundred sets for sale in America were sold by E. P. Dutton for $192 per set. The collected works was reprinted in America by AMS Press in 1968 at $360.

This is the first appearance of Garnett's essay on Hudson.

Following publication of the Collected Edition Dent issued a Popular Edition of thirteen of Hudson's books. *A Traveller in Little Things* appeared in 1923 for 6s. It is gathered in 8's and the leaves measure 202 × 133 mm. Bound in blue cloth with a figure of a bird on a leafy branch blind stamped on the front cover. The author's name with a wavy thick-thin rule underneath, title with a printer's flower underneath, and the publisher's name are stamped in gilt on the spine. All edges trimmed and the top edges stained blue; white wove endpapers. Grey wove dust jacket printed in black.

OTHER EDITIONS

A40d 1932 New Adelphi Library edition no. 61. London, Dent.
A40e n.d. Braille hand-copied edition for the National Library for the Blind (London), three volumes.

A41a

A TIRED TRAVELLER

FIRST EDITION   1921

[*coloured illustration of a Redwing Thrush, reproduced from a painting by H. Grönvold*] / A TIRED TRAVELLER / [*text follows*]

Collation [A]⁴; pp. [1] 2–8; 222 × 141 mm.; printed on wove calendered paper.

Pagination p. [1], title and beginning of text; pp. 2–8, text; on p. 8 'From *Adventures among Birds,* by permission of Messrs J. M. / DENT & SONS, LTD. / Leaflet No. 78. Published by the Royal Society for the Protection of / Birds, 23 Queen Anne's Gate, London, S.W., of whom copies may be / obtained 3d. each; 2/6 per doz.'.

Illustrations Coloured half-tone etching of a Redwing Thrush by H. Grönvold.

Binding Self-wrappers, stapled.

Notes Published at 3d.

This previously appeared in *Saturday Review* 2 January 1909 (C149) and in *Adventures Among Birds* (A31).

A42a

SEAGULLS IN LONDON

FIRST EDITION (1922

[*within a single rule frame*] SEAGULLS / IN / LONDON / BY / W. H. HUDSON

Collation [A]²; pp. [1–4]; 220 × 141 mm.; printed on wove paper.

Pagination p. [1], title; p. [2], '20 *Copies privately printed*'; p. [3], 'SEAGULLS IN LONDON / [*short rule*] / WHY THEY TOOK TO COMING TO TOWN / [*short rule*] / [*text follows*]'; p. [4], '[*double rule*] / SEAGULLS IN LONDON / [*double rule*] / [*text*]'.

Binding Self-wrappers, folded.

Notes Twenty copies privately printed by Clement K. Shorter. This originally appeared as a letter to the Editor in the *Observer* 16 January 1921 (C202). Its first book appearance was in *Dead Man's Plack An Old Thorn & Miscellanea* (A47).

Copies Brotherton; Lilly; Martin; RSPB.

A43a

A HIND IN RICHMOND PARK

FIRST EDITION 1922

A HIND / IN / RICHMOND PARK / BY / W. H. HUDSON / [*orn: two deer beneath an oak tree*] / MCMXXII / LONDON & TORONTO / J. M. DENT & SONS LTD.

Collation π⁸ A–X⁸; pp. [i–iv] v [vi] vii–xv [xvi] 1–335 [336]; 209 × 140 mm.; printed on laid paper.

Pagination p. [i], half-title 'A HIND / IN RICHMOND PARK'; p. [ii], '"There is a magic in Mr. Hudson's style and in / his exquisite sensibility which awakens in his reader / a thousand sleeping memories." / *The Morning Post*.'; p. [iii], title; p. [iv], '*All rights reserved* / PRINTED IN GREAT BRITAIN'; p. v, publisher's note; p. [vi], blank; pp. vii–viii, prefatory note by Morley Roberts dated October 1922; pp. ix–xv, contents; p. [xvi], blank; pp. 1–335, text; at bottom of p. 335, 'PRINTED BY THE TEMPLE PRESS AT LETCHWORTH IN GREAT BRITAIN'; p. [336], blank.

Binding Green cloth. Front cover printed in black with a border of 1 thick and 2 thin rules enclosing the publisher's device; spine stamped in gilt '[*thick-thin rule printed in black*] / [*within a linear frame formed by 2 horizontal rules at top and vertical rules on either side, joining to form a circle at the bottom*] A HIND / IN / RICHMOND / PARK / [*orn: knot*] / W.H.HUDSON / [*orn: knot*] / [*below the frame*] J·M·DENT / &·SONS·L^D / [*thin-thick rule printed in black*]'. All edges trimmed, top edges stained dark green; white wove endpapers. Grey wove dust jacket printed in black.

Notes 2,950 copies published 8 November 1922 at 16s.

"A Hind in Richmond Park," "On the Sense of Smell," and "On the Sense of Direction" previously appeared in *Century Magazine* (New York) July, August and September 1922 (C206, C207, C208).

Hudson was at work on this book at the time of his death, 18 August 1922. The work was complete except for the last chapter which needed revision. Part was in a clean typescript, but the last few pages, amounting to some two thousand words, were in Hudson's handwriting and difficult to decipher. Morley Roberts prepared the closing pages of the book for the press. He described his task in three letters to Margaret Alice Lilly Brooke, Lady Rani of Sarawak. 12 September 1922: "I've been asked to put together the bits of the unfinished chapter of the *Hind*. I doubt if it can be done: much is in pencil & totally illegible even to me. But I may make a note for the end of the book & in any case I think the finished portion practically ends it."

19 September 1922: "The last part of Hudson's script is *impossible*! Still I hope to make out enough to get the book finished & his intentions clear. It is a most melancholy task but one of duty & love also."

6 October 1922: "I arranged the unfinished part of Hudson's book & I think it is all right, though incomplete as some of the M.S. was totally illegible. I have also had to write a short prefatory note for the book explaining what happened & why the principle task fell to me."

Reviews Times Literary Supplement 16 November 1922; *Nation & Athenaeum* 18 November 1922; *New Statesman* 9 December 1922; *Spectator* 16 December 1922.

A43b

FIRST AMERICAN EDITION (1923)

A HIND IN / RICHMOND PARK / BY / W. H. HUDSON / AUTHOR OF "FAR AWAY AND LONG AGO," / "ADVENTURES AMONG BIRDS," / "THE PURPLE LAND," ETC. / [*orn: two deer beneath an oak tree*] / NEW YORK / E. P. DUTTON AND COMPANY / 681 FIFTH AVENUE

Collation [1–20]⁸; pp. [i–iv] v–xxiii [xxiv] [1] 2–296; 207 × 140 mm.; printed on wove paper.

Pagination p. [i], half-title, 'A HIND IN / RICHMOND PARK'; p. [ii], list of thirteen books by the same author; frontispiece portrait by Will Rothenstein; p. [iii], title; p. [iv], 'Copyright, 1923 / By E. P. DUTTON & COMPANY / [*short rule*] / All Rights Reserved / [*short rule*] / Printed in the United States of America / This First (American) Edition is Limited to 1550 Copies of which / only 1500 are for sale'; pp. v–vi, prefatory note by Morley Roberts, dated October, 1922; pp. vii–xii, contents; pp. xiii–xxiii, introduction by Edward Garnett, dated October, 1922; p. [xxiv], blank; pp. [1] 2–296, text.

Binding Red cloth. White circular medallion with profile portrait in centre of front cover, within a single blind rule border; white paper label on spine, printed in green, '[*double rule*] / A HIND / IN / RICHMOND / PARK / BY / W. H. HUDSON / [*figure of a deer*] / [*triple rule*]'. Top edges trimmed, others untrimmed; white wove endpapers.

Notes 1,550 copies published 24 January 1923 at $3.00. Three printings to October 1926.

The introduction by Edward Garnett entitled "The Genius of W. H. Hudson" is reprinted from *Literary Digest*, December 1922. This is its first book appearance.

Reviews Saturday Review 2 December 1922; *Boston Transcript* 3 February 1923; *New York Times Book Review* 18 February 1923; *Springfield Republican* 25 February 1923; *New York World* 4 March 1923; *New York Evening Post* 28 April 1923; *New York Tribune* 29 April 1923; *Catholic World* June 1923; *ALA Booklist* July 1923; *Bookman* December 1923; *Yale Review* 1924.

A43c

COLLECTED EDITION   1923

[*in red*] A HIND / IN / [*in red*] RICHMOND PARK / BY / W. H. HUDSON / [*publisher's device*] / MCMXXIII / LONDON & TORONTO / [*in red*] J. M. DENT & SONS LTD. / NEW YORK: E. P. DUTTON & CO.

Collation π^8 ($\pi 1 + \chi 1$) A–T⁸ U¹⁰ (— U10) (x)⁴; pp. [*two unnumbered pages*] [i–iv] v [vi] vii–xv [xvi] 1–323 [324] 325–330; 220 × 148 mm.; printed on cream laid paper with oval watermark incorporating Hudsons' name, a figure of a tree and two deer.

Pagination p. [*first unnumbered page*], blank; [*second unnumbered page*], 'THIS EDITION IS LIMITED TO 750 COPIES / FOR SALE IN ENGLAND, 100 FOR SALE / IN THE UNITED STATES OF AMERICA, / AND 35 PRESENTATION COPIES'; p. [i], half-title 'THE / COLLECTED WORKS / of / W. H. HUDSON / [*short rule*] / IN TWENTY-FOUR / VOLUMES / A HIND IN RICHMOND PARK'; p. [ii], ' "There is a magic in Mr. Hudson's style and in / his exquisite sensibility which awakens in his reader / a thousand sleeping memories." / *The Morning Post.*'; p. [iii], title; p. [iv], '*All rights reserved* / PRINTED IN GREAT BRITAIN'; p. v, publisher's note; p. [vi], blank; pp. vii–viii, prefatory note by Morley Roberts dated October 1922; pp. ix–xv, contents; p. [xvi], blank; pp. 1–323, text; p. [324], blank; pp. 325–330, index; at bottom of p. 330, 'PRINTED BY THE TEMPLE PRESS AT LETCHWORTH IN GREAT BRITAIN.'.

Binding Green cloth. Gold medallion profile portrait in centre of front cover enclosed within a single blind rule border; spine stamped in gilt 'W. H. / HUDSON / [*leafy branch*] / A Hind / in / Richmond / Park / J·M·DENT / & SONS. LD.'. Blind rule border on back cover. Top edges trimmed and gilt, other edges untrimmed; cream laid endpapers. On front pastedown is a reproduction of pictorial bookplate with Hudson's name and dates. Maroon silk place marker.

Notes This is one of twenty-four volumes of Hudson's collected works. Eight hundred and eighty-five sets were published 1922–1923 for twenty-four guineas per set. The one hundred sets for sale in America were sold by E. P. Dutton for $192 per set. The collected works was reprinted in America by AMS Press in 1968 at $360.

Following publication of the Collected Edition Dent issued a Popular Edition of thirteen of Hudson's books. *A Hind in Richmond Park* appeared in 1929 for 6s. It is gathered in 8's and the leaves measure 202 × 133 mm. Bound in blue cloth with a figure of a bird on a leafy branch blind stamped on the front cover. The author's name with a wavy thick-thin rule underneath, title with a printer's flower underneath, and the publisher's name are stamped in gilt on the spine. All edges trimmed and the top edges stained blue; white wove endpapers. Grey wove dust jacket printed in black.

The Uniform Edition of Hudson's works was published in 1951 by Dent and consists of seven titles: *The Purple Land*; *Nature in Downland*; *A Hind in Richmond Park*; *Green Mansions*; *Adventures Among Birds*; *Far Away and Long Ago*. *Idle Days in Patagonia* was added in 1954.

A Hind in Richmond Park is gathered in 16's and the leaves measure 192 × 124 mm. Bound in red cloth. The author's name, title, a figure of a feather and the publisher's name are stamped in gilt on the spine. All edges trimmed; white wove endpapers. Green and white wove dust jacket printed in black.

OTHER EDITIONS

A43d n.d. Braille hand-copied edition for the National Library for the Blind (London), four volumes.

A44a

RALPH HERNE

FIRST EDITION 1923

[*within a decorative rule frame, within an ornamental frame*] [*open letter*] RALPH / [*open letter*] HERNE / [*decorative rule*] / *By* W. H. HUDSON / [*decorative rule*] / [*type ornaments combined to form a vertical design with the letters B and R on either side*] / [*decorative rule*] / *New York* / ALFRED A. KNOPF / 1923

Collation [1]⁴ [2–11]⁸ [12]⁴; [i–xii] 1–160 [161–162] [2]; 235 × 151 mm.; printed on laid paper. Watermark: 'BORZOI BOOKS' with a figure of a Borzoi at lower right corner recto of every leaf.

Pagination pp. [i–iv], blank; p. [v], half-title '[*type design*] RALPH HERNE [*type design*]'; pp. [vi–vii], facsimile reproduction in blue of Hudson's manuscript; p. [viii], blank; p. [ix], title; p. [x], 'COPYRIGHT 1923 / ALFRED A. KNOPF / NEW YORK'; p. [xi], contents; p. [xii], blank; pp. 1–160 [161], text; p. [162], '*Nine hundred and fifty copies printed from* / *Monotype Caslon type at the Printing House of* / *William Edwin Rudge, Mount Vernon, N.Y.* / *Typography by Bruce Rogers* / [*autograph, number in black ink*]; [2], blank.

Binding Orange paper boards, black cloth spine. Orange paper label on spine printed in black '[*row of 3 circular type ornaments*] / [*decorative rule*] / Ralph / Herne / BY / W·H / HUDSON / [*decorative rule*] / [*row of three circular type ornaments*]'. All edges untrimmed; white laid endpapers with watermark as above. First leaf of first signature pasted down. Second leaf is a free endpaper. End of book has regular positioned endpapers. In publisher's black box with orange paper label on spine printed in black as above.

Notes 950 copies published 15 May 1923 at $7.50.

Ralph Herne first appeared in *Youth* 4 January through 14 March 1888 (c47). Its first appearance in book form in England was in the Collected edition (A21d). The copy of *Ralph Herne* used by Hudson to mark corrections and revisions for the Collected edition is in the G. M. Adams Collection at the University of Michigan.

The manuscript reproduced in facsimile as the frontispiece describes the writing of *Ralph Herne* and the critical reception of Hudson's work.

On 13 November 1921 Hudson wrote to Alfred A. Knopf: "I believe I mentioned to you that I had the Ms. of a story – a short novel – written many years ago & printed in a paper called *Youth* which no longer exists, & that you asked me to send it to you in New York. When I spoke of it to you (Edward) Garnett was with us & remarked that this was a story he had never heard of. I told him that he had heard of it & *read* it, & had expressed the opinion that it would be better for my literary reputation not to issue it in book form. I said there & say now again that I don't care two straws about my literary reputation. When a book of mine [*The Purple Land that England Lost* (A1)] much praised now came out in the eighties it was slated by the reviewers & for 19 years remained dead, then when revived it *was a classic*! I care as little for what they say now as I did then when whatever came from my pen was 'disgusting rubbish.'

I grant that as a love story this early story – written before *A Purple Land* is weak but it has one thing which I think makes it worth saving, & that is a *true* history of the great epidemic which devastated Buenos Ayres in 1871. I did not witness it but my sisters & a brother went through it & it was out of their vivid narratives of their own experience that I wove the tale. In the Argentine where there is a considerable English reading public the story would have a special value.

I am now sending the Ms. for you to read & consider, & if you think it worth publishing let me know as soon as you can if you will buy the American & Canadian rights outright. But my idea is that it would be better for an introduction."

Reviews New York Times Book Review 3 June 1923.

OTHER EDITIONS

A44b 1924   Borzoi pocket books edition. New York, Knopf.

A45a

RARE VANISHING & LOST BRITISH BIRDS

FIRST EDITION   1923

RARE / VANISHING & LOST / BRITISH BIRDS / COMPILED FROM NOTES BY / W. H. HUDSON / BY / LINDA GARDINER / [*illustration of a pheasant*] /

WITH 25 COLOURED PLATES BY / H. GRONVOLD / MCMXXIII / LONDON AND TORONTO / J. M. DENT & SONS LTD. / NEW YORK: E. P. DUTTON & CO.

Collation $\pi^8 \chi^2$ A–G^8 H^4; pp. [i–iv] v–xv [xvi] xvii [xviii] xix [xx] [1] 2–115 [116] 117–120; 221 × 153 mm.; printed on laid paper.

Pagination p. [i], half-title 'RARE, VANISHING, AND LOST / BRITISH BIRDS'; p. [ii], blank; frontispiece; p. [iii], title; p. [iv], '*All rights reserved* / PRINTED IN GREAT BRITAIN'; pp. v–x, foreword by Linda Gardiner dated 22 August 1923; pp. xi–xv, preface to the first edition by W. H. Hudson, dated 1894; p. [xvi], blank; p. xvii, contents; p. [xviii], blank; p. xix, list of coloured plates; p. [xx], blank; pp. [1] 2–109, text; pp. 110–114, Allusions in Poetry; p. 115, List of Writers; p. [116], blank; pp. 117–120, index; at bottom of p. 120, 'PRINTED BY THE TEMPLE PRESS AT LETCHWORTH IN GREAT BRITAIN'.

Illustrations 25 coloured half-tone etchings from original drawings by H. Grönvold tipped in on calendered paper.

Binding Green cloth. Front cover stamped in blind with a single rule border enclosing publisher's device; spine stamped in gilt 'W.H.HUDSON / [*rule*] / RARE / VANISHING / & LOST / BRITISH / BIRDS / [*bird design*] / EDITED BY / LINDA / GARDINER / J.M.DENT / & SONS.L^D'. All edges trimmed, top edges stained green; white wove endpapers. Grey wove dust jacket printed in blue.

Notes 3,200 copies published 7 November 1923 at 10s. 6d.

This is an expansion of Hudson's *Lost British Birds* (A11) completed after his death by Linda Gardiner.

Hudson had been at work on this revised and enlarged edition of *Lost British Birds* for some years. His purpose was to arouse public sentiment about the continuing loss of bird life in England. The earlier edition described thirteen birds held to be practically lost to Britain as breeding species. This edition was to be expanded to include not only those species exterminated in Britain, but also less common species which were becoming excessively scarce through persecution, and rare species which had proved themselves ready to increase and multiply but were invariably killed off while attempting to do so.

Miss Gardiner undertook the task of completing and editing the unfinished manuscript because she had talked and corresponded at length with Hudson and knew his intentions about the book: "In putting [the unfinished manuscript] together I have transcribed every note with the greatest care, and every reference has been looked up and completed. Though the composition was obviously hurried and uncorrected I have left it as it stood rather than alter a word or the form of a sentence. Where it was too broken and incomplete to admit of this I have collated, interpreted, and interpolated, leaving untouched all that had been set down, and adding what I believed the writer would have wished added and meant to add, in order to complete the work as nearly as possible on the lines and in the words he intended."

A lecture with slides reproduced from the illustrations in this book was prepared by H. Vicars Webb for the Royal Society for the Protection of Birds.

A45b

FIRST AMERICAN ISSUE 1923

Same as first edition except issued in a grey wove dust jacket with Dutton's name printed in blue on front and spine.

Notes Published at $4.00. See note to A22c for information on publishing records.

Copies Texas.

A46a

153 LETTERS FROM W. H. HUDSON

FIRST, LIMITED, EDITION 1923)

[*enclosed within a frame formed by one thick rule and two thin rules printed in brown*] 153 LETTERS FROM / W. H. HUDSON / EDITED AND WITH AN / INTRODUCTION AND / EXPLANATORY NOTES / BY EDWARD GARNETT / PUBLISHED MCMXXII / AT THIRTY GERRARD / STREET SOHO W BY / THE NONESUCH PRESS / [*photograph of Hudson*]

Collation [A]² B–M⁸ N¹⁰ (—N 10); pp. [2] [i–ii] 1–10 [11–12] 13–191 [192–194]; 256 × 164 mm.; printed on wove paper.

Pagination [2], blank; p. [i], title; p. [ii], '*This edition, printed and made in England, is / limited to one thousand numbered copies, of which / this is number* [autograph number in black ink] / *The photograph of W. H. Hudson on the title page is by Opie, Redruth.*'; pp. 1–10, introduction by Edward Garnett dated November, 1923; p. [11], section-title, '*The Letters*'; p. [12], blank; pp. 13–191, text of letters;

p. [192], '*Pen sketch referred to in the letter of | July 29th, 1903, page 50.*'; p. [193], pen sketch; p. [194], blank.

Binding Brown buckram. White paper label on spine printed in brown '[*double rule*] | Letters | *from* | W. H. HUDSON | [*double rule*]'. All edges untrimmed; white wove endpapers. Extra label tipped to back free endpaper. Brown wove dust jacket printed in black and red.

Notes 1,000 copies published 26 November 1923 at 25s.

Seven of these letters appeared in the November 1923 issue of *Dial* (see c211).

Reviews Times Literary Supplement 13 December 1923.

A46b

FIRST AMERICAN EDITION 1923)

LETTERS FROM | W. H. HUDSON | *1901–1922* | EDITED AND WITH AN INTRODUCTION | BY | EDWARD GARNETT | [*orn: two deer beneath an oak tree*] | NEW YORK | E. P. DUTTON & COMPANY | 681 FIFTH AVENUE

Collation [1]^6 ($\pm$ 1$_1$; 1$_3$ + χ1); [2–19]^8; pp. [i–vi] [1–2] 3–295 [296]; 206 × 141 mm.; printed on wove paper.

Pagination p. [i], half-title 'LETTERS FROM | W. H. HUDSON'; p. [ii], blank; p. [iii], title; p. [iv], 'Copyright, 1923, / By E. P. DUTTON & COMPANY | [*short rule*] | *All Rights Reserved.* | This first American Edition | is limited to 950 copies, of | which 900 copies only are | for sale. | Printed in the United States of America'; p. [v], contents; p. [vi], blank; p. [1], fly-title, '[*rule*] | *Letters from W. H. Hudson* | [*rule*]'; p. [2], blank; pp. 3–15, introduction by Edward Garnett dated August 1923; p. 16, blank; pp. 17–295, text of letters; p. [296], blank.

Binding Red cloth. White circular medallion with profile portrait in centre of front cover, within a single blind rule border; white paper label on spine printed in green '[*double rule*] | LETTERS | FROM | W. H. HUDSON | *1901–1922* | [*type design*] | *Edited and with* | *an introduction* | BY | EDWARD | GARNETT | [*triple rule*]'. Top edges trimmed, others untrimmed; white wove endpapers. Grey wove dust jacket printed in black. Watermark: D within a double rule diamond above the word DUCHESS.

Notes 950 copies published 10 December 1923 at $7.00.

Reviews New York Times Book Review 13 January 1924; *Springfield Republican* 13 January 1924; *Nation* 16 January 1924; *Outlook* 16 January 1924.

A46c

FIRST ENGLISH TRADE EDITION 1925

[*within a double rule border*] LETTERS / FROM W·H·HUDSON / TO EDWARD GARNETT / PUBLISHED IN LONDON / AND TORONTO BY / J·M·DENT AND / SONS·LTD / [*design*] / MCMXXV

Collation π^8 1–13^8 14^6; pp. [*2*] [i–vii] viii–xiv [1] 2–12 [13] 14–218 [219–220]; 194 × 132 mm.; printed on wove paper.

Pagination [*2*] blank; p. [i], half-title 'LETTERS / FROM W·H·HUDSON'; p. [ii], blank; frontispiece; p. [iii], title; p. [iv], '*A Limited Edition of these Letters / was published in* 1923 / PRINTED IN GREAT BRITAIN'; p. [v], contents; p. [vi], blank; pp. [vii] viii–xiv, preface by Edward Garnett, dated 30 December 1924; pp. [1] 2–12, introduction by Edward Garnett, dated November 1923; pp. [13] 14–218, text of letters; p. [219], pen sketch by Hudson; p. [220], '*Cambridge: printed by W. Lewis at the University Press*'.

Binding Rose cloth. Profile portrait blind stamped in centre of front cover, within a single blind rule border; spine stamped in gilt 'LETTERS / FROM / W. H. / HUDSON / TO / EDWARD / GARNETT / [*design*] / J·M·DENT / &·SONS·L^D'. All edges trimmed, top edges stained green; white wove endpapers. Grey wove dust jacket printed in blue. Pencil sketch of Hudson on front dust jacket.

Variant Publisher's imprint at bottom of spine blind stamped and dust jacket printed in black.

Notes 2,650 copies published 13 February 1925 at 6s.

This edition contains the first appearance of Edward Garnett's preface and one additional letter dated 11 July 1918 that did not appear in the limited edition.

Variant copy Dobie.

OTHER EDITIONS

A46d 1923 London, Chaucer Head.
A46e n.d. New York, Salloch.

A47a

DEAD MAN'S PLACK AN OLD THORN & MISCELLANEA

FIRST EDITION; ALSO COLLECTED EDITION   1923

[*in red*] DEAD MAN'S PLACK / [*in red*] AN OLD THORN / & MISCELLANEA / BY / W. H. HUDSON / [*publisher's device*] / WITH AN APPRECIATION BY / VISCOUNT GREY OF FALLODON / MCMXXIII / LONDON & TORONTO / [*in red*] J. M. DENT & SONS LTD. / NEW YORK: E. P. DUTTON & CO.

Collation π⁸ A–2A⁸ 2B¹⁰; pp. [i–vi] vii–xiii [xiv] xv–xvi [1–2] 3–394 [395–396] 397–399 [400] 401–403 [404]; 220 × 148 mm.; printed on cream laid paper with oval watermark incorporating Hudson's name, a figure of a tree and two deer.

Pagination p. [i], blank; p. [ii], 'THIS EDITION IS LIMITED TO 750 COPIES / FOR SALE IN ENGLAND, 100 FOR SALE / IN THE UNITED STATES OF AMERICA, / AND 35 PRESENTATION COPIES'; p. [iii], half-title 'THE / COLLECTED WORKS / of / W. H. HUDSON / [*short rule*] / IN TWENTY-FOUR / VOLUMES / DEAD MAN'S PLACK / AN OLD THORN / & MISCELLANEA'; p. [iv], blank; frontispiece photograph of Hudson by Marie Leon; p. [v], title; p. [vi], '*All rights reserved* / PRINTED IN GREAT BRITAIN'; pp. vii–xiii, an appreciation of W. H. Hudson by Viscount Grey of Fallodon; p. [xiv], note regarding the error in the date of Hudson's birth as represented on the pictorial bookplate reproduced on the front pastedown of all volumes in the Collected edition; pp. xv–xvi, contents; facsimile of a letter written by Hudson to Edward Garnett 29 May 1920 referring to "Dead Man's Plack"; p. [1], section-title 'DEAD MAN'S PLACK'; p. [2], blank; pp. 3–394, text; p. [395], 'BIBLIOGRAPHICAL / SUMMARY'; p. [396], blank; pp. 397–399, 'PUBLISHERS AND DATES OF PUBLICATION OF / THE FIRST EDITIONS OF THE WORKS IN- / CLUDED IN THIS COLLECTED EDITION'; p. [400], blank; pp. 401–403, index; p. [404], 'PRINTED BY / THE TEMPLE PRESS AT LETCHWORTH / IN GREAT BRITAIN'.

Contents Dead Man's Plack (A39) – An Old Thorn (A39) – Osprey, or, Egrets and Aigrettes (A4) – Bird Catching (A10) – Lost British Birds (A11) – A Linnet for Sixpence! (A24) – On Liberating Caged Birds (A32) – A Thrush that Never Lived (A30) – Roff and a Linnet: Chain and Cage (A35) – Aves (C132) – The Common Crow (C68) – The Feather-Fashion: A Last Word (C99) – Our Wild Birds (C116) – Laughing at a Cat (C133) – Clover Seed (C151) – Little Fishes and Fascination (C187) – In Praise of Owls (C124) – Truth Plain and Coloured (C131) – Our Indian Birds (C140) – Animal Autobiographies (C143) – Preface to Waterton's essay *The Barn Owl* (A13) – Preface to *The Other Side of the Bars* (B4) –

Preface to *The Great Deserts and Forests of North America* (B1) – Unfinished Foreword to *Cloud Castle* (B6) – Feathered Women (A9) – Letter to Clergymen, Ministers, and others (A14) – The Trade in Birds' Feathers (A17) – Sea-Gulls in London (A42) – A Study of the Jaguar (B3) – My Experiences of the Puma (B3) – Do Cats Think? (Parts I and II) (C203) (C205) – Wanted, a Lullaby (C23) – Tom Rainger (C34).

Binding Green cloth. Gold medallion profile portrait in centre of front cover enclosed within a single rule border; spine stamped in gilt 'W. H. / HUDSON / [*leafy branch*] / Dead Man's / Plack / An Old / Thorn & / Miscellanea / J·M·DENT / & SONS. LD.'. Blind rule border on back cover. Top edges trimmed and gilt, other edges untrimmed; cream laid endpapers. On front pastedown is a reproduction of pictorial bookplate with Hudson's name and dates. Maroon silk place marker.

Notes This is one of twenty-four volumes of Hudson's collected works. Eight hundred and eighty-five sets were published 1922–1923 for twenty-four guineas per set. The one hundred sets for sale in America were sold by E. P. Dutton for $192 per set. The collected works was reprinted in America by AMS Press in 1968 at $360.

This is the first appearance of the appreciation of Hudson by Viscount Grey of Fallodon.

"Dead Man's Plack" and "An Old Thorn" first appeared in 1920 (A39). See Contents note above for first appearances of the various shorter pieces. See also A49, the Popular edition of *Dead Man's Plack an Old Thorn & Poems*.

A48a

A HUDSON ANTHOLOGY

FIRST EDITION 1924

A / [*in red*] HUDSON ANTHOLOGY / ARRANGED BY / EDWARD GARNETT / [*publisher's device*] / 1924 / LONDON & TORONTO / [*in red*] J. M. DENT & SONS LTD. / NEW YORK: E. P. DUTTON & CO.

Collation π^8 A–2A^8; pp. [2] [i–vi] vii–xiv [1–2] 3–380 [381–382] [2]; 194 × 129 mm.; printed on wove paper.

Pagination [2], blank; p. [i], half-title 'A HUDSON ANTHOLOGY'; p. [ii], blank; frontispiece; p. [iii], title; p. [iv], '*All rights reserved* / PRINTED IN GREAT BRITAIN'; p. [v], 'DEDICATED / TO ALL LOVERS / OF / W. H. HUDSON'S WRITINGS'; p. [vi], blank; pp. vii–x, preface by Edward Garnett dated August 1924; pp. xi–xiv, contents; p. [1], section-title, 'SOUTH AMERICAN NATURE BOOKS'; p. [2], blank; pp. 3–381, text; at bottom of p. [381], 'PRINTED BY THE TEMPLE PRESS AT LETCHWORTH IN GREAT BRITAIN'; p. [382], blank; [2], blank.

Contents Extracts from the following books: *Far Away and Long Ago* (A34) – *Birds of La Plata* (A38) – *The Naturalist in La Plata* (A5) – *Idle Days in Patagonia* (A7) – *Birds in Town and Village* (A36) – *Birds in London* (A16) – *Nature in Downland* (A19) – *Birds and Man* (A20) – *Hampshire Days* (A22) – *The Land's End* (A26) – *Afoot in England* (A27) – *A Shepherd's Life* (A29) – *Adventures Among Birds* (A31) – *The Book of a Naturalist* (A37) – *A Traveller in Little Things* (A40) – *A Hind in Richmond Park* (A43) – *The Purple Land* (A1) – *A Crystal Age* (A2) – *El Ombú* (A21) – *Green Mansions* (A23) – *A Little Boy Lost* (A25) – *An Old Thorn* (A39) – *Dead Man's Plack* (A39) – *A Linnet for Sixpence* (A24).

Binding Green cloth. Publisher's device stamped in gilt in centre of front cover, within a single blind rule border; spine stamped in gilt '[*within a single rule panel*] A / Hudson / Anthology / [*cross*] / Edited by / Edward / Garnett / [*bird on a leafy branch*] / [*at foot of spine*] J. M. DENT / & SONS, L^D'. All edges trimmed, top edges stained green; white wove endpapers. Front pastedown has a tree design within a double rule border, all printed in green. Grey wove dust jacket printed in black.

Notes 4,000 copies published 7 September 1924 at 7s. 6d. Reissued with a cancel title page in 1936.

Reviews Saturday Review 27 September 1924; *Spectator* 4 October 1924; *Times Literary Supplement* 30 November 1924.

A48b

FIRST AMERICAN ISSUE   1924

Title page, collation, pagination, and *contents* same as first edition.

Binding Green cloth. Front cover stamped in gilt '[*within a single rule panel in upper left corner*] A / Hudson / Anthology / [*cross*] / Edited by / Edward / Garnett / [*bird on a leafy branch*]'; spine stamped in gilt same as front cover with addition of 'E. P. DUTTON / & CO.' at foot of spine. All edges trimmed; white wove endpapers. Cream wove dust jacket printed in green.

Notes Issued at $3.00. See note to A22c for information on publishing records.

Reviews Springfield Republican 10 December 1924; *New York World* 4 January 1925.

A49a

DEAD MAN'S PLACK AN OLD THORN & POEMS

FIRST EDITION (ALSO FIRST POPULAR EDITION) 1924

[*within a single rule frame*] DEAD MAN'S PLACK / AN OLD THORN / & POEMS / [*publisher's device*] / BY / W. H. HUDSON / 1924 / J. M. DENT & SONS LTD. / LONDON & TORONTO / PARIS: J. M. DENT ET FILS

Collation π^4 A–M^8 N^6; pp. [2] [i–iv] v [vi] [1–2] 3–99 [100–102] 103–130 [131–132] 133–140 [141–142] 143–194 1¹–7 [8]; 202 × 132 mm.; printed on wove paper.

Pagination [2], blank; p. [i], half-title 'DEAD MAN'S PLACK / AN OLD THORN / AND / POEMS'; p. [ii], blank; frontispiece; p. [iii], title; p. [iv], '*All rights reserved* / [*notice of previous publication of this book*] / PRINTED IN GREAT BRITAIN'; p. v, contents; p. [vi], blank; p. [1], section-title 'DEAD MAN'S PLACK'; p. [2], blank; pp. 3–99, text; p. [100], blank; p. [101], section-title 'AN OLD THORN'; p. [102], blank; pp. 103–130, text; p. [131], section-title 'POSTSCRIPT / TO / DEAD MAN'S PLACK / & AN OLD THORN'; p. [132], blank; pp. 133–140, text; p. [141], section-title 'POEMS'; p. [142], blank; pp. 143–194, text; at bottom of p. 194 'PRINTED BY THE TEMPLE PRESS AT LETCHWORTH IN GREAT BRITAIN'; pp. 1¹–7 [8], publisher's advertisements for Hudson's works; [2], blank.

Contents Dead Man's Plack – An Old Thorn (first appeared in *English Review* May 1911 (C165)) – Postscript to Dead Man's Plack & An Old Thorn – The London Sparrow (first appeared in *Merry England* July 1883 (C29)) – In the Wilderness (first appeared in *Merry England* June 1884 (C32)) – Gwendoline (first appeared in *Merry England* June 1885 (C38)) – Tecla and the Little Men (first appeared in *Tales of the Pampas* (A33)) – The Old Man of Kensington Gardens.

Illustrations Two line etchings.

Binding Blue cloth. Front cover blind stamped with bird on a leafy branch within a single rule border; spine stamped in gilt 'W. H. HUDSON / [*wavy rule*] / DEAD MAN'S / PLACK / AN OLD / THORN / & POEMS / J·M·DENT / & SONS·L^D'. All edges trimmed, top edges stained blue; white wove endpapers.

Notes 2,500 copies published 3 November 1924 at 6s. Reissued in 1935.

Dead Man's Plack and An Old Thorn was first published in 1920 (A39) and collected together with Hudson's miscellaneous writings as *Dead Man's Plack An Old Thorn & Miscellanea* (A47). The poems were first collected in book form in the Collected edition of Hudson's works, 1922–1923 with the title *A Little Boy Lost Together with the Poems of W. H. Hudson* (A25e).

A50a

MEN, BOOKS AND BIRDS

FIRST EDITION, FIRST ISSUE (1925)

MEN, BOOKS AND / BIRDS / BY / W. H. HUDSON / WITH NOTES, SOME LETTERS, AND AN INTRODUCTION / BY / MORLEY ROBERTS / LONDON / EVELEIGH NASH & GRAYSON / LIMITED

Collation [A]⁸ B–Z⁸; pp. [1–4] 5–368; 214 × 136 mm.; printed on wove paper.

Pagination p. [1], half-title 'MEN, BOOKS AND BIRDS'; p. [2], advertisement for Roberts' biography of Hudson, published by Eveleigh Nash & Grayson uniform with this volume; p. [3], title; p. [4], '*First published in 1925 / Printed in Great Britain*'; pp. 5–13, introduction by Roberts; pp. 14–352, text of letters; pp. 353–368, index; at bottom of p. 368, '[*rule*] / PRINTED IN GREAT BRITAIN BY RICHARD CLAY & SONS, LIMITED, / BUNGAY, SUFFOLK.'

Binding Green cloth. Blind stamped border on front cover; spine stamped in gilt 'Men / Books / and / Birds / W.H. / Hudson / NASH & GRAYSON'. All edges trimmed; white wove endpapers. Blue wove dust jacket printed in black.

Variant Red cloth. Leaves measure 209 × 131 mm. Spine stamped in gilt 'MEN, BOOKS / AND BIRDS / W. H. HUDSON / NASH & / GRAYSON'. All edges trimmed; white wove endpapers.

Notes Published 8 June 1925 at 16s.

Reviews Canadian Forum October 1929.

Variant copy ISU.

A50b

FIRST EDITION, SECOND ISSUE (1932)

[*open letters*] MEN, BOOKS AND / [*open letters*] BIRDS / By / [*open letters*] W. H. HUDSON / With Notes, some Letters, and an Introduction by / [*open letters*]

MORLEY ROBERTS / [*publisher's device*] / [*open letters*] GRAYSON & GRAYSON / CURZON STREET MAYFAIR LONDON

Collation [A]⁸ (— A1 ± A2) B–Z⁸; pp. [3–4] 5–368; 219 × 137 mm.; printed on wove paper.

Pagination p. [3], title; p. [4], '*Published by Grayson & Grayson Ltd.* / *1925* / *Mayfair Miscellany: 1932* / *Printed in Great Britain*'; pp. 5–13, introduction by Roberts; pp. 14–352, text of letters; pp. 353–368, index; at bottom of p. 368, '[*rule*] / PRINTED IN GREAT BRITAIN BY RICHARD CLAY & SONS, LIMITED, / BUNGAY, SUFFOLK.'

Binding Blue cloth. Spine stamped in gilt, '[*rule*] / [*zig-zag design*] / [*open letters*] MEN, BOOKS / [*open letters*] AND / [*open letters*] BIRDS / [*diamond design*] / W. H. / HUDSON / GRAYSON / [*zig-zag design*] / [*rule*]'. All edges trimmed; white wove endpapers.

Notes Cancel title page with the Grayson & Grayson imprint.

Copies Dobie.

OTHER EDITIONS

A50c 1925   Toronto, Ryerson Press.
A50d 1928   Travellers' Library edition. London, Jonathan Cape.
A50e 1932   Mayfair Miscellany. London, Grayson.

A51a

THE DISAPPOINTED SQUIRREL

FIRST EDITION (1925)

THE DISAPPOINTED / SQUIRREL / *and Other Stories from* / "*The Book of a Naturalist*" / BY / W. H. HUDSON / [*illustration*] / *Illustrated by* / MARGUERITE KIRMSE / GEORGE H. DORAN COMPANY / On Murray Hill : : New York

Collation [1–9]⁸; pp. [1–12] 13–22 [23–24] 25–31 [32–34] 35–45 [46–48] 49–57 [58–60] 61–67 [68–70] 71–77 [78–80] 81–93 [94–96] 97–103 [104–106] 107–120 [121–122] 123–132 [133–134] 135–143 [144]; 229 × 154 mm.; printed on wove paper.

Pagination p. [1], half-title 'THE DISAPPOINTED / SQUIRREL *and Other Stories* /

[*drawing of a squirrel*]'; pp. [2-3], blank; p. [4], frontispiece; p. [5], title; p. [6], 'COPYRIGHT, 1919, 1925, / BY GEORGE H. DORAN COMPANY / REPRINTED FROM "THE BOOK OF A NATURALIST" BY PERMISSION / OF THE PUBLISHERS, E. P. DUTTON & COMPANY. / THE DISAPPOINTED SQUIRREL AND OTHER STORIES / – B – / PRINTED IN THE UNITED STATES OF AMERICA'; p. [7], contents and drawing of a bird; p. [8], blank; p. [9], list of illustrations and a drawing of a dog; p. [10], blank; p. [11], section-title 'ONE: Adventures with Foxes / [*drawing of a fox*]'; p. [12], blank; pp. 13-22, text; p. [23], section-title 'TWO: The Disappointed Squirrel / [*drawing of a squirrel*]'; p. [24], blank; pp. 25-31, text; p. [32], '[*drawing of a squirrel*]'; p. [33], section-title 'THREE: Jack Jackdaw and Some Other Birds / [*drawing of a bird*]'; p. [34], blank; pp. 35-45, text; p. [46], '[*drawing of a bird*]'; p. [47], section-title 'FOUR: The Man Who Ate a Heron / [*drawing of a heron*]'; p. [48], blank; pp. 49-57, text; p. [58], blank; p. [59], section-title 'FIVE: My Friend the Pig / [*drawing of a pig*]'; p. [60], blank; pp. 61-67, text; p. [68], '[*drawing of a pig*]'; p. [69], section-title 'SIX: Cristiano: A Horse / [*drawing of horses*]'; p. [70], blank; pp. 71-77, text; p. [78], blank; p. [79], section-title 'SEVEN: Mary's Little Lamb / [*drawing of a lamb*]'; p. [80], blank; pp. 81-93, text; p. [94], blank; p. [95], section-title 'EIGHT: A Friendly Rat / [*drawing of a rat*]'; p. [96], blank; pp. 97-103, text; p. [104], blank; p. [105], section-title 'NINE: The Potato at Home and in England / [*drawing of a potato*]'; p. [106], blank; pp. 107-120, text; p. [121], section-title 'TEN: The Little Red Dog / [*drawing of a dog*]'; p. [122], blank; pp. 123-132, text; p. [133], section-title 'ELEVEN: John-Go-to-Bed-at-Noon / [*drawing of grass*]'; p. [134], blank; pp. 135-143 [144], text.

Contents Adventures with Foxes – The Disappointed Squirrel – Jack Jackdaw and Some Other Birds – The Man Who Ate a Heron – My Friend the Pig – Cristiano: a Horse – Mary's Little Lamb – A Friendly Rat – The Potato at Home and in England – The Little Red Dog – John-Go-to-Bed-at-Noon.

Illustrations Twenty-six black and white drawings and eight full-page coloured reproductions of illustrations by Marguerite Kirmse, the Anglo-American etcher, illustrator and painter.

Binding Yellow cloth. Front cover stamped in green '[*within a panel formed by a decorative wavy border*] THE / DISAPPOINTED / SQUIRREL / W. H. HUDSON / [*coloured reproduction of illustration of a squirrel and a bird on tree limbs, within a decorative border*]; spine stamped in green '[*decorative rule*] / THE / DISAP- / POINTED / SQUIRREL / [*acorn design*] / W. H. / HUDSON / [*decorative rule*] / DORAN'. All edges trimmed; pictorial white wove endpapers printed in tan.

Notes Published 11 September 1925 at $2.50. See note to A37b for information on publishing records.

These stories are selected from *The Book of a Naturalist*. See A37 for notes on previous publications.

Reviews New York Times Book Review 8 November 1925.

Copies LC.

A52a

THREE WATER BIRDS

FIRST EDITION (1926)

'[*coloured illustration*] / THREE WATER BIRDS / [*text begins*]'.

Collation [1]⁴; pp. [1] 2–7 [8]; 224 × 142 mm.; printed on wove paper.

Pagination p. [1], illustration, title, and beginning of text; pp. 2–7, text; at bottom of p. 7, 'Leaflet No. 82 Published by the Royal Society for the Protection of / Birds, 82, Victoria Street, S. W. 1., of whom copies may be obtained / 3d. each; 2/6 per doz.'; p. [8], 'MILES, WARDOUR ST., W. –10,000. 16/9/26.'.

Illustration Coloured half-tone etching by Roland Green from T. A. Coward's *Birds and their Young*.

Binding Self wrappers, stapled. Front wrapper with coloured illustration, title and beginning of text printed in black as above.

Notes 10,000 copies published 16 September 1926 at 3d. each or 2s. 6d. per dozen.
    This first appeared as "Three Common River Birds" in *Hampshire Days* (A22).

A53a

A FAIRY FAUNA

FIRST SEPARATE EDITION 1927

A FAIRY FAUNA / BY W. H. HUDSON / THE NOTARY BINDERS / 5 CHURCH STREET / KENSINGTON / 1927

Collation [A–C]⁴; pp. [6] [i–ii] 1–7 [8–10] [6]; 192 × 150 mm.; printed on laid paper. Watermark: figure of hammer and anvil.

Pagination [6], blank endpapers, the first enclosed within wrapper; p. [i], title; p. [ii], blank; pp. 1–7 [8], text; p. [9], blank; p. [10] 'THANKS ARE DUE TO MESSRS. J. M. DENT AND SONS FOR / PERMISSION TO REPRINT THIS EXTRACT FROM "NATURE IN / DOWNLAND." / THIS EDITION IS LIMITED TO 50 COPIES, OF WHICH THIS IS NO. [*autograph number in black ink*] AND IS PRINTED AND BOUND BY THE NOTARY / BINDERS AT 5 CHURCH STREET, KENSINGTON.' [6], blank endpapers, the last enclosed within wrapper.

Binding Green marbled wrappers. Front cover printed in black 'A FAIRY FAUNA / BY W. H. HUDSON.' Top and bottom edges trimmed, fore edges untrimmed; white laid endpapers.

Notes 50 copies published.
   This first appeared in *Nature in Downland* (A19).

Copies Dartmouth.

A54a

MARY'S LITTLE LAMB

FIRST SEPARATE EDITION (1929)

[*complete title page in open letters*] MARY'S / LITTLE LAMB / BY / W. H. HUDSON / [*picture of a lamb*] / ILLUSTRATED BY / ROBERTA F. C. WAUDBY / LONDON & TORONTO: / J. M. DENT & SONS, LTD.

Collation a–b^8 (a$_4$ + b^8); pp. [1–8] 9–27 [28–30] [2]; 191 × 135 mm.; printed on wove paper.

Pagination pp. [1–4], blank; p. [5], half-title 'MARY'S LITTLE LAMB'; p. [6], frontispiece; p. [7], title; p. [8], 'FIRST PUBLISHED ... 1929 / *All rights reserved* / PRINTED IN GREAT BRITAIN'; pp. 9–27 [28], text; p. [29], ['*line of sheep, diminishing in size from right to left*] / [*open letters*] THE / END'; p. [30], '*Printed by Turnbull & Spears / at Edinburgh in Great Britain*'; [2] blank.

Illustrations Five full-page line etchings and three small line etchings by Roberta F. C. Waudby.

Binding Yellow wrappers printed in black. All edges tirmmed. On back cover is list of six Elian Greeting-Booklets designed and illustrated by Waudby. At bottom of back cover '*Printed in Great Britain at the Temple Press, Letchworth, Herts (Cj536)*'.

Variant Orange wrappers.

Notes 5,350 copies published 31 October 1929 at 1s.
 This first appeared in *The Book of a Naturalist* (A37).

Variant copy Texas.

A55a

BIRDS OF WING AND OTHER WILD THINGS

FIRST EDITION (1930

[*double spread title page, within a wide decorative floriated border*] [*on right*] BIRDS OF / WING / AND OTHER / WILD THINGS / SELECTIONS / FROM THE / WORKS / OF / W. H. HUDSON / [*between two wing designs*] by / H. F. B. FOX B.A. / [*across bottom of page*] J·M·DENT & SONS·LTD·LONDON & TORONTO [*on left*] [*figure of a bird on branch*] / THE STONECHAT / [*across bottom of page*] NEW YORK E·P·DUTTON AND COMPANY

Collation [A]¹⁶ B–H¹⁶; pp. [1–4] 5–256; 150 × 110 mm.; printed on wove paper.

Pagination p. [1], series title '*The* KING'S TREASURIES / OF LITERATURE / GENERAL EDITOR / SIR A · T · QUILLER COUCH'; pp. [2–3], title pages; p. [4], '*All rights reserved* / FIRST PUBLISHED .. 1930 / PRINTED IN GREAT BRITAIN'; pp. 5–6, introduction; pp. 7–8, contents; pp. 9–11, biographical note by Edward Garnett; pp. 12–14, biographical note by John Galsworthy; pp. 15–240, text; pp. 241–242, questions; pp. 243–256, appendices. At bottom of p. 256 'MADE AT THE / TEMPLE PRESS [*figure of a flower*] LETCHWORTH / IN GREAT BRITAIN'.

Contents Selections from *Far Away and Long Ago* (A34) – *Birds in London* (A16) – *Afoot in England* (A27) – *The Land's End* (A26) – *Nature in Downland* (A19) – *Hampshire Days* (A22) – *The Book of a Naturalist* (A37).

Binding Red cloth. Profile portrait stamped in blind in lower right corner of front cover, enclosed within a single blind rule border; spine stamped in gilt '[*reading from bottom to top, within a frame formed by leafy branches*] BIRDS OF WING [*leaf design*] Hudson'. 'J M DENT' is incorporated into the leafy design and '192' is stamped across bottom of spine. All edges trimmed; white wove endpapers. Front endpapers have a design printed in green.

Notes 10,000 copies published 21 March 1930 at 1s. 4d. Edward Garnett's biographical note is reprinted from his note on Hudson's spirit in the collected edition of *A Traveller in Little Things* (A40c). John Galsworthy's biographical note is reprinted from his foreword to the collected edition of *Far Away and Long Ago* (A34c).

Copies BM; Bodleian; RSPB.

A56a

SOUTH AMERICAN ROMANCES

FIRST EDITION (1930)

W. H. HUDSON'S / SOUTH AMERICAN ROMANCES / THE PURPLE LAND; GREEN MANSIONS; EL OMBÚ / DUCKWORTH / 3 HENRIETTA STREET / LONDON W.C.

Collation [A]¹⁶ B–BB¹⁶; pp. [i–viii] [1] 2–355 [356–358] 359–673 [674–676] 677–728 [729–730] 731–745 [746–748] 749–774 [775–776] 777–813 [814–816] 817–823 [824]; 198 × 129 mm.; printed on wove paper.

Pagination p. [i], half-title, 'W. H. HUDSON'S / SOUTH AMERICAN ROMANCES'; p. [ii], blank; p. [iii], title; p. [iv], '*First Published 1930* / *All rights reserved* / *Made and Printed in Great Britain by* / *The Camelot Press Limited,* / *London and Southampton*'; p. [v], contents; p. [vi], blank; p. [vii], section-title 'THE PURPLE LAND / Being the Narrative of one Richard Lamb's / Adventures in the Banda Oriental, in South / America, as told by Himself'; p. [viii], blank; pp. [1] 2–355, text; p. [356], blank; p. [357], section-title 'GREEN MANSIONS / *A Romance of The Tropical Forest*'; p. [358], blank; pp. 359–364, prologue; pp. 365–673, text; p. [674], blank; p. [675], section-title 'EL OMBÚ'; p. [676], dedication to R. B. Cunninghame Graham; pp. 677–728, text; p. [729], section-title 'STORY OF A PIEBALD HORSE'; p. [730], blank; pp. 731–745, text; p. [746], blank; p. [747], section-title 'NIÑO DIABLO'; p. [748], blank; pp. 749–774, text; p. [775], section-title 'MARTA RIQUELME'; p. [776], blank; pp. 777–813, text; p. [814], blank; p. [815], section-title 'APPENDIX TO EL OMBÚ'; p. [816], blank; pp. 817–823, text; p. [824], blank.

Contents The Purple Land – Green Mansions – El Ombú – Story of a Piebald Horse – Niño Diablo – Marta Riquelme – Appendix to El Ombú.

Binding Green cloth. Spine stamped in gilt 'SOUTH / AMERICAN / ROMANCES / W. H. HUDSON / DUCKWORTH'. All edges trimmed; white wove endpapers. Yellow wove dust jacket printed in red and blue.

Notes 10,500 copies published 1 April 1930 at 8s. 6d. Presentation copies in leather bindings at 12s. 6d. (no copy seen).

The Purple Land was first published in 1885 (A1). *Green Mansions* was first published in 1904 (A23). *El Ombú* was first published in 1902 (A21). See notes under main entries for publishing history.

OTHER EDITIONS

A56b 1931 Cheaper edition. London, Duckworth.
A56c 1966 New edition. London, Duckworth. With a new introduction by Ruth Tomalin.
A56d 1966 Leviathan Books edition. London, Duckworth.

A57a

W. H. HUDSON'S LETTERS TO R. B. CUNNINGHAME GRAHAM

FIRST EDITION   1941

W. H. HUDSON'S / LETTERS / TO / R. B. CUNNINGHAME GRAHAM / With a few to / Cunninghame Graham's Mother / Mrs Bontine / Edited, with an Introduction, by / RICHARD CURLE / Drawings of Hudson and / Cunninghame Graham by / Sir William Rothenstein / The Golden Cockerel Press / 1941

Collation A–H^8; pp. [1–6] 7–13 [14] 15 [16] 17–113 [114] 115–128; 190 × 128 mm.; printed on laid paper.

Pagination p. [1], blank; p. [2], frontispiece; p. [3], title; p. [4], 'Printed in Great Britain'; p. [5], 'INTRODUCTION'; p. [6], blank; pp. 7–13, text of introduction by Richard Curle; p. [14], blank; p. 15 'THE LETTERS'; p. [16], drawing of Cunninghame Graham; pp. 17–112, text of letters; p. 113, 'NOTES'; p. [114], blank; pp. 115–127, text of notes; p. 128, 'Printed by Christopher Sandford & Owen Rutter at / The Golden Cockerel Press, Rolls Passage, London, / E. C. 4, and completed on the 5th day of November, / 1941, the Edition is limited to 250 numbered copies, / printed in 13 point Perpetua type on Arnold's mould / made paper. Copy number: [*autograph number in blue ink*]'.

Illustrations Frontispiece caricature of W. H. Hudson and one drawing of Cunninghame Graham by Will Rothenstein, painter and principal of the Royal College of Art. His work covering the years 1889 to 1925, recording over 750 drawings and 135 lithographs, is considered one of the greatest series of contemporary portraits. Hudson was one of his favourite and most frequently drawn subjects. A portrait of Hudson by Rothenstein is in the National Portrait Gallery, London.

Binding Half red morocco and yellow cloth; spine stamped in gilt 'HUDSON'S / LETTERS / [*Golden Cockerel rooster*]'. Top edges gilt, others untrimmed; white laid endpapers.

Notes 250 copies published 5 November 1941 at 30s.
A proof copy is in the Dartmouth College Library.

A58a

TALES OF THE GAUCHOS

FIRST EDITION 1946

Tales of the Gauchos | Stories by W. H. HUDSON *| Compiled and Edited by |* ELIZABETH COATSWORTH *| Illustrated by Henry C. Pitz | [publisher's device] | New York:* ALFRED A. KNOPF 1946

Collation [1-8]^{16} [9]^4; pp. [i-vii] viii [ix-x] [1] 2-251 [252-254]; 229 × 155 mm.; printed on wove paper.

Pagination p. [i], blank; p. [ii], list of '*Other Borzoi Books for Young People*' [4 titles]; p. [iii], half-title, '*Tales of the Gauchos*'; p. [iv], blank; p. [v], title; p. [vi], 'Copyright 1946 by Alfred A. Knopf, Inc. All rights reserved. No part of this / book may be reproduced in any form without permission in writing from / the publisher, except by a reviewer who may quote brief passages or repro- / duce not more than three illustrations in a review to be printed in a magazine / or newspaper. Manufactured in the United States of America. Published / simultaneously in Canada by The Ryerson Press. / FIRST EDITION'; pp. [vii]-viii, contents; p. [ix] fly-title, '*Tales of the Gauchos*'; p. [x], blank; pp. [1] 2-5, foreword by Elizabeth Coatsworth; pp. 6-251, text; p. [252], blank; p. [253], acknowledgments; p. [254], note on the type in which this book was set; last 2 lines read, 'This book was composed and printed by The Plimpton Press, / Norwood, Mass., and bound by H. Wolff.'

Contents Niño Diablo (reprinted from *Tales of the Pampas* (A33)) – The House – A First Walk – Serpent and Child – As to Food (reprinted from *Far Away and Long Ago* (A34)) – Something More (reprinted from *Idle Days in Patagonia* (A7)) – Memory of the Pampa Grass (reprinted from *The Naturalist in La Plata* (A5)) – The Friend of Man – The Guardian Puma – Fear in the Shell – The

Chakar (reprinted from *The Naturalist in La Plata* (A5)) – The Purple Land (reprinted from *The Purple Land* (A1)) – Queen of the Pigs (reprinted from *Idle Days in Patagonia* (A7)) – Cristiano: A Horse – Mary's Little Lamb (reprinted from *The Book of a Naturalist* (A37)) – Don Gregorio Gandara – Fight in the Dark (reprinted from *Far Away and Long Ago* (A34)) – The Old Man of the Sea (reprinted from *A Little Boy Lost* (A25)) – The Voice in the Darkness (reprinted from *Green Mansions* (A23)) – A Troop of Wild Horses (reprinted from *A Little Boy Lost* (A25)) – Manual, Also Called the Fox (reprinted from *The Purple Land* (A1)) – The Serpent With the Cross – The Plains of Patagonia (reprinted from *Idle Days in Patagonia* (A7)) – The Grand Archaic Ostrich – The Dragonfly – About Spiders (reprinted from *The Naturalist in La Plata* (A5)) – Liberty and Dirt (reprinted from *The Purple Land* (A1)) – Story of a Piebald Horse (reprinted from *Tales of the Pampas* (A33)).

Illustrations Line etchings throughout the text and six colour half-tone etchings by Henry C. Pitz, the American etcher, lithographer and illustrator.

Binding Green cloth. Illustration of a snake and a bird surrounded by foliage blind stamped in centre of front cover; spine stamped in gilt '[*from top to bottom*] Tales of the Gauchos W. H. HUDSON Knopf'. All edges trimmed, top edges stained brown; coloured illustrated wove endpapers. Coloured illustrated wove dust jacket.

Notes 6,000 copies published 14 March 1946 at $3.00.

Reviews Bulletin from *Virginia Kirkus' Bookshop Service* 15 January 1946; *Saturday Review of Literature* 9 March 1946; *ALA Booklist* 15 March 1946; *Library Journal* 15 March 1946; *Weekly Book Review* 17 March 1946; *New York Times Book Review* 7 April 1946; *Chicago Book Week* 26 May 1946; *Hornbook* May 1946.

OTHER EDITIONS

A58b 1954 Borzoi Books for Young People edition. New York, Knopf.

A59a

FOREWORD

FIRST EDITION 1947

FOREWORD / BY / W. H. HUDSON / [*figure of a hat*] / TEMPE / EDWIN B. HILL / 1947

Collation π²; pp. [1–4]; 180 × 126 mm.; printed on laid paper.

Contents p. [1], wrapper title; pp. [2–3], text; p. [4], 'Messrs. Duckworth & Co., London, England, have kindly permitted the re-publication of the 'Foreword' to Edward Thomas's / 'Cloud Castle,' the last, though uncompleted, paper by Henry [*sic*] H. / Hudson. Forty copies have been printed by Edwin B. Hill on his / private press at 27 East Sixth Street, Tempe, Arizona.

Binding Self wrappers, folded.

Notes 40 copies printed in Tempe Arizona.
    See B6 for first appearance.

Copies Dartmouth; Houghton.

A60a

THE BEST OF W. H. HUDSON

FIRST EDITION   1949

The Best of / w. h. hudson / Edited by / Odell Shepard / [*publisher's device*] / New York · 1949 / E. P. Dutton and Company, Inc.

Collation [1–10]¹⁶; pp. [1–4] 5–15 [16–18] 19–317 [318] [2]; 212 × 142 mm.; printed on wove paper.

Pagination p. [1], half-title, '*The Best of* / w. h. hudson'; p. [2], blank; p. [3], title; p. [4], '*Copyright, 1949, by E. P. Dutton & Co., Inc. / All rights reserved. Printed in the U.S.A. /* FIRST EDITION */ No part of this book may be reproduced / in any form without permission in writing / from the publisher, except by a reviewer / who wishes to quote brief passages in con- / nection with a review written for inclusion in / magazine or newspaper or radio broadcast.*'; pp. 5–12, introduction by Odell Shepard; pp. 13–15, contents; p. [16], blank; p. [17], fly-title, '*The Best of* / w. h. hudson'; p. [18], blank; pp. 19–317, text; p. [318], blank; [2], blank.

Contents Publisher's note: "It will be noticed by readers familiar with W. H. Hudson's works that some of the extracts here presented have title-headings which are not to be found in Mr. Hudson's text.
    These headings have been added by the Editor of the volume as guide marks for the readers."
Extracts from *The Purple Land* (A1) – *Idle Days in Patagonia* (A7) – *Nature in Downland* (A19) – *Birds and Man* (A20) – *Hampshire Days* (A22) – *The Land's End*

(A26) – *Afoot in England* (A27) – *A Shepherd's Life* (A29) – *An Old Thorn* (A39) – *Far Away and Long Ago* (A34) – *The Book of a Naturalist* (A37) – *Birds in Town and Village* (A36) – *A Traveller in Little Things* (A40) – *A Hind in Richmond Park* (A43).

Binding Green cloth. Publisher's triangular device blind stamped in lower right corner of front cover; spine stamped in gilt, '[*triple rule*] / [*Green letters, in relief, on a gold panel*] THE / BEST OF / W. H. / HUDSON / *Edited by* / ODELL / SHEPARD / [*below panel*] DUTTON / [*square design*]'. All edges trimmed; white wove endpapers. Rose wove dust jacket printed in white.

Notes Published 11 October 1949 at $4.00. See note to A22c for information on publishing records.

Reviews Bulletin from Virginia Kirkus' Bookshop Service 1 September 1949; *New York Times Book Review* 30 October 1949; *Springfield Republican* 20 November 1949; *San Francisco Chronicle* 2 December 1949; *New Yorker* 10 December 1949; *Chicago Sunday Tribune* 25 December 1949; *New York Herald Tribune Book Review* 15 January 1950.

A61a

LETTERS ON THE ORNITHOLOGY OF BUENOS AYRES

FIRST EDITION, AMERICAN ISSUE (1951)

LETTERS ON / *The Ornithology* / *of Buenos Ayres* / BY W. H. HUDSON / [*wavy rule*] / *Edited by* DAVID R. DEWAR, *with* / *a Foreword by* HERBERT F. WEST / PUBLISHED BY PERMISSION OF THE / ZOOLOGICAL SOCIETY OF LONDON / *Cornell University Press* / ITHACA, NEW YORK

Collation [1–7]⁸; pp. [i–vi] vii–xv [xvi–xviii] 1–85 [86] 87–93 [94]; 218 × 140 mm.; printed on wove paper; watermark 'WARREN'S OLDE STYLE'.

Pagination p. [i], half-title '*Letters on the Ornithology of Buenos Ayres*'; p. [ii], blank; p. [iii], title; p. [iv], '*Copyright 1951 by Cornell University* / *Cornell University Press* / *London: Geoffrey Cumberlege* / *Oxford University Press* / PRINTED IN THE UNITED STATES OF AMERICA BY THE / VAIL-BALLOU PRESS, INC., BINGHAMTON, NEW YORK'; p. [v], dedication; p. [vi], blank; pp. vii–viii, foreword by Herbert Faulkner West dated 1950; pp. ix–xv, introduction by David R. Dewar dated October 1950; p. [xvi], blank; p. [xvii], contents; p. [xviii], blank; pp. 1–85, text; p. [86], blank; pp. 87–90, postscript; pp. 91–93, index; p. [94], blank.

Binding Blue cloth. Design blind stamped in lower right corner of front cover; spine stamped in gilt '[*reading from top to bottom*] W. H. HUDSON 〉〉 LETTERS ON THE / ORNITHOLOGY OF BUENOS AYRES [*across bottom of spine*] Cornell'. All edges trimmed; white wove endpapers. Glassine dust jacket and publisher's grey paper-board box with white label printed in blue.

Variant Cancel title page.

Notes 784 copies published 5 April 1951 at $2.75.

These letters were written in the Argentine Republic in 1869 and 1870. Twelve were published in the *Proceedings of the Zoological Society of London* between 1870 and 1871 as "Letters on the Ornithology of Buenos Ayres." (C5–C16) and first collected in *Argentine Ornithology* (A3). The corrected text of seven letters is here printed from the originals in the library of the Zoological Society of London. The text of the other five is reprinted from the *Proceedings of the Zoological Society of London*. These letters were never reprinted during Hudson's life. Two letters to Philip L. Sclater are included here that were not previously published.

Reviews Chicago Sunday Tribune 17 June 1951; *New York Times Book Review* 22 July 1951.

Variant copy Texas.

A61b

FIRST EDITION, ENGLISH ISSUE (1951)

An undetermined number of copies of the first edition were forwarded to Oxford University Press for distribution in England. A question was raised about who controlled the copyright of this volume in England, with the resolution that permission for publication should be in the name of the Royal Society for the Protection of Birds and not the Zoological Society of London. A permissions slip was printed and pasted over the permissions notice on the title page. The new permissions slip reads: 'PUBLISHED BY PERMISSION OF THE / ROYAL SOCIETY FOR THE PROTECTION OF BIRDS'.

In a letter dated 27 May 1973 David R. Dewar wrote: "The note on the title page, so far as I am aware, appeared originally on all the copies whether intended for sale in the United States or in Great Britain. When the British batch was about to be released a question arose about the precise copyright position of the letters and when they were distributed another note was pasted over the original reference to the Zoological Society and reads 'published by permission of the Royal Society for the Protection of Birds.' . . . I cannot give particulars of how this alteration was decided upon as I received no letters about it from the parties concerned. I do not know how many sheets were sent from Cornell to the Oxford Press – or indeed if sheets were sent. There is – apart from the substitute note – absolutely no distinction between the copies I have seen. They are identical as if some copies had been simply 'exported' from Cornell."

Notes Issued August 1951 at 22s.

Reviews Times Literary Supplement 16 November 1951.

Copies No copy seen. Information from David R. Dewar.

A62a

TWO LETTERS ON AN ALBATROSS

FIRST EDITION (1955)

[*fancy*] Two / [*fancy*] Letters / [*fancy*] On An] [*fancy*] Albatross / by William Henry Hudson / and Robert Bontine Cunninghame Graham / *Edited with an Introduction by* / *Herbert Faulkner West* / WESTHOLM PUBLICATIONS / Hanover, New Hampshire

Collation [1–3]^4; pp. [1–20] [4]; 217 × 140 mm.; printed on laid paper; watermark: '*Hamilton Kilmory*'.

Pagination p. [1], half-title 'TWO LETTERS ON AN ALBATROSS'; p. [2], blank; p. [3], title; p. [4], 'Copyright 1955 by Herbert Faulkner West'; p. [5], dedication to Angus, Olave, and Patricia; p. [6], blank; pp. [7–11], introduction by Herbert Faulkner West dated August 1955; p. [12], blank; pp. [13–18], text; p. [19], blank; p. [20], '*Two hundred copies, of which this is* / *No.* [autograph number in black ink] / *Printed by offset lithography from Fotosetter Bodoni Book* / *at Sequoia Press, Kalamazoo, Michigan.* / *Design by William Stone*'; [4] blank.

Binding Yellow, red, blue, and white patterned boards; black cloth spine; spine stamped in gilt '[*reading from top to bottom*] TWO LETTERS ON AN ALBATROSS [*circular design*] Westholm'. All edges trimmed; white laid endpapers.

Notes 200 copies published 1 December 1955 at $5.00.

These two letters were written in response to an article about cruelty to birds that appeared in *Nature: A Weekly Illustrated Journal of Science* (25 October 1900). Hudson's letter first appeared in the *Saturday Review*, 24 November 1900 (C100) and Graham's first appeared in the *Saturday Review*, 1 December 1900.

A63a

WILLIAM HENRY HUDSON'S DIARY

FIRST EDITION 1958

WILLIAM HENRY HUDSON'S / DIARY CONCERNING HIS VOYAGE / FROM BUENOS AIRES TO SOUTHAMPTON / ON THE *EBRO* / FROM I APRIL 1874 TO 3 MAY 1874 / WRITTEN TO HIS BROTHER / ALBERT MERRIAM HUDSON / WITH NOTES BY / DOCTOR JORGE CASARES / OF BUENOS AIRES / MCMLVIII / WESTHOLM PUBLICATIONS / HANOVER · NEW HAMPSHIRE

Collation [1]⁸ [2]⁴ [3]⁸; pp. [i–vi] vii–ix [x–xii] 13–34 [35–40] [*2*]; 184 × 114 mm.; printed on laid paper: Watermark 'AMALFI'.

Pagination p. [i], half-title 'WILLIAM HENRY HUDSON'S / DIARY CONCERNING HIS / VOYAGE ON THE *EBRO*'; p. [ii], blank; p. [iii], verso of frontispiece, blank; p. [iv], frontispiece, previously unpublished photograph of Hudson; p. [v], title; p. [vi], 'Copyright, 1958, by / Hubert Rockwood Hudson'; pp. vii–ix, foreword by Herbert Faulkner West dated June 1958; p. [x], blank; p. [xi], fly-title 'WILLIAM HENRY HUDSON'S / DIARY CONCERNING HIS / VOYAGE ON THE *EBRO*'; p. [xii], blank; pp. 13–34, text; pp. [35–36], blank; p. [37], list of eight books by Westholm Publications; p. [38], blank; p. [39], '[*woodcut of ship at sea with initials WHH*] / 250 copies / of this book have been printed / on handmade Amalfi paper / by The Stinehour Press / Lunenburg, Vermont / 1958;' p. [40], blank; [*2*], blank.

Binding Orange cloth. Front cover stamped in gilt [*within a gilt stamped compartment formed by crescent shaped tool*] 'WILLIAM HENRY HUDSON'S / DIARY CONCERNING HIS / VOYAGE ON THE *EBRO*'; spine stamped in gilt '[*reading from top to bottom*] [*crescent shaped tool*] WILLIAM HENRY HUDSON'S DIARY [*crescent shaped tool*]'. Top edges trimmed; others untrimmed; off-white laid endpapers. Glassine dust jacket.

Notes 250 copies published 10 October 1958 at $5.00.

A64a

GAUCHOS OF THE PAMPAS AND THEIR HORSES

FIRST EDITION 1963

[*in red*] GAUCHOS OF THE PAMPAS / [*in red*] AND THEIR HORSES / BY W. H.

HUDSON AND / R. B. CUNNINGHAME GRAHAM / FOREWORD BY J. FRANK DOBIE / [*illustration, in grey*] WESTHOLM PUBLICATIONS / HANOVER / N. H. / 1963

Collation [1–7]⁶ 8⁴; pp. [1–11] 12–28 [29–31] 32–47 [48] 49–52 [53] 54–65 [66] 67–86 [87–88] [4]; 223 × 151 mm.; printed on wove paper with watermarks 'BIBLIOPHILE SOCIETY' and 'MADE IN HOLLAND'.

Pagination pp. [1–2], blank; p. [3], half-title 'GAUCHOS OF THE PAMPAS / AND THEIR HORSES'; p. [4], blank; p. [5], title; p. [6], blank; p. [7], acknowledgments; p. [8], blank; p. [9], contents; p. [10], blank; pp. [11] 12–28, foreword by J. Frank Dobie; p. [29], fly-title '[*illustration, in grey*] / [*in red*] GAUCHOS OF THE PAMPAS / [*in red*] AND THEIR HORSES'; p. [30], blank; pp. [31] 32–47, Story of a Piebald Horse; pp. [48] 49–52, 'CRISTIANO: A HORSE'; pp. [53] 54–65, The Horse of the Pampas; pp. [66] 67–86, San José; p. [87], 'COLOPHON [*printer's flower*] This book has been designed by Caroll Cole- / man and printed at The Prairie Press in Iowa City. The body / type is Garamond, with American Uncial for the display. Both / are hand-set. The book has been printed on a mould-made rag / paper imported from Holland. The edition is limited to four hun- / dred copies. Completed in September, nineteen hundred sixty-three.'; p. [88], blank; [4], blank.

Contents Hudson's contributions include 'Story of a Piebald Horse' (text from *Tales of the Pampas* (A33)) and 'Cristiano: the Sentinel Horse' (text from *The Book of a Naturalist* (A37)). Graham's contributions include 'The Horse of the Pampas' (text from *Father Archangel of Scotland*) and 'San José' (text from *Progress*).

Binding Light grey patterned boards, green cloth spine; spine stamped in gilt '[*reading from top to bottom*] GAUCHOS OF THE PAMPAS AND THEIR HORSES'. Top edges trimmed, others untrimmed; brown wove endpapers. Tan wove dust jacket printed in brown.

Notes 400 copies published September 1963 at $5.00.

A65a

BIRDS AND GREEN PLACES

FIRST EDITION (1964)

Birds And Green Places / A selection from the writings of / W. H. Hudson / [*illustration of two birds*]

Collation [A–G]⁸ [H]² [I]⁸; pp. [1–5] 6–9 [10] 11–63 [64] 65 [66] 67–78 [79–80] 81 [82] 83–93 [94] 95 [96] 97–105 [106] 107 [108] 109–115 [116] 117–130 [131–132]; 210 × 141 mm.; printed on wove paper.

Pagination p. [1], half-title '*Birds And Green Places*'; p. [2], '© THE ROYAL SOCIETY FOR THE / PROTECTION OF BIRDS. / Printed by De Volharding, Amsterdam, / the Netherlands, and published by / THE ROYAL SOCIETY FOR THE PROTECTION OF BIRDS / The Lodge, Sandy, Bedfordshire. 1964.'; p. [3], title; p. [4], 'Illustrations by Robert Gillmor'; p. [5], contents; p. 6, selectors' note by P. E. Brown and P. H. T. Hartley and illustration of Hudson memorial in Hyde Park; pp. 7–9, introduction by P. H. T. Hartley; p. [10], illustration; pp. 11–12, contents of part 1, "Birds in Green Places"; pp. 13–63, text of part 1; p. [64], illustration; p. 65, contents of part 2, "Bird Song"; p. [66], illustration; pp. 67–78 [79], text of part 2; p. [80], illustration; p. 81, contents of part 3, "Some Other Animals"; p. [82], illustration; pp. 83–93, text of part 3; p. [94], illustration; p. 95, contents of part 4, "Small Fry"; p. [96] illustration; pp. 97–105, text of part 4; pp. [106], illustration; p. 107, contents of part 5, "Wild Flowers"; p. [108], illustration; pp. 109–115, text of part 5; p. [116], illustration; p. 117, contents of part 6 "Green Places"; pp. 118–130, text of part 6; p. [131], illustration; p. [132], blank.

Contents Selections of Hudson's writings from the following books: *Birds in a Village* (A8) – *British Birds* (A12) – *Birds in London* (A16) – *Nature in Downland* (A19) – *Birds and Man* (A20) – *Hampshire Days* (A22) – *The Land's End* (A26) – *Afoot in England* (A27) – *A Shepherd's Life* (A29) – *Adventures Among Birds* (A31) – *The Book of a Naturalist* (A37) – *A Traveller in Little Things* (A40) – *A Hind in Richmond Park* (A43).

Illustrations Fifteen black and white drawings by Robert Gillmor.

Binding Smooth white paper boards with green cloth spine. Front cover printed in black 'BIRDS / AND / GREEN / PLACES / [*illustration of bird at right*] / [*illustration of 4 birds in a line*] / [*illustration of a bird*] / [*at right*] A SELECTION / FROM THE / WRITINGS / OF / W. H. HUDSON'; spine stamped in gilt from top to bottom 'BIRDS AND GREEN PLACES'. All edges trimmed; white wove endpapers.

B

Contributions to Books

B1a

THE GREAT DESERTS AND FORESTS OF NORTH AMERICA

FIRST EDITION 1901

THE GREAT / DESERTS AND FORESTS / OF NORTH AMERICA / BY / PAUL FOUNTAIN / WITH A PREFACE BY W. H. HUDSON, F.Z.S. / Author of "The Naturalist in La Plata," etc. / LONGMANS, GREEN, AND CO. / 39 PATER-NOSTER ROW, LONDON / NEW YORK AND BOMBAY / 1901

Collation ✱^{4} b^2 A–S^8 T^4; pp. [2] [i–iv] v–vii [viii] ix [x] [1] 2–295 [296]; 222 × 143 mm.; printed on wove paper.

Binding Rose cloth. Front cover stamped in gilt 'THE GREAT DESERTS / AND FORESTS OF / NORTH AMERICA / [at lower right corner] PAUL FOUNTAIN'; spine stamped in gilt '[three leafy flowers stemming from a horizontal rule] / THE GREAT / DESERTS / AND / FORESTS / OF / NORTH / AMERICA / [horizontal rule] / [branch design with tops touching rule] / PAUL / FOUNTAIN / LONGMANS'. Top edges trimmed and stained green, others untrimmed; white wove endpapers; three free endpapers front and back.

Contains Preface, pp. v–vii.

Notes This was collected in *Dead Man's Plack An Old Thorn & Miscellanea* (A47).

B2a

THE BOOK OF THE OPEN AIR

FIRST EDITION 1907

THE BOOK OF THE / OPEN AIR / EDITED BY / EDWARD THOMAS / Author of 'Horae Solitariae,' 'Oxford,' 'Beautiful Wales,' / 'The Heart of England,' and Editor of 'The / Pocket Book of Poems and Songs / for the Open Air.' / HODDER AND STOUGHTON / LONDON MCMVII

Collation Twelve parts as follows: parts 1–6 signed a^4 [b]^4 1–2^8 3^4 a^4 4–5^8 6^4 a^4 7–8^8 9^4 a^4 10–11^8 12^4 a^4 13–14^8 15^4 a^4 16–17^8 18^4; parts 7–12 signed a^4 1–2^8 3^4 a^4 4–5^8 6^4 a^2 7–8^8 9^4 a^2 10–11^8 12^4 a^2 13–14^8 15^4 a^2 16–17^8 18^4; pagination (not including preliminaries in each part) parts 1–6: [i–iv] v–vii [viii] [1–2] 3–240; parts 7–12: 1–240; 295 × 209 mm.; printed on wove paper.

Illustrations Fifty coloured illustrations tipped in.

Binding Green paper wrappers printed in blue. Coloured illustration pasted to front cover of each part.

Contains A four-line quote from Hints to Adder-seekers, part 1 p. v (collected in *The Book of a Naturalist* (A37)) – Blue Columbine and Chequered Daffodil, part 3 pp. 110–115 (first appeared in *Speaker* 21 November 1903 (C112) and collected in *The Book of a Naturalist* (A37)) – The Little Red Dog, part 6 pp. 212–216 (first appeared in *Speaker* 24 December for 26 December 1903 (C113) and collected in *The Book of a Naturalist* (A37)).

Notes The twelve parts were bound into two volumes and published by Hodder & Stoughton in 1907 as *British Country Life in Spring & Summer* (parts 1–6) and *British Country Life in Autumn & Winter* (parts 7–12).

B3a

HARMSWORTH NATURAL HISTORY

FIRST EDITION 1910–1911

[*within a wide grey border with figures of animals' heads in colour at each corner*] / [*in green*] HARMSWORTH / [*in green*] NATURAL HISTORY / A COMPLETE SURVEY OF THE ANIMAL KINGDOM / WITH THOUSANDS OF PHOTOGRAPHS FROM LIFE, / AND AN UNRIVALLED SERIES OF COLOUR PLATES / [*printer's device*] / CHIEF CONTRIBUTORS / RICHARD LYDEKKER, F.R.S. / SIR HARRY JOHNSTON / PROFESSOR J. R. AINSWORTH-DAVIS, M. A. / [*figure of elephant's head in colour*] / FIRST VOLUME / [*printer's device*] / PUBLISHED AT / CARMELITE HOUSE, LONDON, E.C. / 1910

Collation Three volumes composed of thirty-nine parts as follows: volume 1, parts 1–13, pp. 1–676; volume 2, parts 14–26, pp. 677–1350; volume 3, parts 27–39, pp. 1351–2018; 263 × 194 mm.; printed on wove paper.

Illustrations 'The colour plates, about 150 in number, are unique among animal pictures, and the hundreds of black and white drawings by the same famous artist, William Kuhnert, in addition to the photographs from real life – some of them reproduced by direct colour photography, so that we thus have Nature in her own colours – enrich the book with an unrivalled series of illustrations.' [*from the introductory note in Volume 1*].

Binding (1) Three-fourths Persian leather dyed brown; spine stamped in gilt '[double rule] / HARMSWORTH / NATURAL / HISTORY / [double rule] / [six vertical rules] / [double rule] / [volume and inclusive page numbers]'. (2) Green cloth. Front cover stamped in gilt '[within a single rule border] HARMSWORTH / NATURAL HISTORY / [lion's head]; spine stamped in gilt 'HARMSWORTH / NATURAL / HISTORY / [lion's head] / [volume and inclusive page numbers]'.

Bindings provided by the publisher at 3s. 6d. for the leather and 1s. 6d. for the cloth.

Contains Volume 1, "A Study of the Jaguar", pp. 389–391 and "My Experiences of the Puma", pp. 394–397.

Notes Volumes 2 and 3 do not contain contributions by Hudson. The thirty-nine parts were intended to be bound into three volumes and title pages and table of contents were provided by the publisher; volumes 1 and 2 are dated 1910; volume 3 is dated 1911.

"A Study of the Jaguar" was collected in *Dead Man's Plack An Old Thorn & Miscellanea* (A47). "My Experiences of the Puma" first appeared in *Longman's Magazine* September 1886 (C44), was collected in *The Naturalist in La Plata* (A5) and again in *Dead Man's Plack An Old Thorn & Miscellanea* (A47).

B4a

THE OTHER SIDE OF THE BARS

FIRST EDITION 1911

The Other / Side of the Bars / The Case of the Caged Bird / BY / ERNEST BELL / WITH A PREFACE BY / W. H. HUDSON / HUMANITARIAN LEAGUE / 53, CHANCERY LANE, LONDON / 1911

Collation [A]¹²; pp. [1–5] 6–7 [8–9] 10–24; 211 × 137 mm.; printed on wove paper.

Illustrations Fifteen pen and ink drawings by Alf Priest throughout text.

Binding Brown wove paper wrappers, stapled. Front cover printed in black '[within a single wide rule frame] [fancy] The Other Side / [fancy] of the Bars / The Case of the Caged Bird / [within a wide single rule frame] [coloured country scene with birds in flight; inset picture of caged bird in lower left corner]'.

Contains Preface, pp. 5–7.

Notes This was collected in *Dead Man's Plack An Old Thorn & Miscellanea* (A47).

B5a

MOLLY AND MARGARET

FIRST EDITION   1912

MOLLY / AND MARGARET / BY / PAT / WITH INTRODUCTION BY W. H. HUDSON / COLOURED FRONTISPIECE / AND 8 ILLUSTRATIONS BY / T. BAINES, JNR. / LONGMANS, GREEN AND CO. / 39 PATERNOSTER ROW, LONDON / NEW YORK, BOMBAY, AND CALCUTTA / 1912 / All rights reserved

Collation π^8 A–J^8 K^6; pp. [i–iv] v–xiii [xiv] xv [xvi] [1] 2–155 [156]; 185 × 126 mm.; printed on wove paper.

Illustrations Coloured frontispiece and eight black and white drawings, tipped in on calendered paper, by T. Baines, Jr.

Binding Green cloth. Figure of a girl walking on green grass, with blue sky in back ground, all within a single white rule border. Beneath the girl and within a white panel, printed in red 'MOLLY / AND / MARGARET / By PAT'; spine stamped in gilt '[*double rule*] / MOLLY / AND / MARGARET / By / PAT / LONGMANS / [*double rule*]. All edges trimmed; white wove endpapers.

Contains Introduction, pp. v–xii.

B6a

CLOUD CASTLE AND OTHER PAPERS

FIRST EDITION   (1922)

CLOUD CASTLE / AND OTHER PAPERS / BY EDWARD THOMAS / With a Foreword by W. H. HUDSON / [*publisher's device*] / LONDON: DUCKWORTH & CO. / 3, HENRIETTA STREET, COVENT GARDEN

Collation [π]^4 1–12^8 13^4; pp. [i–iv] v–vii [viii] [1–2] 3–197 [198] [2]; 216 × 139 mm.; printed on wove paper.

Binding Blue cloth. Front cover stamped in blind 'CLOUD CASTLE / AND OTHER PAPERS / By EDWARD THOMAS / WITH A FOREWORD By W. H. HUDSON'; spine stamped in gilt 'CLOUD / CASTLE / AND / OTHER / PAPERS / EDWARD / THOMAS / DUCKWORTH'. Publisher's device blind stamped in lower left corner of back cover. All edges trimmed; white wove endpapers. Yellow wove dust jacket printed in black.

Contains Foreword, pp. v–vi.

Variant Blue cloth. Front cover stamped in black '[*within a single rule border*] CLOUD CASTLE / AND OTHER PAPERS / By EDWARD THOMAS / WITH A FOREWORD By W. H. HUDSON'; spine stamped in black 'CLOUD / CASTLE / AND / OTHER / PAPERS / EDWARD / THOMAS / DUCKWORTH'. All edges trimmed; white wove endpapers.

Notes "A few days before his sudden death, Mr. W. H. Hudson undertook to write an Introduction for this collection of essays by the late Edward Thomas. This fragment was found among his papers after his death, and is now printed as being of interest to the admirers of both these authors." (*editor's note*).

Hudson wrote to Morley Roberts in July 1922: "Mrs. Edward Thomas has collected some of the tales and sketches by her husband and wants me to write a preface. I have a proof of the book – a rather slim affair – and must try to do it as he was a friend and most lovable fellow. And was killed."

Hudson's foreword was reprinted in a four-page leaflet by Edwin B. Hill in 1947 (see A59). It was collected in *Dead Man's Plack An Old Thorn & Miscellanea* (A47).

B7a

LOOKING BACK AN AUTOBIOGRAPHICAL EXCURSION

FIRST EDITION 1933

LOOKING BACK / AN AUTOBIOGRAPHICAL / EXCURSION / By / NORMAN DOUGLAS / Volume I [Volume II] [*illustration*] / LONDON / CHATTO AND WINDUS / 1933

Collation Volume I: a⁶ A–Q⁸ R⁶; pp. [i–viii] ix–xi [xii] 1–268 [4]; 233 × 161 mm.; printed on laid paper.
Volume II: a⁴ s–2K⁸ 2L⁴; pp. [i–vi] vii [viii] 269–527 [528] [4]; 233 × 161 mm.; printed on laid paper.

Illustrations Eight photographs.

Binding Reddish-brown and white decorative boards. Reddish-brown buckram spine stamped in gilt 'LOOKING / BACK / AN AUTOBIOGRAPHICAL / EXCURSION /

NORMAN / DOUGLAS / VOLUME I [II]. Top edges gilt, others untrimmed; white laid endpapers. Cream wove dust jacket printed in reddish-brown.

Contains Volume II contains one letter dated 7 June 1914 and a short extract from another to Douglas, pp. 406–407.

Notes This edition is limited to 535 sets; 500 are for sale.

B8a

THE LIFE AND LETTERS OF JOHN GALSWORTHY

FIRST EDITION (1935)

The / LIFE AND LETTERS / OF / JOHN / GALSWORTHY / *By* / H. V. MARROT / [*publisher's device*] / [*rule*] / WILLIAM HEINEMANN LTD / LONDON :: TORONTO

Collation π^8 [A]^8 B–3D^8 3E^{10}; pp. [i–viii] ix–xv [xvi] [1–2] 3–819 [820]; 217 × 139 mm.; printed on wove paper.

Illustrations Sixty-five photographs.

Binding Purple cloth stamped in gilt on front cover with coat of arms; spine stamped in gilt '*The* / LIFE & LETTERS / OF / JOHN / GALSWORTHY / H. V. MARROT / HEINEMANN'. Publisher's device blind stamped on lower right corner of back cover. All edges trimmed; wove pictorial endpapers. Tan wove dust jacket printed in black and green.

Contains Five letters to Galsworthy, 31 January 1904, pp. 160–161; 11 October 1906; pp. 197–198; 3 March 1907, pp. 206–207; 19 March 1909, pp. 243–244; 22 June 1922, p. 520.

B9a

LETTERS FROM LIMBO

FIRST EDITION (1936)

ERNEST RHYS / [*diamond design*] [*thick-thin rule*] [*diamond design*] / LETTERS FROM LIMBO / *With 63 Reproductions* / *of Letters* / London / J. M. DENT AND SONS LTD.

Collation [A]^{10} B–S^8 T^{10}; pp. [2] [i–iv] v–xi [xii] xiii–xvii [xviii] [1–2] 3–289 [290–292]; 209 × 134 mm.; printed on laid paper.

Illustrations Facsimiles of selected letters.

Binding Rose cloth. Spine stamped in gilt '[*within a double rule panel*] LETTERS / FROM LIMBO / [*below panel*] ERNEST / RHYS / [*in blind*] DENT'. All edges trimmed, top edges stained rose; white laid endpapers.

Contains Letter to Rhys dated 9 September 1911 (?), Rhys note regarding the letter, and a facsimile photo of the last page of the letter, pp. 55-56.

B10a

THE WORTHING CAVALCADE: WILLIAM HENRY HUDSON A TRIBUTE

FIRST EDITION 1947

[*within a decorative border*] THE WORTHING CAVALCADE / [*the following four lines set in a script face type with swash caps*] William Henry Hudson / A Tribute / by / Various Writers / *Edited by* / SAMUEL J. LOOKER / *With a Frontispiece and* / 31 *other Illustrations* / 1947 / Published under the Worthing Art Development Scheme by / Aldridge Bros., 35, Warwick Street, Worthing, Sussex. / Printed and Made in Great Britain by / Frederick Steel & Co., Ltd., Stroud, Glos.

Collation [A–K]⁸ [L]⁶; pp. [1–15] 16–169 [170] [2]; 257 × 190 mm., printed on calendered wove paper.

Illustrations Thirty-three photographs.

Binding Limp blue cloth. Front cover stamped in gilt '*WORTHING CAVAL- CADE* / *WILLIAM HENRY HUDSON* / *A TRIBUTE* / [*decorative rule*]'; spine stamped in gilt '*WILLIAM HENRY HUDSON · A TRIBUTE*'. All edges trimmed; cream wove endpapers.

Contains Letter to James Guthrie dated 26 January 1921, pp. 46–47; three letters to Violet Hunt, 11 September 1920, 30 March 1921, 4 April 1921, pp. 113–117.

B11a

THE LAST PRE-RAPHAELITE

FIRST EDITION (1948)

THE LAST / PRE-RAPHAELITE / *A Record of the Life and Writings* / *of* / FORD

MADOX FORD / by / DOUGLAS GOLDRING / London / MACDONALD & CO. (Publishers) LTD.

Collation [A]⁸ B–S⁸; pp. [i–iv] v–xiii [xiv] xv [xvi] 17–228; 216 × 142 mm.; printed on wove paper.

Binding Blue cloth. Spine stamped in gilt over red compartment '[rule] / The Last / Pre- / Raphaelite / DOUGLAS / GOLDRING / [rule] / [at foot of spine] MacDonald'. All edges trimmed, top edges stained red; white wove endpapers. White wove dust jacket printed in blue, red, and black.

Contains Four letters to Ford, 1904, pp. 119–124.

B12a

W. H. HUDSON

FIRST EDITION (1954)

W. H. HUDSON / By / RUTH TOMALIN / [publisher's device] / PHILOSOPHICAL LIBRARY

Collation [A]⁸ B–I⁸; pp. [1–4] 5–7 [8] 9–143 [144]; 196 × 134 mm.; printed on wove paper.

Illustrations Frontispiece photograph of W. H. Hudson at age 27.

Binding Red cloth. Publisher's circular device printed in black on front cover; spine printed in black 'W. H. / HUDSON / RUTH / TOMALIN / PHILOSOPHICAL / LIBRARY'. All edges trimmed, top edges stained blue; white wove endpapers.

Contains Letter to Spencer Fullerton Baird, Assistant Secretary, Smithsonian Institution, 5 September 1866, pp. 52–53.

B13a

A DESCRIPTIVE CATALOGUE OF THE W. L. LEWIS COLLECTION

FIRST EDITION (1970)

[within a rule] A / Descriptive / Catalogue / of / The W. L. Lewis / Collection / [ornament] / by Lyle H. Kendall, Jr. / [ornament] / Part One / Manuscripts / Inscriptions / Art

Collation [1–5]¹⁶ [6]¹² [7]¹⁶; pp. [i–ix] x–xi [xii–xiii] xiv [1–2] 3–196 [197–198] [4]; 250 × 163 mm.; printed on wove paper.

Illustrations Ten illustrations of manuscripts.

Binding Black cloth. Front cover stamped in gilt '*The W. L. Lewis Collection— Part One* / [*rectangular illustration of four shelves of books; on illustration "by Lyle H. Kendall, Jr."*] / TEXAS CHRISTIAN UNIVERSITY PRESS'; spine stamped in gilt '[*reading from top to bottom*] *The W. L. Lewis Collection – Part One Texas Christian University* [*across bottom of spine*] TCU / PRESS'. All edges trimmed; white wove endpapers.

Contains Letter to Miss Newton, 30 November 1920, p. 52.

C

Contributions to Periodicals

INTRODUCTORY NOTE concerning Hudson's contributions to the *Proceedings of the Zoological Society of London*:

Hudson's first published work appeared in the *Proceedings of the Zoological Society of London*. His contributions there may, for convenience, be divided into three parts: 1) a series of three lists of birds collected by Hudson in Conchitas, Argentine Republic, with introductory remarks by Philip L. Sclater and Osbert Salvin and an extract of a letter from Hudson to Sclater about bird collecting (C1–C4); 2) a series of twelve letters about the ornithology of Buenos Aires (C5–C16); 3) a series of eleven articles about the birds of the Argentine Republic (C17–C22; C24–28).

Hudson's contributions to the *Proceedings* were incorporated with slight textual changes into *Argentine Ornithology*, published by Sclater and Hudson in 1888–1889 (A3). In Sclater's preface to Volume I Hudson is credited with all the personal observations while Sclater takes the responsibility for the arrangement, nomenclature and scientific portions of the work. A brief list of Hudson's contributions to the *Proceedings* and the *Ibis* (with the omission of "On the Habits of the Vizcacha", (C20)) is included in the appendix to *Argentine Ornithology*, Volume II, pp. 226–227.

In 1920 Hudson's portion of *Argentine Ornithology* was published as *Birds of La Plata* (A38), again with minor textual changes.

The series of twelve letters on the ornithology of Buenos Aires was not reprinted in Hudson's lifetime and was excluded from the Collected edition of Hudson's works published in 1922–1923 by J. M. Dent. The twelve letters, together with two previously unpublished letters to Sclater, were first collected and published in book form in *Letters on the Ornithology of Buenos Ayres*, 1951 (A61).

C1 [Classified list of birds with brief notes on their identities] *Proceedings of the Zoological Society of London* part 1 (13 February 1868) 137–146. In "List of Birds collected at Conchitas, Argentine Republic, by Mr. William H. Hudson", by P. L. Sclater and Osbert Salvin.

C2 [Second classified list of birds with brief notes on their identities] *Proceedings of the Zoological Society of London* part 1 (11 March 1869) 158–162. In "Second List of Birds collected at Conchitas, Argentine Republic, by Mr. William H. Hudson; together with some Notes upon another Collection from the same locality", by P. L. Sclater and Osbert Salvin.

C3 [Extract of a letter to the Secretary of the Zoological Society of London dated 30 April 1869 read at the meeting of the Zoological Society 24 June 1869] *Proceedings of the Zoological Society of London* part 2 (24 June 1869) 432–433.

C4 [Third classified list of birds with brief notes on their identities] *Proceedings of the Zoological Society of London* part 3 (9 December 1869) 631–636. In "Third List of Birds collected at Conchitas, Argentine Republic, by Mr. William H. Hudson", by P. L. Sclater and Osbert Salvin.

C5 [First letter on the ornithology of Buenos Ayres] *Proceedings of the Zoological Society of London* part 1 (10 February 1870) 87–89.

C6 [Second letter on the ornithology of Buenos Ayres] *Proceedings of the Zoological Society of London* part 1 (24 February 1870) 112–114.

C7 [Third letter on the ornithology of Buenos Ayres] *Proceedings of the Zoological Society of London* part 1 (24 March 1870) 158–160.

C8 [Fourth letter on the ornithology of Buenos Ayres] *Proceedings of the Zoological Society of London* part 2 (26 May 1870) 332–334.

C9 [Fifth letter on the ornithology of Buenos Ayres] *Proceedings of the Zoological Society of London* part 2 (23 June 1870) 545–547.

C10 [Sixth letter on the ornithology of Buenos Ayres] *Proceedings of the Zoological Society of London* part 2 (23 June 1870) 548–550.

C11 [Seventh letter on the ornithology of Buenos Ayres] *Proceedings of the Zoological Society of London* part 3 (1 November 1870) 671–673.

C12 [Eighth letter on the ornithology of Buenos Ayres] *Proceedings of the Zoological Society of London* part 3 (15 November 1870) 748–750.

C13 [Ninth letter on the ornithology of Buenos Ayres] *Proceedings of the Zoological Society of London* part 3 (6 December 1870) 798–802.

C14 [Tenth letter on the ornithology of Buenos Ayres] *Proceedings of the Zoological Society of London* part 1 (3 January 1871) 4–7.

C15 [Eleventh letter on the ornithology of Buenos Ayres] *Proceedings of the Zoological Society of London* part 2 (21 March 1871) 258–262.

C16 [Twelfth letter on the ornithology of Buenos Ayres] *Proceedings of the Zoological Society of London* part 2 (2 May 1871) 326–329.

C17 "On the Birds of the Rio Negro of Patagonia", *Proceedings of the Zoological Society of London* part 2 (26 April 1872) 534–548.

C18 "On the Habits of the Swallows of the Genus *Progne* met with in the Argentine Republic", *Proceedings of the Zoological Society of London* part 2 (7 May 1872) 605–609.

C19 "Notes on the Habits of the Churinche (*Pyrocephalus rubineus*)", *Proceedings of the Zoological Society of London* part 3 (5 November 1872) 808–810.

C20 "On the Habits of the Vizcacha (*Lagostomus trichodactylus*)", *Proceedings of the Zoological Society of London* part 3 (19 November 1872) 822–833. Collected in *The Naturalist in La Plata* (A5).

C21 "Further Observations on the Swallows of Buenos Ayres", *Proceedings of the Zoological Society of London* part 3 (19 November 1872) 844–846.

C22 "Notes on the Habits of the Pipit of the Argentine Republic", *Proceedings of the Zoological Society of London* part 3 (2 December 1873) 771–772.

C23 "Wanted, A Lullaby", *Cassell's Family Magazine* n.s. 1 (February 1874) 213–215. Signed "Maud Merryweather". Collected in *Dead Man's Plack An Old Thorn & Miscellanea* (A47). This is the first publication of a poem by Hudson and the first thing he wrote in England. He expressed his feelings about poetry in a letter to R. B. Cunninghame Graham twenty-five years later, on 15 July 1908, after referring to Mrs Cunninghame Graham's self doubts about her own poetic talents: "It is a feeling I suffered much from in long past days and eventually caused me to give up what I valued above everything, the desire to express myself in Verse. I could never satisfy myself that I would ever be able to master that delicate, and difficult instrument and so destroyed it. That is to say, I destroyed what I had done and set myself to overcome the wish. Nevertheless the belief remains fixed in my mind that our deepest emotions and the best in us cannot be expressed in any other way."

C24 "Notes on the Procreant Instincts of the three Species of *Molothrus* found in Buenos Ayres", *Proceedings of the Zoological Society of London* part 2 (3 March 1874) 153–174.

C25 "On the Habits of the Burrowing Owl (*Pholeoptynx cunicularia*), *Proceedings of the Zoological Society of London* part 3 (19 May 1874) 308–311.

C26 "On the Herons of the Argentine Republic, with a Notice of a curious Instinct of *Ardetta involucris*", *Proceedings of the Zoological Society of London* part 4, (16 November 1875) 623–631.

C27 "Note on the Spoonbill of the Argentine Republic", *Proceedings of the Zoological Society of London* part 1 (4 January 1876) 15.

C28 "Notes on the Rails of the Argentine Republic", *Proceedings of the Zoological Society of London* part 1 (18 January 1876) 102–109.

C29 "The London Sparrow", *Merry England* 1 (July 1883) 223–228. Collected in *A Little Boy Lost Together with the Poems of W. H. Hudson* (A25e) and in *Dead Man's Plack An Old Thorn & Poems* (A49).

C30 "Settler's Recompense", *Merry England* 1 (September 1883) 377–384. Collected in *Idle Days in Patagonia* (A7).

C31 "Pelino Viera's Confession", *Cornhill Magazine* 1 (October 1883) 337–356. Collected in *Tales of the Pampas* (A33).

C32 "In the Wilderness", *Merry England* 3 (June 1884) 85–87. Collected in *A Little Boy Lost Together with the Poems of W. H. Hudson* (A25e) and in *Dead Man's Plack An Old Thorn & Poems* (A49).

C33 "Spiders", *Gentleman's Magazine* 257 (July 1884) 80–92.

C34 "Tom Rainger", *Home Chimes* 1 (9 August 1884) 441–445. Collected in *Dead Man's Plack An Old Thorn & Miscellanea* (A47).

C35 "Idle Days in Patagonia", *Gentleman's Magazine* 257 (November 1884) 478–487. Collected in *Idle Days in Patagonia* (A7).

C36 "A Versatile Hawk", *Gentleman's Magazine* 258 (January 1885) 70–77.

C37 "Concerning Eyes", *Gentleman's Magazine* 258 (April 1885) 384–393. Collected in *Idle Days in Patagonia* (A7).

C38 "Gwendoline", *Merry England* 5 (June 1885) 124. Collected in *A Little Boy Lost Together with the Poems of W. H. Hudson* (A25e) and in *Dead Man's Plack An Old Thorn & Poems* (A49).

C39 "Notes on the Birds of the Genus *Homorus* observed in the Argentine Republic", *Ibis* 5th series 3 no. 11 (July 1885) 283-286. Collected in *Argentine Ornithology* (A3).

C40 "Life in Patagonia", *Gentleman's Magazine* 259 (July 1885) 75-87. Collected in *Idle Days in Patagonia* (A7).

C41 "The Crested Screamer", *Gentleman's Magazine* 259 (September 1885) 280-287. Collected in *The Naturalist in La Plata* (A5).

C42 "South American Bird-Music", *Nature* 33 (31 December 1885) 199-201. Collected in *Idle Days in Patagonia* (A7).

C43 "Humming-birds", *Longman's Magazine* 8 (May 1886) 72-80. Collected in *The Naturalist in La Plata* (A5).

C44 "The Puma", *Longman's Magazine* 8 (September 1886) 553-564. Collected in *The Naturalist in La Plata* (A5), *Dead Man's Plack An Old Thorn & Miscellanea* (A47) and *Harmsworth Natural History* (B3).

C45 "Far Away", *Gentleman's Magazine* 261 (November 1886) 502-510.

C46 "Chanticleer", *Longman's Magazine* 10 (December 1887) 201-210. Collected in *Birds in a Village* (A8) and *Birds in Town & Village* (A36).

C47 *Ralph Herne*, *Youth* vol. 12 no. 437 to vol. 12 no. 447 (4 January 1888 to 14 March 1888) as follows:
    chapters 1 and 2, vol. 12 no. 437 (4 January 1888) 1-3.
    chapters 3 and 4, vol. 12 no. 438 (11 January 1888) 17-19.
    chapters 5 and 6, vol. 12 no. 439 (18 January 1888) 33-36.
    chapters 7 and 8, vol. 12 no. 440 (25 January 1888) 49-51.
    chapter 9   vol. 12 no. 441 (1 February 1888) 65-66.
    chapter 10   vol. 12 no. 442 (8 February 1888) 81-82.
    chapter 11   vol. 12 no. 443 (15 February 1888) 97-98.
    chapter 12   vol. 12 no. 444 (22 February 1888) 113-114.
    chapter 13   vol. 12 no. 445 (29 February 1888) 129-131.

chapter 14   vol. 12 no. 446 (7 March 1888) 145-146.
chapter 15   vol. 12 no. 447 (14 March 1888) 161-162.
See A44 for separate publication. First book appearance in England was in the Collected edition, A21d.

C48 "The Eagle and the Canary", *Gentleman's Magazine* 264 (February 1888) 171-177. Collected in *Birds in a Village* (A8) and *Birds in Town & Village* (A36).

C49 "Sight in Savages", *Longman's Magazine* 12 (July 1888) 279-287. Collected in *Idle Days in Patagonia* (A7).

C50 "Exotic Birds for Britain", *Murray's Magazine* 5 (March 1889) 373-387. Collected in *Birds in a Village* (A8) and *Birds in Town & Village* (A36).

C51 "The Great Dog-Superstition", *Macmillan's Magazine* 59 (April 1889) 458-467. Collected in *The Book of a Naturalist* (A37).

C52 "Seen and Lost", *Longman's Magazine* 14 (August 1889) 399-411. Collected in *The Naturalist in La Plata* (A5).

C53 "Nino Diablo", *Macmillan's Magazine* 61 (February 1890) 303-313. Collected in *El Ombú* (A21).

C54 "The Naturalist on the Pampas", *Nineteenth Century* 27 (February 1890) 268-283.

Hudson wrote to George Gissing 12 June 1905: "I can say nothing about Mr. Knowles; my experience of him is very little and dates a long time back and was not satisfactory. It is true he used one long paper of mine, but I was without a title or sword or plume and therefore in his eyes a person of no importance."

C55 "Music and Dancing in Nature", *Longman's Magazine* 15 (April 1890) 597-610. Collected in *The Naturalist in La Plata* (A5).

C56 "The Plains of Patagonia", *Universal Review* 7 no. 28 (August 1890) 549-563. Collected in *Idle Days in Patagonia* (A7).

C57 "Some Habits of the Spider", [letter to The Editor] *Nature* 43 (18 December 1890) 151.

C58 "The Dying Huanaco", *Longman's Magazine* 17 (March 1891) 557-566. Collected in *The Naturalist in La Plata* (A5).

C59 "The Strange Instincts of Cattle", *Longman's Magazine* 18 (August 1891) 389–400. Collected in *The Naturalist in La Plata* (A5).

C60 "The Bruised Serpent", *Macmillan's Magazine* 67 (April 1893) 451–457. Collected in *The Book of a Naturalist* (A37).

C61 "The Serpent's Tongue", *Fortnightly Review* 60 n.s. 54 (August 1893) 198–206. Collected in *The Book of a Naturalist* (A37).

C62 "Feathered Women", [letter to The Editor] *The Times* no. 34,084 (17 October 1893) 6. See A9 for separate publication.

C63 "Feathered Women", *Nature Notes: The Selborne Society's Magazine* 4 (November 1893) 212–213. A reprint of Hudson's article by the same title that appeared in *The Times* 17 October 1893 (C62) and separately published the same year by the Society for the Protection of Birds (A9).

C64 "The Serpent's Strangeness", *Fortnightly Review* 61 n.s. 55 (April 1894) 528–537. Collected in *The Book of a Naturalist* (A37).

C65 "Sea-Bird Shooting", [letter to The Editor] *The Times* no. 34,329 (30 July 1894) 7.

C66 "The Last of the Ospreys", [letter to The Editor] *The Times* no. 34,425 (19 November 1894) 14.

C67 "The Adder Controversy", *Saturday Review* 79 (2 March 1895) 279. Published anonymously; reference to this article in Hudson's notebook in the Library of the Royal Society for the Protection of Birds.

C68 "The Common Crow", *Fortnightly Review* 63 n.s. 57 (May 1895) 793–799. Collected in *Dead Man's Plack An Old Thorn & Miscellanea* (A47).

C69 "My First Caged Bird", *Sunday Magazine* 24 (October 1895) 667–669. Collected in *Adventures Among Birds* (A31). See also C161.

C70 "An Appeal to the Clergy", *Nature Notes: The Selborne Society's Magazine* 7 (January 1896) 26–28. A reprint of *Letter to Clergymen, Ministers, and Others* (A14).

C71 "Selborne", *Contemporary Review* 69 (February 1896) 277–284. Collected in *Birds and Man* (A20).

C72 "The Vision of the Great Spoonbill", *Sunday Magazine* 25 (March 1896) 198–201. Collected in *A Little Boy Lost* (A25).

C73 "Tree-felling and Philosophy", *Saturday Review* 81 (28 March 1896) 322–323. Published anonymously; reference to this article in Hudson's notebook in the Library of the Royal Society for the Protection of Birds and in a letter to R. B. Cunninghame Graham 29 March 1896 (see A57).

C74 [on Egret's plumes] [letter to The Editor] *The Times* no. 34,938 (9 July 1896) 8.

C75 "Abbotsbury", *Saturday Review* 82 (5 September 1896) 255–256. Collected in *Afoot in England* (A27).

C76 "The Threshold of England", [letter to The Editor] *The Times* no. 35,006 (26 September 1896) 8.

C77 "The Wood Wren", *Longman's Magazine* 28 (October 1896) 590–597. Collected in *Birds and Man* (A20).

C78 "Ravens in Somersetshire", *Longman's Magazine* 28 (October 1896) 150–156. Collected in *Birds and Man* (A20).

C79 "Birds and Man", *Longman's Magazine* 29 (December 1896) 143–152. Collected in *Birds and Man* (A20).

C80 "London Birds in Winter", *Saturday Review* 83 (13 March 1897) 264–265. Collected in *Birds in London* (A16).

C81 "Early Spring in Savernake Forest", *Longman's Magazine* 29 (April 1897) 512–520. Collected in *Birds and Man* (A20).

C82 "Afoot in Quiet Places", *Sunday Magazine* 26 (July 1897) 436–442.

C83 "The Best Scenery I Know", *Saturday Review* 84 (17 July 1897) 53–54.

C84 "Wolmer Forest", *Longman's Magazine* 30 (August 1897) 342–353. Collected in *Hampshire Days* (A22).

C85 "The Trade in Birds' Feathers", [letter to The Editor] *The Times* no. 35,396 (25 December 1897) 5. See A17 for separate publication.

C86 "The Visionary", *Nature Notes: The Selborne Society's Magazine* 9 (March 1898) 53–54. Collected in *A Traveller in Little Things* (A40).

C87 "The Secret of the Willow-Wren", *Longman's Magazine* 31 (March 1898) 422–429. Collected in *Birds and Man* (A20).

C88 "The Queen's Private Grounds at Kew", [letter to The Editor] *The Times* no. 35,488 (12 April 1898) 8.

C89 "The Living Garment of the Downs", *Longman's Magazine* 32 (May 1898) 32–41. Collected in *Nature in Downland* (A19).

C90 "Owls in a Village", *Idler* 13 (June 1898) 641–646. Collected in *Birds and Man* (A20).

C91 "El Pato", *Badminton Magazine of Sports and Pastimes* 7 (October 1898) 402–416. Collected in *El Ombú* (A21).

C92 "Branscombe and its Birds", *Longman's Magazine* 32 (October 1898) 543–549. Collected in *Afoot in England* (A27).

C93 "London Birds", *Longman's Magazine* 33 (March 1899) 461–472. Collected in *Birds and Man* (A20).

C94 "The Human in Floral Colours", *Saturday Review* 87 (11 March 1899) 296–297. Collected in *Birds and Man* (A20).

C95 "Geese: An Appreciation and a Memory", *Badminton Magazine of Sports and Pastimes* 9 (October 1899) 388–396. Collected in *Birds and Man* (A20).

C96 "Summer in the Forest", *Longman's Magazine* 35 (January 1900) 263–276. Collected in *Hampshire Days* (A22).

C97 "The Dartford Warbler: How To Save Our Rare Birds", *Humane Review* 1 (April 1900) 28–38. Collected in *Birds and Man* (A20).

C98 "Kew Gardens and Old Deer Park", [letter to The Editor] *The Times* no. 36,116 (14 April 1900) 11. See A18 for separate publication.

C99 "The Feather-Fashion: A Last Word", *Humane Review* 1 (October 1900) 223–232. Collected in *Dead Man's Plack An Old Thorn & Miscellanea* (A47).

C100 "Destruction of the Albatross", *Saturday Review* 90 (24 November 1900) 650. See A62 for separate publication.

C101 "A More or Less Happy Family", *Badminton Magazine of Sports and Pastimes* 12 (May 1901) 526–532. Collected in *Hampshire Days* (A22).

C102 "A Summer's End on the Itchen", *Longman's Magazine* 38 (May 1901) 17–30. Collected in *Hampshire Days* (A22).

C103 "Wild Musk", *Argosy* 74 (June 1901) 279–285.

C104 "A Talk About Parrots", *Saturday Review* 91 (15 June 1901) 765–766. Collected in the second edition of *Birds and Man* (A20b).

C105 "Through Cobbett's Country", *Saturday Review* 92 (28 December 1901) 800–802. Collected in *Afoot in England* (A27).

C106 "Selborne Revisited", *Longman's Magazine* 39 (March 1902) 413–425. Collected in *Hampshire Days* (A22).

C107 "The Last Hampshire Ravens", *Animal Life and the World of Nature* 1 (July 1902) 14–16.

C108 "A Shepherd of the Downs", *Longman's Magazine* 40 (September 1902) 452–464. Collected in *A Shepherd's Life* (A29).

C109 "A Thrush that Never Lived", *Humane Review* 2 (October 1902) 208–210. See A30 for separate publication.

C110 "A Shepherd of the Downs", *Longman's Magazine* 40 (October 1902) 509–521. Collected in *A Shepherd's Life* (A29).

C111 "A Cold Day at Silchester", *Speaker* 9 (31 October 1903) 104–106. Collected in *Afoot in England* (A27).

C112 "Blue Columbine and Chequered Daffodil", *Speaker* 9 (21 November 1903) 190–191. Collected in *The Book of the Open Air* (B2) and in *The Book of a Naturalist* (A37).

C113 "The Little Red Dog", *Speaker* 9 (24 December for 26 December 1903) 314–315. Collected in *The Book of the Open Air* (B2) and in *The Book of a Naturalist* (A37).

C114 "Salisbury and its Doves", *Speaker* 9 (9 January 1904) 359–360. Collected in *Afoot in England* (A27).

C115 "In Praise of the Cow", *Speaker* 9 (6 February 1904) 445–447. Collected in *Afoot in England* (A27).

C116 "Our Wild Birds", *Speaker* 9 (27 February 1904) 510–511. Collected in *Dead Man's Plack An Old Thorn & Miscellanea* (A47).

C117 "On the Use of Guide-books", *Speaker* 10 (2 April 1904) 11–12. Collected in *Afoot in England* (A27).

C118 "The Comfort of Ruins", *Speaker* 10 (30 April 1904) 112–114.

C119 "The Collector in Guiana", *Saturday Review* 97 (18 June 1904) 787. A review of *A Naturalist in the Guianas* by Eugene André. Anonymous review; Hudson mentions this review in his letter to Morley Roberts, 24 June 1904.

C120 [On Bird-catching and Collecting], *Bird Notes and News* 1 (December 1904) 53.

C121 "Bats", *Speaker* 11 (24 December 1904) 314–316. A review of *The Mammals of Great Britain and Ireland* by J. G. Millais. Collected in *The Book of a Naturalist* (A37).

C122 "The Vanishing Curtsey", *Speaker* 11 (7 January 1905) 351–352. Collected in *A Traveller in Little Things* (A40).

C123 "Bath and Wells Revisited", *Speaker* 11 (18 March 1905) 584–585. Collected in *Afoot in England* (A27).

C124 "In Praise of Owls", *Speaker* 12 (15 April 1905) 67–69. A review of *Bird*

Life and Bird Lore by R. Bosworth Smith. Collected in *Dead Man's Plack An Old Thorn & Miscellanea* (A47).

C125 "An Easter Walk on Whitesheet Hill", *Speaker* 12 (27 May 1905) 204–205. Collected in *Afoot in England* (A27).

C126 "Wasps", *Speaker* 12 (24 June 1905) 301–303. A review of *Wasps Social and Solitary* by George W. Peckham and Elizabeth G. Peckham. Collected in *The Book of a Naturalist* (A37).

C127 [On Wheatears and Elder-trees], *Bird Notes and News* 1 (July 1905) 72.

C128 "The Serpent in Literature", *Monthly Review* 20 (August 1905) 118–130. Collected in *The Book of a Naturalist* (A37).

C129 "The Return of the Native", *Speaker* 12 (30 September 1905) 615–616. Collected in *Afoot in England* (A27).

C130 "Wild Wings", *Speaker* 13 (11 November 1905) 142 and 144. A review of *Travels of a Naturalist in Northern Europe* by J. A. Harvie-Brown and *Wild Wings* by Herbert Keightley Job.

C131 "Truth Plain and Coloured", *Speaker* 13 (9 December 1905) 248–249. A review of *Ways of Nature* by John Burroughs and *Red Fox* by Charles G. D. Roberts. Collected in *Dead Man's Plack An Old Thorn & Miscellanea* (A47).

C132 "Aves", *Wild Fauna and Flora of the Royal Botanic Gardens, Kew*. Bulletin of Miscellaneous Information, Additional Series (1906) 2–10. Collected in *Dead Man's Plack An Old Thorn & Miscellanea* (A47).

C133 "Laughing at a Cat", *Speaker* 13 (13 January 1906) 365–366. Collected in *Dead Man's Plack An Old Thorn & Miscellanea* (A47).

C134 "Winter at St. Ives", *Speaker* 13 (3 February 1906) 430–431. Hudson wrote to Edward Garnett 4 February 1906, "I was rather surprised on reading my St. Ives article to find that I was capable of being very dull."

C135 "Something Pretty in a Glass Case", *Saturday Review* 101 (10 February 1906) 168–169. Collected in the second edition of *Birds and Man* (A20b).

C136 "Gulls at St. Ives", *Speaker* 13 (24 February 1906) 497–499. Collected in *The Land's End* (A26).

C137 "Lady Grey as Nature Lover", *Speaker* 13 (3 March 1906) 519–520.

C138 "Cornwall's Connemara", *Speaker* 13 (24 March 1906) 593–595. Collected in *The Land's End* (A26).

C139 "Bolerium", *Speaker* 14 (28 April 1906) 67–68. Collected in *The Land's End* (A26).

C140 "Our Indian Birds", *Speaker* 14 (26 May 1906) 185–186. A review of *Bombay Ducks* by Douglas Dewar. Collected in *Dead Man's Plack An Old Thorn & Miscellanea* (A47).

C141 "A Cyclist on Walking", *Speaker* 14 (14 July 1906) 337–339. Collected in *Afoot in England* (A27).

C142 "A Present of a Walnut", *Speaker* 14 (25 August 1906) 476. Collected in *A Traveller in Little Things* (A40).

C143 "Animal Autobiographies", *Saturday Review* 102 (1 December 1906) 675. A review of *The Life Story of a Fox* by J. C. Tregarthen. Collected in *Dead Man's Plack An Old Thorn & Miscellanea* (A47).

C144 "Gannets Fishing", *Saturday Review* 103 (16 February 1907) 200–201. Collected in *The Land's End* (A26).

C145 "Bird Life at the Land's End", *Saturday Review* 103 (9 March 1907) 298–300.

C146 "The Preservation of British Birds", [letter to The Editor] *Morning Post* (London) no. 42,348 (14 February 1908) 5. Letter signed by Hudson and five other persons on the Watchers' Committee of The Royal Society for the Protection of Birds.

C147 "The Sacred Bird", *Saturday Review* 106 (3 October 1908) 415–416. Collected in *Adventures Among Birds* (A31).

C148 "Stonehenge", *English Review* 1 (December 1908) 60–68. Collected in *Afoot in England* (A27).

C149 "A Tired Traveller", *Saturday Review* 107 (2 January 1909) 12–14. See A41 for separate publication. Collected in *Adventures Among Birds* (A31).

C150 "Goldfinches at Ryme Intrinsica", *English Review* 2 (May 1909) 246–254. Collected in *Adventures Among Birds* (A31). Reprinted in *English Review* July 1925.

C151 "Clover Seed", *Saturday Review* 107 (26 June 1909) 812–814. Collected in *Dead Man's Plack An Old Thorn & Miscellanea* (A47).

C152 "A Spray of Southernwood", *Saturday Review* 108 (14 August 1909) 192–193. Collected in *A Traveller in Little Things* (A40).

C153 "At Porchester", *Saturday Review* 108 (21 August 1909) 225. Collected in *A Traveller in Little Things* (A40).

C154 "The Immortal Nightingale", *Cornhill Magazine* 101 (April 1910) 552–563. Collected in *Adventures Among Birds* (A31).

C155 "Wells-next-the-sea", *Saturday Review* 109 (30 April 1910) 557–558. Collected in *Adventures Among Birds* (A31).

C156 "White Duck', *English Review* 5 (May 1910) 267–275. Collected in *Adventures Among Birds* (A31).

C157 "The Wood by the Sea", *Saturday Review* 109 (21 May 1910) 655–656. Collected in *Adventures Among Birds* (A31).

C158 "Some Clever Birds", *Saturday Review* 109 (28 May 1910) 688–689.

C159 "Proposed Extermination of a Crane", [letter to The Editor] *The Times* no. 39,292 (7 June 1910) 13.

C160 "Extermination of Cranes", [letter to The Editor] *The Times* no. 39,299 (15 June 1910) 8.

C161 "Cardinal; the Story of my First Caged Bird", *Cornhill Magazine* 102 (July 1910) 37–44. Collected in *Adventures Among Birds* (A31). See also c69.

C162 "Axe Edge and Its Birds – I", *Saturday Review* 111 (21 January 1911) 78–80. Collected in *Adventures Among Birds* (A31).

C163 "Axe Edge and Its Birds – II", *Saturday Review* 111 (28 January 1911) 110–112. Collected in *Adventures Among Birds* (A31).

C164 "Axe Edge and Its Birds – III", *Saturday Review* 111 (4 February 1911) 141–142. Collected in *Adventures Among Birds* (A31).

C165 "An Old Thorn", *English Review* 8 (May 1911) 192–207. Collected in *Dead Man's Plack and An Old Thorn* (A38).

C166 "A Patriarch of the Pampas", *Eye-Witness* 1 (7 September 1911) 368–370. Collected in *Far Away and Long Ago* (A34).

C167 "The Wonderful Story of a Mackerel", *Saturday Review* 112 (9 September 1911) 325–326. Collected in *A Traveller in Little Things* (A40).

C168 "Temples of the Hills", *Cornhill Magazine* 105 (March 1912) 352–363. Collected in *Adventures Among Birds* (A31).

C169 "A Memory of the Ancient Time", *English Review* 11 (June 1912) 349–365.

C170 "In a Green Land", *Saturday Review* 113 (29 June 1912) 811–812. Collected in *Adventures Among Birds* (A31).

C171 "In a Green Land", *Saturday Review* 114 (6 July 1912) 13–14. Collected in *Adventures Among Birds* (A31).

C172 "In a Green Land", *Saturday Review* 114 (20 July 1912) 79–80. Collected in *Adventures Among Birds* (A31).

C173 "In a Green Land", *Saturday Review* 114 (27 July 1912) 109–111. Collected in *Adventures Among Birds* (A31).

C174 "A Plea for the Osprey", [letter to The Editor] *Field* 120 (14 December 1912) 1232.

C175 "Wild Wings", *English Review* 13 (January 1913) 213–225. Collected in *Adventures Among Birds* (A31). Reprinted in *English Review* August 1925 (C214).

C176 "My Neighbour's Bird Stories", *New Statesman* 1 (4 October 1913) 817–819. Collected in *The Book of a Naturalist* (A37).

C177 "In a Churchyard", *New Statesman* 2 (18 October 1913) 51–52.

C178 "Moths", *New Statesman* 2 (8 November 1913) 147–148.

C179 "Spring Sadness", *New Statesman* 3 (23 May 1914) 211–212.

C180 "The Strenuous Mole", *New Statesman* 3 (18 July 1914) 468–469. Collected in *The Book of a Naturalist* (A37).

C181 "On Liberating Caged Birds", *Bird Notes and News* 6 (Spring 1915) 69–71. See A32 for separate publication.

C182 "A Sentimentalist on Foxes", *Country Life* 37 (17 April 1915) 525–526. Collected in *The Book of a Naturalist* (A37).

C183 "Dogs in London", *National and English Review* 65 (May 1915) 381–391. Collected in *The Book of a Naturalist* (A37).

C184 "Roff and a Linnet", *New Statesman* 5 (29 May 1915) 183–184. See A35 for separate publication.

C185 "The Thrush as Mimic", *Country Life* 37 (5 June 1915) 784–785.

C186 "The Old Man's Delusion", *New Statesman* 5 (4 September 1915) 519. Collected in *A Traveller in Little Things* (A40).

C187 "Little Fishes and Fascination", *Country Life* 38 (18 September 1915) 399–400. Collected in *Dead Man's Plack An Old Thorn & Miscellanea* (A47).

C188 "The Mole Question", *Country Life* 38 (6 November 1915) 622–623. Collected in *The Book of a Naturalist* (A37).

C189 "The Toad as Traveller", *Country Life* 38 (13 November 1915) 656–657. Collected in *The Book of a Naturalist* (A37).

C190 "Early Memories", *English Review* 22 (January 1916) 11–20. Collected in *Far Away and Long Ago* (A34). On 13 March 1916 Hudson wrote Lady Margaret Brooke, Rani of Sarawak: "You remember my article in the *English Review* – Early Memories & my account of the 'jester' Don Eusebio? Also all I have told you about Rosas, the Nero of South America & his one child, his beloved daughter *Manuelita*? Well, the *son of that daughter*, Terrero, a wealthy English gentleman, has just written me a long letter to say how astonished he was to read my article. His brother – there are two grandsons of Rosas – sent it to him to read, & he tells me how his mother, the famous Manuelita, used to tell them about 'El loco, Don Eusebio' but he had never seen the famous court fool in the vivid way I had brought him back."

C191 "The Story of a Skull", *Country Life* 39 (1 January 1916) 8. Collected in *A Traveller in Little Things* (A40).

C192 "Little Girls I Have Met", *Cornhill Magazine* 113 (February 1916) 207–220. Collected in *A Traveller in Little Things* (A40).

C193 "The Discontented Squirrel", *Chambers's Journal of Popular Literature, Science and Art* 7th series, vol. 6 (11 March 1916) 225–227. Collected in *The Book of a Naturalist* (A37).

C194 "The Friendly Rat", *The Times* no. 41,115 (15 March 1916) 11. Collected in *The Book of a Naturalist* (A37).

C195 "On Some Increasing Birds", *Country Life* 39 (20 May 1916) 614–615.

C196 "Life in a Pine Wood (People, Birds, and Ants)", *National and English Review* 67 (June 1916) 576–583. Collected in *The Book of a Naturalist* (A37). Hudson wrote to Lady Rani of Sarawak in June 1916: "The Editor of the Nat. Institute for the Blind has written two or three times to me the last few days about my Life in a Pine Wood paper. He is having it printed in embossed type for the use of the blind! It strikes me as curious that a paper like that should be wanted for such readers!"

C197 "Daws in West Cornwall", *Country Life* 40 (22 July 1916) 93–94.

C198 "My Friend the Pig", *National and English Review* 69 (March 1917) 72–76. Collected in *The Book of a Naturalist* (A37).

C199 "The Misused Potato", *National and English Review* 60 (April 1917) 237–241. Collected in *The Book of a Naturalist* (A37).

C200 "A Lost Village", *Reveille* 2 (November 1918) 281–284. Collected in *A Traveller in Little Things* (A40).

C201 "Dandy", *Animals' Friend* 25 (August 1919) 161–162. Collected in *A Traveller in Little Things* (A40).

C202 "Seagulls in London", [A letter to The Editor] *Observer* no. 6,764 (16 January 1921) 5. See A42 for separate publication.

C203 "Do Cats Think?" *Cornhill Magazine* 123 (May 1921) 597–608. Reprinted in *Strand Magazine*, August 1921. Collected in *Dead Man's Plack An Old Thorn & Miscellanea* (A47).

C204 "Do Cats Think?" *Strand Magazine* 62 (August 1921) 161–167. Hudson wrote to Edward Garnett 14 May 1921: "That paper, 'Do Cats Think?' has brought me a lot of letters, and the editor of the *Strand* has bought the second serial rights to put it into his magazine. A funny thing for him to do!"

C205 "Do Cats Think", *Strand Magazine* 62 (February 1922) 164–169. Collected in *Dead Man's Plack An Old Thorn & Miscellanea* (A47).

C206 "A Hind in Richmond Park", *Century Magazine* (New York) 104 (July 1922) 338–344. Collected in *A Hind in Richmond Park* (A43).

C207 "On the Sense of Smell", *Century Magazine* (New York) 104 (August 1922) 497–506. Collected in *A Hind in Richmond Park* (A43).

C208 "On the Sense of Direction", *Century Magazine* (New York) 104 (September 1922) 693–701. Collected in *A Hind in Richmond Park* (A43).

C209 "[Letter to Philip Gosse], *Bookman's Journal and Print Collector* 7 (October 1922) 1–2. In "W. H. Hudson: An Impression –" by Philip Gosse.

C210 [Partial letter to Sir Montagu Sharpe dated 3 May 1922], *Annual Report*, Royal Society for the Protection of Birds (1 January – 31 December 1922) 28.

C211 "Letters from W. H. Hudson to Edward Garnett", *Dial* 75 (November 1923) 417-429. Collected in *153 Letters from W. H. Hudson* (A46).

C212 [Letter to Viscount Grey of Fallodon dated 12 February 1922], *Annual Report*, Royal Society for the Protection of Birds (1 January–31 December 1923) 38–39.

C213 "Goldfinches at Ryme Intrinsica", *English Review* 41 (July 1925) 33-43. See C150 for first appearance.

C214 "Wild Wings", *English Review* 41 (August 1925) 229-241. See C175 for first appearance.

C215 [Letter to Spencer F. Baird], *Saturday Review of Literature* 30 (12 April 1947) 16. In "W. H. Hudson's Lost Years" by Edwin Way Teale and R. Gordon Wasson.

D

Translations

CHINESE
D1 NIAO YÜ SHOU. Taipei: Taiwan Book Company, 1947. Translation by Liu Wen-chen of *Birds and Man*.

CZECH
D2 ZELENÉ PALÁCE. ROMÁN Z VENEZUELSKÝCH PRALESŮ. Prague: F. Topič, 1926. Translation by Elsie Havlasová of *Green Mansions*.

D3 EL OMBÚ. Přerov: Bohuslav Durych, 1930. Translation by A. Skoumal of *El Ombú*.

D4 PURPUROVÁ ZEMĚ. Prague: Rudolf Škeřík, 1930. Translation by Jan Čep of *The Purple Land that England Lost*.

D5 ZELENÝ RÁJ. Prague: Lidová Demokracie, 1961. Translation by Jaroslav Žabka of *Green Mansions*.

D6 PURPUROVÁ ZEMĚ. Prague: Vyšehrad, 1971. Translation by Václav Čep of *The Purple Land that England Lost*.

DANISH
D7 LØVSLOTTET. Copenhagen: Jarl Borgen, 1949. Translation by Elsa Gress of *Green Mansions*.

DUTCH
D8 DE GEHEIMZINNIGE VROUW IN HET WOUD. Amsterdam: Meulenhoff, 1924. Translation by W. T. van de Reemur of *Green Mansions*.

D9 DE KLEINE ZWERVER. Amsterdam: De Arbeiderspers, 1931. Translation by Henk van Laar of *A Little Boy Lost*.

D10 RIMA, KIND VAN DE WILDERNIS. The Hague: Zuid-Hollandsche Uitgevers Maatschappij, 1959. Translation by E. Baronesse van Heemstra of *Green Mansions*.

ESTONIAN
D11 ROHELISED MAJAD. Tartu: Tapper, 1930. Translation by Marta Sillaots of *Green Mansions*.

D12 SINIMAA. Tartu: Ilukirjandus ja Kunst, 1941. Translation by Auguste Pärn of *The Purple Land*.

D13 GOLUBAIA ZEMLIA. Tartu: Gosudarstvennoe Izdatel'stvo Khudozhestvennoi Literatury i Iskusstva, 1941. Translation by A. Piarn of *The Purple Land*.

FINNISH
D14 VIHANNISSA ASUNNOISSA. Porvoo: Söderström, 1927. Translation by I. K. Inha of *Green Mansions*.

FRENCH
D15 LE PAYS POURPRE. Paris: Librairie Plon, 1927. Translation by Victor Llona of *The Purple Land*.

D16 UN FLÂNEUR EN PATAGONIE. Paris: Librairie Stock; Delamain et Boutelleau, 1929. Translation by Victor Llona of *Idle Days in Patagonia*.

D17 VERTES DEMEURES. Paris: Librairie Plon, 1929. Translation by Victor Llona of *Green Mansions*.

D18 LE NATURALISTE À LA PLATA. Paris: Librairie Stock, 1930. Translation by Victor Liona of *The Naturalist in La Plata*.

D19 AU LOIN . . . JADIS . . . HISTOIRE DE MON ENFANCE. Paris: Librairie Stock, 1933. Translation by H. Archambaud-Fauconnier of *Far Away and Long Ago*.

D20 EL OMBÚ. Paris: Mercure de France, 1964. Translation by Pierre Leyris of *El Ombú*.

GERMAN
D21 ROMAN IN URUGUAY. Berlin: Zsolnay, 1930. Translation by Ellinor Drösser of *The Purple Land*.

D22 RIMA. DIE GESCHICHTE EINER LIEBE AUS DEM TROPENWALD. Zurich: Manesse-Verlag, 1958. Translation by Kuno Weber of *Green Mansions*.

GREEK
D23 I CORI TIS ZOUNGLAS. Athens: Pechlivanidis, 1954. Translation of *Niño Diablo*.

HEBREW
D24 HEKHALE YEREQ. Tel Aviv: Mizpeh, 1934. Translation by Simon Halkin of *Green Mansions*.

D25 HAYELED HAOVED. Tel Aviv: Shtibel, 1934–35. Translation by Simon Ginzburg of *A Little Boy Lost*.

D26 HAYELED HAOVED. Tel Aviv: Masada, 1956. Translation by Simon Ginzburg of *A Little Boy Lost*.

D27 HEKHALE YEREQ. Tel Aviv: M. Newman, 1960. Translation by Simon Halkin of *Green Mansions*.

D28 HEKHALE YEREQ. Tel Aviv: Am Oved, 1961. Translation by Simon Halkin of *Green Mansions*.

ITALIAN

D29 LA BANDA ORIENTALE. Milan: Rizzoli, 1945. Translation by Orsola Nemi of *The Purple Land*.

D30 VERDI DIMORE. Milan: Edizioni Allegranza, 1945. Translation by Maria Martone of *Green Mansions*.

D31 VERDI DIMORE. Milan: Valentino Bompiani Editore, 1945. Translation by Angelo Bianco of *Green Mansions*.

D32 VERDI DIMORE. Milan: A. Mondadori, 1958. Translation by Maria Martone of *Green Mansions*.

D33 VERDI DIMORE. in SELEZIONE DEL LIBRO. Milan: Selezione dal Reader's Digest, 1959. Translation by Mariella Filiasi Carcano of *Green Mansions*.

D34 LA TERRA DI PORPORA. Milan: Rizzoli, 1963. Translation by Niní Anfosso of *The Purple Land*.

JAPANESE

D35 NO NO TORI NO SEIKATSU. Tokyo: Tenjinsha, 1931. Translation by Miki Kimura of selections from *Adventures Among Birds, Idle Days in Patagonia, Far Away and Long Ago, Birds in Town and Village* and *Birds in London*.

D36 HAKUBUTSU MONOGATARI. Tokyo: Taihosha, 1932. Translation by Shizuo Machino of selections from *The Book of a Naturalist*.

D37 RA PURATA NO HAKUBUTSUGAKUSHA. Tokyo: Iwanami Shoten, 1934. Translation by Ryokichi Iwata of *The Naturalist in La Plata*. There is also a 1954 edition.

D38 KOYA NO SEIKATSU FUKEI. Tokyo: Shokyu Shobo, 1936. Translation by Shunzo Kashiwakura of *El Ombú*. This volume also contains MADARAGOMA MONOGATARI, "*Story of a Piebald Horse*," and MARUTA RIKERUME, "*Marta Riquelme*."

D39 HARUKANA KUNI TÔI MUKASHI. Tokyo: Iwanami Shoten, 1937. Translation by Shizu Jugaku of *Far Away and Long Ago*. There is also a 1950 edition.

D40 KOTORI O TOMO TO SHITE. Tokyo: Kaizosha, 1937. Translation by Ki Kimura of *Adventures Among Birds*.

D41 MIDORI NO YAKATA: NETTAIRIN ROMANCE. Tokyo: Iwanami Shoten, 1937. Translation by Yuzo Murayama of *Green Mansions*. There is also a 1951 edition.

D42 HAKUBUTSUGAKUSHA NO SHUKI. Tokyo: Toyo Shokan, 1941. Translation by Tetsu Ishuin of *The Book of a Naturalist*.

D43 HAKUBUTSU MONOGATARI. Tokyo: Taihôsha, 1942. Translation by Machino Shizuo of *The Book of a Naturalist*.

D44 YUME O OU KO. Tokyo: Iwanami Shoten, 1951. Translation by Kiku Amino of *A Little Boy Lost*.

D45 LA PLATA NO HAKUBUTSU GAKUSHA. Tokyo: Iwanami Shoten, 1952. Translation by Ryôkichi Iwata of *The Naturalist in La Plata*.

D46 KOTORI O TOMO TO SHITE. Tokyo: Sogensha, 1954. Translation by Ki Kimura of *Adventures Among Birds*.

D47 MAJO NO MORI: MIDORI NO YAKATA. Tokyo: Kaiseisha, 1954. Translation by Shigeru Kayama of *Green Mansions*.

D48 URUWASHIKI KANA SOGEN. Tokyo: Eihôsha, 1954. Translation by Shunzô Kashiwakura of *The Purple Land*.

D49 RÔBOKU AIWA ERU ONBU. Tokyo: Eihôsha, 1956. Translation by Shunzô Kashiwakura of *El Ombú*. This volume also contains ROBOKU AIWA, "*An Old Thorn*", MADARAGOMA MONOGATARI, "*Story of a Piebald Horse*", and MARUTA RIKERUME, "*Marta Riquelme*".

D50 MIDORI NO YAKATA. Tokyo: Mikasa Shobô, 1959. Translation by Shirô Aoki of *Green Mansions*. There is also a 1966 edition.

D51 MIDORI NO YAKATA. Tokyo: Shinchosha, 1959. Translation by Tadae Fukizawa of *Green Mansions*.

D52 MIDORI NO YAKATA: NETTAIRIN NO ROMANCE. Tokyo: Kadokawa Shoten, 1959. Translation by Yoichi Moriya of *Green Mansions*.

D53 MIDORI NO YAKATA: NETTAIRIN NO ROMANCE. Tokyo: Akimoto Shobô, 1959. Translation by Hinako Nagai of *Green Mansions*. There is also a 1968 edition.

D54 MIDORI NO YAKATA. Tokyo: Kaiseisha, 1960. Translation by Kaisaku Noda of *Green Mansions*.

D55 MIDORI NO YAKATA. Tokyo: Shûeisha, 1967. Translation by Kiyoko Nishikawa of *Green Mansions*.

D56 MIDORI NO YAKATA. Tokyo: Kaiseisha, 1968. Translation by Shigeru Kayama of *Green Mansions*.

D57 PAPURU RANDO. Tokyo: Eihosha, 1971. Translation by Shunzo Kashiwakura of *The Purple Land*.

PORTUGUESE
D58 VERDES MORADAS. Pôrto Alegre: Edição da Livraria do Globo, 1942. Translation by M. Deabreu of *Green Mansions*.

D59 LONGE E HÁ MUITO TEMPO. Rio de Janeiro: Gráfica Editôra Brasileira, 1952. Translation by Nair Lacerda of *Far Away and Long Ago*.

RUSSIAN
D60 ZELENYE DVORTSY. Moscow: Knigoizdatel'stvo "Sovremennye Problemy" N. A. Stolliar, Tipografiia Izdatel'stva MGSPS "Trud i Kniga", 1926. Translation by P. Okhrimenko of *Green Mansions*.

D61 DEVUSHKA-PTITSA. Moscow: Aktsioner-noe Izdatel'skoe Obshchestvo "Zemlia i Fabrika", Tipografiia "Gudok", 1927. Translation of *Green Mansions*.

D62 ZELENYE DVORTSY. Moscow: Knigoizdatel'stvo "Sovremennye Problemy" N. A. Stolliar, Gosudarstvennaia Tipografiia imeni Evg. Sokolovoi v Leningrade, 1928. Translation by P. Okhrimenko of *Green Mansions*.

SERBIAN
D63 ZELENI DVORI. Belgrad: Dom i Skola, 1947. Translation by Živojin V. Simić of *Green Mansions*.

D64 ZELENI ZAMAK. Novi Sad: Bratstvo-Jedinstvo, 1953. Translation by Živojin V. Simić of *Green Mansions*.

D65 ZELENI DVORI. Cetinje: Obod, 1960. Translation by Živojin V. Simić of *Green Mansions*.

SPANISH
D66 EL OMBÚ Y OTROS CUENTOS RÍOPLATENSES. Buenos Aires: Agencia General de Librería y Publicaciones, 1928. Translation by Eduardo Hillman of *El Ombú*.

D67 LA TIERRA PURPÚREA (UN IDILIO URUGUAYO). Madrid: Sociedad General Española de Librería, 1928. Translation by Eduardo Hillman of *The Purple Land*.

D68 LA TIERRA PURPÚREA. Buenos Aires: La Nación, 1928. Translation of *The Purple Land*.

D69 EL OMBÚ Y OTROS CUENTOS RIOPLATENSES. Buenos Aires: Librería Anaconda, 1933. Translation by Eduardo Hillman of *El Ombú*.

D70 ALLÁ LEJOS Y HACE TIEMPO: RELATOS DE MI INFANCIA. Buenos Aires: Jacobo Peuser, 1938. Translation by Fernando Pozzo and Celia Rodríguez de Pozzo of *Far Away and Long Ago*. Other printings by Peuser appeared in 1942, 1945, 1947, 1948, 1953.

D71 MANSIONES VERDES. Santiago de Chile: Empresa Editora Zig-Zag, 1938. Translation by Ernesto Montenegro of *Green Mansions*. There is also a 1949 edition.

D72 DIAS DE OCIO EN LA PATAGONIA. Buenos Aires: Joaquín Gil Editor, 1940. Translation by J. Hubert of *Idle Days in Patagonia*.

D73 ANTOLOGÍA DE GUILLERMO ENRIQUE HUDSON: Precedida de Estudios críticos sobre su Vida y su Obra por Fernando Pozzo, E. Martínez Estrada, Jorge Casares, Jorge Luis Borges, H. J. Massingham, V. S. Pritchett y Hugo Manning. Buenos Aires: Editorial Losada, 1941. Contains selections from *Far Away and Long Ago*; *Idle Days in Patagonia*; *The Naturalist in La Plata*; *El Ombú*; *Adventures Among Birds*.

D74 EL OMBÚ Y OTROS CUENTOS RIOPLATENSES. Buenos Aires: Espasa-Calpe, 1941. Translation by Eduardo Hillman of *El Ombú*.

D75 LA TIERRA PURPÚREA (UN IDILIO URUGUAYO). Buenos Aires: Biblioteca "Pluma de Oro", 1941. Translation by Eduardo Hillman of *The Purple Land*.

D76 CARTAS DE W. H. HUDSON A CUNNINGHAME GRAHAM Y A LA SRA. DE BONTINE 1890-1922. Buenos Aires: Editorial Bajel, (n.d., 1942). Translation by Ignacio Covarrubias of *W. H. Hudson's Letters to R. B. Cunninghame Graham*.

D77 AVENTURAS ENTRE PÁJAROS. Buenos Aires: Santiago Rueda, 1944. Translation by Ricardo Attwell de Veyga of *Adventures Among Birds*.

D78 UNA CIERVA EN EL PARQUE DE RICHMOND. Buenos Aires: Editorial Claridad, 1944. Translation by Fernando Pozzo of *A Hind in Richmond Park*.

D79 ALLÁ LEJOS Y HACE TIEMPO. Buenos Aires: Jacobo Peuser, 1945. Translation by Fernando Pozzo and Celia Rodríguez de Pozzo of *Far Away and Long Ago*. With a prologue by R. B. Cunninghame Graham. The Spanish equivalent of the Limited Editions Club edition (A34f).

D80 EL LIBRO DE UN NATURALISTA. Buenos Aires: Santiago Rueda, 1946. Translation by Máximo Siminovich of *The Book of a Naturalist*.

D81 EL NIÑO PERDIDO. Buenos Aires: Guillermo Kraft, 1946. Translation by Celia Rodríguez de Pozzo and F. C. Scholes of *A Little Boy Lost*.

D82 PÁJAROS DE LA CIUDAD Y LA ALDEA. Buenos Aires: Santiago Rueda, 1946. Translation by Federico López Cruz of *Birds in Town and Village*.

D83 UN VENDEDOR DE BAGATELAS. Buenos Aires: Editorial Sudamericana, 1946. Translation by Francisco Uriburu of *A Traveller in Little Things*.

D84 VIDA DE UN PASTOR. Buenos Aires: Santiago Rueda, 1946. Translation by Ricardo Attwell de Veyga of *A Shepherd's Life*.

D85 FAN. HISTORIA DE UNA NIÑA. Buenos Aires: Santiago Rueda, 1947. Translation by Carlos A. Massini of *Fan*.

D86 LA TIERRA PURPÚREA. Buenos Aires: Santiago Rueda, 1951. Translation by Eduardo Hillman of *The Purple Land*.

D87 MANSIONES VERDES. Buenos Aires: Santiago Rueda, 1952. Translation by Ernesto Montenegro of *Green Mansions*.

D88 LA SELVA MARAVILLOSA. Madrid: Editorial Tesoro, 1952. Translation by Joaquin Rodriguez Castro of GREEN MANSIONS.

D89 EL NATURALISTA EN EL PLATA. Buenos Aires: Emecé, 1953. Translation by M.C. of *The Naturalist in La Plata*.

D90 EL OMBÚ Y OTROS CUENTOS. Buenos Aires: Guillermo Kraft, 1953. Translation by Alfredo M. Santillan of *El Ombú*.

D91 ALLÁ LEJOS Y HACE TIEMPO. Buenos Aires: 1954. Translation by Gonzalo Fernández of *Far Away and Long Ago*.

D92 LA TIERRA PURPÚREA. Montevideo: Editorial Surcos, 1954. A dramatization by Carlos Lermitte of *The Purple Land*.

D93 DÍAS DE OCIO EN LA PATAGONIA. Buenos Aires: Ediciones Agepe, 1956. Translation by Emilio Züberbühler of *Idle Days in Patagonia*.

D94 LA TIERRA PURPÚREA. Buenos Aires: Guillermo Kraft, 1956. Translation of *The Purple Land*.

D95 LA TIERRA PURPÚREA. Buenos Aires: Editorial Anaconda, 1956. Translation by Eduardo Hillman of *The Purple Land*.

D96 ALLÁ LEJOS Y HACE TIEMPO. Buenos Aires: Sopena, 1957. Translation by Mariá A. L. de Córdoba of *Far Away and Long Ago*.

D97 ALLÁ LEJOS Y HACE TIEMPO, RELATOS DE MI INFANCIA. Buenos Aires: Guillermo Kraft, 1958. Translation by Juan Antonio Brusol of *Far Away and Long Ago*.

D98 LA TIERRA PURPÚREA. Montevideo: Ministerio de Instrucción Pública y Prevision Social, 1965. Translation by Eduardo Hillman of *The Purple Land*.

D99 PAJAROS NUESTROS. Buenos Aires: Guillermo Kraft, n.d. Translation of *Birds of La Plata*.

SWEDISH

D100 I OMBÚTRÄDETS SKUGGA. Stockholm: Wahlström and Widstrand, 1922. Translation by Karin Jensen of *El Ombú*.

D101 GRÖNSKANDE BONINGAR. Stockholm: Wahlström and Widstrand, 1923. Translation by Karin Jensen of *Green Mansions*.

D102 URSKOGENS HEMLIGHET. Stockholm: Svenska andelsförlaget, 1923. Translation by Senta Centervall of *Green Mansions*.

D103 URSKOGENS HEMLIGHET. Helsinki: Söderström, 1923. Translation of *Green Mansions*.

D104 DET PURPURSTÄNKTA LANDET. Stockholm: Wahlström and Widstrand, 1924. Translation by Karin Jensen of *The Purple Land*.

D105 I FJÄRRAN LAND FÖR LÄNGE SEN. Stockholm: Wahlström and Widstrand, 1925. Translation by Karin Jensen of *Far Away and Long Ago*.

D106 I FÅGLARNAS RIKE. Stockholm: Wahlström and Widstrand, 1926. Translation by Karin Jensen of *Adventures Among Birds*.

D107 URSKOGENS HEMLIGHET. Stockholm: Billow, 1929. Translation by Senta Centervall of *Green Mansions*.

D108 DET BLODRÖDA LANDET. Stockholm: Natur o. kultur, 1944. Translation by Karin Jensen of *The Purple Land*.

D109 DET BLODRÖDA LANDET. Helsinki: Söderström, 1944. Translation by Karin Jensen of *The Purple Land*.

D110 GRÖNSKANDE BONINGAR. in DET BÄSTAS BOKVAL. Stockholm: Reader's Digest Aktiebolag, 1959. Translation by Lily Vallquist of *Green Mansions*.

DIII I FJÄRRAN LAND FÖR LÄNGE SEN. Stockholm: Natur o. kultur, 1961. Translation by Gustav Sandgren of *Far Away and Long Ago*.

THAI
D112 [*Far Away and Long Ago*] Bangkok: Ministry of Education, n.d.

TURKISH
D113 YEŞIL MALIKÂNELER. Istanbul: Türkiye Yayinevi, 1961. Translation by Özay Sunar of *Green Mansions*.

E

Books about W. H. Hudson

Wilson, G. F. *A Bibliography of the Writings of W. H. Hudson*. London, The Bookman's Journal, 1922.

Roberts, Morley. *W. H. Hudson. A Portrait*. London, Nash & Grayson, 1924.

Goddard, Harold. *W. H. Hudson: Bird-Man*. New York, Dutton, 1928.

B., C. de. *A Naturalist and Immortality*. Whetston, London, Bellchi Press, 1937.

Pozzo, Fernando. *Semblanza de Hudson*. Buenos Aires, Edicion del Instituto de Conferencias del Banco Municipal, 1940.

Gudino Kramer, Luid. *Exaltacion de los Valores Humanos en la Obra de Hudson y Noticias sobre nuestro Folklore*. Parana (Entre Rios), Edicion del autor, 1942.

Wells, Carlton F. *The G. M. Adams – W. H. Hudson Collection*. Ann Arbor, Michigan, William L. Clements Library, 1943.

Hamilton, Robert. *W. H. Hudson. The Vision of Earth*. London, Dent, 1946.

Liandrat, Francisque. *W. H. Hudson 1841–1922. Naturaliste. Sa Vie et son Oeuvre*. Lyon, M. Audin, 1946.

Mendoza, Angelica. *Guillermo Enrique Hudson (1841–1922) Vida y Obra – Bibliografia – Antologia*. New York, Hispanic Institute, 1946.

Looker, Samuel J. *William Henry Hudson: A Tribute by Various Writers*. Worthing, Sussex, Worthing Art Development Scheme, 1947.

West, Herbert Faulkner. *W. H. Hudson's Reading*. Privately printed, 1947.

Dominquez, Maria Alicia. *Presencia del Paisaje en la Obra de Guillermo Enrique Hudson*. Buenos Aires, Ministerio de Hacienda, Economia y Prevision, Direccion de Turismo y Parques, 1949.

Espinoza, Enrique. *Tres Clásicos Ingleses de la Pampa. F. B. Head, William Henry Hudson, R. B. Cunninghame Graham*. Santiago de Chile, Babel, 1951.

Martinez Estrada, Ezequiel. *El Mundo Maravilloso de Guillermo Enrique Hudson*. Mexico – Buenos Aires, Fondo de Cultura Económica, 1951.

Schultz de Mantovani, Fryda. *Fábula del Niño en el Hombre*. Buenos Aires, Editorial Sudamericana, 1951. (Colección Ensayos Breves.)

Costa Herrera, Luis. *Un Viaje por "La Tierra Purpúrea"*. Buenos Aires, Ediciones Medina, 1952.

Velasquez, Luis Horacio. *Hudson Vuelve. Sentido de Nostalgia y Soledad.* La Plata, Ediciones Llanura, 1952.

Ara, Guillermo. *Guillermo E. Hudson: El Paisaje Pampeano y su Expresión.* Buenos Aires, Ministerio de Educación, Universidad de Buenos Aires, 1954.

Hardacre, Kenneth. *W. H. Hudson: A Shepherd's Life.* London, James Brodie, 1954. (Notes on Chosen English Texts Series.)

Haymaker, Richard E. *From Pampas to Hedgerows and Downs. A Study of W. H. Hudson.* New York, Bookman Associates, 1954.

Smith, Thomas Warnock. *W. H. Hudson: Far Away and Long Ago.* London, James Brodie, 1954. (Notes on Chosen English Texts Series.)

Tomalin, Ruth. *W. H. Hudson.* London, Witherby, 1954. (Great Naturalist Series.)

Franco, Luis. *Hudson a Caballo.* Buenos Aires, Editorial Alpe, 1956.

West, Herbert Faulkner. *For a Hudson Biographer.* Hanover, New Hampshire, Westholm Publications, 1958.

Franco, Luis. *Guillermo Enrique Hudson, Escritor Argentino de Lengua Inglesa.* Buenos Aires, Ediciones Peuser, 1959. Originally appeared in Rafael Alberto Arrienta's *Historia de la Literatura Argentina.* Buenos Aires, 1959, volume V, pp. 397–432.

Antonio Moncaut, Carlos. *Reminiscencias del Gaucho Guillermo Enrique Hudson y Breviario de sus Pajaros del Plata.* La Plata, 1961.

Tsuda, Masao. *Las Huellas de Guillermo Enrique Hudson.* Buenos Aires, Americalee, Editora e Impresora, 1963.

Velazquez, Luis Horacio. *Guillermo Enrique Hudson.* Buenos Aires, Ediciones Culturales Argentinas, Ministerio de Educación y Justicia, Dirección General de Cultural, 1963.

Ross, Waldo. *Dos Momentos de la Libertad de la Pampa: William Henry Hudson y Ricardo Güiraldes.* Oxford, Dolphin Book Company, 1964.

Azcoaga, Juan E., editor. *Guillermo Enrique Hudson.* Buenos Aires, Centro Editor de America Latina, 1969. (Enciclopedia del Pensamiento Esencial, no. 41.)

Degiuseppe, Alcides, editor. *Hudson en Quilmes y Chascomus.* Buenos Aires, Ministerio de Educacion, Subsecretaria de Cultura, 1971.

Jurado, Alicia. *Vida y Obra de W. H. Hudson*. Buenos Aires, Argentina Fondo Nacional de las Artes, Coleccion Ensayos, 1971.

Barroso, Haydee M. Jofre. *Genio y Figura de Guillermo Enrique Hudson*. Buenos Aires, Editorial Universitaria de Buenos Aires, 1972.

Frederick, John T. *William Henry Hudson*. New York, Twayne, 1972. (Twayne's English Authors Series.)

Index

Most items are indexed by main entry numbers. Page numbers, where given, are in *italics*. Items in **Bold** type are for main entries of Hudson's major works in Sections A and B. Titles of books and periodicals are in *italics*. Titles of contributions to periodicals and chapters in books are in quotation marks.

"Abbotsbury" A27, C75
Abel A23
Aberdeen Free Press A2, A31
Aberdeen: The University Press A29
"About Spiders" A58
Academy A1, A2, A7, A8, A16, A19
Academy & Literature A21, A22
Achtenhagen, Olga A23
Adams Collection. *See* G.M. Adams Collection
"Adder Controversy, The" C67
Adler, Elmer A26
Adventures Among Birds A31
Adventures Among Birds xiv, A1, A7, A19, A23, A34, A40, A41, A43, A48, A65, C69, C147, C149, C150, C154, C155, C156, C157, C161, C162, C163, C164, C168, C170, C171, C172, C173, C175, D35, D40, D46, D73, D77, D106
"Adventures with Foxes" A51
Afoot in England A27
Afoot in England 1, A27, A48, A55, A60, C75, C92, C105, C111, C114, C115, C117, C123, C125, C129, C141, C148
"Afoot in Quiet Places" C82
Ainsworth-Davis, J.R. B3
Airmont Classic, An A23
Airmont, publishers A23
Alabama Institute for Deaf and Blind A23
ALA Booklist A2, A7, A23, A25, A27, A29, A34, A36, A37, A40, A43, A58
Aldridge Bros. B10
Amalfi, watermark A63
Amateur Photographer A19
Ambassador Books A23
Americalee, Editora e Impresora 225
American Review of Reviews A2, A7, A25, A33
American Uncial type A64
Amino, Kiku D44

Amsco School Publications A23
AMS Press A1, A2, A5, A6, A7, A12, A16, A19, A20, A21, A22, A23, A25, A26, A27, A29, A31, A34, A36, A37, A38, A40, A43, A47
Anderson, Carl J.H. A23
Anfosso, Ninì D34
Anglo-Argentine A21
Angus A62
"Animal Autobiographies" A47, C143
Animal Life and the World of Nature C107
Animals Friend A20, A22, C201
Animals' Friend, The A40
Annual Report, Royal Society for the Protection of Birds C210, C212
An Old Thorn A19, A39, A47, A48, A49, A60
"An Old Thorn" C165, D49
Antonio Moncaut, Carlos 225
Aoki, Shirô D50
"Appeal to the Clergy, An" C70
"Appendix to El Ombú" A21, A28, A33, A56
"Apple Blossoms and a Lost Village" A40
Appleby, publishers A23
Appleton-Century-Crofts *xi*, A5
Ara, Guillermo 225
Archambaud-Fauconnier, H. D19
Argentina Fondo Nacional de las Artes, Coleccion Ensayos 226
Argentine Ornithology A3
Argentine Ornithology 1, 3, A1, A3, A4, A5, A7, A38, A61, *194*, C39
Argentine Republic A3, *194*
Argo A34
Argosy C103
Armed Services edition A1, A2, A23, A33
Arrienta, Rafael Alberto 225
Art-Type edition A23
"As a Tree Falls" A40

228 / INDEX

Asociacion Ornitologica del Plata *xi*
"Aspects of the Valley" A7
"As to Food" A58
Athenaeum A1, A5, A6, A7, A8, A12, A16, A19, A20, A21, A22, A26, A27, A34, A36, A39
Atlanta [Georgia] Journal A23
"At Last, Patagonia!" A7
"At Porchester" C153
Attwell de Veyga, Ricardo D77, D84
Audin, M., publisher *224*
Auk A31, A36, A38
"Autumn" A19
"Autumn, 1912" A31
"Avalon and a Blackbird" A31
Aveleyra, Miss Romola A1
"Aves" A47, C132
"Axe Edge and Its Birds – I" C162
"Axe Edge and Its Birds – II" C163
"Axe Edge and its Birds – III" C164
Azcoaga, Juan E. *225*

Babel, publishers *224*
"Back to the West Country" A31
Badminton Magazine of Sports and Pastimes, The A20, A21, A22, C91, C95, C101
Baines, T., Jnr. B5
Baird, Spencer Fullerton *5*, B12
Bali A23
Ballantyne, Hanson & Co. A19, A22
Banda Oriental A1
Bantam A23
Bantam Classics edition A23
Bantam Pathfinder edition A23
Barker, Carlos A23
Barn Owl, The A13
Barn Owl, The 3, A13, A47
Barroso, Haydee M. Jofre *226*
Barry Shurlock A22
Bates, H.E. A23
"Bath and Wells Revisited" A27, C123
"Bats" A37, C121
Bauer, George W. *xi*
Bayswater edition A20, A27
Bazaar Exchange & Mart A40
B., C. de *224*
"Beautiful Hawk-Moths" A37
Beautiful Wales B2

"Beauty of the Fox" A37
Beck Engraving Company, The A23
Beddard, Frank E. A12
Bedford Street *xv*
Beebe, William A23
Bellchi Press *224*
Bell, Ernest *6*, B4
Bennett Book Studio A23
Bennett, Joe *xi*
Best Books edition A23
Best of W.H. Hudson, The A60
Best of W.H. Hudson, The A60
"Best Scenery I Know, The" C83
Bewick, Thomas A31
Bianco, Angelo D31
Bibliography of the Writings of W.H. Hudson, A *224*
Bibliophile Society, watermark A64
Billing and Sons, Ltd. A2
"Biography of the Vizcacha" A5
Birch, Reginald A23
Bird and Tree Competition *3*
Bird-Catching A10
Bird-Catching 3, A10, A47
"Bird-Catching" A10
"Bird Life at the Land's End" C145
"Bird Life in Winter" A26
"Bird Music" A31
"Bird Music in South America" A7
Bird Notes and News A32, C120, C127, C181
Bird Protection Act *3*
Birds and Green Places A65
Birds and Green Places A65
Birds and Man A20
Birds and Man 5, A20, A22, A48, A60, A65, C71, C77, C78, C79, C81, C87, C90, C93, C94, C95, C97, C104, C135, D1
"Birds and Man" A20, C79
"Birds and the Book, The" A16
Birds and their Young A52
"Birds at their Best" A20
"Birds for London" A16
Birds from my Homeland A38
"Birds in a Cornish Village" A36
"Birds in Authority" A31
Birds in a Village A8
Birds in a Village 1, A4, A8, A11, A36, A65, C46, C48, C50

"Birds in a Village" A8, A36
"Birds in Green Places" A65
Birds in London A16
Birds in London A16, A18, A19, A20, A48, A55, A65, C80, D35
"Birds in London" A20
Birds in Town & Village A36
Birds in Town & Village A8, A36, A39, A48, A60, C46, C48, C50, D35, D82
Birds of La Plata A38
Birds of La Plata 3, A3, A11, A38, A48, *194*, D99
"Birds of the Peak" A31
"Birds of the Rio Negro of Patagonia" A7
Birds of Wing and Other Wild Things A55
Birds of Wing and Other Wild Things A55
"Bird Song" A65
Birmingham Daily Post A22, A31
Birmingham, University of *xi, 5*
Black and White A7
Black Jacket series A37
Blas and Bearded A1
"Blood: A Story of Two Brothers" A40
Blow, Kathleen *xi*
"Blue Columbine and Chequered Daffodil" B2, C112
Bodleian Library *ix, 9*, A1, A4, A6, A10, A11, A13, A23, A24, A35, A55
Bogan, Louise A23
"Bolerium" C139
"Bolerium: The End of all the Land" A26
Bombay Ducks C140
Boni and Liveright A23
Bonner & Co. A35
"Book: An Apology, The" A31
Book Buyer A2
Book League of America, The A23
Bookman A2, A20, A23, A26, A27, A29, A31, A34, A36, A39, A43
Bookman Associates *225*
Bookman's Journal, The A4, *224*
Bookman's Journal and Print Collector, The A6, A22, C209
Book of a Naturalist, The A37
Book of a Naturalist, The A37, A48, A51, A54, A55, A58, A60, A64, A65, B2, C51, C60, C61, C64, C112, C113, C121, C126, C128, C176, C180, C182, C183, C188, C189, C193, C194, C196, C198, C199, D36, D42, D43, D80
Book of The Open Air, The B2
Book of the Open Air, The A37, B2, C112, C113
Borges, Jorge Luis D73
Borzoi A23, A33
Borzoi Books A58
Borzoi books edition A25
Borzoi Books for Young People edition A58
Borzoi Books, watermark A44
Borzoi Classics edition A23
Borzoi Pocket Book edition A23, A33, A44
Boston Herald A23
Boston Transcript A1, A2, A7, A19, A23, A25, A27, A33, A34, A36, A37, A43
Bournemouth Graphic A22
"Boyhood's End" A34
Brack, O.M. *xii*
"Branscombe" A27
"Branscombe and its Birds" C92
British Birds A12
British Birds A12, A15, A65
British Birds, by William Yarrell A13
British Country Life in Autumn & Winter B2
British Country Life in Spring & Summer B2
British Museum *ix, 9*, A1, A2, A3, A7, A9, A10, A13, A14, A15, A17, A22, A23, A24, A26, A27, A31, A35, A38, A55
British Ornithologists' Union A11
"British Pelican, The" A26
British Publishers Guild A27
British Weekly A23
Brooke, Margaret Alice Lilly, Lady Rani of Sarawak *4, 5, 6*, A27, A43, C190, C196
Brotherton Collection, The. *See* Edward Allen Brotherton Collection, University of Leeds
Brotherton Library, The. *See* Edward Allen Brotherton Collection, University of Leeds
Brown, P.E. A65
"Bruised Serpent, The" A37, C60
Brusol, Juan Antonio D97
Buenos Aires *194*

Bulletin from Virginia Kirkus Bookshop Service A58, A60
Burleigh Press, The A20
Burleigh Ltd. A20
Burroughs, John C131
Butler, Horacio A23
Buxton, Sydney A17
"By Swallowfield" A27

Cagle, William R. *x*
Camborne Literary Society A26
Cambridge University Press A46
Camelot Press, The A1, A23, A56
Cameo Classics A1, A23
Campfield Press, The A30
Canadian Forum A50
Canton, William 5
Caravansary and Conversation A31
Carcano, Mariella Filiasi D33
Cardavon Press *xi*, A23
"Cardinal: The Story of My First Caged Bird" A31, C161
Carlton House, publishers A23
Carmania xv
Carmelite House B3
"Carrion Crow in the Balance, The" A16
Casares, Jorge A38, A63, D73
Case of the Caged Bird, The. See *Other Side of the Bars, The*
Cassell's Family Magazine 1, C23
"Castles by the Sea" A26
Castro, Joaquin Rodriguez D88
Catholic World A7, A43
"Cat Question, The" A16
Caxton House, publishers A23
Centervall, Senta D102, D107
Centro Editor de America Latina 225
Century Magazine, The A43, C206, C207, C208
Čep, Jan D4
Čep, Václav D6
"Chaker, The" A58
Chamber's Journal of Popular Literature, Science and Art A37, C193
"Chanticleer" A8, A36, C46
Chapman & Hall A5, A6, A7, A8, A11
Chariot/FineWove, watermark A35
"Charm of the Downs" A19

Charta Regia Britannica A18
Chatto and Windus B7
Chaucer, publishers A46
"Chequered Daffodil, The" A37
Chicago BookWeek A58
Chicago News A23
Chicago Sunday Tribune A60, A61
Chicago Tribune A23
Chicago, University of, Library 9, A1, A8, A23
Chicago, University of, Special Collections *xi*
"Chichester" A19
Chiswick Press A4
"Chitterne Churchyard, In" A40
Chosen English Texts Series 225
Christopher Sandford & Owen Rutter A57
Church Family Newspaper A31
"Churchyard, In a" C177
Classics Book Club A23
Classics illustrated edition A23
[Classified lists of birds with brief notes on their identities] C1, C2, C4
"Clerk and the Last Ravens, The" A31
Clodd, Edward 5
Cloud Castle A47, A59
Cloud Castle and Other Papers B6
Cloud Castle and Other Papers B6
Clovernook Printing House for the Blind A1, A34
"Clover Seed" A47, C151
Coatsworth, Elizabeth A58
Cobb, Lee J. A23
Coker, Willie Belle *xi*
"Cold Day at Silchester, A" A27, C111
Coleman, Carroll A64
Collected Works of W.H. Hudson, The 3, 5, A1, A2, A5, A6, A7, A12, A16, A19, A20, A21, A22, A23, A25, A26, A27, A29, A31, A34, A36, A37, A38, A39, A40, A43, A44, A47, 194, *See also* Popular Edition, Readers' Library Edition, New Readers' Library Edition and Uniform Edition.
"Collector in Guiana, The" C119
Collins, A.L. A26
Collins Classics edition A23

Collins, publishers A23
Colonial issue, *Green Mansions* A23
Colorgraphic Offset Company A23
"Comfort of Ruins, The" C118
"Coming of Spring, The" A26
"Common Crow, The" A47, C68
"Concerning Eyes" A7, C37
"Concerning Lawns and Earthworms" A37
Conchitas, Argentine Republic *194*
Contemporary Review A20, C71
Cooper, R.M. *xi*, A12
Cornell University Press *xi*, A61
Cornhill Magazine A21, A31, A33, A40, C31, C154, C161, C168, C192, C203
"Cornish Humour" A26
Cornishman, The A26
"Cornwall's Connemara" A26, C138
Costa Herrera, Luis *224*
Couch, A.T. Quiller A55
Country Life A16, A29, A37, A40, C182, C185, C187, C188, C189, C191, C195, C197
Country Life Press *xiii*
Court Book Company A23
Covarrubias, Miguel A23, D76
Coward, T.A. A52
"Crested Screamer, The" A5, C41
"Cristiano: A Horse" A37, A51, A58, A64
"Cristiano: the Sentinel Horse" A64
Critic A12, A16
"Cromer Beach, On" A40
Crowell, Cedric R. A23
Crown Library edition A20
"Crows in London" A16
Crusoe, Robinson A1
Cruz, Federico López D82
Crystal Age, A A2
Crystal Age, A A1, A2, A7, A21, A34, A40, A48
Cullen, John *xi*
Curle, Richard A27, A31, A38, A57
Current Opinion A34
C. Whittingham and Co. A4
"Cyclist on Walking, A" C141

Daglish, Eric Fitch A19, A27, A34
Daily Chronicle A5, A7, A8, A16, A21, A22, A23, A25, A26, A27, A29

Daily Express A31
Daily Mail A22
Daily News A1, A19, A20, A23, A27, A29, A40
Daily News and Leader A31, A34
Daily Telegraph A16, A19, A22, A23, A26, A29, A31
"Dandy" C201
"Dandy: A Story of a Dog" A40
D. Appleton and Co. A5, A26
"Dartford Warbler, The" A20
"Dartford Warbler: How to Save Our Rare Birds, The" C97
Dartmouth College Library, Special Collections *xi*, *4*, *9*, A1, A2, A3, A6, A8, A22, A23, A29, A38, A39, A53, A59
David & Charles (Publishers) A16
"Daws in the West Country" A20
"Daws in West Cornwall" C197
Deabreu, M. D58
"Dead and the Living, The" A40
Dead Man's Plack A1, A40, A47, A48, A49
"Dead Man's Plack" A39
Dead Man's Plack and An Old Thorn A39
Dead Man's Plack and an Old Thorn A39, A47, A49, C165
Dead Man's Plack An Old Thorn & Miscellanea A47
Dead Man's Plack An Old Thorn & Miscellanea A4, A9, A10, A11, A13, A14, A17, A24, A30, A32, A35, A42, A47, A49, B1, B3, B4, B6, C23, C34, C44, C68, C99, C116, C124, C131, C132, C133, C140, C143, C151, C187, C203, C205
Dead Man's Plack An Old Thorn & Poems A49
Dead Man's Plack an Old Thorn & Poems A47, A49, C29, C32, C38
"Death-feigning Instinct, The" A5
de Córdoba, Mariá A.L. D96
"Dedication to all who love the beautiful and mourne over the senseless and cruel destruction of bird life and beauty, A" A17
Degiuseppe, Alcides *225*
Dell, publishers A23

de Martelly, John A23
Demetria A1
Dent, J.M. *xi, 4, 194*
Denton, John *xi,* A2
Descriptive Catalogue of the W.L. Lewis Collection, A B13
Descriptive Catalogue of the W.L. Lewis Collection, A B13
"Desert Pampas, The" A5
"Destruction of the Albatross" C100
Detmold, E.J. *3,* A36
De Volharding A65
Dewar, David *xii,* A7, A61
Dewar, Douglas C140
Dial A1, A12, A19, A23, A29, A31, A34, A37, A46, C211
"Dimples" A40
Disappointed Squirrel and Other Stories from "The Book of a Naturalist", The A51
Disapointed Squirrel and Other Stories from "The Book of a Naturalist", The A37, A51
"Disappointed Squirrel, The" A51, C193
"Discontented Squirrel, The" A37
Diversions of a Naturalist A37
Dobie Collection. *See* J. Frank Dobie Collection, Humanities Research Center, University of Texas at Austin
Dobie, J. Frank *xi,* A64
"Do Cats Think?" A47, C203, C204, C205
Dodd, Mead A23
"Dog in Exile, A" A7
"Dogs in London" A37, C183
Dolores A1
Dominquez, Maria Alicia 224
"Don Gregorio Gandara" A58
Doric Books A2
Dos Momentos de la Libertad de la Pampa: William Henry Hudson y Ricardo Güiraldes 225
Doubleday & Company A37
Doubleday, Doran & Co. *xi,* A23
Doubleday, Page and Co. *xiii*
Douglas, Norman B7
"Dragonfly, The" A58
"Dragon-Fly Storms" A5
Dresser, H.E. A15
Drösser, Ellinor D21

Dublin Evening Herald A39
Duchess, watermark A46
Duckworth & Co. A20, A21
Duckworth, Gerald *xi*
Duckworth's Greenback Library A21
Duo-tone classics, library edition A23
Durward, Quentin A1
Duvoisin, Roger A. A33
Dwoskin, Charles A23
"Dying Huanaco, The" A5, C58

"Eagle and the Canary, The" A8, A36, C48
"Earliest Memories" A34
"Early Memories" C190
"Early Spring in Savernake Forest" A20, C81
Eastbourne Gazette A19
"Easter Walk on Whitesheet Hill, An" C125
"East London" A16
Ebenezer Baylis & Son A16, A22
Ebro, The A63
Edgar A39
Edicion del Instituto de Conferencias del Banco Municipal 224
Ediciones Culturales Argentinas, Ministerio de Educación y Justicia, Dirección General de Cultural 225
Ediciones Llanura 225
Ediciones Medina 224
Ediciones Peuser 225
Edinburgh Library edition A37
Editions for the Armed Services A1, A2, A23, A33
Editorial Alpe 225
Editorial Sudamericana 224
Editorial Universitaria de Buenos Aires 226
Educational Series. Society for the Protection of Birds A15
Edward Allen Brotherton Collection, University of Leeds *xi, 5, 9,* A1, A6, A20, A23, A42
Elfrida A39
Elian Greeting-Booklets A54
El Ombú A21
El Ombú A1, A21, A28, A33, A40, A48, A56, C53, C91, D3, D20, D38, D49, D66, D69, D73, D74, D90, D100

"El Ombú" A28, A33, A56
El Ombú and other South American Stories A21
"El Pato" C91
Enciclopedia del Pensamiento Esencial *225*
English Review, The A27, A31, A34, A39, A49, C148, C150, C156, C165, C169, C175, C190, C213, C214
E.P. Dutton & Co. *xi, xv,* A1, A2, A5, A6, A7, A12, A16, A19, A20, A21, A22, A23, A25, A26, A27, A29, A31, A34, A36, A37, A38, A39, A40, A43, A45, A46, A47, A48, A51, A55, A60, *224*
Ernest Benn *xi,* A2
Espinoza, Enrique *224*
Estrada, E. Martínez D73
Eusebio, Don C190
Evans, D.W. *xi*
Eveleigh Nash & Grayson A50
Evening Standard A27, A29, A31
Everyman's Library A1, A23
Everyman's Library edition A29, A34
Exaltacion de los Valores Humanos en la Obra ae Hudson y Noticias sobre nuestro Folklore 224
"Exotic Birds for Britain" A8, A36, C50
"Expulsion of the Rooks" A16
"Extermination of Cranes" C160
[Extract of a letter to the Secretary of the Zoological Society of London dated 30 April 1869 read at the meeting of the Zoological Society 24 June 1869] C3
Eyebrows A1
Eye Witness A34, C166
Eyre Methuen *xi*

Fábula del Niño en el Hombre 224
"Facts and Thoughts about Spiders" A5
Fairy Fauna, A A53
Fairy Fauna, A A53
"Fairy Fauna, A" A19
Family Herald A27
Fan A6
Fan 3, 5, A6, D85
"Far Away" C45
Far Away and Long Ago A34
Far Away and Long Ago 4, A1, A7, A19, A23, A31, A34, A36, A39, A40, A43,
A48, A55, A58, A60, C166, C190, D19, D35, D39, D59, D70, D73, D79, D91, D96, D97, D105, D111, D112
Far Town Road A23
Father Archangel of Scotland A64
"Fear in Birds" A5
"Fear in the Shell" A58
Feathered Women
Feathered Women 3, A9, A47
"Feathered Women" C62, C63
"Feather-Fashion: A Last Word, The" A47, C99
Fernández, Gonzalo D91
Ferrer, Mel A23
Field A19, A20, A22, A27, A29, A31, A38, C174
Field Museum of Natural History, Library *xi, 9,* A13, A14, A15
Figaro A1
"Fight in the Dark" A58
Fine Editions Press A23
"First Walk, A" A58
Fishing Gazette A22
Fitter, Richard A16
F.J. Head & Co. A23
Förlag, A B Ljus A27
Foley, Cornelia B. *xi*
"Following a River" A27
Fondo de Cultura Económica *224*
For a Hudson Biographer 225
Ford, Ford Madox B11
Forest and Stream A16
Foreword A59
Foreword A59
Fortnightly Review A37, C61, C64, C68
Fotosetter Bodoni Book A62
Fountain, Paul B1
Four Novels for Adventure A23
4/6 Series of Novels, The A2
Fox, H.F.B. A55
Franco, Luis *225*
Franklin Printing Company, The A23
Franklin Watts A23
Frasconi, Antonio A38
"Freckles" A40
Frederick, John T. *226*
Frederick Steel & Co. B10
Freese, Walter E. *xi,* A37

"Friendly Rat, A" A37, A51, C194
"Friend of Man, The" A58
"Friendship in Animals" A31
From Pampas to Hedgerows and Downs. A Study of W.H. Hudson 225
Fukizawa, Tadae D51
Fuller, Edmund A23
"Further Observations on the Swallows of Buenos Ayres" C21
"Furze in its Glory, The" A26
"Furze-Wren or Furze-Fairy, The" A31

Galsworthy, John *vi, xiii, xiv*, 2, 5, A23, A33, A34, A40, A55, B8
"Gannets Fishing" C144
Garamond type A64
Gardiner, Linda 4, A45
Garnett, Edward *xv*, 4, 5, A1, A6, A19, A20, A21, A22, A23, A29, A33, A34, A39, A40, A43, A44, A46, A47, A48, A55, C134, C204, C211
Garnett, Richard *xi*
Gauchos of the Pampas and Their Horses A64
Gauchos of the Pampas and their Horses A64
"Geese: An Appreciation and a Memory" A20, C95
Genio y Figura de Guillermo Enrique Hudson 226
"Genius of W.H. Hudson, The" A43
Gentleman's Magazine 1, A5, A7, A8, A36, C33, C35, C36, C37, C40, C41, C45, C48
Geoffrey Cumberlege A61
Geographical Journal A34
George H. Doran A37, A51
Gerald Duckworth & Co. *xiv* A1, A2, A16, A22, A23, A25, A28, A33, A56, A59, B6
Gilbert and Rivington, Ld. A5, A7
Gilberton, publishers A23
Gillmor, Robert A65
Ginzburg, Simon D25, D26
Gissing, George A17, A25, C54
Glasgow Evening News A27
Glasgow Herald A20
Glixon, David M. *xi*
Globe A16, A23, A26, A27, A31
Gloucester Journal A20, A39

G.M. Adams Collection, Department of Rare Books and Special Collections, University of Michigan 5, 9, A1, A2, A3, A6, A7, A8, A15, A16, A22, A23, A29, A38, A44
G.M. Adams – W.H. Hudson Collection, The 224
Goddard, Harold 224
Golden Cockerel Press, The A57
Golden Ass, The A33
"Goldfinches at Ryme Intrinsica" A31, C150, C213
Goldring, Douglas B11
Good Words A19
Gosse, Philip C209
Gotch, Bernard C. A29
G.P. Putnam *xiv*
G.P. Putnam's Sons *xi*, A23
Graham, Mrs. Bontine 4, A25, A57, C23, D76
Graham, R.B. Cunninghame 2, 4, A1, A7, A21, A25, A28, A34, A38, A56, A57, A62, A64, C23, C73, D76, D79
Grainger, Edmund A23
"Grand Archaic Ostrich, The" A58
Graphic A1, A8, A19, A22, A27
Grayson & Grayson A50
"Great Bird Gatherings" A31
Great Deserts and Forests of North America, The B1
Great Deserts and Forests of North America, The A47, B1
"Great Dog Superstition, The" A37, C51
"Great Frost, A" A26
"Great Illustrated Classics edition" A23
Great Naturalist Series 225
Greenback Library, The A21, A28
"Green Country in Quest of Rare Songsters, In a" A31
"Green Land, In a" C170, C171, C172, C173
Green Mansions A23
Green Mansions xiii, xiv, xv, 2, 5, A1, A2, A7, A19, A21, A23, A25, A28, A31, A33, A34, A37, A40, A43, A48, A56, A58, D2, D5, D7, D8, D10, D11, D14, D17, D22, D24, D27, D28, D30, D31, D32, D33, D41, D47, D50, D51, D52,

D53, D54, D55, D56, D58, D60, D61,
D62, D63, D64, D65, D71, D87, D101,
D102, D103, D107, D110, D113
"Green Places" A65
Green, Roland A52
Gress, Elsa D7
Grey, Edward, (Viscount Grey of Fallodon)
   A1, A20, A22, A47, C212
Grey, Lady A22
Grönvold, H. *3*, A30, A32, A38, A41, A45
Grosset and Dunlap A1, A23
Guardian A19, A20, A26, A27, A29
"Guardian Puma, The" A58
Gudino Kramer, Luid 224
"Guide Books: An Introduction" A27
Guild Books A27
Guild Books edition A27
*Guillermo E. Hudson: El Paisaje Pampeano y
   su Expressión* 225
Guillermo Enrique Hudson 225
*Guillermo Enrique Hudson (1841–1922) Vida
   y Obra-Bibliografía-Antología* 224
*Guillermo Enrique Hudson, Escritor
   Argentino de Lengua Inglesa* 225
Guillermo Kraft A34
"Gulls at St. Ives" A26, C136
Gunther, Dr. A18
Gurney & Jackson A13
Guthrie, James B10
"Gwendoline" A39, A49, C38

"Half-hour breathing intervals of a
   laborious Naturalist" A37
Halkin, Simon D24, D27, D28
Hall, C. V. 2, 4, A9, A10, A11, A13
Halle, Louis J., Jr. A23
Hamilton Kilmory, watermark A62
Hamilton, Robert 224
hammer and anvil, watermark A53
Hampshire Days A22
Hampshire Days A21, A22, A48, A52, A55,
   A60, A65, C84, C96, C101, C102, C106
"Hampshire Village, In a" A31
Hampton Court edition A23
Hants Chronicle A22
Hardacre, Kenneth 225
Harford, Henry A6
Harmsworth Natural History B3

Harmsworth Natural History A5, B3, C44
Harper & Brothers A23
Harper's *xiv*
Harper's Modern Classics A23
Harper's Weekly A23
Hartley, Alfred *3*, A7
Hartley, P.H.T. A65
Hartsdale House, publishers A23
Harvard University *9*
Harvie-Brown, J.A. C130
"Haunter of Churchyards, A" A40
Havlasová, Elsie D2
Haymaker, Richard E. 225
Hazell, Watson & Viney A31
Heart of England, The B2
Heinemann, William A21, B8
Henderson, Keith A1, A23
Henry Lindenmeyr & Sons A27
Hepburn, Audrey A23
Heritage Club, The A23
Heritage Press, The A23
Heritage Press edition, The A23
Heritage Reprint series, The A23
Hernando de Soto A21
"Heron: A Feathered Notable, The" A37
"Heron as a Table-Bird, The" A37
"Her Own Village" A40
Hill, Edwin B. A59, B6
Hillman, Eduardo D66, D67, D69, D74,
   D75, D86, D95, D98
Hind in Richmond Park, A A43
Hind in Richmond Park, A 5, A1, A7, A19,
   A23, A31, A34, A39, A43, A48, A60,
   A65, C206, C207, C208, D78
"Hind in Richmond Park, A" A43, C206
"Hints to Adder-Seekers" A37, B2
Hispanic Institute 224
Historia de la Literatura Argentina 225
History of British Birds, A A31
Hodder and Stoughton *xi*, A37, B2
Home Chimes C34
"Homeless" A40
Homorus A3
Hook, Bryan A16
Hooper, Wynnard *6*
Horae Solitariae B2
Horder, Lord (Baron Horder) *xi*, A1
Hornbook A58

"Horse and Man" A5
"Horse of the Pampas, The" A64
Houghton Library, Harvard University 9, A59
"House, The" A58
"How I Became an Idler" A7
"How I Found My Title" A40
Hubbard, Mrs. George 4, A23
Hubert, J. D72
Hudson a Caballo 225
Hudson, Albert 4, A63
Hudson Anthology, A A48
Hudson Anthology, A A48
Hudson, Emily 4
Hudson en Quilmes y Chascomus 225
Hudson, Hubert Rockwood A63
Hudson Vuelve. Sentido de Nostalgia y Soledad 225
Hudson, W.H. Chronology of major publications 7, 8
Huellas de Guillermo Enrique Hudson, Las 225
Humane Review, The A20, A21, C97, C99, C109
"Human in Floral Colours, The" C94
Humanitarian A26, A31
Humanitarian League A35, B4
Humanities Research Center xi, 4, 9, A2, A19, A22, A23, A34
"Humble-Bees and other Matters" A5
"Humming-Birds" A5, C43
Humphries, publishers A23
Hunt, Violet B10
Hutchinson & Co. A26, A27, A31
Hutchinson Publishing Group *xi*, A26
H. Wolff Estate A20
Hyde Park A65

Ibis A3, A20, *194*, C39
"Idle Days" A7
Idle Days in Patagonia A7
Idle Days in Patagonia A1, A7, A8, A19, A22, A23, A31, A34, A36, A43, A48, A58, A60, C30, C35, C37, C40, C42, C49, C56, D16, D35, D72, D73, D93
"Idle Days in Patagonia" C35
"Idle Hours of a Naturalist" A37
Idler A20, C90

Illinois State University 9, A1, A2, A6, A8, A16, A19, A22, A36, A37, A50
Illustrated Classics A23
Illustrated editions A23
Illustrated London News A7, A23
Illustrated Modern Library edition A23
"Immortal Nightingale, The" A31, C154
"Impression of Axe Edge, An" A31
"Impression of Penzance, An" A26
"In a Garden" A8
Inconsequent Demi-semi Divagations of Indolescence A37
Independent Review A2
Indiana University, Bloomington, Indiana 9
Indian Field A20
Inha, I.K. D14
International Collectors Library edition A23
Inter-Society Color Council-National Bureau of Standards centroid color charts *x*
"In the Wilderness" A25
Irish Times A27, A31
Ishuin, Tetsu D42
Isthumas of Tehuantepec A23
Iwata, Ryôkichi D37, D45

Jacket Library edition A23
"Jack Jackdaw and Some Other Birds" A51
James Brodie, publishers 225
Jameson, Harriet C. *xi*
J.B. Lippincott Co. A8
Jefferies, Richard A25
Jensen, Karin D100, D101, D104, D105, D106, D108, D109
Jewish World A2
J. Frank Dobie Collection, Humanities Research Center, University of Texas at Austin 9, A1, A2, A3, A8, A22, A23, A29, A34, A38, A40, A46, A50
J.M. Dent & Sons Ltd. *xv*, A1, A2, A5, A6, A7, A12, A16, A19, A20, A21, A22, A23, A25, A26, A27, A29, A31, A34, A36, A37, A38, A39, A40, A41, A43, A45, A46, A47, A48, A49, A53, A54, A55, B9, *224*
J. Miles & Co. A32

Job, Herbert Keightley C130
John Crerar Library, The *xi*, A22
"John-Go-To-Bed-At-Noon" A37, A51
John O'London's Weekly A39
Johnston, Harry B3
Jonathan Cape A50
Jugaku, Shizu D39
Jurado, Alicia *xii, 226*

Kanter, Albert L. A23
Kashiwakura, Shunzô D38, D48, D49, D57
Kauffer, E. McKnight A23
Kayama, Shigeru D47, D56
Keane, A.H. A1
Kendall, Lyle H., Jr. B13
Kennerley, Mitchell *xiv*, A31
Keulemans, J.K. *3*, A3
Kew A18
Kew Gardens and Old Deer Park A18
Kew Gardens and Old Deer Park 3, A18
"Kew Gardens and Old Deer Park" C98
Kimura, Ki D40, D46
Kimura, Miki D35
King Penguin Books edition, The A38
Kingsley, Dorothy A23
King's Treasuries of Literature A8
King's Treasuries of Literature edition A31, A55
Kirmse, Marguerite A51
Knickerbocker Press A23
Knopf, Alfred A. *vi, vii, xi, xv, 2, 5*, A20, A21, A23, A25, A26, A27, A31, A33, A44, A58
Knopf, Blanche *xiv, xv*, A23
Knowledge A16
Knowles, Mr. C54
Koshland, William A. *xi*, A20
Kraft, Alberto A34
Kraft, publishers A38
Kuhnert, William B3

Lacerda, Nair D59
Lady A21
"Lady Grey as Nature Lover" C137
"Lake Village, The" A31
Lamb, Richard A1
Lancer Books A23
Lancet A22

Land and Water A5, A7, A20
Land's End, The A26
Land's End, The A26, A48, A55, A60, A65, C136, C138, C139, C144
Lankester, Ray, A37
Large type edition A23
"Last Hampshire Ravens, The" C107
"Last of his Name, The" A27
"Last of the Ospreys, The" C66
Last Pre-Raphaelite, The B11
Last Pre-Raphaelite, The B11
Lathrop, Dorothy P. A25
"Laughing at a Cat" A47, C133
Leeds, University of *xi, 5*
Leisure Hour A7, A22
Lemon, Mrs. Frank E. *4*, A4, A9, A10, A11, A13, A14, A15, A18
Leon, Marie A47
Lermitte, Carlos D92
Lerner, Alan Jay A23
Lesser, [Joseph] A23
Letters From Limbo B9
Letters from Limbo B9
Letters from W.H. Hudson 1901–1922 A46
Letters from W.H. Hudson 1901–1922 A46
Letters from W.H. Hudson to Edward Garnett A46
Letters from W.H. Hudson to Edward Garnett A46
"Letters from W.H. Hudson to Edward Garnett" C211
Letters on the Ornithology of Buenos Ayres A61
Letters on the Ornithology of Buenos Ayres A3, A38, A61, *194*
"Letters on the Ornithology of Buenos Ayres" A61
[Letters on the ornithology of Buenos Ayres] C5 to C16
Letter to Clergymen, Ministers, and Others A14
Letter to Clergyman, Ministers, and Others 3, A14, A47, C70
"[Letter to Philip Gosse]" C209
"[Letter to Spencer F. Baird]" C215
"[Letter to Viscount Grey of Fallodon dated 12 February 1922]" C212

Leviathan Books edition A56
Lewis, W.L. B13
Lewis, W., printer A46
Leyris, Pierre D20
Liandrat, Francisque *224*
Liberating Caged Birds, On A32
Liberating Caged Birds, On A32, A47
"Liberating Caged Birds, On" C181
"Liberty and Dirt" A58
Library Journal A58
Library of Congress *ix*, A1, A3, A5, A7, A15, A22, A31, A36, A51
Life and Letters of John Galsworthy, The B8
Life and Letters of John Galsworthy, The B8
"Life in a Pine Wood" A37
"Life in a Pine Wood (People, Birds, and Ants)" C196
"Life in Patagonia" A7, C40
Life Story of a Fox, The C143
Lilly Library, Indiana University, Bloomington *xi, 9*, A1, A2, A7, A8, A22, A23, A26, A29, A31, A42
Limited Editions Club, The A23
Limited Editions Club edition, The A23, A34, D79
Linnet for Sixpence, A A24, A47, A48
"Linnets, Larks and Goldfinches" A10
"List of Birds collected at Conchitas, Argentine Republic, by Mr. William H. Hudson" C1
Literary Digest, The A43
Literary Gazette A16
Literary Guild of America A23
Literary World A1, A2, A19, A20, A22, A23
Literature A16, A19
Literature of Yesterday and Today edition A19, A34
Little Boy Lost, A A25
Little Boy Lost, A A21, A25, A40, A48, A58, C72, D9, D25, D26, D44, D81. *See also* A39
Little Boy Lost Together with the Poems of W.H. Hudson, A A25, A39, A49, C29, C32, C38
"Little Fishes and Fascination" A47, C187
"Little Girl Lost, A" A40

"Little Girls I Have Met" A40, C192
"Little Red Dog, The" A37, A51, B2, C113
Liverpool Courier A27
Liverpool Daily Post A22, A31
"Living Garment, The" A19
"Living Garment of the Downs, The" C89
Llona, Victor D15, D16, D17, D18
Lodge, G.E. A12
Lodge, R.B. A12, A16
"London Birds" C93
"London Birds in Winter" C80
"London Daw, The" A16
London Quarterly Review A22
"London's Little Birds" A16
"London Sparrow, The" *1*, A25, A39, A49, C29
Longmans, Green and Co. A12, A16, A19, A20, A22, B1, B5
Longman Group *xi*
Longman Group Limited A12
Longman's Magazine 1, A5, A7, A8, A19, A20, A22, A27, A29, A36, B3, C43, C44, C46, C49, C52, C55, C58, C59, C77, C78, C79, C81, C84, C87, C89, C92, C93, C96, C102, C106, C108, C110
Looker, Samuel J. B10, *224*
Looking Back an Autobiographical Excursion B7
Looking Back An Autobiographical Excursion B7
Los Angeles Times A23
Lost British Birds A11
Lost British Birds 3, A11, A45, A47
"Lost Village, A" C200
Lucas, E.V. *5*
Lusty, Robert *xi*, A26
Lydekker, Richard B3

McClelland and Stewart, publishers A34
McCormick, A.D. *3*, A11, A16, A23, A25, A27
MacDonald & Co, publishers B11
Macdonald, Lesley *xii*
Machino, Shizuo D36
Macmillan, *xi*
Macmillan's Magazine A21, A37, C51, C53, C60
Macrae, John Jr. *xi, xv*

Macy, George A23, A34
Macy, George, Archives A34
Made in Holland, watermark A64
McFee, William A1
Magno, S. *xi*, A38
Magnum Easy Eye Books edition A23
Mammals of Great Britain and Ireland, The C121
Manaton *xiii*
Manchester Guardian A8, A20, A22, A27, A31, A38, A39, A40
"Manners and Morals" A26
Manning, Hugo D73
"Manual, Also Called the Fox" A58
Manuelita C190
"Man Who Ate a Heron, The" A51
"Maritime District, The" A19
Marrot, H.V. B8
"Marsh Warbler's Music, The" A31
Marshall, J.L. *xi*
"Marta Riquelme" A21, A28, A33, A56, D38, D49
Martinez Estrada, Ezequiel 224
Martin, H. Bradley, Library *xii, 5, 9*, A3, A4, A9, A10, A23, A42
Martone, Maria D30, D32
Mary's Little Lamb A54
Mary's Little Lamb A54
"Mary's Little Lamb" A37, A51, A58
Masefield, John *4*
Massinghame, H.J. *4*, D73
Massini, Carlos A. D85
Maurice, Charles A36
Mayfair Miscellany A50
"Memory of the Ancient Times, A" C169
"Memory of the Pampa Grass" A58
Men, Books and Birds A50
Men, Books and Birds A50
Mendoza, Angelica 224
"Mephitic Skunk, The" A5
Meredith A31
Merry England 1, A7, A25, A49, C29, C30, C32, C38
Merryweather, Maud C23
Methuen & Co. A29
Metro-Goldwyn-Mayer A23
Mewton-Wood, Noel, A34
Meynell, Francis *xi*

Michigan, University of *5, 9*, A6, A44
Michigan, University of, Department of Rare Books and Special Collections *xi*
Millais, J.G. C121
"Millicent and Another" A40
"Mimicry and Warning Colours in Grasshoppers" A5
Ministerio de Educación 225
Ministerio de Educacion, Subsecretaria de Cultura 225
Ministerio de Hacienda, Economia y Prevision, Direccion de Turismo y Parques 224
"Misused Potato, The" C199
Modern Classics edition A29
Modern Library, The A1, A23
"Mole Question, The" A37, C188
Molly and Margaret B5
Molly and Margaret B5
Montenegro, Ernesto D71, D87
Monthly Review, The A37, C128
"Moor-hens in Hyde Park" A8, A36
"More or Less Happy Family, A" A22, C101
Moriya, Yoichi, D52
Morning Leader A21
Morning Post A20, A27, A29, A40, A43, C146
"Mosquitoes and Parasite Problems" A5
"Moths" C178
"Movements of London Birds" A16
Mundo Maravilloso de Guillermo Enrique Hudson, El 224
Murayama, Yuzo D41
Murray's Magazine A8, A36, C50
"Music and Dancing in Nature" A5, C55
"My Experiences of the Puma" A47, B3
"My First Caged Bird" C69
"My Friend Jack" A27
"My Friend the Pig" A37, A51, C198
"My Neighbour's Bird Stories" A37, C176

Nagai, Hinako D53
Nannichi, Yoshio A29
Nan-un-do, publishers A34
Nash & Grayson 224
Nation A2, A5, A7, A12, A20, A23, A25, A26, A27, A29, A33, A34, A38, A39,

A40, A46
Nation & Athenaeum A40, A43
National and English Review A37, C183, C196, C198, C199
National Home Library A23
National Institute for the Blind C196
National Library for the Blind A1, A5, A8, A19, A21, A22, A23, A25, A27, A29, A31, A34, A39, A40, A43
National Physical Laboratory A18
National Portrait Gallery A57
"Native Naturalist, A" A26
Naturalist and Immortality, A 224
Naturalist in La Plata, The A5
Naturalist in La Plata, The A4, A5, A7, A8, A20, A21, A37, A48, A58, B1, B3, C20, C41, C43, C44, C52, C55, C58, C59, D18, D37, D45, D73, D89
Naturalist in the Guianas, A C119
"Naturalist on the Pampas, The" C54
Natural Science A5
Nature A3, A5, A7, A8, A11, A12, A16, A19, A20, A22, A23, A34, A36, A37, A62, C42, C57
Nature in Downland A19
Nature in Downland A1, A7, A19, A20, A21, A22, A23, A28, A31, A34, A39, A43, A48, A53, A55, A60, A65, C89
Nature Notes A9, A14, A16, A22, A40, C63, C70, C86
"Nature's Night-lights" A5
Navy & Army Illustrated A19
Nelson, publishers A37
Nemi, Orsola D29
New Adelphi Library edition A40
New Age A2, A29
Newcastle Weekly Chronicle A31
New Gallery A17
New popular edition A38
New Readers' Library, The A1, A2, A16, A20, A21, A22, A23
New Readers' Library edition, The A1, A2, A16, A20, A21, A22, A23
New Readers' Library, pocket edition A23
New Republic A1, A23, A33
New Statesman 1, A31, A35, A37, A40, A43, C176, C177, C178, C179, C180, C184, C186

Newton, Miss E.A. 5, B13
New York Call A7
New York Commercial Advertiser A19
New Yorker A60
New York Evening Post 5, A25, A27, A38, A43
New York Evening Sun A1, A23
New York Freeman A27
New York Herald Tribune Book Review A60
New York Independent A1, A2, A7, A23
New York Metropolitan *xiii*
(*New York*) *Nation* A1
New York Sun A23
New York Times Book Review A1, A2, A6, A7, A8, A20, A22, A23, A25, A26, A27, A29, A31, A33, A34, A36, A37, A38, A39, A40, A43, A44, A46, A51, A58, A60, A61
New York Tribune A19, A22, A43
New York Weekly Review A36, A37
New York World A43, A48
Nineteenth Century A5, C54
"Niño Diablo" A21, A28, A33, A56, A58, C53, D23
Nishikawa, Kiyoko D55
"Noble Wasp, A" A5
Nobusada, I. A34
Noda, Kaisaku D54
Nonesuch Press, The *xi*, A23, A46
"North-West and North London" A16
Norton, publishers A23
Notary Binders, The A53
"Note on Hudson's Literary Art, A" A19
"Note on Hudson's Romances, A" A23
"Note on Hudson's Spirit, A" A40
"Note on the Spoonbill of the Argentine Republic" C27
"Note on W.H. Hudson, A" 5
"Notes on the Birds of the Genus *Homorus* observed in the Argentine Republic" C39
"Notes on the Habits of the Churinche (*Pyrocephalus rubineus*)" C19
"Notes on the Habits of the Pipit of the Argentine Republic" C22
"Notes on the Procreant Instincts of the three Species of *Molothrus* found in Buenos Ayres" C24

"Notes on the Rails of the Argentine
  Republic" C28
Nottingham Guardian A31
Nottinghamshire Daily Guardian A20, A22
Nuflo A23

Observer A5, A27, A29, A31, A36, A38,
  A40, A42, C202
Okhrimenko, P. D60, D62
Olave A62
Olivia A1
"Old Cornish Hedges" A26
"Old Garden, In an" A36
"Old Man in [sic] Kensington Gardens,
  The" 6
"Old Man of Kensington Gardens, The"
  A25, A39, A49
"Old Man of the Sea, The" A58
"Old Man's Delusion, The" A40, C186
"Old Road Leading Nowhere, An" A27
Old Thorn, An A29
"Old Thorn, An" A39
"[on Bird-catching and Collecting]" C120
"[on Egret's plumes]" C74
153 Letters from W.H. Hudson A46
153 Letters from W.H. Hudson A46, C211
"On Going Back" A27
"On the Birds of the Rio Negro of
  Patagonia" C17
"On the Habits of the Burrowing Owl
  (*Pholeoptynx cunicularia*)" C25
"On the Habits of the Swallows of the
  Genus *Progne* met with in the Argentine
  Republic" C18
"On the Habits of the Vizcacha (*Lagostomus
  trichodactylus*)" *194*, C20
"On the Herons of the Argentine Republic,
  with a Notice of a curious Instinct of
  Ardetta involucris" C26
"On the Sense of Direction" A43
"On the Sense of Smell" A43
"On the Use of Guide-books" C117
"[On Wheatears and Elder-trees]" C127
Open-Air Library edition A19, A27
Opie, photographs A46
Osprey; Or, Egrets and Aigrettes A4
Osprey; Or, Egrets and Aigrettes 2, 3, A4,
  A47

Other Side of the Bars, The B4
Other Side of the Bars, The A47, B4
"Our Indian Birds" A47, C140
"Our Wild Birds" A47, C116
Out-Door World Library A12
Outlook A19, A20, A25, A26, A29, A31,
  A34, A36, A37, A39, A40, A46
"Owls in a Village" A20, C90
Oxford B2
Oxford University Press A61

Pájaros Nuestros A38
Palliser, Edith *4*
Pall Mall Gazette A19, A20, A22, A23,
  A27, A31
Palmer, Roger *xi*, A37
"Parental and Early Instincts" A5
Parker, C.C. *xv*
Parnassus, publishers A23
Pärn, Auguste D12
"[Partial letter to Sir Montagu Sharpe
  dated 3 May 1922]" C210
Pasadena [Texas] Star-News A23
Pat, author of *Molly and Margaret* B5
"Patriarch of the Pampas" A34, C166
Patricia A62
Pawling, Sydney *xv*
Payne, James A33
Pears, Peter A34
Peckham, Elizabeth G. C126
Peckham, George W. C126
"Pelican, The" *4*
"Pelino Vieras Confession" A21, A33, C31
Penguin Books A1, A27, A38
Penguin Books edition A27
"People and the Farms, The" A26
Percy Lund, Humphries & Co. A21
"Perfume of an Evening Primrose" A7
Perkins, Anthony A23
"Perplexed Lady, A" A17
Peter Pauper Press A23
Philadelphia Inquirer A23
Phillips, Mrs. Edward *2*, *4*, A1, A8, A9,
  A10, A11, A13
Philosophical Library, publishers B12
Piarn, A. D13
"Pilgrims at The Land's End" A26
Pilot A19, A22

Pipits A15
Pipits A15
Pittsburgh Monthly Bulletin A2
Pitz, Henry C. A58
Plain English A39
"Plains of Patagonia, The" A7, A58, C56
Planet A27
"Plea for the Osprey, A" C174
Plimpton Press, The A23, A27, A58
Pocket Book of Poems and Songs for the Open Air, The B2
Poems of W.H. Hudson, The. See A Little Boy Lost together with the Poems of W.H. Hudson
"Poetic Spirit, The" A26
Popular Classics of the World A23
Popular edition A34
Popular Edition of W.H. Hudson A5, A7, A16, A19, A20, A22, A26, A27, A31, A34, A36, A37, A40, A43, A47, A49
Popular Science A7, A12
"Porchester Churchyard, In" A40
Portland, Duchess of 2
"Postscript to An Old Thorn" A39
"Postscript to Dead Man's Plack" A39
"Postscript to Dead Man's Plack & An Old Thorn" A49
"Potato at Home and in England, The" A37, A51
Pozzo, Fernando D70, D73, D78, D79, 224
Prairie Press, The A64
"Praise of Cows, In" A47
"Praise of Owls, In" C124
"Praise of the Cow, In" A27, C115
Presencia del Paisaje en la Obra de Guillermo Enrique Hudson 224
"Present of a Walnut, A" C142
"Preservation of British Birds, The" C146
Priest, Alf B4
Pritchett, V.S. D73
Proceedings of the Zoological Society of London 1, A3, A5, A7, A61, 194, C1 to C22, C24 to C28
Prochovnick, Ammiel xi
Progress A64
"Proposed Extermination of a Crane" C159
"Protection of Birds in The Parks" A16

Public Opinion A19, A22
Publisher's Weekly A23, A34
"Puma, The" C44
"Puma, or Lion of America, The" A5
Punch A29
Purple Land, The A1
Purple Land, The A1, A2, A7, A19, A21, A23, A28, A31, A33, A34, A36, A39, A40, A43, A44, A48, A56, A58, A60, D12, D13, D15, D21, D29, D34, D48, D57, D67, D68, D75, D86, D92, D94, D95, D98, D104, D108, D109
"Purple Land, The" A58
Purple Land that England Lost, The A1
Purple Land that England Lost, The A1, A21, A44, D4, D6
Putnam, Lee xi
Pyle, Howard A23

Quarterly Review A5
Queen A31
"Queen of the Pigs" A58
Queen's Private Grounds at Kew, The" C88
Quinn & Boden Company, The A26

R. & R. Clark, Limited A20, A37
Ralph Herne A44
Ralph Herne 3, A21, A44
"Ralph Herne" 5, A44, C47
Randall, David A. xi
Random House A23
Rankin, Thomas E. A23
Ransom, Harry H. xi
Rare Vanishing & Lost British Birds A45
Rare Vanishing & Lost British Birds 4, A11, A45
"Ravens in Somerset" A20, C78
Readers Club, The A23
Readers' Digest Condensed Books edition A23
Readers' Library, The A1, A2, A7, A21, A23
Readers' Library edition, The A1, A2, A7, A21, A23
"Real First Edition of Hudson's Hampshire Days, and Other Notes, The" A22
"Recent Colonists" A16

Red Cross *xiv*
Red Fox C131
Redway, Agnes *4*
Registered Guild library edition A23
"Remarkable Book on the Habits of Animals, A" A5
Reminiscencias del Gaucho Guillermo Enrique Hudson y Breviario de sus Pajaros del Plata 225
Republic of Uruguay A1
"Return of the Chiff-Chaff, The" A40
"Return of the Native, The" A27, C129
Reveille A40, C200
Review of Reviews A1, A23
R. Folkard and Son A21
R.H. Porter A3
Rhys, Ernest A29, B9
Richard Clay & Sons, Limited A6, A34, A39, A50
Rima A23
"Ring-Ouzel as a Songster, The" A31
Roberts, Charles G.D. C131
Roberts, F.W. *xi*
Roberts, Morley *1, 2, 3, 4, 5,* A1, A6, A7, A11, A20, A23, A26, A27, A36, A37, A38, A39, A43, A50, B6, C119, *224*
Rodríguez de Pozzo, Celia D70, D79, D81
Roff and a Linnet: Chain and Cage A35
Roff and a Linnet: Chain and Cage A35, A47
"Roff and a Linnet" C184
Rogers, Bruce A44
"Roman Calleva" A27
Romola A1
Roodenko, Igal A38
Rook, Dorothy *xii*
Roosevelt, Theodore A1, A40
Rosarivo, Raúl W. A34
Rosas C190
Rosenthal, Robert *xi*
Ross, Waldo *225*
Rothenstein, William A1, A43, A57
Royal Academy A25
Royal College of Art A57
Royal National Institute for the Blind A23, A25, A29, A34
Royal Palace *xv*
Royal Society for the Protection of Birds *xii, 2, 4, 5, 9,* A2, A3, A4, A6, A8, A12, A13, A14, A15, A16, A18, A22, A23, A26, A30, A32, A35, A41, A42, A45, A52, A55, A61, A65, C67, A73, C146
RSPB. *See* Royal Society for the Protection of Birds
Rudge, William Edwin A44
"Rural Rides" A27
Rutter, Owen. *See* Christopher Sandford & Owen Rutter
Ruzicka, Rudolph A23
Ryerson Press A23, A25, A50, A58

"Sacred Bird, The" A31, C147
"Salisbury and its Doves" A27, C114
"Salisbury Revisited" A27
Salloch, publishers A46
Salvin, Osbert *194,* C1, C2, C4
"Samphire Gatherer, The" A40
Sampson Low, Marston, Searle, and Rivington A1
Sandford, Christopher. *See* Christopher Sandford & Owen Rutter
Sandgren, Gustav D111
San Francisco Chronicle A23, A60
"San Jose" A64
Santillan, Alfredo M. D90
Saturday Review 1, A1, A3, A7, A16, A20, A22, A23, A26, A27, A29, A31, A36, A40, A41, A43, A48, A62, C67, C73, C75, C80, C83, C94, C100, C104, C105, C119, C135, C143, C144, C145, C147, C149, C151, C152, C153, C155, C157, C158, C162, C163, C164, C167, C170, C171, C172, C173
Saturday Review of Literature A1, A58, C215
Saxton, Eugene *xiv*
Scholes, F.C. D81
School edition A34
Schultz de Mantovani, Fryda *224*
Schwarz, Louis A23
Science A5, A7
Scientific American A5
Sclater, P.L. A3, A4, A61, *194,* C1, C2, C4
Scotsman A20, A26
"Sea-Bird Shooting" C65
Seagulls in London A42
Seagulls in London A42, A47
"Seagulls in London" C202

"Second List of Birds collected at Conchitas, Argentine Republic, by Mr. William H. Hudson; together with some Notes upon another Collection from the same locality" C2
"Second Story of Two Brothers, A" A40
"Secret of the Charm of Flowers, A" A20
"Secret of the Willow Wren, The" A20, C87
"Seeking a Shelter" A27
"Seen and Lost" A5, C52
Seibundo Press, The A29
"Selborne" A20, C71
"Selborne Revisited" A22, C106
Semblanza de Hudson 224
"Sense of Direction, On the" C208
"Sense of Smell, On the" C207
"Sentimentalist on Foxes, A" A37, C182
Sequoia Press A62
"Serpent and Child" A58
"Serpent in Literature, The" A37, C128
"Serpent's Strangeness, The" A37, C64
"Serpent's Tongue, The" A37, C61
"Serpent With the Cross, The" A58
"Settler's Recompense, The" A7, C30
Sharp, Becky A1
Sharpe, Montagu C210
Sharpe, R. Bowdler A3
Sheffield Telegraph A21
Shepard, Odell A60
"Shepherd of the Downs, A" A19, A29, C108, C110
"Shepherds and Wheatears" A19
Shepherd's Life, A A29
Shepherd's Life, A A2, A7, A29, A31, A48, A60, A65, C108, C110, D84
Shizuo, Machino D43
Shorter, Clement K. A42
"Shuddering Angel, The" A17
"Sight in Savages" A7, C49
"Silence and Music" A19
Sillaots, Marta D11
Simić, Živojin V. D63, D64, D65
Siminovich, Máximo D80
"Simple Story, A" 4
Singapore Free Press A2
Sketch A7
Skoumal, A. D3

"Small Fry" A65
Smith, R. Bosworth C124
Smithsonian Institution 5, B12
Smith, Thomas Warnock 225
Smit, J. A5, A7, A22, A24
Smyth, Clifford A2, A40
"Snow and the Quality of Whiteness" A7
Sociedad Ornitológica del Plata A38
Society for the Protection of Birds 2, 3, A1, A4, A9, A10, A11, A13, A14, A15, A17, A18, A24, C63. *See also* Royal Society for the Protection of Birds
Society of Authors, The *xii*
"Some Clever Birds" C158
"Some Curious Animal Weapons" A5
"Some Early Flowers" A26
"Some Habits of the Spider" C57
"Some Increasing Birds, On" C195
"Some Other Animals" A65
"Something about the Owl" A13
"Something More" A58
"Something Pretty in a Glass Case" A20, C135
"South American Bird Music" C42
South American Romances A56
South American Romances A1, A21, A28, A33, A56
South American Sketches A28
South American Sketches A2, A21, A28, A31, A33
"South-East London" A16
"South-West London" A16
South Wind A23
Spater, George *xii*, 9, A2, A16, A26
Speaker 1, A16, A19, A20, A22, A23, A25, A26, A27, A37, A40, B2, C111, C112, C113, C114, C115, C116, C117, C118, C121, C122, C123, C124, C125, C126, C129, C130, C131, C133, C134, C136, C137, C138, C139, C140, C141, C142
Spectator A1, A5, A6, A7, A12, A16, A19, A20, A21, A23, A25, A26, A27, A29, A31, A34, A36, A43, A48
Spencer, Robert *xi*, A5
"Spiders" C33
Spingarn, Joel B. *xiii*
Spottiswoode and Co. A12, A16
"Spray of Southernwood, A" A40, C152

Springfield Republican A7, A23, A33, A36, A40, A43, A46, A48, A60
Springfield Sunday Union-Republican A23
"Spring Sadness" C179
Standard A16, A19, A20, A22, A23, A26
Stern, Mrs. Emma (Gelders) A23
Stinehour Press, The A63
St. James Gazette A19, A22
"Stonehenge" 4, A27, C148
Stone, William A62
"Story of a Jackdaw, A" A40
"Story of a Piebald Horse" A1, A21, A28, A33, A56, A58, A64, D38, D49
"Story of a Skull, The" A40, C191
"Story of a Walnut, A" A40
"Story of Long Descent, A" A40
"Story of Three Poems, A" A40
Strand Magazine C203, C204, C205
"Strange and Beautiful Sheldrake, The" A20
"Strange Instincts of Cattle" A5, C59
"Strangers Yet" A40
Stratford Press, The A23
Strato Publications A23
"Strenuous Mole, The" A37, C180
Students' Library of Contemporary Fiction edition A23
Studio A22
"Study of the Jaguar, A" A47, B3
Sulman, D. A22
"Summer Days on the Otter" A27
"Summer Heat" A19
"Summer in the Forest" A22, C96
"Summer's End on the Itchen, A" A22, C102
Sunar, Özay D113
Sunday Magazine A25, A31, C69, C72, C82
Sunday Sun A26
Sunday Times A40
Sun Dial Press A23
"Surrey Village, A" A40
"Survey of the Parks: West London, A" A16
"Swallows and Churches" A19
Swiveller, Dick A1
Syracuse, University of A22

Tales of the Gauchos A58

Tales of the Gauchos A58
Tales of the Pampas A33
Tales of the Pampas A21, A25, A28, A33, A49, A58, A64, C31
"Talk About Parrots" C104
Targ, William *xi*, A23
Tatler A27, A29, A39, A40
Taylor and Francis, printers A3
Teale, Edwin Way A23, C215
"Tecla and the Little Men" A21, A25, A33, A39, A49
Teitel, N.R. A23
Telegraph A26
Temple Press at Letchworth, The A1, A2, A5, A6, A7, A12, A16, A19, A20, A21, A22, A23, A25, A26, A27, A29, A31, A34, A36, A37, A38, A40, A43, A45, A47, A48, A49, A54, A55
"Temples of the Hills, The" A31, C168
Terrero, C190
Texas Christian University Press B13
Texas, University of Texas at Austin *xi, 4, 9*, A1, A2, A3, A5, A6, A7, A8, A16, A20, A22, A23, A36, A38, A39, A45, A54, A61
The Times A1, A9, A16, A17, A18, A21, A22, A23, A26, A27, A29, A37, C62, C65, C66, C74, C76, C85, C88, C98, C159, C160, C194
"Third List of Birds collected at Conchitas, Argentine Republic, by Mr. William H. Hudson" C4
"Third Story of Two Brothers, A" A40
"Thistle-Down" A19
Thomas, Edward A37, A59, B2, B6
Thomas, Mrs. Edward B6
Thompson, T. A13
Thorburn, A. A12
Thorne, Will A26
"Three Common River Birds" A22, A52
Three Sirens Press A1, A23
Three Water Birds A52
Three Water Birds A22, A52
"Threshold of England, The" C76
"Through Cobbett's Country" C105
"Thrush as Mimic, The" C185
Thrush that Never Lived, A A30
Thrush that Never Lived, A A30, A47

"Thrush that Never Lived, A" C109
Times Literary Supplement A2, A20, A31, A34, A36, A37, A38, A39, A40, A43, A46, A48, A61
Times of India A20
Tippett, Michael A34
Tired Traveller, A A41
Tired Traveller, A A41
"Tired Traveller, A" C149
"Tired Traveller, A (*Turdus iliacus*)" A31
"Toad as Traveller, The" A37, C189
To-day A23
Tomalin, Ruth A56, B12, 225
"Tom Rainger" 4, A47, C34
T.P.'s Weekly A27
Trade in Bird's Feathers, The A17
Trade in Bird's Feathers, The A17, A47
"Trade in Birds' Feathers, The" C85
Traveller in Little Things, A A40
Traveller in Little Things, A A40, A48, A55, A60, A65, C86, C122, C142, C152, C153, C167, C186, C191, C192, C200, C201, D83
Travellers' Library edition A50
Travels of a Naturalist in Northern Europe C130
"Tree-felling and Philosophy" C73
Tregarthen, J.C. C143
Tres Clásicas Inglesas de la Pampa. F.B. Head, William Henry Hudson, R.B. Cunninghame Graham 224
Tribune A2
Tridgould, Winifred A37
Trinity Press, The A16
"Troop of Wild Horses, A" A58
"Troston" A27
Truth A26, A27, A29, A31
"Truth Plain and Coloured" A47, C131
Tsuda, Masao 225
Tupper, H.G. *xi*
Turnbull and Spears A20, A25, A54
Twayne, publishers *226*
Twayne's English Authors Series *226*
Two Letters on an Albatross A62
Two Letters on an Albatross A62
Two shilling net series A28
"Two White Houses: A Memory, The" A40

"Unbleached Arnold", watermark A34
Uniform Edition of W.H. Hudson, The A1, A7, A19, A23, A31, A34, A43
Universal Braille Press A27
Universal Library A23
Universal Review A7, C56
University Classics edition A23
University of Birmingham. *See* Birmingham, University of
University of Chicago. *See* Chicago, University of
University of Leeds. *See* Leeds, University of
University of Michigan. *See* Michigan, University of
University of Syracuse. *See* Syracuse, University of
University of Texas. *See* Texas, University of Texas at Austin
Un Viaje por "La Tierra Purpúrea" 224
Unwin, T. Fisher A2
Uriburu, Francisco D83
Uruguay. *See* Republic of Uruguay

Vail-Ballou Co. A20, A27
Vail-Ballou Press, The A61
"Valley of the Black River" A7
Vallquist, Lily D110
Van de Reemur, W.T. D8
Van Doren, Carl A23
Van Heemstra, E. Baronesse D10
"Vanishing Curtsey, The" A40, C122
Vanity Fair A23
Van Laar, Henk D9
Velazquez, Luis Horacio 225
"Versatile Hawk, A" C36
"Vert-Vert; or Parrot Gossip" A20
Vida y Obra de W.H. Hudson 226
"Village and 'The Stones', The" A27
Villager A34
"Visionary, The" A40, C86
"Vision of the Great Spoonbill, The" A25, C72
"Voice in the Darkness, The" A58

"Walking and Cycling" A27
Wallace, Alfred R. A5
"Wanted, A Lullaby" *1*, A47, C23

Warde, Frederic A23
Warren's Olde Style, watermark A25, A61
"War with Nature, The" A7
Washington D.C. Evening Star A23
"Wasp at Table, A" A40
"Wasps" A37, C126
"Wasps and Men," A40
Wasps Social and Solitary C126
Wasson, R. Gordon C215
Waterton, Charles A13, A47
Watts, G.F. A17
Waudby, Roberta F.C. A54
"Wave of Life, A" A5
Wayfarer's Library edition A27
Ways of Nature C131
W.C. Hamilton & Sons, paper manufacturers, A26
Webb, H. Vicars A45
Weber, Kuno D22
Weekly Book Review A58
Week's Survey A22, A23
Wells, Carlton F. *224*
"Wells-next-the-sea" C155
"Wells-Next-The-Sea, Where Wild Geese Congregate" A31
Wen-chen, Liu D1
West, Herbert Faulkner *xii*, A61, A62, A63, *224, 225*
Westholm Publications A62, A63, A64, *225*
Westminster Budget A19
Westminster Gazette A31, A40
Westminster Review A7
"West of the Adur" A19
W.F. Etherington A20, A26
W.H. Hudson B12
W.H. Hudson B12, *225*
"W.H. Hudson: An Impression" C209
W.H. Hudson. A Portrait 224
W.H. Hudson: A Shepherd's Life 225
W.H. Hudson: Bird-Man 224
W.H. Hudson 1841–1922. Naturaliste. Sa Vie et son Oeuvre 224
W.H. Hudson: Far Away and Long Ago 225
W.H. Hudson's Letters to R.B. Cunninghame Graham A57
W.H. Hudson's Letters to R.B. Cunninghame Graham A57, D76

"W.H. Hudson's Lost Years" C215
W.H. Hudson's Reading 224
W.H. Hudson. The Vision of Earth 224
"White Duck" A31, C156
Whitehall Review A1
"Whitesheet Hill" A27
Whittle, Eric S. *xii*
"Wilderness, In the" A39, A49, C32
Wild Fauna and Flora of the Royal Botanic Gardens, Kew C132
"Wild Flowers" A65
"Wild Flowers and Little Girls" A40
"Wild Life" A19
"Wild Musk" C103
Wild Wings C130
"Wild Wings" C130, C175, C214
"Wild Wings: A Farewell" A31
William Brendon and Son A1, A23, A26, A27
William Clowes and Sons A1, A8
William Henry Hudson 226
William Henry Hudson: A Tribute by Various Writers 224
William Henry Hudson's Diary A63
William Henry Hudson's Diary 4, A63
William L. Clements Library *224*
Wilson, Edward A. A23
Wilson, G.F. *xii*, A4, A6, A22, *224*
Wilson, Jean A. A23
Wilson Library Bulletin A2, A23, A27, A37
"Wiltshire Village, A" A40
Windsor Press A23
"Wind, Wave, and Spirit" A27
Wingrave, Horace A40
Wingrave, J. A23
Wingrove, Alfred A3
Wingstone, *xiii*
"Winter Aspects and a Bird Visitation" A26
"Winter at St. Ives" C134
"Wintering in West Cornwall" A26
"Winter in West Downland" A19
Witherby & Co. A24
Witherby, publishers *225*
Wolff, H. A58
"Wolmer Forest" A22, C84
"Wonderful Story of a Mackerel, A" A40, C167

"Wood by the Sea, A" A31, C157
"Woodhewer Family, The" A5
Woodroffe, W.L. A10
"Wood Wren, The" C77
"Wood Wren at Wells, A" A20
Work of the Book World A22
World A22
World Publishing Co. A1, A23
World's Popular Classics A23
World's Work A22
Worthing Art Development Scheme B10, 224
Worthing Cavalcade: William Henry Hudson A Tribute, The B10
Worthing Cavalcade: William Henry Hudson A Tribute, The B10
Wright, George Edward A17
Wright, Walter W. *xi*

Yale Review A7, A43
Youth 5, A21, A44, C47

Žabka, Jaroslav D5
Zoological Society of London, The 9, A8, A22, A61
Züberbühler, Emilio D93

OHIO UNIVERSITY LIBRARY

soon as you
avoid a
late